PENGUIN BOOKS

STROLLING THROUGH VENICE

John Freely was born in New York in 1926. He joined the US Navy at the age of seventeen and served with a commando unit in Burma and China during the last months of the Second World War. He received a PhD in physics from New York University in 1960, and since then he has lived in New York, Boston, London, Athens, Istanbul and Venice. His first book was *Strolling Through Istanbul* (1972, with Hilary Sumner-Boyd). He has subsequently written twenty other travel books, most of them about Greece and Turkey. Also published by Penguin are *Classical Turkey* and *Strolling Through Athens*.

JOHN FREELY

Strolling Through Venice

PENGUIN BOOKS

PENGUIN BOOKS

Published by the Penguin Group
Penguin Books Ltd, 27 Wrights Lane, London w8 5tz, England
Penguin Books USA Inc., 375 Hudson Street, New York, New York 10014, USA
Penguin Books Australia Ltd, Ringwood, Victoria, Australia
Penguin Books Canada Ltd, 10 Alcorn Avenue, Toronto, Ontario, Canada m4v 3b2
Penguin Books (NZ) Ltd, 182–190 Wairau Road, Auckland 10, New Zealand

Penguin Books Ltd, Registered Offices: Harmondsworth, Middlesex, England

First published 1994
10 9 8 7 6 5 4 3 2 1

Maps and plans by Nigel Andrews

Filmset in 11/13.5 pt Monotype Bembo by
Datix International Limited, Bungay, Suffolk
Printed in England by Clays Ltd, St Ives plc

For Toots
Another Dream

Contents

I would like to express my deep gratitude to the friends who helped me in so many ways while I was working in Venice on this book, particularly Roderick Conway Morris and Christine Danagher, Michael and Liliana Gluckstern, Alessandro and Patricia Bonelli, and Lady Ashley Clarke. I am grateful to Anthony Baker for having provided all of the photographs that illustrate the book. I would also like to thank Esther Sidwell for all the very careful work that she has done in editing my manuscript.

Introduction

Strolling Through Venice is a guide to the city and its lagoon, both as they were in times past and as they are today. The book begins with a description of the topography of the Venetian lagoon and a brief outline of the city's history, covering the time from its founding up until the present day. The chapters that follow include a score of walking tours through the labyrinthian streets and squares of Venice, as well as a trip up and down the Grand Canal by vaporetto and an exploration of the islands of the lagoon. These tours will visit every one of the 115 churches of Venice and its thirty-three museums, as well as identifying some three hundred of the city's *palazzi*, the most notable of which will be described in some detail.

The appendixes include a glossary of Italian words and technical terms that are frequently used in the text and a list of the opening hours of monuments and museums.

But Venice is not treated as if it is an outdoor museum, for the emphasis throughout is on the life of the city, as it is now and as it was in the days of the Serenissima, the Serene Republic that for more than a thousand years prided itself as the 'Bride of the Sea'. Venice is very much alive, despite the much publicized concerns that it is a dying city sinking inexorably into the lagoon from which it was first created. The discovery of this living Venice is one of the purposes of the book, linking the city of today with the monuments of the illustrious Venetian past that are described in the guide.

[I] The Lagoon and the City

Venetians sing of their beautiful city as '*Gemm' adriatica/Sposa del mar*', 'Gem of the Adriatic/Bride of the sea'. Those fortunate enough to arrive in Venice by ship see the city literally emerging from the lagoon, its domes and campaniles silhouetted against the Euganean Hills if the day is clear; on halcyon days in midwinter the snow-plumed peaks of the Dolomites rise up behind *terraferma* to create a dramatic mountainous backdrop to the sea-girt scene. The city takes form as the ship crosses the lagoon and enters the Bacino San Marco, the old port of Venice. On the right are the Palazzo Ducale and the Basilica of San Marco with its towering campanile; to the left on its islet is the church of San Giorgio Maggiore and straight ahead on the Grand Canal is the church of Santa Maria della Salute. We have arrived in Venice, and if the timing is right all the city's bells will toll the hour as we pass through the Bacino and head down the Giudecca Canal towards the Stazione Marittima. And deep among them we will hear the sonorous tone of Marangona, the great bell of San Marco, which for more than a thousand years has marked the hours when Venetians begin and end their working day, or pealed the alarm for a great fire or the appearance of an enemy fleet off the islands of the lagoon, or tolled the death of a Doge – it is the deepest sound of Venice and we hear its profound message as we enter the Venetian labyrinth.

Venice is indeed a labyrinth, a doubly convoluted maze, with a hundred or more islets threaded with canals and linked by some four hundred bridges. One labyrinth is formed by the canals, most of which are known as *rio*, or, if they are smaller, *riello*. The second labyrinth is formed by the walkways of Venice, which has no proper streets, but a maze of alleys and squares with uniquely Venetian names. (Even the spelling of these names is unique, because of the many differences between the Venetian dialect and standard Italian.) A *calle* is a rather long and narrow street, which in any other city would be considered a mere alley. A *calle larga* is a wide street. A *ramo* is a short extension of a *calle*. A *salizzada* is one of the principal *calli* in each parish, one of the first to be paved (in Venetian, *salizai*) with brick *c*. 1260. Some of the older *calli* are called *ruga* or *rughetta* (said to be derived from the French *rue* or the Portugese *rua*). A *sottoportego* is a *calle* that passes under a building or an arcade. A *fondamenta* is a sidewalk along the bank of a canal, as is a *riva*. A *crosera* is a cross street. A *campo* is a square, generally next to a church. Many of the *campi* are very large and elsewhere in Italy might be known as *piazze*, but only Piazza San Marco is so called in Venice. A *piazzetta* is a smaller *piazza*, of which there are just two in Venice, both of them appendages of Piazza San Marco. A *campiello* is a smaller *campo*, or if it is very small and forms a cul-de-sac it is known as a *corte*, or sometimes, if it is a larger court, it is called a *cortile*. A *campazzo* is a formerly abandoned area now serving as a *campiello*. A *chiovere* is a *campiello* that formerly served as a dyer's drying-ground. A *rio terà* is a street formed from a filled-in canal; a *piscina* is one laid out on what was once a pond; while a *paludo* is a former marsh. A *lista* is a street that once passed in front of a consulate, such as Lista da Spagna. A *marzaria* is one of the original market streets that led into Piazza San Marco. The longest and widest 'avenue' in Venice is Strada Nova, which was laid out on a filled-in canal in the 19C as were other straight and wide 'streets' such as Calle Larga XXII Marza and Rio Terà Garibaldi. But even the oldest of the *calli* and *campi* and *campielli* of Venice were originally laid out on filled-in land, for Venice was created from marshland, surrounded by the all-embracing lagoon from which the city was formed some fifteen centuries ago and into which it may one day disappear. '*Il mare la chiama*', the Venetians say when a wind from the Adriatic stirs the green waters of the lagoon, 'the sea is calling', calling eternally for his bride.

The lagoon of Venice is shaped like a great crescent lune concave outwards towards the sea, with the inner circular segment along the shore of *terraferma* serrated by innumerable inlets, streams, estuaries, channels and canals, the outer seaward arc a series of three long and narrow *lidi*, or sand-bars, Litorale di Pellestrina to the south, Litorale di Lido in the centre, and Litorale del Cavallino to the north. The area of the lagoon so enclosed is some 160 square miles, measuring about 30 miles between the two horns of the lune to north and south, and its width varying from 5 to 10 miles. Venice itself is nearly at the centre of the lagoon, its westernmost point about $3\frac{1}{2}$ miles from the mainland, to which it is now linked by railway and road bridges. Most travellers today come to Venice along these bridges, an approach that Thomas Mann compared to entering a palace through the back door, for the grand entrance to the city is Porto di San Nicolò, the channel between the Lido island and the Cavallino peninsula.

Porto di San Nicolò is one of three channels into the lagoon. Porto di Malamocco separates the Lido and Pellestrina islands, while Porto di Chioggia passes between Pellestrina and the southern horn of the lagoon at the town of Chioggia. These three *porti* are the main channels for the water that surges in and out of the lagoon with the tides in the Adriatic. Within the lagoon the saline water of the sea mixes with the fresh water that pours into it from the rivers and streams from the Dolomites. The major rivers that originally emptied into the lagoon were the Brenta, the Sile and the Piave, but all three of them have long since been diverted to lessen the depositing of silt and also to eliminate the creation of malarial swamps. The Piave now enters the Adriatic north of the lagoon; the Sile flows in the old bed of the Piave and is channelled around the north end of the lagoon to flow directly into the sea; while most of the waters of the Brenta flow into the sea just south of Chioggia, with one of its tributary streams entering the lagoon opposite Venice at Fusina.

The lagoon and the sand-bars, none of them more than half a mile wide, are the combined creation of the Adriatic and the three rivers that flowed into it around what is now the city of Venice. This is evident in the composition of the bars, which are sea sand on their Adriatic shores and river mud along the lagoon. The silt-bearing fresh waters of the three rivers intermingled with the salt water of the Adriatic within the lagoon after the creation of the sand-bars, and in the diurnal ebb and flow of the tides the deposit of alluvial soil created a myriad of mud-banks and islands separated by a labyrinth of channels. These channels, once formed by the swirling action of the tides, are marked out by some 20,000 *pali*, wooden stakes driven into the mud bottom and constantly renewed, markers that date back to the first dwellers in the lagoon. These *pali* were also used by the first Venetians to define and protect the periphery of the islands in the lagoon, as one can see in the islets like Torcello that are now barely inhabited. They also used these stakes as foundations for their dwellings, using higher-standing *pali* for walls, laying larchwood logs across them for floors and covering their cottages with thatched roofs. Other *pali* served as mooring-posts for their boats, for the first Venetians lived on and from the sea, fishing in the Adriatic and the lagoon, hunting for waterfowl in the swamps and estuaries along the fringes of *terraferma*, creating salt from the sea water left in shallow pools on the mud-flats, trading their salt and fish up-river with towns in the Veneto, and eventually venturing out across the ocean in maritime commerce. Thus did Venice become the Bride of the Sea.

The earliest mention of the lagoon people is by the Greek geographer Strabo, writing *c.* 8 BC, who refers to them as Eneti or Veneti. The first to describe the life of the early lagoon-dwellers is the Roman official Cassiodorus, who wrote to them *c.* 525:

For you live like sea-birds, with your homes dispersed, like the Cyclades, across the surface of the water. The solidity of the earth on which they rest is secured only by osier and wattle; yet you do not hesitate to oppose so frail a bulwark to the wildness of the sea. Your people have one great wealth – the fish which suffices for them all.

Between the times of Strabo and Cassiodorus the population of the lagoon had greatly increased, as refugees fled from the mainland towns to escape from the barbarian tribes that invaded Italy in the later Roman imperial era. The most destructive of these invaders were the Visigoths under Alaric, who in 410 sacked Rome, and the Huns under Attila, who in 452 took Aquileia after a three-month siege and utterly destroyed the town, with Altino, Concordia, Opitergium and Padua soon suffering the same fate. But the Venetian islands were untouched by these invasions, protected by the treacherous waters of the lagoon which only the islanders themselves could navigate.

Venetian tradition dates the birth of the city to 421, when three consuls from Padua are supposed to have founded a trading post at Rivo Alto, 'High Bank', which came to be known as Rialto. The Città di Riva Alto, or Rialto, is one of twelve island townships listed in the earliest extant history of Venice, a chronicle written at the beginning of the 11C by John the Deacon. Tradition holds that in 466 these twelve townships sent representatives to an assembly at Grado, where they elected tribunes, one to govern each of the islands. The tribunes were subservient to the Emperor of the East in Constantinople. During the reign of Justinian (527–65) the lagoon townships constituted the Byzantine Provincia Venetarium. In the 7C the capital of the lagoon confederacy became Heraclea, where in 726 Orso Ipato was elected as the first Doge of Venice, a title deriving from the Latin *dux*. Orso reigned as Doge until 737, when he was killed in a civil war between Heraclea and Jesolo. An interregnum of five years followed before Orso's son Teodato was elected Doge, whereupon he transferred the centre of government from Heraclea to Malamocco on the Lido. The capital remained in Malamocco until 810, when Charlemagne's son, King Pépin, invaded the region and almost succeeded in conquering Venice before he was driven off. The following year, under Doge Agnello Partecipazio, the capital was shifted from Malamocco to the Rialtine islands, thenceforth to be known as Rialto. Thus Rialto became the capital of the lagoon, and in the sixteen years of his reign Doge Agnello laid the foundations of the great city that thenceforth would be the capital of the Serenissima, the Serene Republic of Venice.

One of Agnello's first acts as Doge was to appoint a committee of three men to build the new capital: one to fortify the sand-bars; a second to dredge canals, stake out the boundaries of the Rialtine islands and prepare plots of land for building sites; and a third to supervise the erection of the buildings themselves, which, like the cottages of the original lagoon dwellers, were built on foundations of *pali* driven into the ground. The first public building to be erected was the Palazzo Ducale, erected on the site of the present Doge's Palace. This and many other edifices were completed by the time that Agnello passed on in 827, to be succeeded as Doge by his son Giustiniano Partecipazio.

The reign of Giustiniano began with an event of great symbolic importance to Venice. This was the arrival of the remains of St Mark the Apostle, whose body had been stolen from its tomb in Alexandria by two Venetian merchants and enshrined in a chapel between the Doge's Palace and the church of San Teodoro. Mark then supplanted Theodore as the patron saint of Venice. The chapel was replaced by a series of larger churches, culminating with the present Basilica of San Marco, which was completed in the reign of Doge Vitale Falier (1084–96).

Venice began its rise to greatness under Doge Pietro Orseolo II (991–1008). During the first year of his reign he
signed treaties with both the Emperor of the West, Otto II,
and the Byzantine Emperor Basil II, the latter giving Venetian
merchants very advantageous trading rights in Constantinople. The trade of Venice expanded rapidly because of this
agreement, its sea-borne commerce extending throughout the
eastern Mediterranean, including the Muslim world; its river
boats making their way upstream to towns like Pavia, from
where the goods were transported overland to northern
Europe. As a chronicler of the time remarked: 'to the fair at
Pavia came the Venetians, bringing with them from overseas
all the riches of the Orient'. The only hindrance to this trade
came from the Slav pirates on the Dalmatian coast, but in the
year 1000 the Doge succeeded in putting them down. The
following Ascension Day the anniversary of the Doge's departure on his victorious voyage was commemorated in a
ceremony that began at the cathedral of San Pietro di Castello,
where the bishop accompanied the Doge and his council,
followed by all the populace, as they sailed out to Porto di
San Nicolò. There the bishop in a simple ceremony gave
thanks to God, ending with this plea: 'Grant O Lord, that for
us, and for all who sail thereon, the sea may be calm and
quiet; this is our prayer, Lord hear us.' As time passed the
ritual became far more elaborate, and at its climax the Doge
cast a gold ring into the waves, the symbolic Marriage with
the Sea. This ceremony continued down to the end of the
Republic, as Venice annually renewed her vows as Sposa del
Mar, the Bride of the Sea.

Thus did Venice begin the second millennium of the Christian era, and during the following centuries she acquired
widespead possessions both on the mainland of Italy and
overseas. At her peak, the possessions of Venice on *terraferma*
comprised much of north-eastern Italy, the core of it being
the Veneto. Her maritime empire, much of which fell to her
after the Venetians under Doge Enrico Dandolo joined the

knights of the Fourth Crusade in capturing Constantinople in 1204, included the Ionian Isles, Crete, Cyprus, the Cyclades and a string of ports and fortresses along the shores of Greece and Albania.

In 1171 Venice was divided into its present six *sestieri*, or 'sixths', three on either side of the Grand Canal, the two shores being referred to as *citra* (this) and *ultra* (that) in relation to Piazza San Marco. The *sestieri* on the *citra* side are San Marco, Castello and Cannaregio; those on the *ultra* side Dorsoduro, San Polo and Santa Croce. Soon afterwards the Venetians made a number of reforms in their government. The nobility in each of the *sestieri* were ordered to elect two representatives, each of whom nominated forty representatives for a general assembly. This assembly, the Maggior Consiglio, or Great Council, thenceforth appointed all of the chief officials of the Republic, including the twelve representatives of the *sestieri*. Another reform was to increase the number of the Doge's counsellors from two to six, and they, with him, formed an inner council of state that came to be known as the Signoria. The next step was to strengthen the Pregadi, or Senate, which had assisted the Doge when he asked for advice, now giving it a role in all important decisions, particularly in foreign affairs. A decade later another body was created – the Quarantia, or Council of Forty – which occupied the administrative ground between the Maggior Consiglio and the Signoria. Then in 1297 the Maggior Consiglio was enlarged to include all adult male members of the nobility. At the same time the ranks of the nobility were closed to all but the oldest and most powerful families, who from 1311 onwards were listed in the Libro d'Oro, the Golden Book. Nevertheless in later years wealthy families were able to buy their way into the nobility, so that in the mid 16C the Maggior Consiglio numbered some 2,500, more than 6 per cent of the adult males in a total population of about 175,000 in the city.

The acquisition of its land and maritime empires involved

the Republic in numerous wars both in Italy and overseas. The most notable of the conflicts in Italy were the war of Chioggia in 1379–80, in which Venice emerged victorious over Genoa; and the war against the League of Cambrai in 1509–29, in which the Venetians held their own against a powerful coalition that included the Emperor Maximilian, the Kings of France, Spain and Hungary, the Dukes of Savoy and Ferrara, and the Papacy. Overseas the Republic fought seven major wars against the Ottoman Empire, the first beginning in 1463 and the last ending in 1718, in the course of which the Venetians lost all their maritime empire to the Turks except the Ionian Isles. During that time Venice was the only power that continued to oppose the relentless advance of the Ottoman Empire, and her one great moment of triumph came when the Venetian contingent led the Christian fleet that defeated the Turks at the battle of Lepanto on 5 October 1571. But this did little to stem the Ottoman tide, for the year before Cyprus had fallen to the Turks, and a century later Crete fell as well, leaving Venice with only a few island outposts in the eastern Mediterranean. Venice made a comeback in its sixth war against the Ottomans in 1684–99, when her forces, under Francesco Morosini, reconquered the Morea (Peloponnesus). But in the last war with the Ottoman Empire, in 1713–18, the Venetians lost all their overseas possessions except the Ionian Isles.

These endless wars and the loss of much of her maritime trade left Venice bankrupt and powerless, no longer able to defend herself when the French army under Napoleon invaded Italy in 1796. On 12 May 1797 Doge Lodovico Manin and his government surrendered to the French without a struggle, ending the long and illustrious history of the Venetian Republic.

The French occupied Venice for five months until 17 October 1797, when the city was ceded to Austria in accordance with the Treaty of Campo Formio. The Austrians took possession of Venice on 18 January 1798. Their first occupation of the city lasted only until 1805; after Napoleon's victory at the battle of Austerlitz, Venice became part of the new French Kingdom of Italy. Napoleon's stepson, Eugène de Beauharnais, was appointed Viceroy of the Kingdom, with the title of Prince of Venice. Within the next two years the French authorities in Venice closed twenty-six churches, all but one of which were subsequently demolished; they also suppressed forty-eight monasteries and convents, and 385 guilds and confraternities, most of which never reopened.

Then in 1814 the Austrians recaptured Venice from the French. The second Austrian occupation of Venice lasted for more than half a century, though interrupted for nineteen months in 1848–9, when the Venetians rebelled under Daniele Manin and succeeded in establishing an independent state known as the Republic of San Marco. But the Austrians besieged the city and forced Manin and his supporters to surrender on 19 August 1849. The Austrians then resumed their occupation of the city, which lasted until 1866, when Venice was united with the rest of Italy under King Victor Emmanuel II.

Venice has changed greatly since the fall of the Republic, but in many ways it remains the same. In 1797 there were 153 churches in Venice, of which 128 were built before the end of the 15C, all of the latter appearing in Jacopo de' Barbari's extraordinary bird's-eye view of the city done in 1500. One hundred and fifteen of the churches dating from the time of the Republic remain standing, all but a few of them still functioning, and though many of their monasteries and convents have closed the buildings themselves survive. There are also some three hundred *palazzi* dating from the days of the Republic, many of them identifiable in Barbari's view, along with other structures such as market and administrative buildings, dwellings of the *cittadini*, or citizen class, guildhalls (*scuole*), bridges and well-heads, not to mention the Arsenal, the great shipyard of the Republic.

There are those who say that Venice is a dying city, for the population has dropped from 135,000 in 1945 to 75,000 in 1990, with most of those departing being young people seeking better opportunities on *terraferma*. There is also serious concern that Venice is sinking into the lagoon from which it originally arose, particularly because of the catastrophic *acqua alta*, or high water, which inundated the city on 4 November 1966, when the level of the lagoon rose 1.94 m higher than normal. This gave rise to a number of conservation programmes, most notably the Venice in Peril Fund, which has restored several monuments that were damaged in the flood.

Thus Venice endures, very much alive, with her bewitching beauty compensating for the vanished glory of the Serenissima. As the French ambassador to the Republic remarked in the mid 18C: 'The great days of Venice are over; the city, however, remains a perpetual delight.'

And in that spirit we begin our exploration of the Venetian labyrinth.

[2] Piazza San Marco

Piazza San Marco has been the centre of Venice and Venetian life since the earliest days of the city. The Piazza and its two wings, the Piazzetta on the seaward side, fronted by the Molo, and the much smaller Piazzetta dei Leoni to the northeast of the square, together make up a vast forecourt to the two greatest edifices in Venice, the Basilica of San Marco and the Palazzo Ducale. The present pavement of the Piazza and the Piazzetta, made of trachyte with rectangular patterns in white Istrian stone, was laid down by Andrea Tirali in 1722.

The Piazza is 175.7 m in length along its central axis, which extends from the Basilica of San Marco on the east to the edifice known as Ala Napoleonica on the west. Its width ranges from 82 m on the east to 57 m on the west, its north side formed mostly by the Procuratie Vecchie and its south by the Procuratie Nuove. These two monumental buildings were so named because they originally housed the Procurators of San Marco, the highest-ranking magistrates in the Republic after the Doge, the Procuratie Vecchie being their original home and the Procuratie Nuove the later one.

The Piazza was created in the first great building programme in 811, when the capital was shifted from Malamocco to the Rialtine islands. The original Piazza was a little less than half as long as the present square, bounded on its western side by the Canale Batario. The square was known as Brolo, or the Orchard, because it was planted with fruit trees and vines. Doge Sebastiano Ziani (1172–8) acquired the western side of the Brolo from the convent of San Zaccaria, whereupon he filled in the Canale Batario to extend the Piazza to its present length.

The Procuratie Vecchie in its original form was designed by Mauro Coducci and completed in 1499, with the building comprising the present arcade and the loggia on the second storey. The upper loggia on the third storey and the attic above it were added in 1517–26 by Bartolomeo Bon and Guglielmo Bergamasco, while the north-west wing was completed in 1532 by Jacopo Sansovino. Two decades later Sansovino erected the church of San Geminiano next to the north-west wing of the Procuratorie Vecchie. The church was demolished in 1807, along with the western wings of both the Procuratie Vecchie and the Procuratie Nuove, to make way for Ala Napoleonica.

The Procuratie Vecchie was the first monumental public building in Venice to be erected in a purely classical style. It is 152 m long and 18 m high and its arcade has fifty arches, each of the two loggias above having a hundred arches on their facade, with two window bays over each arch of the portico. After the completion of the Procuratie Nuove, the Procurators moved over to the south side of the Piazza, whereupon the various chambers of the Procuratie Vecchie were let out to tenants. The chambers under the arcade were converted into shops, as they still are, the oldest being the Caffè Quadri, which has been there since c. 1730.

The Procuratie Nuove was designed by Vincenzo Scamozzi, and building was started in 1586. By that time work was almost completed on Sansovino's Libraria Marciana, the library of San Marco, which had been erected on the west side of the Piazzetta facing the Palazzo Ducale. Scamozzi oriented the Procuratie Nuove so that it joined the library at right angles on a line with the eastern side of the campanile of San Marco, making a harmonious junction between the edifices at that corner of the Piazza. Scamozzi began the construction of the new building at the corner where it joined the library, and by the time of his death in

1616 he had completed the first ten arches. Marco Carità then continued the project until 1640, when Baldassare Longhena was put in charge and completed the building, which comprised the remaining twenty-six arches along the southern side of the Piazza and seven on the western end that linked it with the church of San Geminiano. The building is 133 m long and 22 m high. All three orders of classical Graeco-Roman architecture appear on its facade, for the arcade is Doric, the second storey Ionic and the third Corinthian. After the fall of the Republic in 1797 it became Palazzo Reale, the royal palace of the Napoleonic Kingdom of Italy. After 1866 it passed to the Kingdom of Italy and King Victor Emmanuel II, until finally, after the First World War, it was given to the state by Victor Emmanuel III. Most of the two upper floors of the palace now house the Correr Museum and the Archaeological Museum. As in the Procuratie Vecchie, the arcade is occupied mostly by shops, with the central part housing the famous Florian's, an elegant café dating to 1720.

The entire western end of the Piazza is occupied by the edifice known as the Ala Napoleonica, the Napoleonic Wing. This palatial structure occupies the site of Sansovino's church of San Geminiano and the flanking wings of the old and new buildings of the Procuratie. These were all demolished in 1807, on Napoleon's orders, to make way for the entrance, reception hall and ballroom of the Palazzo Reale. The Napoleonic Wing was begun soon afterwards by Giovanni Antolini; after 1810 it was continued by Giuseppe Maria Soli; and then, following the restoration of Austrian control in Venice in 1814, it was completed by Lorenzo Santi. The facade is in the same style as the Procuratie Nuove on the first two storeys, with the arcade in the Doric order and the loggia in the Ionic order, but in place of a third storey there is an attic floor with statues of Roman emperors and reliefs of mythological and allegorical figures. The entrance – to the right under the central portico – is known as the Nuovo Atrio, and a double stairway known as the Scala Maggiore leads up to the anteroom of the former Palazzo Reale, now the Correr Civic Museum, which we will visit after exploring the rest of the Piazza.

We now walk back across the Piazza towards the Torre dell'Orologio, or clock tower, at the north-eastern corner of the Piazza proper, where the old market street named Marzaria de l'Orologio passes through it in a round-arched sottoportego. The original Torre dell'Orologio was designed by Mauro Coducci and completed in 1499. A pair of side wings were added to the tower in 1506 by Pietro Lombardo, and then additional floors were built by Giorgio Massari in 1755. Above the archway is the great clock, its face adorned with gilt and blue enamels, the twelve signs of the zodiac shown in a band within the outer circle of the twenty-four hours, along with the spheres of the sun and moon. On the mezzanine floor above the clock a little semicircular terrace fronts a classical *naiskos*, which frames a gilded relief in beaten copper representing the Virgin and Child, a work attributed to Alessandro Leopardi. The *naiskos* is flanked by two panels in which the time is shown digitally, with Roman numerals for the hours and Arabic numbers for the minutes, at intervals of five minutes. During Ascension week a little side door opens up beside the *naiskos* on the hour, whereupon the three Magi are led out by a herald angel and bow before Mary and Jesus. Above this, on the uppermost floor, the winged Lion of St Mark stands against a blue enamel background with gold stars. On the rooftop terrace above this is the huge bell, surmounted by a cross and the two muscular figures who strike the hours ponderously with their mallets. Known as the 'Moors' because of the dark patina on the bronze, they were cast in 1494 by Ambrogio delle Ancore, probably from models by Paolo Savin.

Piazzetta dei Leoni is the extension of the Piazza in the area between the Basilica of San Marco and the northern side of the square. Part of this area was originally occupied by the church of San Teodoro, but in 889 that was demolished and rebuilt as a chapel on a site behind the present Basilica of San Marco. The Piazzetta dei Leoni takes its name from the statues of the two lions in pink Verona marble at the entrance of the square, done in 1722 by Giovanni Bonazza. The lions rest on pedestals flanking the three-stepped approach to a low platform centred on a *vera da pozzo*, or well-head, built in 1722 by Andrea Tirali.

These well-heads, among the most characteristic elements of the Venetian scene, are usually situated in the centre of a *campo* or *corte* to serve those living around them. There were originally 6,782 well-heads in the city, of which 256 are still to be seen in public places. They were the only sources of water in Venice up until the mid 19C, when a number of artesian wells came into use. Then after the completion of an aqueduct from the mainland in 1884 the *vere da pozzo* eventually fell into disuse. They are not true wells, for the well-head stands above a cement-walled cistern that collects rain-water filtering down through a mixture of sand and gravel before reaching the central well-shaft. The catchment area of the cistern is usually marked by strips of white Istrian stone, with the rain-water entering through marble grilles. The *vere da pozzo* are minor monuments in their own right, most of them decorated with carvings and reliefs; almost all once bore a symbol of the Lion of St Mark, but these were removed by the French when they occupied the city in 1797.

On the northern side of Piazzetta dei Leoni is the former church of San Basso. The original church on this site was erected in 1076. The present building was built in 1665, and is attributed to Baldassare Longhena. The church was closed by the French in 1810; it is now used occasionally for lectures and art exhibitions.

The large edifice at the rear of the square is the Palazzo Patriarcale, the headquarters of the Patriarchate of Venice, which in 1807 was transferred here from the church of San Pietro di Castello. The palace was originally the Canonica of San Marco, the residence of the clergy of the Basilica, built in stone in 1618–35 to replace an earlier wooden building. The Canonica was rebuilt in 1837–50, by Lorenzo Santi.

We now head across the eastern end of the Piazza, passing the three flag-poles that stand in front of the Basilica of San Marco. The flag-poles are shown in Giovanni Bellini's painting of *The Procession of the Cross*, dated 1496, but without the present bronze bases, which were done in 1505 by Alessandro Leopardi. The bases are decorated with reliefs of allegorical figures representing the various virtues of the Serenissima, and on the central one there is a profile of Doge Leonardo Loredan, during whose reign the bases were put in place.

The campanile of San Marco stands isolated near the southeastern end of the piazza. The entrance to the campanile is through the Loggetta, the elegant little structure on the east side of the tower. The observation deck commands a sweeping view of Venice and its surrounding waters and isles. As Thomas Coryat wrote after his visit to Venice in 1608: '... whatsoever thou art ... forget not to go to the top of St Mark's tower before thou comest out of the city'.

The present campanile, completed in 1912, is a replica of the original, which collapsed in 1902. Francesco Sansovino, who wrote the first full-length printed guidebook to Venice, published in 1581, writes that the foundations of the original campanile were laid in 888; the shaft of the tower was completed in 1148, while the bell chamber seems to have been added *c.* 1170. The tower was struck by lightning in 1489 and its summit destroyed by fire. Doge Leonardo Loredan assigned the restoration to Bartolomeo Bon, who in 1510–13 built the new bell chamber, attic and pyramid, including the installation of the gilded copper statue of the Archangel Gabriel on its pinnacle, which survived the collapse of the original campanile

The height of the original campanile was 98.6 m, measured from the base to the head of the Archangel Gabriel; its width at the base of the tower was 12.8 m and one metre less at the top: all these dimensions are the same in the present campanile.

The original belfry contained four bells, which are described thus by the Procurators of San Marco: 'In the said campanile are four bells, all of an excellent sound; the smallest is called Trottiera, the next is known as Mezza Terza, the third as Nona, and the fourth and largest is Marangona.' According to Francesco Sansovino, there was also a fifth bell, a small one called Ringhiera. Each bell had its own distinctive sound, which was heard and recognized throughout Venice. Marangona received its name from the fact that it signalled the hours when work began and ended for the *marangoni*, the various guilds of Venice; it was tolled at midnight and, on occasion, to celebrate victories or announce emergencies. It also served as a first notice for meetings of the Maggior Consiglio, followed by the tolling of Trotteria, which was so called because at its sound the nobles who were behind schedule had to put their horses to the trot in order to reach the Palazzo Ducale on time. Nona rang at midday, and Mezza Terza announced meetings of the Senate, while Ringhiera, also known as Maleficio, was sounded only when an execution was to take place. All but one of these bells were shattered when the campanile collapsed in 1902, with only Marangona surviving intact to be rehung in 1910 in the new belfry, where it still tolls the hours, reminding one of the antiquity of this city.

The Loggetta at the base of the tower on its eastern side was rebuilt during the restoration of the campanile in 1902–12, using the materials that had survived from Sansovino's structure. The original Loggetta was built at the base of the campanile in the 15C as a 'Ridotto dei Nobili', or meeting-place for nobility, replacing the lean-to market shambles that had been built around the tower. This building was destroyed in 1489, when the lightning bolt that struck the campanile brought down part of the belfry and crushed the Loggetta. A new Loggetta was erected in the years 1537–49 by Sansovino, who also supervised the sculptural decoration. After 1589 the Loggetta ceased to be a Ridotto dei Nobili; instead it was set aside for the Procuratore di San Marco and his guard, who kept watch there during meetings of the Maggior Consiglio. After the fall of the Republic the Loggetta was used for the drawing of the government lottery, which took place every Saturday afternoon at three.

The Piazzetta took its present form around the same time as the Piazza. The square is bounded to its east by the Palazzo Ducale and to its west by Sansovino's library.

The library was erected to house the celebrated collection of books and manuscripts that had been bequeathed to Venice in 1468 by Cardinal Bessarion, a Greek from Trebizond who had been an archbishop in the Orthodox Church in Constantinople. Sansovino's original design called for the library, which he began in 1537, to be covered with a great Roman vault, with a two-storeyed facade of twenty-one arches along the west side of the Piazzetta, a short north wing of three arches on the Piazza, and three arches on the south side along the Molo. Starting from the campanile, work was progressing satisfactorily on the side of the building facing the Piazzetta, until suddenly, on 18 December 1545, the great vault of the library collapsed. Sansovino was held personally responsible for the disaster and was imprisoned, charged with paying the entire cost of the repairs. With the help of his many friends he was finally released after promising to pay for the repairs, which took him twenty years. When he resumed work he repaired the library, replacing the vault with a wooden-beamed ceiling. Sixteen arches of the building along the Piazzetta had been erected by 1554, when work was interrupted once again, to be completed in 1588 by Vincenzo Scamozzi.

The building is 18 m high and 81 m in length on the side facing the Piazzetta, with the lower colonnade in the Doric order and the upper in the Ionic. The building is surmounted by a classical parapet with statues of mythological deities above the columns of the colonnades and slender obelisks at the corners. The statues are by a number of Venetian and Tuscan artists, most notably Alessandro Vittoria and Bartolomeo Amannati. As well as Bessarion's library, the building also contains the Archaeological Museum, and gives entrance to the Biblioteca Nazionale Marciana, which is housed in the Zecca, or mint, the edifice behind the library.

The Zecca abuts the library on its seaward side, its facade stretching as far as Rio dei Giardinetti. From the Molo the Zecca extends inwards behind the library as far as the fifteenth column on the facade along the Piazzetta.

Venice was minting coins as early as the mid 9C, and in 1283 the Republic coined its first gold ducat, the famous zecchino. The original mint was demolished to make way for the present building, which was begun in 1536 by Jacopo Sansovino. The original design called for a ground floor with a facade of nine round arches, and a piano nobile of half-columns in the Doric order, but then Sansovino added a third storey with Ionic half-columns. The arches and columns are boldly rusticated. The Zecca functioned as a mint until 1870, and then it reopened in 1905 to house the Biblioteca Nazionale Marciana.

The twin columns on the Molo at the seaward end of the Piazzetta are among the oldest and most distinctive landmarks in Venice, appearing in the earliest extant representations of the city. The winged Lion of St Mark stands on the column to the east and St Theodore on the one to the west, holding a shield in his right hand and a lance in his left, standing on the back of an amphibian resembling a crocodile, but probably meant to represent a dragon. The statue of St Theodore is a copy of the original, which is preserved in the courtyard of the Palazzo Ducale, the one here having been put in its place in 1991. The columns are monoliths, the one on the east made of grey granite and that on the west of red Egyptian granite, both of them surmounted by huge Veneto-Byzantine capitals with crosses on the sides and palmette leaves on the corners. The two columns were brought back to Venice in 1172 by Doge Vitale Michiel II after a campaign in the Aegean, and were undoubtedly taken from the ruins of an ancient Graeco-Roman temple. According to tradition, they were erected on the Molo by Nicolò Baratieri, the engineer who built the first Rialto bridge in wood. As a reward, Baratieri was allowed to set up gambling booths between the columns for a card game he ran, called *barrato*, so that this part of the Molo came to be known as the Baratieri. At times when a public execution was held the gallows was erected on the Baratieri between the two columns. Both columns were stabilized in 1891, when they seemed in imminent danger of toppling over. The columns, which weigh 80 tons each, were then reset on their original pedestals.

We now walk back along the arcade of the library. The portal in the fifth bay of the arcade from the Molo is the entrance to the Biblioteca Nazionale Marciana, open only to readers. The portal in the eleventh bay is the entrance to the Libreria Sansoviniano itself, and is flanked by two caryatids done by Alessandro Vittoria with the assistance of Lorenzo Rubini. The library is open only for exhibitions.

The portal in the sixteenth bay of the arcade is the entrance to the Archaeological Museum. The core of the museum's collections are the antiquities that were bequeathed to the Republic by Cardinal Domenico Grimani in 1523 and by his nephew Giovanni Grimani, Patriarch of Aquileia, in 1593. The collection has since 1918 been housed in its present location, with the entrance hall leading into the easternmost courtyard of the Procuratie Nuove, that part of the palace completed by Vincenzo Scamozzi in the years 1586–1616. The most prominent antiquity in the courtyard is a colossal statue thought to be of Marcus Vipsanius Agrippa, the first minister of Augustus. A staircase on the right leads up from the courtyard to the museum proper, with the various antiquities displayed in a congeries of twenty rooms. The exhibits are mostly sculptures from the Graeco-Roman era, including statues, busts, figurines and funerary reliefs, jewellery, bronzes, pottery and other ceramics, inscriptions and coins. There is also one room devoted to Babylonian, Assyrian and Egyptian antiquities.

We now walk back to the central portico at the eastern end of the Piazza, where we ascend the Scala Maggiore to enter the Correr Civic Museum. The museum is named after Teodoro Correr (1750–1830), who devoted his lifetime to collecting works of art, documents, memorabilia and other items of interest associated with the history of Venice. The collection of the Correr Museum has now grown so large that it has been spread out over a number of other locations, which together are known as the Venetian Civic Museums of Art and History. The Correr Museum itself comprises two major sections: the Historical Section, on the first floor, and the Quadreria, or picture gallery, on the second floor. The Museum of the Risorgimento, devoted to Venice in the period of its unification with the modern Italian state, is in a separate section on the second floor.

The lobby of the museum is in the former antechamber of the Royal Palace, with the Ballroom directly ahead, though this is the last room one passes through in visiting the museum, which we enter through the door on the left. On the wall to the left in the antechamber is a full-size copy of Barbari's view of Venice in 1500, the original blocks of which are preserved in the museum.

The first gallery that we enter is the Napoleonic Loggia of the Royal Palace, after which we turn left and pass in turn through the next two galleries, the Throne Room and Dining Hall, before going on through the rest of the Historical Section. The Throne Room and Dining Hall contain recently salvaged panels of the early-19C frescoes that decorated the Royal Palace, including works by Francesco Hayez and Giancarlo Bevilacqua. Also exhibited here are marble statues of Orpheus and Eurydice done by Antonio Canova in 1776.

The galleries that follow on the first floor are identified as follows in the museum catalogue: the altar-frontal room; the Lion of St Mark; the Doge; dogal festivals; the Theatine

Bookcases, their shelves filled with books and manuscripts of the 16–18C; costumes; portraits of Doges; collections of coins and medals; portraits; the battle of Lepanto; the Bucintoro, the great barge used by the Doge on state occasions; the Arsenal; trade with the Orient; the Armoury; the Doge Francesco Morosini Rooms. Beyond these are several new galleries that opened in the spring of 1993, their exhibits including paintings depicting the various guilds of Venice; card games and other games of chance; portraits of boatmen victorious in regattas; as well as prints and models showing the Forze d'Ercole, the human pyramids formed in Piazza San Marco at times of festival.

The paintings in the Quadreria and elsewhere in the museum include four by Giovanni Bellini, three by Vittore Carpaccio, including his *Two Court Ladies*, which Ruskin described as 'the best picture in the world', two each by Paolo Veneziano, Lorenzo Veneziano, Stefano Veneziano and Bartolomeo Vivarini, and individual works by Jacopo Bellini, Gentile Bellini, Cosmè Tura, Alvise Vivarini, Andrea Mantegna, Lorenzo Lotto, Jacopo del Fiore, Giambattista Cima da Conegliano, Palma il Giovane and Michele Giambono, to mention only the most famous Italian painters.

The exhibits in the Museum of the Risorgimento include paintings, portrait busts, prints, documents, letters, manuscripts, proclamations, cartoons, caricatures, coins, medals, swords, rifles, military uniforms and other memorabilia, ranging in date from the fall of the Republic in 1797 to the union of Venice with the Kingdom of Italy in 1866.

After visiting the museums one is usually ready for a drink at Florian's or Quadri's. While relaxing there one might reflect upon all the historic events that have taken place in this great square, which Napoleon called 'the finest drawing-room in Europe', as well as the fêtes that have been celebrated here since the early years of the Serenissima and which continue today, the most spectacular modern festival being the world-famous Venetian Carnival. Thomas Coryat describes the scene in his *Crudities*, published in 1611, where he calls Piazza San Marco 'the fairest place of all the citie':

Truely such is the stupendious (to use a strange Epipheton for so strange and rare a place as this) glory of it, that at my first entrance thereof it did even amaze or rather ravish my senses. For here is the greatest magnificence of architecture to be seene, that any place under the sunne doth yeelde. Here you may both see all manner of fashions of attire, and hear all the languages of Christendome, besides those that are spoken by the barbarous Ethnickes; the frequencie of people being so great twise a day, betwixt sixe of the clocke in the afternoon and eight, that, as an elegant writer saith of it, a man may very properly call it rather Orbis rather than Urbis forum, that is a market place of the world, not of the citie.

[3] The Basilica of San Marco

The present basilica is the third church dedicated to St Mark to stand upon this site. When the body of the Evangelist was brought to Venice in 829 Doge Giustiniano Partecipazio first placed it in a chapel within the Palazzo Ducale. The Doge began the construction of a church to enshrine the saint, and this was completed in 836 by Doge Giovanni Partecipazio I. This church was destroyed by fire in 976. A new church was begun in 976 by Doge Pietro Orseolo I and completed towards the close of the 10C by Doge Pietro Orseolo II. Construction of the present edifice was begun in 1063 by Doge Domenico Contarini, and it was completed by Doge Vitale Falier (1084–96).

The original plan of the present building was based on that of the now-vanished church of the Holy Apostles in Constantinople, erected by Justinian c. 530. Like the Holy Apostles, San Marco is in plan a Greek cross, with a slight prolongation of the western arm. The intersection of the arms of the cross is covered by a central dome, with four other domes of somewhat unequal sizes surrounding it near the ends of the two axes. All five domes are hemispheres, the lofty bell-shaped cupolas with lanterns that we see today being added in the 13C. The interior domes are supported by huge quadripartite piers and, in the case of the north, south and east domes, by the corners of solid walls, strengthened in the transept by arches resting on twin columns. The space beneath the west dome is flanked to north and south by three columns on each side, which, together with the arched openings in the piers, form a

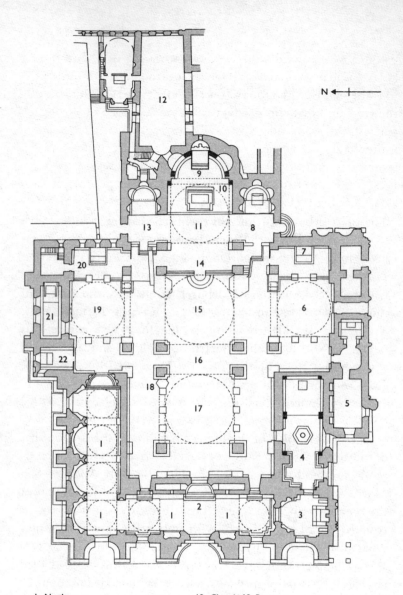

N ←

1. Narthex
2. Main Porch
3. Zen Chapel
4. Baptistery
5. Treasury
6. Dome of St Leonard
7. Altar of the Sacrament
8. Chapel of St Clement
9. Main Apse
10. Pala d'Oro
11. East Dome
12. Sacristy

13. Chapel of St Peter
14. Iconostasis
15. Dome of the Ascension
16. West Vault
17. West Dome
18. Il Capitello
19. Dome of St John the Evangelist
20. Chapel of the Virgin Nicopeia
21. Chapel of St Isodore
22. Chapel of the Madonna dei Mascoli

The Basilica of San Marco

colonnade that divides the western end of the nave into three aisles. Similar colonnades divide the north and south transepts into three spaces, the central ones domed. The eastern arm of the cross terminates in a semicircular apse covered by a conch, flanked by apsidal side chapels. The western arm of the cross is preceded by a narthex. In the 13C the narthex was extended around the north and south sides of the western arm of the cross, with the first bay on the southern side becoming the Zen Chapel and the remainder the baptistery. The extension of the narthex around the sides of the building, along with the addition of the lofty outer cupolas, was only part of the remodelling of the church in the 13C, when the sack of Constantinople in 1204 brought Venice such vast wealth that she lavished adornments on her cathedral. Precious marbles brought back from Constantinople were used to embellish the facade of the basilica, along with other treasures such as the four bronze horses which were set on the balcony over the main entrance. Thus in the second quarter of the 13C the plain Byzantine facades of the church began to disappear under what Ruskin described as its 'incrustation of brick with more precious materials', giving it what Otto Demus termed its 'plastic' shape, the outstanding feature being 'the lavish use of columns', which 'all but smother the architectural body with their massed bundles'. The dense rows of columns of rare marbles were placed in two orders, surmounted by Byzantine capitals ranging in date from the 6C to the 11C. This adornment of the facades went on for two centuries, reaching its climax in the first half of the 15C.

Five great portals with bronze doors originally led from the Piazza into the narthex, but the one on the far right was later changed into a window. The portals are set in large arched niches between projecting piers with clusters of columns in two orders. There are mosaics in each of the five coves of the arches above the portals, and also in the lunettes of all but the central arch in the upper zone of the facade. Only one of these mosaics is part of the original 13C decoration, that over the first door on the left, Porta Sant'Alipio, the others being replacements of the originals done by artists from the 17C to the 19C. The original mosaic, which is dated to 1260–70, depicts the Translation of the Body of St Mark into the Basilica. This scene is the earliest extant representation of the basilica, showing the facade essentially as it is today. The mosaics above the other doorways are, from left to right: St Mark Venerated by the Venetian Magistrates, Christ in Glory and the Last Judgement, the Body of St Mark Received by the Venetians and the Stealing of St Mark's Remains.

The arched portals themselves are of interest, as are the four doors that are still in place, all of them in bronze. The central door is Byzantine and is believed to be of the 6C, while the other three are identified by an inscription as works of a Venetian goldsmith named Bertucci, dated 1300. The intricate reliefs in the arches of the portals range in date from the beginning of the 13C to the early 14C. The sculptural decoration of the central porch consists of the reliefs of its three arches, including both their soffits and frontage, making six series in all. Two of the three archivolts surmount the door itself; the third and outermost surrounds the mosaic of the Last Judgement in the apse-like niche of the porch. The soffit of the great outer arch contains an astonishing catalogue of the trades and occupations of Venice. On the face of the arch, Christ is shown in benediction, flanked by the figures of the Prophets among vines and volutes. In the lunette over the door a relief depicting the Dream of St Mark is framed in an arch.

A terrace, erected in the 12C, extends around the whole length of the facade, dividing it into two zones. The four bronze horses taken from Constantinople were set up on pedestals at the centre of the terrace over the central portal, and they are shown there in the mosaic over Porta Sant'Alipio. The bronze horses one sees on the terrace today are copies of the originals, which are protected from the elements inside the basilica in the Museo Marciano. The four side arches are decorated with mosaics done in 1617 to replace earlier ones with the same subjects; they are, from left to right: the Descent from the Cross, the Harrowing of Hell, the Resurrection and the Ascension.

The five great arches in the upper zone of the western facade spring from double columns that are part of the original structure of the 11C basilica. Above the original round arches is the Gothic crown of pointed cusps, floral reliefs, statues, pinnacles and *aediculae*, or kiosks, an embellishment begun in the late 14C and continued in the first decades of the 15C. This was done under the direction of the Dalle Masegne, a family of Venetian builders, with the later assistance of master-builders from the Veneto and Lombardy and stonecutters from Tuscany, among whom the Florentine family of Lamberti played a prominent part. The gilded Lion of St Mark in the starred lune between the round and pointed arches is part of the 13C decoration.

The south facade of the basilica was also richly decorated, since it flanked the main entrance to the Palazzo Ducale and could be seen from the Piazzetta. The Treasury of the basilica juts out from the facade just beside the Porta della Carta, the entrance to the Palazzo Ducale. At the corner of the treasury wall is the porphyry group known as the Tetrarchs, another part of the loot removed from Constantinople in 1204. The group consists of four imperial figures who stand in a circle embracing one another, each with one hand on his sword. This is a representation of the Tetrarchy established by Diocletian in AD 293, showing himself and his co-emperor and their two caesars (sub-emperors). The left foot of one of the Tetrarchs was missing and was replaced in white stone. Excavations in Istanbul in 1965 resulted in the discovery of the missing porphyry foot by the archaeologists Martin Harrison and Nezih Firatli. A short way to the west of the Tetrarchs there are two large pillars known as the Pilastri Acritani. The name comes from the supposed origin of the pillars, for it was believed that they had been acquired by the Venetians in 1256 when they captured the city of Acre in Syria. The 1965 excavations in Istanbul by Harrison and Firatli revealed that in fact the pillars originally stood in the 6C church of St Polyeuktos in Constantinople, destroyed in 1204 by the Venetians and Crusaders.

At the south-west corner of the facade there is an isolated stump of a porphyry column known as the Pietra del Bando, the Proclamation Stone, so called because the public herald stood there when reading edicts from the Doge and the Signoria. The Pietra del Bando was also supposed to have been brought back from Acre in 1256, but it too undoubtedly came from Constantinople.

The northern facade of the basilica can be viewed from the Piazzetta dei Leoni. The fourth arch from the corner is the Porta dei Fiori, the Flower Gate, which leads into the easternmost bay of the north side of the narthex. The portal takes its name from the intertwined foliage in the reliefs on and within the trefoil arch above the door, as well as in the great circular arch above. In the lunette of the arch a trefoil foliate border frames a beautiful relief depicting the Nativity. The facade of the north transept has a large arch at its centre. A niche within the arch contains the sarcophagus of Daniele Manin, leader of the Venetian revolution against Austria in 1848–9. Manin died in exile in Paris in 1857, and his ashes were brought back to Venice in 1868.

We enter the narthex through the central portal. The other bays of the narthex are covered by blind domes and are connected to one another by arches and vaults flanked by arcades; the floor is paved in variegated mosaics with intricate geometrical patterns. The southern end of the narthex now terminates at the funerary chapel of Cardinal Giambattista Zen (d. 1501). The mosaics in the vault, twelve scenes from the Life of St Mark, were done in the 1270s.

Aside from the central bay, the mosaics in the rest of the narthex date back to the 13C decoration of the basilica, though there have been replacements, additions and restorations. The work commenced at the beginning of the 13C in the first bay, next to the Zen Chapel, and it continued from there through the west and north sides of the narthex, with those in the last bay completed towards the end of the century. The iconographic cycle begins in the first bay with the Creation; it goes on to the History of Noah and the Deluge, interrupted by the first bay; continuing with the Building of the Tower of Babel, the History of Abraham and the Histories of Joseph and Moses, concluding in the last bay on the north side.

Each of the vaulted bays on either side of the main entrance has a tomb built within a niche in its western wall, the oldest funerary monuments in Venice. The tomb to the right is that of Doge Vitale Falier (d. 1096); the one to the left is that of the Dogaressa Felicita (d. 1101), wife of Doge Vitale Michiel I. At the north-west corner of the narthex there is a blind niche that contains a suspended sarcophagus, the tomb of Doge Bartolomeo Gradenigo (d. 1342). There is another sarcophagus in the blind niche on the northern side of the fifth bay, the tomb of Doge Marin Morosini (d. 1253). In the blind niche of the sixth bay is the tomb of Bartolomeo Ricoverati, Dean of San Marco (d. 1420).

We now return to the central bay of the west narthex, which has above it a great open vault known as Il Pozzo, the Well, covered by the Arco del Paradiso. The surfaces of this aperture are covered with 16C mosaics depicting the Crucifixion, the Deposition in the Sepulchre, the Raising of Lazarus, the Death of the Virgin, the Four Evangelists and eight Prophets. Two ranges of niches flanking the door contain mosaic portraits, with the Virgin and Child flanked by eight Apostles in the upper order and in the lower one the four Evangelists. These mosaics are dated c. 1070, and are among the earliest in the basilica. The two side doors in the apse lead to the galleries and the Museo Marciano.

On entering the nave we pass under Arco dell'Apocalisse, the Arch of the Apocalypse, which takes its name from the five mosaics of the Vision of St John the Evangelist, done in 1570–89 by the brothers Francesco and Arminio Zuccato. Looking back, we see the Arco del Paradiso, decorated with mosaics depicting the Last Judgement; these were done in 1557–1619 from cartoons by Tintoretto, Antonio Vassilacchi and Maffeo da Verona. Above the door there is a 13C mosaic representing Christ the Saviour between the Virgin and St Mark.

We then come under the Dome of the Pentecost. This was the first of the domes to be decorated with mosaics, in the first half of the 12C, representing the Feast of Pentecost. In the crown of the dome the Holy Spirit is symbolized by a dove, enthroned along with the Gospel, with rays of light descending radially on the heads of the twelve Apostles.

High on the walls of both aisles there is a frieze of *pinakes*, or tablets, five on either side, all dating from the first half of the 13C. Christ Emmanuel is depicted on the central tablet on the left and the Virgin in the centre on the right, each of them flanked by prophets. On the wall and arch above the frieze on the left wall are scenes from the Life of Christ and the Apostles, done in 1619–24 from cartoons by Tizianello, Padovanino, Vassilacchi and Palma il Giovane. On the wall of the south aisle above the frieze is a large mosaic representing the Agony in the Garden dating from the early 13C. In the upper order, flanking the windows and in the arch above, is a mosaic representing the Lives of the Apostles dated *c.* 1200. At the western end of the south wall, to the right of the door leading into the baptistery (now closed for restoration), there is a relief showing Christ flanked by the Virgin and St John the Baptist, a Byzantine work of the late 10C.

Near the front of the aisle on the left is the tiny chapel known as 'Il Capitello'. This is a kiosk with a circular arcade of six columns of precious marbles topped by gilded Byzantine capitals, covered by a pyramidal marble roof surmounted by a huge agate. The chapel enshrines a painted wooden crucifix of Byzantine origin.

We now pass under the west vault of the central dome, whose mosaics depict the Passion and Resurrection, dating from the mid 13C. We then continue on to the transept, where the central dome covers the crossing point of the two arms of the Greek cross. This is known as the Dome of the Ascension, because of the theme of its mosaic decoration, dating from the early 13C.

The mosaic in the centre of the south vault of the central dome is the Eternal Father in Glory, done in the first half of the 17C. The other four mosaics on the vault are scenes from the Life of Christ, done at the end of the 12C or the beginning of the 13C.

The two piers that support the central dome to the east anchor between them the iconostasis, or rood screen, which separates the nave from the chancel. Above its centre is a huge silver and bronze crucifix, done in the second half of the 14C by Jacopo di Marco Bennato. On either side are marble statues of the Virgin, St John the Baptist and the twelve Apostles, signed in 1390 by Jacobello and Pier Paolo Dalle Masegne. The iconostasis is flanked by two pulpits set against the eastern piers of the central dome, both of them dating from the 13C. On the pier above the pulpit on the right is a 15C statue of the Virgin and Child.

The end of the right transept is covered by the Dome of St Leonard. This is named for one of the eight saints who are depicted in mosaics in the dome and its pendentives, surrounding a simple cross within a golden orb in the crown. The original mosaics were done in the 13C, but three figures are 15–16C replacements.

The vault on the west side of the Dome of St Leonard is decorated with mosaics depicting Acts of the Virgin, originally done in the 13C and replaced by the present works in the 17C. On the wall below are two 13C mosaics depicting the miraculous rediscovery of the body of St Mark in the Basilica in 1094, after it had been lost in the rebuilding of the church. On the west face of the pier supporting the Dome of

St Leonard on that side there is a 12C relief known as 'The Madonna of the Kiss'.

At the end of the aisle is the entrance to the Tesoro, or Treasury, for which there is a separate admission fee. The doorway is surmounted by a trefoil ogive arch framing a statuette representing the Risen Christ, flanked by two mosaic angels, a work that predates the destruction of the old treasury in 1231. The exhibits in the Treasury constitute only a tiny fraction of the treasures in San Marco, the most precious of which are part of the loot from the sack of Constantinople in 1204.

In the lunette above the door at the end of the transept there is a 13C mosaic portrait of St Mark. The tympanum wall has a superb Gothic rose window of the 15C. The soffit of the arch that springs from double columns on either side of the niche has mosaics of Sts Anthony, Bernardino, Vincent and Paul the Hermit, all mid 15C.

The eastern vault of the Dome of St Leonard is decorated with mosaics depicting the Parables and Miracles of Christ, originally done c. 1200, with some replaced in the 15C. The Miracles of Christ continue on the end wall, along with scenes depicting the Acts of St Leonard, remade in the 17C after a cartoon by Pietro Vecchia.

The eastern vault covers the Altar of the Sacrament, designed in 1617 by Tommaso Contino. Built up against the pier to the left is the little Altar of St James, commissioned by Doge Cristoforo Moro (1462–71). The statue of St James and other adornments on the altar are works by Lombard masters of the third quarter of the 15C.

The arch between this pier and the one to its left leads to the Chapel of St Clement. A flight of steps leads up to the doorway of an iconostasis in Verona marble, formed by a balustrade with four columns surmounted by an architrave. On the architrave there are statues of the Virgin and Child between Sts Christina, Clara, Catherine and Agnes, all done in 1397 by Jacobello and Pier Paolo Dalle Masegne. In the lower arch is a mosaic depicting St Philip and St James, and in the conch one of St Clement, both 12C.

A separate admission fee is charged for admittance to the chancel, whose public entrance is on the north side of the chapel of St Clement. On either side of the sanctuary inside the iconostasis are the *cantorie*, the galleries used by the singers and musicians. Their balustrades are decorated with eight reliefs depicting Acts and Miracles in the Life of St Mark, signed by Jacopo Sansovino and dated 1537. On the side walls there are six statues of saints in bronzed terracotta, attributed to Pietro da Salò. The mosaics in the vault linking the central and eastern domes depict the Annunciation and four scenes from the life of Christ, done in 1587–9 by Giannantonio Marini from a cartoon by Tintoretto.

The mosaics in the eastern dome were originally done in the first quarter of the 12C. The central figure in the crown of the dome, Christ Emmanuel, was destroyed in the fire of 1419 and was redone *c.* 1500. The other figures are arrayed around the base of the dome above the windows, with the Virgin at Prayer facing west and around her thirteen prophets carrying scrolls with biblical inscriptions, while the pendentives are decorated with the symbols of the four Evangelists. The vaults between the eastern dome and the side chapels to its north and south are decorated with 12C mosaics depicting episodes from the Life of St Mark and the Translation of Mark's Relics. On the end wall, there are 12C mosaics depicting episodes from the Life of St Clement. Above the side door leading to the Palazzo Ducale there is an 11C mosaic of Cain and Abel offering gifts to the Eternal Father.

The high altar stands isolated in the inner half of the area beneath the eastern dome. On the variegated marble balustrades at the sides are eight bronze statuettes. The inner ones are the four Evangelists, done by Jacopo Sansovino in 1550–52; they are flanked by four Doctors of the Church, signed by Girolamo Pagliari and dated 1614. The altar table covers the sarcophagus of St Mark, which was removed from the crypt and placed here on 26 August 1835. The altar is surrounded by four alabaster columns with 12C capitals supporting a verd-antique ciborium. At the top of the ciborium in front there are three marble statues, with three more behind. The statues in front represent Christ between St Mark and St John; those behind are of the Redeemer between St Mark and St Luke. The statues are all dated to the 13C except that of the Redeemer, which was done in the 18C. The ciborium columns are carved with deeply incised reliefs representing scenes from the New Testament, dating from the mid 13C.

Behind the altar, facing the apse of the church, is the famous Pala d'Oro, one of the most remarkable products of the goldsmith's art that has survived from the medieval world. The original Pala d'Oro was commissioned by Doge Pietro Orseolo I (976–8) and was made to order in Constantinople. The altarpiece was sent back to Constantinople in 1105 by Doge Ordelafo Falier in order to be enlarged and embellished, and in 1209 Doge Pietro Ziani had it adorned further, using precious materials looted from Byzantium. The Pala d'Oro achieved its present form under Doge Andrea Dandolo, who in 1345 commissioned the goldsmith Gianpolo Boninsegna to rework it. The altarpiece is decorated with 176 sculptured cloisonné enamel panels and medallions of various sizes and shapes bordered in gold frames set with precious stones.

In the centre of the conch of the apse there is a huge 16C mosaic of the Pantocrator enthroned, and below this, flanking the three windows, are the figures of Sts Nicholas, Peter, Mark and Hermagoras, dating from the late 11C. Placed against the central niche of the apse is the small Altar of the Sacrament, with an architrave supported by six columns. The statuettes on either side of the altar are of St Francis and St Bernardino, done at the beginning of the 16C by Lorenzo Bregno. On the door of the tabernacle there is a superb relief in gilded bronze showing Christ between Angels, by Jacopo

Sansovino. The bronze doors of the sacristy in the niche to the left, with reliefs of the Resurrection and Deposition, are also by Sansovino.

The chapel to the left of the chancel is dedicated to St Peter. The approach passage to the chapel is decorated with mosaics of Moses and Elijah, done in 1593 by Lorenzo Ceccato. The chapel is preceded by a four-column iconostasis whose architrave supports five statues, with the Virgin between Sts Mary Magdalene, Cecilia, Helena and Margaret. The statues date from the end of the 14C and are attributed to the Dalle Masegne brothers. In the conch of the apse above the altar there is a restored mosaic of St Peter, done originally in the mid 12C.

We now go on into the left transept, starting with the vault that links the central and northern domes. The mosaics in this vault depict the Last Supper and five Miracles of Christ. These are replacements of the original mosaics, and were done in the 16–17C from cartoons by Veronese, Tintoretto and Salviati. Set up against the pier to the left of the Chapel of St Peter is the little Altar of St Paul, commissioned by Doge Cristoforo Moro and made by a Lombard master during the 1460s. The 16C statue of St Paul is attributed to Danese Cattaneo.

Beyond the north arch is the Dome of St John the Evangelist. The main theme of the mosaic decoration in the dome is the Life of St John the Evangelist, dating from the end of the 12C. The mosaics in the pendentives depict four Church Fathers. Beyond the Altar of St Paul a vault shielded by a three-arched iconostasis leads to the Altar of the Virgin. The mosaics in the vault, most of them redone in the 17C, depict Episodes and Miracles in the Life of Christ. The altar was reconstructed in its present form in 1617 to enshrine the miraculous icon of the Virgin Nicopeia, Our Lady of Victory, taken from Constantinople in 1204.

At the end of the north transept a door leads into the chapel of St Isidore, originally a depository. Doge Andrea

Dandolo decided to convert it into a chapel to enshrine the body of St Isidore, brought back from Chios in 1125 by Doge Domenico Michiel, and the work was finished in 1355 under Doge Giovanni Gradenigo. The mosaics in the chapel date from the mid 14C and are almost untouched by restorers. Above the altar is Christ between St Mark and St Isidore; on the opposite side, the Virgin and Child between St Nicholas and St John the Baptist. On the vault and side wall to the right the mosaics show episodes of the life of St Isidore and on the left the removal of his remains to Venice. The vault above the chapel is decorated with mosaics depicting the Miracles of Christ, dated c. 1300. On the end wall a huge mosaic depicts the Genealogical Tree of the Virgin, done by Vincenzo Bianchini in 1542–51 from a cartoon by Salviati.

To the left of the door to the Chapel of St Isidore is the Chapel of the Madonna dei Mascoli. The chapel takes its name from the Confraternita dei Mascoli, founded in the 12C; their original place of assembly was in the crypt, but in 1618 they began using this as a place of prayer. An inscription on the altar records that it was erected in 1430; in niches there are statues of the Virgin and Child between St Mark and St John by Bartolomeo Bon. The vault of the chapel is decorated with a mosaic cycle begun c. 1430 by Michele Giambono and still in progress in 1450. The mosaics, depicting five episodes in the Life of the Virgin, are based on cartoons by Jacopo Bellini and possibly Andrea Mantegna and Andrea del Castagno; these are among the first important works of Renaissance painting in Venice. On the wall to the right of the chapel there is a 13C relief of the Virgin at Prayer.

The side aisle of the north transept opens into the north end of the narthex through Porta di San Giovanni. The west vault and the end wall of the transept are decorated with mosaics depicting the Acts of the Virgin and the Infancy of Christ, dating from the end of the 12C and the beginning of the 13C, with some later restoration. The mosaics in the lower order on the end wall tell the story of St Susanna, done in 1588–91 from cartoons by Tintoretto and Palma il Giovane.

Above Porta di San Giovanni there is a trefoil ogive arch framing a mosaic portrait of St John the Evangelist. The reliefs in the arch show Christ Emmanuel at the apex and half figures of angels in the spandrels. The arch and its relief and the mosaic portrait have all been dated to the third quarter of the 13C.

There are two reliefs on the pier that forms the south-west corner of the area under the Dome of St John. On the south face of the pier is the Madonna dello Schioppo, a 13C relief of the Virgin and Child, which has an old rifle fixed to the left side of its frame. The rifle is a dedicatory offering from a detachment of Venetian marines who were miraculously saved from an Austrian bomb at Fort Marghera on 10 May 1849, during the siege of Venice. On the west face of the pier there is an 11C Byzantine relief known as the Madonna della Grazia.

We now walk up the north aisle of the nave to look at the pavement there, which includes the most striking examples of the floor mosaics in the basilica, done in the 12C. The pavement mosaics are mostly in elaborate geometrical patterns, as well as panels with confronted peacocks and doves, an eagle attacking a rabbit, a swan with a snake in its beak, a lion biting a wolf, and a winged horse.

Next we visit the Museo Marciano, gallery and balcony. (Another admission fee is charged.) The main room of the museum is used to exhibit the four bronze horses that formerly stood on the balcony over the main entrance to the basilica. Originally part of a quadriga, or four-horse chariot, they are masterpieces of Greek bronzework of the 4C BC, taken from Greece to Constantinople by Constantine the Great after he established his capital there in AD 330.

Only the front part of the gallery is now open to the public, but from there one can look out over the nave and take a closer look at the mosaics in the upper zone of the basilica, including those in the Arco del Paradiso. One can also walk out on to the balcony above the front and south side of the church, commanding a sweeping view of the Piazza and Piazzetta and their surrounding buildings.

[4] The Palazzo Ducale

Our next tour will take us through the Palazzo Ducale, the Doge's Palace. The Palazzo Ducale was the residence of the doge, as well as the headquarters of the executive, legislative and judicial organs of government, the centre of the political world of the Venetian Republic.

The original Palazzo Ducale was erected by Doge Agnello Partecipazio (811–27). The palace was destroyed by fire in 976, and it was rebuilt soon afterwards by Doge Pietro Orseolo I. The exterior of the palace began to take on its present form during a radical rebuilding programme that began in 1340 and ended in 1419. This comprised that part of the present palace facing the Molo and extending northwards along the Piazzetta as far as the seventh arch of the facade. The next stage of construction began in 1424, under Doge Francesco Foscari, when the facade along the Piazzetta was extended to its present length, along with the addition of the Gothic crown of crenellations, spires, pinnacles and *aediculae* to match those on the facade of the basilica. A fire in 1483 destroyed the old east wing of the palace along Rio de Palazzo. A new east wing was then begun under the supervision of Antonio Rizzo, who was succeeded as architect in 1498 by Giorgio Spavento and Scarpagnino, with the decorative work under the direction of Pietro Lombardo. The east wing was completed in 1550, with work on the interior decoration taking another decade. The Palazzo delle Prigioni, the Palace of the Prisons, was built as an annexe to the Palazzo Ducale on the other side of Rio de Palazzo in

1563–1614, with the two buildings connected by the famous Ponte dei Sospiri, the Bridge of Sighs.

The Gothic arcades along the Molo and the Piazzetta are of almost equal length, the first 71 m long with seventeen arches and the second 74 m with eighteen arches. Both are 25 m high, the crenellations rising another 2 m. The arcades are formed by thirty-six marble columns that stand without pedestals on the original pavement 0.4 m below the present ground level. Pointed arches spring from the capitals of the arcade to support the loggia, which forms a balcony that runs almost completely around the palace, fronted by a marble balustrade between the columns. There are twice as many columns in the portico of the piano nobile as in the lower arcade, with ogive arches springing from their capitals and supporting between them the quadrifoliate roundels character-istic of Venetian Gothic architecture. Above the piano nobile the facade is revetted in a lozenge pattern of white Istrian stone and pink Verona marble, pierced by seven large win-dows on each of the two sides, the central ones opening on to balconies. The balcony over the Molo is the work of Pier Paolo and Jacobello Dalle Masegne in 1400–1404. The top ornament, a tripartite *aedicula* with statues of Sts Peter, Mark and Paul in the niches, was rebuilt in 1579, with the statue of Venice as Justice on the pinnacle added by Alessandro Vittoria. The balcony over the Piazzetta was done in 1536 by Pietro da Salò and Danese Cattaneo. The huge relief above the window shows Doge Andrea Gritti kneeling before the Lion of St Mark; this is a modern work which replaced the original destroyed by the French in 1797. The statue of Venice as Justice on the pinnacle above was done in 1579 by Alessandro Vittoria.

There are reliefs on the three corners of the facades at arch level of the arcades on both the ground level and the piano nobile, as well as on the capitals of the thirty-six columns of the lower portico. The first that we will examine is on the corner of the facade on the Molo by the Ponte de la Paglia.

Ruskin called this the 'angle of the Vine'; the corner between the Molo and the Piazzetta he named the 'angle of the Fig Tree' and the one beside the Basilica the 'Judgement angle'. The upper relief at the angle of the Vine shows Tobias and the Archangel Raphael, a work dating from the 14C. The lower relief depicts the Drunkenness of Noah, who is shown on the front of the angle, while two of his two sons, who are trying to cover his nakedness, are on the side, with a third son shown on the other side of the arch opening on to the canal; this is dated to the end of the 14C or the beginning of the 15C, and may be by Matteo Raverti.

The reliefs on the eighteen capitals on the ground-level arcade along the Molo, as well as the first seven along the Piazzetta, were done by Lombard masters and Venetian stonemasons in the first phase of the construction of the Gothic facades, 1340–1419, while the remaining eleven were done in the second building phase, 1424–38. The sculptures on the angle of the Vine show the Archangel Michael above on the loggia, and below Adam and Eve and the Serpent.

The first seven reliefs on the capitals of the facade along the Piazzetta date from the same building stage as those on the Molo, while the remaining eleven are from the later stage. The roundel above the thirteenth column in the loggia has a relief showing Venice as Justice. The transition point between the two building stages along the Piazzetta can be seen at the centre of the eighth arch from the Fig Tree angle.

Both reliefs on the Judgement angle date from the first half of the 15C; the lower one is the Judgement of Solomon, by the Lamberti family; the upper one is the Archangel Gabriel, by Bartolomeo Bon.

We enter the Palazzo Ducale through the Porta della Carta, the Paper Gate. The gate probably takes its name from the fact that it was the station of the scribes who wrote petitions and other legal papers for those who had dealings with the Signoria. It was commissioned by Doge Francesco Foscari, and was built in 1438–43 by Giovanni Bon and his

Ground Floor

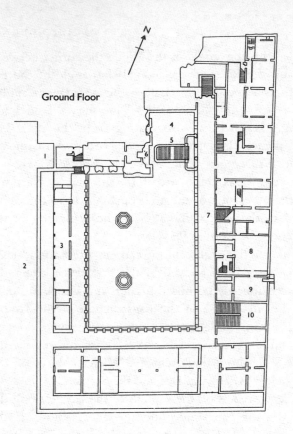

The Palazzo Ducale

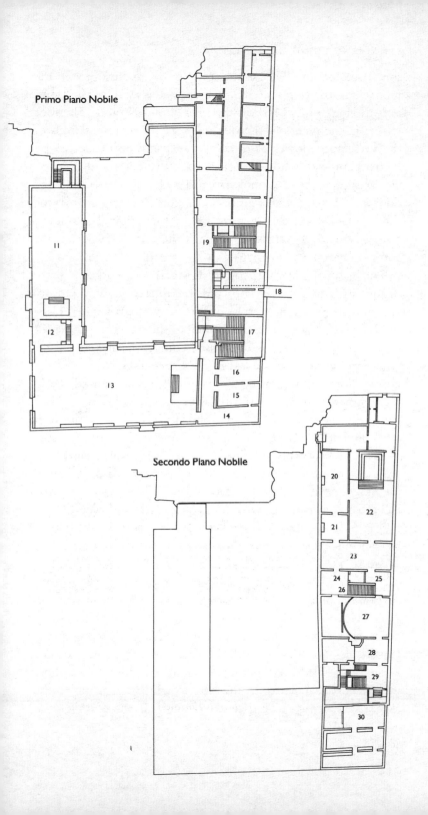

Primo Piano Nobile

Secondo Piano Nobile

son Bartolomeo. The statue of Venice as Justice on the pinnacle of the trefoil arch above the gateway is by the Bons, as is the bust of St Mark in the medallion below it. The four statues in the niches of the side pilasters are representations of the Virtues; the lower pair, Temperance and Fortitude, are by Pietro Lamberti, while the upper two, Prudence and Charity, are attributed to Antonio Bregno. The group above the doorway shows Doge Francesco Foscari kneeling before the Lion of St Mark; this is a replica of the original sculpture, which was destroyed by the French in 1797. The portal was completely restored in 1976–9 by the Venice in Peril Fund.

The gateway leads to Arco Foscari, the Foscari Porch, begun by the Bon family and completed after 1440 by Antonio Bregno. The porch consists of six cross-vaulted bays, the last five of which open on their right into the portico of the Cortile di Palazzo, the inner courtyard of the palace. After emerging from the last bay we turn back to look at the Foscari Porch. This was begun by the Bons and completed in the reign of Doge Cristoforo Moro (1462–71) by Stefano Bon di Nicolò of Cremona; the sculptural decoration is attributed to a number of artists from Lombardy and the Veneto, most notably Antonio Bregno and Antonio Rizzo.

Directly opposite the Foscari Porch is the Scala dei Giganti, the Stairway of the Giants, named for the colossal statues that flank its upper landing, with Mars on the left and Neptune on the right. The stairway and its reliefs were done in 1484–1501 by Antonio Rizzo, with the statues of Mars and Neptune added in 1566 by Jacopo Sansovino. The Scala dei Giganti is part of the Renaissance wing of the palace. The ornate decoration of the facade was begun by Pietro Lombardo in 1498, with Scarpagnino finishing the project in 1550–60. The little courtyard to the left of the Scala dei Giganti is the Cortile dei Senatori, so called because the members of the Senate assembled there before public ceremonies. From there we ascend the stairway to the left, which brings us up to the loggia, a balcony that extends around all the sides of the

Cortile di Palazzo except the north. The abbreviated north side, which stops short of the Scala dei Giganti, is in two parts; at its end, to the right, is the north facade of the Arco Foscari, and to the left is the so-called Clock Facade. The latter, built in 1603–14 by Bartolomeo Monopola with the help of Pietro Cittadella, is a classical three-storeyed facade with a clock in the centre of the upper storey, surrounded with niches containing statues of robed figures in ancient dress. The north facade of the Arco Foscari is topped on its Gothic spires with allegorical figures of the Arts, and at its base there is a large marble statue of an armed figure, a representation of the *condottiere* Francesco Maria della Rovere (1490–1538), Duke of Urbino, done in 1587 by Giovanni Bandini. The south side of the courtyard opens up at its centre into the Porta del Frumento, the Wheat Gate; this was built in the early 17C by Bartolomeo Monopola, who also rebuilt the south and west facades of the courtyard in their present form. The gate takes its name from the fact that above it on the loggia was the Ufficio delle Biade, the office of the magistrate who controlled the wheat trade. In the south-east corner of the courtyard we see the original marble statue of St Theodore that formerly stood atop one of the two columns on the Molo. In the centre of the courtyard there are two superb bronze *vere da pozzo*, dating from the mid 16C.

The interior of the palace is reached by an archway in the middle of the east loggia. The archway opens on to the Scala d'Oro, the Golden Stairway, designed by Jacopo Sansovino in 1554 and completed by Scarpagnino in 1559. The stairway is named for its vaulted ceiling, decorated with white and gilt stuccoes by Alessandro Vittoria and frescoes by Giovan Battista Franco. The door on the left on the first landing, the Primo Piano Nobile, leads into the Doge's Apartments, which are open only for special exhibitions.

At the top of Scala d'Oro we come to the Secondo Piano Nobile. Here we enter Atrio Quadrato, an anteroom to the state rooms beyond built in the reign of Doge Girolamo Priuli (1559–67). The painting in the centre of the carved and gilded ceiling was done by Jacopo Tintoretto, and shows the Doge receiving the scales and sword from Justice, with the Virgin and St Jerome.

We now enter the large gallery known as the Sala delle Quattro Porte. This was originally the Collegio, the meeting place of the Signoria, but it was destroyed on 12 May 1574 in the great fire that ravaged the Renaissance wing of the palace. After being restored it served as a public anteroom for those waiting to be admitted to the presence of the Senate. The restoration, carried out during the reign of Doge Marino Grimani (1595–1605) by Antonio da Ponte, was based on designs by Andrea Palladio and was supervised by Giovanni Antonio Rusconi. The frescoes on the ceiling were painted by Tintoretto in 1578–81. One of the notable paintings on the walls, *Doge Antonio Grimani Kneeling before Faith and St Mark in Glory*, was begun by Titian in 1555 and finished probably by his nephew Marco Vecellio. Another is *Neptune Offering Venice the Riches of the Sea*, done by Giambattista Tiepolo in 1749–50.

The next room is the Anticollegio. This was also restored after the fire of 1574, by Antonio da Ponte, to a design by Palladio, and supervised by Rusconi, with sculptural decoration by Vincenzo Scamozzi, Tiziano Aspetti and Alessandro Vittoria. The octagonal panel in the centre of the ceiling, representing *Venice Conferring Rewards and Honours*, was done by Veronese *c.* 1578. On the wall facing the windows are: *The Rape of Europa* by Veronese (1580) and *The Return of Jacob and his Family* by Jacopo Bassano. The paintings flanking the two doors were done by Tintoretto in 1577–8; they are *Mercury and the Three Graces*, *The Forge of Vulcan*, *Bacchus Crowning Ariadne with the Corona Borealis* and *Pallas Protecting Peace and Abundance while Fending Off Mars*.

Next is the Sala del Collegio. This was the meeting place of the Signoria, a group of thirteen that consisted of the Doge and his six councillors, the three chiefs of the Quarantia and the three additional members, known as *savi*, or sages. The Signoria served as a steering committee for all matters brought before the Senate, and it also functioned as the Doge's cabinet. The Sala del Collegio was restored after the 1574 fire under the direction of Antonio da Ponte. The new hall was designed by Palladio and its restoration was carried out between 1575 and 1578 under the supervision of Rusconi. The paintings on the ceiling were done in 1575–7 by Veronese. Veronese also did the painting on the wall above the Doge's throne in the tribune, depicting Sebastiano Venier's thanksgiving for victory after the battle of Lepanto in 1571. The four large paintings on the wall facing the windows and the one facing the tribune were done by Tintoretto and his students in 1581–4; in them the Doges Francesco Donà, Nicolò da Ponte, Alviso Mocenigo and Andrea Gritti appear as donors.

The following room is the Sala del Senato. Originally the number of senators was fixed at sixty, elected annually, but later the Senate was enlarged by the inclusion in it of the Quarantia, or Council of Forty, and by the addition of sixty more members called the Zonta. Ambassadors and high-ranking naval officers were also admitted to the Senate, so that eventually the number allowed to attend its meetings rose to some 300, of whom about 230 had the right to vote, with those who actually voted averaging 180. The Sala del Senato was restored after the fire of 1574 by Antonio da Ponte, and all but two of the paintings that decorate the room were done in 1581–95. The large central panel within volutes in the ceiling represents *The Exaltation and Triumph of Venice* by Jacopo and Domenico Tintoretto. Above the Doge's throne there is a large painting by Jacopo Tintoretto and his school, *The Dead Christ Supported by Angels, Adored by Doges Pietro Lando and Marcantonio Trevisan*. Other paintings on the ceiling and walls of the room include eight works by Palma il Giovane, two by Jacopo Tintoretto, and one by Giandomenico Tiepolo.

We now leave the Sala del Senato and walk back through

the Sala delle Quattro Porte, after which we go through an L-shaped passageway to enter the Sala del Consiglio dei Dieci. The Consiglio dei Dieci was established in 1310 after the abortive revolt of Bajamonte Tiepolo, and had ten members, including three Capi, or Heads. The initial responsibilities of the Ten were to guard against subversion, to supervise the security police, and to carry out sentences of exile. Subsequently it was used by the Signoria to deal with matters whose urgency and secrecy made it preferable to have them handled by the Ten rather than by the whole Senate. Beginning in the late 16C the Ten increased its control over criminal matters by creating a special committee of three state inquisitors, who at first were concerned only with guarding state secrets but later assumed jurisdiction over all crimes committed by the nobility, which made them the most feared and hated institution in Venice.

The Council of Ten convened in the Sala del Consiglio dei Dieci; the chamber beyond, the Sala della Bussola, served as the anteroom, with a door leading to an inner chamber, not open to the public, where the Capi held their secret deliberations. All three rooms were restored early in the 16C, with Pietro Lombardo beginning the project and Scarpagnino completing the work in 1516. The most notable paintings in the Hall of the Ten are two works by Veronese, *Venice receives the Ducal Cap from Juno* and *An Old Oriental Man with a Young Woman.*

After the Sala della Bussola, which takes its name from the wooden entrance screen in the corner to the right, we go into an anteroom at the head of the Scala dei Censori. We then follow a corridor to the left of the stairway, which brings us into the Armoury of the Council of Ten. The collection comprises over two thousand pieces, including Venetian weapons from as early as the 14C, captured armaments and trophies, and important objects presented by foreign visitors.

After passing through the Armoury we return to the Scala dei Censori, by which we descend to the Primo Piano Nobile.

There we turn left to enter the long and lofty Andito del Maggior Consiglio. The passageway is flanked with elaborately carved stalls and covered with an open-beam ceiling, painted and gilded at the end of the 16C. At the centre of the wall on the left there is a painting of *The Transfiguration* by Domenico Tintoretto; and on the front wall, *Doge Marcantonio Memmo before the Virgin along with the Patron Saints of Venice*, signed by Palma il Giovane and dated 1615.

On the left side of the passageway there are two large rectangular rooms, the first of which is the Sala della Quarantia Civil Vecchia, the branch of the Forty dealing with civil law in Venice. On the left wall there is a tabernacle with a 15C painting of the Virgin and Child. The second room is the Sala dell'Armamento, which was originally an ammunition depot for the Armoury on the floor above. On the walls there are the remnants of a vast fresco painted by Guariento of Padua in 1365–7 above the Doge's throne in the Hall of the Great Council: *Paradise, the Coronation of the Virgin and the Court in Heaven*. This fresco was badly damaged in the fire of 1577, and was covered over by Tintoretto's *Il Paradiso*. When restoration of Tintoretto's painting began in 1903 the surviving fragments of the earlier fresco by Guariento were removed and placed here.

At the end of the passageway we come to a transverse corridor known as the Liago, an antechamber used by the nobility during meetings of the Maggior Consiglio. The end of the Liago to the left is now roped off as a gallery to exhibit three marble statues that once stood in niches on the Arco Foscari, now replaced there by bronze replicas: these are Adam and Eve, signed in 1476 by Antonio Rizzo, and the Reggiscudo, or Shield-bearer, attributed to Rizzo.

We now enter Sala del Maggior Consiglio, by far the largest chamber in the palace, 54 m long, 25 m wide and 15.4 m high. The hall on its present scale was begun in 1340, and it was inaugurated on 30 July 1419. The vastness of this chamber reflects the size of the Maggior Consiglio, which after 1297 had a membership that ranged from 1,100 to 1,600, comprising virtually all the adult males of the nobility. The Doge, flanked by the Signoria, sat in his throne at the centre of the dais, while the members of the Council sat in the stalls along the other three walls and in the nine double rows of benches that occupied the main area of the hall. The hall was restored after the fire of 1577 under the direction of Antonio da Ponte, and the leading artists of Venice were commissioned to decorate it with paintings.

The huge ornate ceiling, designed by Cristoforo Sorte, has fifteen major paintings, all of which were completed between 1578 and 1585. The middle section of the ceiling contains three large oval paintings depicting the glorification of Venice, while each of the two side sections has six smaller pictures showing historical episodes in the Republic's conquest of its mainland territories and overseas empire. These include four works by Francesco Bassano, three each by Veronese and Palma il Giovane, and three by Tintoretto and his pupils.

The frieze under the ceiling contains the portraits of seventy-six Doges, in pairs. The series begins with Obelario degli Antenori (804–11), the seventh Doge; it then continues down to Francesco Venier (1554–6), with the last forty-two Doges portrayed in the frieze of Sala dello Scrutinio. The commission for painting the Doges' portraits, most of which are imaginary, was given to Jacopo Tintoretto, but they were actually carried out almost entirely by his son Domenico and pupils. The portrait of Doge Marin Falier (1354–5) is missing; in its place there is an inscription on a black background recording that he was decapitated for treason against the Republic.

The end wall above the tribune is entirely covered with Tintoretto's great painting, *Il Paradiso*. This is the largest oil-painting in the world, 22 m wide and 7 m high, depicting Christ and the Virgin at the zenith of a vast empyrean surrounded by circles of angels, saints and the blessed. Tintoretto and his assistants, who included his son Domenico and

Palma il Giovane, began the painting in 1588 in the Scuola della Misericordia, completing its several sections and then assembling them two years later in the Sala del Maggior Consiglio, with the final touches completed by 1593.

Along the other three walls there are twenty-one paintings, some of which are copies of the originals. These depict episodes in the history of Venice, idealized and sometimes anachronistic, grouped in three great cycles: *Venice and the Struggle between the Papacy and the Empire* (1176–7), *Venice and the Fourth Crusade* (1202–4) and *Victory of Venice over Genoa in the War of Chioggia* (1379–80). They include four works by Andrea Vicentino, three by Domenico Tintoretto, two by Palma il Giovane, two by Benedetto and Carlo Caliari, and one each by Paolo Veronese, Leandro Bassano, Francesco Bassano and Antonio Vassilacchi. The rear of the hall has a number of display cases and old prints, many of them associated with the Sala del Maggior Consiglio.

The door at the far right-hand corner of the hall leads into the Sala della Quarantia Civil Nova, the branch of the Forty dealing with civil law in the mainland territories of the Republic. The hall was damaged in the fire of 1577 and was restored shortly afterwards. Above the alcove there is a gilded tabernacle with an early-16C painting of the Virgin.

We now pass into the Sala dello Scrutinio. From 1532 onwards this hall was devoted to the counting (*scrutinio*) of the votes cast in elections for the Maggior Consiglio; it was also used for meetings of the various committees involved in the election of the Doge and other officials of the Republic. After the 1577 fire it was restored under the direction of Antonio da Ponte. The richly decorated ceiling has thirty-three panels in carved gilt frames, with the five large ones along the central axis containing paintings depicting *The Struggle between Venice and the Other Italian Maritime Republics*, the smaller pictures clustering around them representing allegorical scenes, trophies and other associated subjects. The main paintings on the ceiling include two by Antonio

Vassilacchi, two by Giulio del Moro and one each by Andrea Vicentino, Nicolò Bambini and Francesco Bassano. The frieze under the ceiling contains portraits of the last forty-two Doges, completing the series in Sala del Maggior Consiglio, beginning with Lorenzo Priuli (1556–9) and ending with Lodovico Manin (1789–97). The first seven portraits were painted by Jacopo Tintoretto and his pupils, while the remainder were done by painters chosen by the successive Doges themselves.

The entire wall above the tribune is covered with a *Last Judgement* by Palma il Giovane. In the eight lunettes above the painting there are portraits of the four Evangelists and four prophets by Andrea Vicentino. On the opposite end wall, framing the door leading to a stairway, the Scalone dello Scrutinio, there is a triumphal arch built in 1694 to honour Doge Francesco Morosini (1688–94). The arch was designed by Palladio and decorated with six symbolic paintings by Gregorio Lazzarini. On the two long walls there are ten large paintings depicting battles won on land and sea by the Venetians. These include four paintings by Andrea Vicentino and one each by Jacopo Tintoretto, Sante Peranda, Antonio Vassilacchi, Marco Vecellio, Pietro Bellotti and Pietro Liberi. There are also allegorical paintings by Sebastiano Ricci, Antonio Vassilacchi and Marco Vecellio.

Returning to Sala del Maggior Consiglio, we then pass through the doorway to the left of the tribune. There we are channelled along a walkway that brings us to the Bridge of Sighs, where we cross to the Palace of the Prisons, which comprises eighteen vaulted cells built of large blocks of Istrian stone.

After completing our brief tour of the prisons we walk back across the Bridge of Sighs and go down a flight of steps to the Sala dei Censori, the Hall of the Censors. The Censori were a group of officials created in the early 16C to enforce new laws designed to prevent the manipulation of elections and the buying and selling of high offices. They are depicted in nine of the ten paintings on the walls, which include five works by Domenico Tintoretto.

We then enter the Sala dei Notai, part of the Avogadria, or Department of City Lawyers. The lawyers are depicted in all the eleven paintings on the walls of the room, which include four works by Domenico Tintoretto and one by Leandro Bassano.

The door from the Sala dei Notai leads out on to the loggia overlooking the Cortile di Palazzo on its east side. This concludes our tour of Palazzo Ducale, which we leave by the Porta del Frumento, bringing us out on to the Molo. There we might stand back and look at the Palazzo Ducale, whose pink marble walls reflect the full light of the sun at all hours of the Venetian day. As Henry James wrote in *Italian Hours*:

There is no brighter place in Venice – by which I mean that on the whole there is none half so bright. The reflected sunshine plays up through the great windows from the glittering lagoon and shimmers and twinkles over gilded walls and ceilings. All the history of Venice, all its splendid stately past, glows around you in a strong sea-light.

[5] The Grand Canal

This tour will take us along the Grand Canal, known to Venetians as the Canalazzo. We will go on the No. 1 *vaporetto*, beginning and ending at the San Marco *pontile*, or *vaporetto* station, first looking at the buildings on the right, or San Marco side of the Canal, and then on the return journey examining those on the other shore. The best vantage point is one of the seats at the front of the boat at the right side of the *vaporetto*, both on the outward and return voyages, between which one must change boats at Pontile Piazzale Roma.

The Grand Canal was originally the ancient bed of a river that flowed between the Rialtine islands, and as the city developed it became the main maritime thoroughfare of Venice. It is about 4 km in length, winding its way in an inverted S-shape as it makes its way from the Bacino San Marco to the lagoon west of Venice, varying in width from 30 m to 70 m, with a maximum depth of 5 m.

As an aid in identifying the various *palazzi*, nearly two hundred in all, they are grouped between the intervening *calli, campi, canali* and *pontili*, and they are identified by number on the map on pp. 58–9. Some of the most important *palazzi* along the Grand Canal and all the churches are described in more detail in subsequent itineraries. Other points of reference are the *traghetto* stations along the canal, where gondolas ferry passengers across as soon as the boat is full, standing room only. These *traghetto* services go back to the earliest days of the city, when each of them formed a guild with its own officers and constitution; some of the documents have been preserved in their parish churches. The number of working *traghetto* stations has greatly diminished in the past century, and now there are only half a dozen left on the Grand Canal, one of them beside Pontile San Marco.

Setting out from Pontile San Marco, the first building that we pass on the right is the 19C Hotel Monaco and Grand Canal (1). The hotel is housed in a *palazzo* that belonged originally to the Vallaresso and then in the 18C passed to the Erizzo, a family who produced one Doge.

Then, after Calle del Ridoto, we see Ca' Giustinian (2), a late Gothic palace of the 15C. The palace belonged originally to the Giustinian, an ancient family who traced their lineage back to the Emperor Justinian, and who gave one Doge to Venice; for a time it was the home of St Lorenzo Giustinian, who in 1451 became the first Patriarch of Venice. In the 16C it passed to the Morosini, who restored and altered the building. The Morosini were one of the 'apostolic' families, the twelve who in 697 at Heraclea elected Paulicus as *dux*, the predecessor of the first Doge; they produced four Doges and two cardinals, while two women of the line married kings and three wed Doges. Like all the great Venetian families, the Morosini and Giustinian had several branches, and a number of other palaces bear their names along the Grand Canal and elsewhere in Venice.

After Calle dei Tredici Martiri we pass the Hotel Bauer Grünwald (3), a 19C neo-Gothic building. Just past Rio San Moisè we see Palazzo Treves-Barozzi (4), built in the early 17C to a design by Bartolomeo Monapola. Its original owners were the Barozzi, who in the 15–16C ruled Naxos, Paros and Santorini as barons under the aegis of Venice.

Next is the Hotel Europa & Regina (5), housed in the 17C Palazzo Badoer-Tiepolo. The *palazzo* was built by the Badoer, who were originally known as the Partecipazio, another of the apostolic families, who in the 9–10C produced seven Doges. In the 18C the palace passed to the Tiepolo, another apostolic family, who gave two Doges to

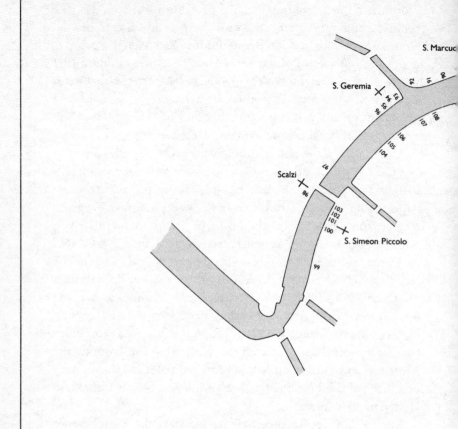

S. Marcuo

S. Geremia

Scalzi

S. Simeon Piccolo

The Grand Canal

S. Stae

Ponte de Rialto

S. Maria Zobenigo

S. Samuele

S. Vitale

Hotel Gritti

Palace

Hotel Europa + Regina

Hotel Bauer Grünwald

Hotel Monaco + Grand Canal

S. Gregorio

S. Maria della Salute

Ponte de l'Accademia

the Republic. In the 19C the palace became a hotel, the Europa. Among the famous literary figures who stayed at the Europa were Théophile Gautier, Marcel Proust, Alfred de Musset and George Eliot, who came here with her husband John Cross on their honeymoon in the spring of 1880. A few weeks after their arrival the somewhat demented Cross jumped from the balcony of their room into the Grand Canal and had to be hauled out by the gondoliers, ending their holiday.

The part of the hotel that was formerly the Regina was before that known as Casa Alvise and was owned by Katherine de Kay Bronson, a wealthy New Yorker. Both Robert Browning and Henry James stayed here for a time in the 1880s as guests of Mrs Bronson. Browning dedicated to Mrs Bronson his last work, *Asolando*, which was published just prior to his death on 12 December 1889. James cast her as Mrs Prest in *The Aspern Papers*.

We now pass Calle del Tragheto, named for an abandoned *traghetto* station from which passengers were formerly ferried across to Punta Dogana on the other side of the Grand Canal. Until the end of the 11C a massive iron chain was suspended across the Grand Canal here as a deterrent to pirate raids.

Beyond Calle del Tragheto we pass two modern buildings before coming to the 17C Palazzo Gaggia (6). Next to that is Palazzo Contarini (7), a 15C Gothic palace. This is one of several palaces on the Grand Canal that at one time or another belonged to the Contarini, a family who produced eight Doges. The next building is another of the family's residences, Palazzetto Contarini-Fasan (8), a beautiful little Gothic palace dating from the mid 15C. The palace was built for a Contarini who was given the nickname Fasan because of his fondness for shooting pheasants (in Venetian, *fasan*). Venetian folklore calls this the House of Desdemona, after the heroine of Shakespeare's *Othello*, a legend he seems to have taken from Giraldi Cinthio's *Hecatommithi*, published in 1565. The legend appears to be based on a true story dating back to the medieval era, for the Venetian chronicles tell of a patrician lady named Desdemona who was murdered by her jealous husband, a member of the Moro family.

Next is Palazzo Manolesso-Ferro (9), a late Gothic palace of the 15C with Renaissance additions. Adjacent to it is Palazzo Flangini-Fini (10), completed in 1688, its design attributed to Alessandro Tremignon.

Just beyond Rio de l'Albero we pass the Hotel Gritti Palace (11). This is housed in Palazzo Pisani-Gritti, a Gothic structure erected at the beginning of the 15C, its facade once decorated with frescoes by Giorgione. The original owners were the Pisani, who had one Doge in the family; later it passed to the Gritti, who also produced a Doge. Among the literary luminaries who stayed in the Hotel Gritti Palace were Somerset Maugham, Graham Greene and Ernest Hemingway. John Ruskin and his wife Effie had an apartment in the *palazzo* in 1851–2, when it was the Casa Wetzler, and it was here that he wrote the second volume of *The Stones of Venice*.

Next is Campo del Tragheto, where gondolas still take passengers across the canal to the *traghetto* station of San Gregorio. Just beyond the *campo* we stop at Pontile Santa Maria del Giglio.

After Rio de Santa Maria del Giglio is the Palazzo Barbarigo (12), built in the 17C by a family who gave two Doges to Venice. Next to it is Palazzo Minotto (13), a Gothic structure erected in the 15C on the site of an earlier Veneto-Byzantine palace.

After Rio di San Maurizio we come to the regal Palazzo Corner della Ca' Grande (14). The *palazzo* was commissioned by Jacopo Corner, nephew of Caterina Cornaro, Queen of Cyprus; it was built in the years 1553–6 by Jacopo Sansovino, who created here what is generally considered to be the finest of his palaces. The Corner family produced four Doges and a queen, Caterina Cornaro, who ruled Cyprus from 1472 until 1488, when she ceded the island to her native Venice. The palace remained in the possesion of the Corner family until 1812, and now houses the Prefecture of Venice.

At the far end of the garden beyond the palace is the 18C Casa delle Rose (15), formerly the property of Prince Hohenlohe. Antonio Canova had his first studio here in the 1770s, and from 1915 to 1919 it was the home of Gabriele D'Annunzio. Beyond it is the 19C Casa Chiodo (16), followed by Calle del Dose Da Ponte; then the contiguous Casa Stecchini (17) and Palazzo Succi (18), both dating from the 17C.

After Rio del Santissimo we pass Palazzetto Pisani (19), a wing of the much larger palace of the same name on Campo Pisani. The palace was built *c.* 1615 and enlarged after 1728; in 1751 it was acquired by the Pisani, a family who had given one Doge to Venice. Separated from Palazzetto Pisani by Ramo Pisani is the 18C Palazzo Benzon-Foscolo (20).

Next are two *palazzi* of the Barbaro family, the first built as a much later wing of the second. The first, Palazzo Barbaro (21), was erected in 1694–8 to a design by Antonio Gaspari, who built a grand ballroom at the level of the second piano nobile. The second, Palazzo Barbaro-Curtis (22), was completed in 1425 to a design by Giovanni Bon; later it was decorated with canvases by Giambattista Piazzetta and Sebastiano Ricci as well as frescoes by Giambattista Tiepolo. The second name of the palace comes from Daniel Sargent Curtis, a Bostonian who purchased it in 1885. John Singer Sargent had a studio in the palace, and it was here that he painted the portrait of the Curtis family now in the Royal Academy in London. The aged Claude Monet used the studio in the 1920s, and while here he painted his views of Venice. Robert Browning gave readings of his poetry in the 18C Barbaro library, where Henry James wrote *The Aspern Papers*. James used Palazzo Barbaro-Curtis as a setting in *The Wings of the Dove*, calling it the Palazzo Leporelli.

Beyond Rio de l'Orso is Palazzo Cavalli-Franchetti (23), a 15C Gothic structure restored and enlarged at the end of the 19C. During the early 19C it was the residence of the Archduke Frederick of Austria, who died here in 1836. Later it was acquired by the Comte de Chambord, who demolished the house beyond it to create the pretty garden we see today. The garden borders Campo San Vidal, where we pass under Ponte de l'Accademia.

We then pass Rio de San Vidal and the 17C Palazzo Civran-Badoer (24), now the German Consulate. This is separated by Calle Giustinian from Palazzo Giustinian-Lolin (25), a youthful work of Baldassare Longhena, the greatest of baroque architects in Venice, who completed it *c.* 1623. The original owner, Giovanni Lolin, left it to his daughter Francesca; she then married a member of the Giustinian family, and their descendants remained in possession of the palace until the early 19C. The last Duchess of Parma, the Regent Luisa Maria, lived in apartments here until her death in 1864. The palace now houses the music library of Ugo and Olga Levi, its last private owners, part of the centre for musical studies that they created in their bequest.

Next, after Calle Vitturi, is Palazzo Falier (26), a 15C Gothic building erected by a family who produced three Doges. The Falier family lived here until the 20C, when it became extinct. The palace is distinguished by its charming *liagi*, two projecting colonnaded balconies flanking a garden. A plaque on the *calle* facade of the palace records that this was the residence of the American writer William Dean Howells when he was American consul in Venice, 1861–5. During that time he wrote the delightful *Venetian Life*, published in 1866.

After Rio del Duca we pass Ca' del Duca (27), a 19C house erected on the site of a palatial edifice designed in the mid 15C by Bartolomeo Bon for the Cornaro family. Before the building was completed it was acquired in 1461 by Francesco Sforza, Duke of Milan, but he eventually abandoned the half-finished palace. Titian used one of the rooms of the abandoned palace as a studio in 1514, when he was working on his paintings for Palazzo Ducale. The present Ca' del Duca incorporates some elements of the original palace, including the bases of the colonnade and the rusticated masonry on the ground floor.

We then see the garden belonging to Palazzo Malipiero-Cappello (28), rebuilt in 1622 on a plan attributed to Baldassare Longhena. This brings us to Campo San Samuele and the *pontile* of the same name. On the far side of the *campo* is Palazzo Grassi (29), built in 1748–72 to a plan by Giorgio Massari. Next is an isolated modern building, and then the huge Palazzo Moro-Lin (30), the 'palace of the thirteen windows'. This was created *c.* 1670 according to a design by the painter Pietro Liberi, who linked two earlier *palazzi* and built a new facade. The original owners were the Lin, from whom it passed in 1788 to the Moro, a family who produced one Doge. Next is a rebuilt house and then Palazzo Da Lezze (31), a restored Gothic structure of the 15C. Here the canal bends sharply to the right, the *volta del canal*, completing the first turn in the inverted S of the Canalazzo.

We now pass Palazzo Erizzo (32), a partly reconstructed 15C Gothic building, named for a family who produced one Doge. Next to it is Palazzo Contarini delle Figure (33), so called because of the two tiny caryatids under the balcony. This elegant Lombardesque palace was built for Jacopo Contarini; it was begun *c.* 1504 by Giorgio Spavento and completed before 1546 by Scarpagnino. Contarini was a patron of the arts and sciences, and had here a collection of astronomical instruments, a celebrated library and a collection of paintings that included works by Titian, the Bassano family, Veronese, Tintoretto and Palma il Giovane, as well as architectural drawings by his close friend Andrea Palladio, who was often a guest at the palace. Richard Wagner and his wife Cosima lived here for a month in the autumn of 1880.

After Calle Mocenigo we come to a group of four palaces (34–7) known as Case Mocenigo. These were erected by the Mocenigo, a family who produced seven Doges. The first of the four is Ca' Vecchia, a 15C Gothic structure remodelled in the 17C; the fourth one is Ca' Nuova, erected in 1579; the twin palaces in between were built in the early 18C to join those at the ends. The philosopher Giordano Bruno was a guest of Giovanni Mocenigo in 1591 at Ca' Vecchia. But after a stay of five months Bruno was denounced to the Inquisition by Mocenigo; seven years later he was convicted of heresy and burned at the stake in Rome. Venetian folklore has it that Bruno's ghost still haunts Ca' Vecchia.

A plaque on the second of the twin Mocenigo *palazzi* records that Byron lived there in 1818–19. Byron's life here was an endless series of love affairs, beginning with his tempestuous housekeeper, 'La Fornarina' (whom he described as having a fine body 'fit to breed gladiators from') and ending with the Countess Teresa Guiccioli, his 'last Passion'. But throughout these romances and his constant carousing he somehow found time to write, and it was here that he began *Don Juan*. The spirit of Byron's Venetian life comes through in the last lines of a letter that he wrote to the Irish poet Thomas Moore, dated 1 June 1818: 'Good night or rather good morning. It is four, and the dawn gleams over the Grand Canal and unshadows the Rialto. I must be to bed; up all night – but as George Philpot says, "It's life, though, damme it's life!"'

Years after Byron left Venice, the Countess Albrizzi recorded that he was once seen, 'on leaving a palace situated on the Grand Canal, instead of entering his own gondola, to throw himself into the water dressed as he was and swim to his lodging'. She added that, in order to avoid the oars of the gondoliers, he carried a torch in his left hand when he swam in the canal at night.

The building following Ca' Nuove is Palazzo Corner-Gheltof (38), dating from the 16–17C. Just beyond it there is a modern *palazzo* and then a one-storey commercial building. Then, after Calle del Tragheto, we see Palazzo Garzoni (39), a much-restored 15C Gothic building.

After Rio de Ca' Garzoni, we pass two modern buildings and come to Pontile Sant'Angelo and Campiello del Teatro. The *campiello* takes its name from the fact that it was the site of the Teatro di Sant'Angelo, which was founded in 1676 and continued in operation until the last decade of the 18C. Some twenty of Vivaldi's operas were produced here in the years 1714–39. The building on the far side of the *campiello* is Palazzo Corner-Spinelli (40). This was built in the last decade of the 15C by Mauro Coducci, who created here one of the first distinctly Renaissance palaces in Venice. In 1535 it was purchased by Giovanni Corner, nephew of Queen Caterina Cornaro, who commissioned Giorgio Vasari to redecorate the palace and Michele Sanmichele to remodel its ground-floor hall, transforming it into a Roman atrium with Tuscan columns. The palace later passed to the Spinelli, a family of the *cittadini* class who had become wealthy in the textile industry, buying their way into the Venetian nobility in 1718.

After Rio de Ca' Corner we pass in turn the 17C Palazzo Curti (41) and the 19C Casa Tornielli (42). Then, after Rio de Ca' Michiel we see the 16C Palazzo Benzon (43). Here in the early 19C the Countess Marina Benzon created a celebrated literary salon, including among her guests Manzoni, Stendhal, Pindemonte, Byron, Thomas Moore and Longfellow. It was at Palazzo Benzon, at the beginning of April 1818, that Byron met and fell in love with the Countess Teresa Guiccioli, as he notes in a letter that he wrote the following day to John Cam Hobhouse: 'I have fallen in love with a Romagnola Countess from Ravenna, who is nineteen years old, and has a Count of fifty, whom she seems disposed to qualify, the first year of marriage being just over . . . and I have hopes, sir – hopes.' And then a few weeks later he describes his new mistress in a letter to Lord Kinnaird: '. . . she is as fair as sunrise and as warm as noon, we had but ten days to manage our little matters in beginning, middle and end; and I have done my duty with proper consummation.'

After Calle Benzon, two modern houses, and Calle del Tragheto, we pass Palazzo Martinengo (44), whose main building was erected in the early 16C, with the much smaller left wing added *c.* 1663. The main facade was once decorated with frescoes by Pordenone, now vanished. Then come

Palazzo Tron (45) and Palazzetto Tron (46), both Gothic buildings of the 15C, erected by a family who produced one Doge. After that comes Palazzo Corner-Contarini dai Cavalli (47), a Gothic palace of the mid 15C, the last part of its name deriving from the two horses on the coats of arms on its facade.

After Rio de San Luca is the magnificent Palazzo Grimani (48), built by a family who produced two Doges. It was built for Girolamo Grimani by Michele Sanmichele, who began construction in 1556. Sanmichele completed the ground floor and the first piano nobile by the time of his death in 1559; the second floor was added by Gian Giacomo dei Grigi in 1559–61, and the palace was finally completed in 1575 by Giovanni Antonio Rusconi. Giovanni Grimani served as Procurator and was head of the Council of Ten, and he missed being elected Doge by three votes. His son Marino was elected Doge in 1595 while he was living in this palace, reigning until his death in 1605. Marino's wife Morasina was formally installed as Dogaressa on 4 May 1597, an honour that had been accorded only twice before in Venetian history. This was marked by a three-day celebration, at the climax of which the Doge and Dogaressa and their party watched from the balcony of Palazzo Grimani as they reviewed the passing warships of Venice, England, Holland and Flanders, followed by a regatta on the Grand Canal. The palace was acquired by the Municipality of Venice in 1807, and today it serves as the Court of Appeal.

Just beyond Palazzo Grimani are Palazzo Corner-Valmarana (49) and Palazzo Martinengo-Ravà (50), both dating from the 17C. Then comes the beginning of Riva del Carbon, followed by Riva del Ferro, two *fondamente* that extend all the way to the Rialto Bridge. We will walk along these *fondamente* later, examining their *palazzi* at close range, so now as we pass in the *vaporetto* we will merely date the buildings and identify some of their former owners.

After Calle Cavalli we pass Palazzo Farsetti-Dandolo (51),

built in the 12–13C and in the 14C acquired by the Dandolo, a family who produced four Doges. Next is Palazzo Piscopia o Loredan (52), which was erected in the 13C, was acquired in the 14C by a branch of the Corner family called the Piscopia and in 1703 passed to the Loredan, who gave three Doges to Venice. An inscription on the side facade records that this was the birthplace of Elena Lucrezia Corner Piscopia, the earliest known poetess in Venice; she received a degree in Aristotelian philosophy at the University of Padua in 1678, the first woman ever to be so honoured.

On the next block is the 14C Palazzetto dei Dandolo (53); this is built on the site of an earlier palace that was the birthplace of Doge Enrico Dandolo, who led the Latin forces that captured Constantinople in 1204, after which he styled himself 'lord of a quarter and a half of the Roman Empire'. Then, just after the summer landing-stage of the No. 1 *vaporetto*, we pass Palazzo Bembo (54), built in the 15C by a family who produced a Doge, a cardinal and a saint, along with two others who were beatified. Then, just beyond Rio de San Salvador, we pass Palazzo Dolfin-Manin (55), built in the second quarter of the 16C for the Dolfin, a family who produced one Doge, and in the late 18C acquired by Lodovico Manin, the last Doge of Venice. Just beyond the palace is the landing-stage used by the No. 1 *vaporetto* in months other than the summer. This marks the beginning of Riva del Ferro, along which there are half a dozen nondescript 19C buildings between the *vaporetto* stations and the Ponte de Rialto.

We now pass under the Ponte de Rialto, built in the late 16C to replace the last of a series of wooden bridges dating back to the last quarter of the 12C. One of the earliest descriptions of the present Rialto Bridge is that of John Evelyn, who was in Venice from May 1645 until March 1646, recording his impressions of the city in his diary:

The first public building I went to see was the Rialto, a bridge of one arch over the Grand Canal, so large as to admit a galley to row under it, built of good marble, and having on it, besides many pretty shops, three ample and stately passages for people without any inconvenience, the two outmost nobly balustred with the same stone; a piece of Architecture much to be admired. It was evening, and the Canal where the Noblesse go to take the air, as in our Hyde Park, was full of ladies and gentlemen . . . Here they were singing, playing on harpsicords, and other music, and serenading their mistresses; in another place racing and other pastimes upon the water, it being exceedingly hot.

The enormous building beyond the bridge is Fontego dei Tedeschi (56), an inn and commercial edifice for the German merchants in Venice completed in 1508.

After Rio del Fontego dei Tedeschi we pass Palazzo Ruzzini (57), built in the 19C by a family who earlier had produced a Doge; this was the site of a commercial building for Iranian merchants called Fontego dei Persiani, demolished in 1830. Next is Casa Perducci (58), a 15C Gothic structure; then Palazzo Civran (59), built c. 1700 on the site of a Byzantine palace, its design attributed to Giorgio Massari. Next are a group of small modern houses followed by the 19C Palazzo Sernagiotto (60); beyond that are two more undistinguished buildings, followed by Campiello Remer and then a modern dwelling.

After Rio de San Giovanni Grisostomo we pass the 16C Palazzo Bollani-Erizzo (61). Next is Palazzo Dolfin (62), consisting of two linked 15C Gothic houses with upper floors added in the 17C. Then comes Ca' da Mosto (63), a Veneto-Byzantine palace that Ruskin described as 'simple, gracious and vigorous, the most original and perfect' of the city's earliest extant civic buildings. The first piano nobile dates from the 12–13C, while the upper two floors were added in the 17C. From the 16C to the 18C it was a luxurious hotel known as the Albergo del Lion Bianco, where visiting royalty were put up when they came to Venice.

After Rio dei Santissimi Apostoli we pass the 18C Palazzo Mangilli-Valmarana-Smith (64). Next is Palazzo Michiel dal Brusà (65), a Gothic structure rebuilt after a fire (*brusà*) in 1774; it still has apartments richly decorated with stuccos and frescoes, most of the paintings being by Jacopo Guarana. After an intervening modern house we then pass Palazzo Michiel dalle Colonne (66), so called because of the colonnade on its ground floor. The palace was erected in the latter half of the 17C to a design attributed to Antonio Gaspari; both this and the preceding palace were built for the Michiel, a family who produced three Doges. Then, after another modern house, we pass the 15C Palazzo Foscari (67), a little Gothic palace built by a family who produced one Doge; in 1520 it was the residence of the Duke of Mantua.

We then come to Campo Santa Sofia, named for the church at its inner end, which in its present form dates to the 17C. The *campo* is the station of the Santa Sofia *traghetto*, one of the oldest in Venice, founded in the 12C. On the far side of the *campo* is Palazzo Sagredo (68), a Gothic structure of the 13–14C, erected on the site of a Veneto-Byzantine palace and rebuilt in the 18C. The palace was built for the Morosini and at the beginning of the 18C it passed to the Sagredo, a family who produced a Doge, a patriarch of Venice and a saint, San Gherardo Sagredo, who was martyred at Buda in 1067. Next to it is Palazzo Pesaro (69), a Gothic building of the 15C, erected by a family who gave one Doge to Venice.

Next comes the Pontile Ca' d'Oro. This is named for Ca' d'Oro (70), the Golden House, a very beautiful 15C Gothic palace that now houses a museum, the Franchetti Gallery. Just beyond Ca' d'Oro is Palazzo Giusti (71), built to a design by Antonio Visentini in 1776; it is now an annexe to the Franchetti Gallery.

We then come to Palazzo Fontana-Rezzonico (72), built in the 16C by an architect working in the style of Jacopo Sansovino. Carlo Rezzonico, the future Pope Clement XIII, was born here in 1693.

After Rio de San Felice we pass two modern houses followed by Calle del Tragheto. We then pass Palazzo Contarini-Pisani (73), rebuilt in the 17C from a Veneto-Byzantine structure. Next to it is Palazzo Boldù (74), also rebuilt in the 17C from an earlier structure. Beyond that is the 16C Palazzo Da Lezze (75), which stands at the rear of a pretty garden.

After Rio de Noal we pass Palazzo Gussoni-Grimani (76). This was erected in the 16C, perhaps to a design by Michele Sanmichele, and its facade was decorated with frescoes by Jacopo Tintoretto, now vanished. During the years 1614–18 this was the residence of Sir Henry Wotton, ambassador from James I to Venice. During his three terms as ambassador, the first of which began in 1604 and the last ending in 1625, Wotton spent much of his time buying up paintings for the king and the Duke of Buckingham. It was Sir Henry who coined the oft-quoted phrase, which nearly ruined his own career, that 'An ambassador is an honest man sent to lie abroad for the good of his country.'

Next is a modern house, followed by three palaces: the 17C Palazzo Ruoda (77); the 17C Palazzo Zulian (78); and the 16C Palazzo Barbarigo (79), still preserving on its facade fragmentary 16C frescoes.

After Rio de la Madalena there is a succession of five palaces: Palazzo Molin (80), built in the 17C by a family who produced one Doge; the 17C Palazzo Emo (81); Palazzo Soranzo (82), a 16C Lombardesque palace erected by a family who had one Doge; Palazzo Erizzo (83), a 15C Gothic building with later modifications; and Palazzo Marcello (84), rebuilt in the 18C by another family who gave one Doge to Venice.

We then pass the splendid Palazzo Vendramin-Calergi (85), the east wing of which stands at the rear of its canal-side garden. The palace was built for Andrea Loredan at the beginning of the 16C by Mauro Coducci, who worked on it until his death in 1504; the project was then carried through to completion in 1509 by the workshop of the Lombardo family. The interior of the palace was originally decorated with frescoes by Giorgione and Titian, now vanished. In 1581 it was purchased by the Duke of Brunswick, who three years later sold it to the Marquis of Mantua. In 1589 the palace was purchased by Vittore Calergi, and then in 1608 it passed by marriage to Vincenzo Grimani, who soon afterwards commissioned Vincenzo Scamozzi to erect an east wing as a residence for his three sons. But when the sons were found guilty of murder they were exiled and the new wing was demolished, only to be re-erected in 1660. The palace later passed to the Vendramin, a family who produced one Doge, and then in 1844 it was acquired by the Duchesse de Berry, widow of the Duc de Berry, pretender to the throne of his father, Charles X of France. Richard Wagner lived in the east wing during his last stay in Venice, and he died there on 13 February 1883. The palace now serves as the Venice Casino except during the summer, when it is occasionally open for exhibitions. It still retains much of its original decor, most notably frescoes by Nicolò Bambini.

After Rio de San Marcuola we pass Casa Gatti–Casazza (86), a double house restored in the style of the 18C, after which we come to Pontile San Marcuola and the *campo* of the same name. At the rear of the *campo* is the church of San Marcuola (87). At the far side of the *campo* is the 17C Palazzo Martinengo-Mandelli (88). This was built on the site of a palace erected in the 10C by Doge Tribuno Memmo (979–91), who lived there while the first Palazzo Ducale was under construction.

After an intervening house we pass the 17C Palazzo Gritti (89), whose facade bears the coats of arms of the Gritti and Dandolo families. We then pass two small houses and a garden before coming to the 17C Palazzo Correr-Contarini (90). Then, after Campiello del Remer, we pass the 19C Palazzo Querini (91), also called Ca' dei Cuori because of the hearts in the coats of arms on its facade. The Duke of Savoy stayed here in 1687. Just beyond is the 18C Palazzo Emo (92), at the junction of the Grand Canal and the Cannaregio Canal. On the other side of the Cannaregio Canal we pass the end facade of the Palazzo Labia (93). The Labia, who originated in Spain, were one of the richest families in 18C Venice, having bought their way into the nobility in 1646. The side of the palace overlooking the Cannaregio Canal was built towards the end of the 17C, while the other side, on Campo San Geremia, was completed in the mid 18C. Just beyond the palace is the church of San Geremia (94). The building just beyond the church is the Scuola dei Morti (95), built in 1689 for a confraternity devoted to saying prayers for the dead. Just beyond it is Palazzo Flangini (96), built in 1664–82 to a design by Giuseppe Sardi.

We then pass a number of modern houses, followed by Rio Terà dei Sabioni. Following this there is another row of houses along Fondamenta Crotta, all of them modern except the second and third, Gothic *palazzetti* of the 15C. At the end of the *fondamenta* we pass the long Palazzo Calbo-Crotta (97), a restored 15C Gothic structure.

After the Ponte dei Scalzi we pass the church of Santa Maria di Nazareth degli Scalzi (98); just beyond the church is Pontile Ferrovia, the *vaporetto* stop for the railway station.

The *vaporetto* now goes on past the railway station and rounds the second bend of the Grand Canal, after which it crosses to Pontile Piazzale Roma. There we disembark and board another *vaporetto*, one headed back down the Grand Canal.

Going back around the bend of the Grand Canal, we pass Rio Novo and then the Papadopoli Gardens, beyond which we pass Rio de la Croce. We then pass a row of modern buildings along Fondamenta San Simeon before we come to the 17C Palazzo Emo-Diedo (99). A short way farther along we pass the church of San Simeon Piccolo (100).

Between the church and Ponte dei Scalzi we pass in succession three small 16C palaces: Casa Adoldo (101), Palazzo

Foscari-Contarini (102) and Palazzo Foscari (103). After going under the bridge we pass Rio Marin and then, after three intervening houses, the first two with a canal-side garden, we see Campo San Simeon Grande.

Two blocks beyond the *campo* is the beginning of Riva di Biasio, where after Calle Correra we pass Palazzo Gritti (104) and Palazzo Corner (105), both dating from the 16C. Then, after an intervening house, we pass the 17C Palazzo Donà-Balbi (106). After two more intervening houses we pass Palazzo Zen (107), rebuilt after being destroyed in the 1849 Austrian bombardment. We then stop at Pontile Riva di Biasio. A block beyond the *pontile*, where Riva di Biasio ends, is the 17C Palazzo Marcello-Todorini (108). Just beyond Rio de San Zan Degolà is Palazzo Giovanelli (109), a 15C Gothic building.

After the first *calle* we pass the huge Fontego dei Turchi (110), a heavily restored 13C structure that now houses the Natural History Museum. The Fontego takes its name from the fact that it was the emporium of the Turkish merchants in Venice, who were in residence there from 1621 until 1838.

We then pass Rio del Megio, which is named for the huge edifice just beyond, the Depositi del Megio (111), or millet storehouse, erected in the 15C as a public granary. The large figure of the Lion of St Mark high on the facade is a modern work by Carlo Lorenzetti, replacing the original relief destroyed in 1797 by the French, who effaced virtually every such symbol of the Serenissima soon after they occupied the city. Beyond the granary is the monumental Palazzo Belloni-Battagia (112), built for Girolamo Belloni in the years 1647–63 by Baldassare Longhena.

After Rio Ca' Tron we see the splendid Palazzo Tron (113), a palace in the classical style erected at the end of the 16C. The interior was decorated with frescoes by Jacopo Guarana, most notably the great ballroom where the Emperor Joseph II of Austria was fêted in 1775. Next to it is Palazzo Duodo (114), a Gothic building of the late 14C restored in

1938. Beyond it is a garden belonging to a 19C house built on the style of the ancient Palazzo Contarini. Next is Palazzo Priuli (115), a Gothic edifice erected towards the end of the 15C by a family who produced three Doges.

We now stop at Pontile San Stae in front of the handsome neoclassical church of San Stae (116). On the other side of Rio de San Stae is the 16C Palazzo Foscarini (117). Doge Marco Foscarini (1762–3) was born here in 1695.

After Rio de la Pergola we come to the magnificent Ca' Pesaro (118). The *palazzo* is built on the site of an earlier palace in which Doge Giovanni Pesaro (1658–9) was born in 1590. In 1652 the future Doge demolished the original Palazzo Pesaro and commissioned Baldassare Longhena to build a new palace. Work was interrupted by Longhena's death in 1652; the project was then resumed under the direction of Antonio Gaspari, who completed the present palace in 1710. The palace still preserves frescoes by Nicolò Bambini and Girolamo Brusaferro; it now houses the Museums of Modern Art and Oriental Art.

After Rio de le Do Torre we pass Palazzetto Donà (119), erected in the 18C by a family who produced three Doges. Next to it is the Palazzo Correggio (120), an 18C palace designed by Andrea Tirali. Then after Calle de Ca' Corner comes the great Palazzo Corner della Regina (121), erected in the second quarter of the 18C. Queen Caterina Cornaro was born in an earlier palace on this site in 1454. Then after Calle de la Rosa we pass Casa Bragadin-Favretto (122), a 14C Gothic building with a cornice from an 11C Veneto-Byzantine palace.

After Rio de San Cassan we pass Palazzetto Jona (123), a neo-Gothic house built at the beginning of the 19C, an intervening building and then the 15C Palazzo Morosini-Brandolin (124).

After Rio de le Becarie we see the arcaded Pescaria, or fish market (125). Beyond it is Campo de la Pescaria and then three 16C buildings of the Rialto market: Fabbriche Nuove di Rialto (126), Fabbriche Vecchie di Rialto (127) and Palazzo dei Camerlenghi (128).

We now pass once again under Ponte de Rialto, after which we see on our right the 200 m Riva del Vin. The only building of interest along this *fondamenta* is the first one by the foot of the bridge, the 16C Palazzo dei Dieci Savi (129).

Beyond Riva del Vin we come to Pontile San Silvestro. Just beyond it is Palazzo Barzizza (130), a 13C Veneto-Byzantine palace rebuilt in the 15C. After an intervening alley is the 17C Palazzo Lanfranchi (131). Adjacent to this is Palazzo Businello-Giustiani (132), a 12–13C Veneto-Byzantine palace rebuilt in the 17C.

After Rio dei Meloni we pass the impressive Palazzo Coccina-Tiepolo-Papadopoli (133). The palace was built in the early 1560s by Gian Giacomo dei Grigi for the Coccina family, wealthy jewel dealers from Bergamo who were members of the *cittadini* class. After the Coccina died out in 1748 the palace passed to a branch of the Tiepolo, and from them in 1864 it passed to the Papadopoli, who had come to Venice from Crete when the island fell to the Turks in 1669.

Then after a canal-side garden and Calle Tiepolo we see in turn Palazzo Donà (134), and Palazzo Donà della Madonnetta (135), two 13C Veneto-Byzantine palaces much altered in later times. The relief of the Madonna on the facade of Palazzo Donà della Madonnetta was set in place when the palace was remodelled in the 15C, at which time the upper loggia was added. The name 'Madonnetta' does not stem from this relief, however, but from an ancient shrine of the Virgin on the bridge across Rio de la Madoneta, the next side canal beyond the palace.

Just beyond Rio de la Madoneta is Palazzo Bernardo (136), built in 1442 to a design attributed to Giovanni and Bartolomeo Bon. The Bernardo, who owned the palace until 1868, were not patricians but members of the *cittadini* class, wealthy merchants in colours and dyes whose shop was at the sign of the pumpkin in the Rialto market. In the mid 15C the

Bernardo rented the palace for a time to Francesco Sforza, Duke of Milan, and his wife Bianca Visconti.

We then pass a series of three contiguous *palazzi*, beginning with the 17C Palazzo Querini-Dubois (137). The second is Palazzo Grimani (138), a 13C structure rebuilt in the Lombardesque style at the beginning of the 16C to a design attributed to Giovanni Buora. The third is Palazzo Cappello-Layard (139), a 16C Renaissance palace once decorated with frescoes by Paolo Veronese and Giambattista Zelotti. The palace was once the home of Sir Austin Layard, whose renowned collection of paintings passed to the National Gallery in London on the death of Lady Layard in 1915.

Just beyond Rio de San Polo is Palazzo Barbarigo della Terrazza (140), so called because of the garden terrace above the ground floor. This neoclassical palace was erected *c.* 1568–9 to a design attributed to Bernardino Contino. A catalogue of the paintings in Palazzo Barbarigo in 1845 included seventeen by Titian, two by Giovanni Bellini, and individual works by Giorgione, Palma il Vecchio, Jacopo Bassano, Jacopo Tintoretto, Giuseppe Salviati, Alessandro Varottari, Girolamo da Santacroce, Peter Paul Rubens and other 16–17C artists. This collection of paintings was sold in 1850 to Tsar Nicholas I of Russia and is now in the Hermitage Museum in St Petersburg.

After an intervening house we pass the splendid Palazzo Pisani-Moretta (141). This huge Gothic palace was erected in the 1470s and restored early in the 16C; it was adorned with canvases by Gentile and Giovanni Bellini, Palma il Vecchio, Jacopo Tintoretto, Paolo Veronese and Giambattista Piazzetta, as well as frescoes by Giambattista Tiepolo and Jacopo Guarana, and statues by Antonio Canova and other sculptors. Piazzetta's great painting, *The Death of Darius*, is now on display in Ca' Rezzonico; Veronese's *The Family of Darius at the Feet of Alexander the Great* is now in the National Gallery in London; Canova's statue of *Daedalus and Icarus* is in the Correr Museum.

We then pass two contiguous *palazzi* of the Tiepolo family. The first is Palazzo Tiepolo (142), a 16C Renaissance palace whose facade still has traces of frescoes by Andrea Schiavone. The second is Palazzo Tiepoletto-Passi (143), a Gothic palace of the late 15C altered in the 16C. Then, after two intervening houses, comes Palazzo Giustinian-Persico (144), a 16C Lombardesque palace.

After Rio de San Tomà there are two contiguous palaces. The first of these is the 17C Palazzo Marcello dei Leoni (145), so called because of the sculptures of the two lions set into its facade, Romanesque works of the 13C. The second is Palazzo Dolfin (146), a much-altered Gothic palace of the 15C, with the family crest and coat of arms over the door.

We now stop at Pontile San Tomà, just beyond which there are two contiguous palaces. The first is Palazzo Dandolo-Paolucci (147), a 17C structure with a top floor added in 1924. The second is Palazzo Civran-Grimani (148), a 17C edifice reconstructed in the first half of the 18C, probably to a design by Giorgio Massari. After Rio de la Frescada and two tiny intervening houses comes Palazzetto Caotorta-Angaran (149), erected at the beginning of the 17C and reconstructed in 1924. Next to it is the grandiose Palazzo Balbi (150), a huge white edifice with two obelisks above its cornice. The palace was built for Nicolò Balbi in 1582–90, probably to a design by Alessandro Vittoria; it still retains its original frescoes, including paintings by Jacopo Guarana. The *palazzo* is called *in volta del canal*, because of its dominating position on the great bend in the Grand Canal, which is here joined by Rio de Ca' Foscari. It was from the balcony of Palazzo Balbi that Napoleon watched the regatta held in his honour on the Grand Canal on 2 December 1807, a decade after his conquest of the Serenissima. When regattas are now held on the Grand Canal, the reviewing stand called 'la Machina' is set up in front of the palace.

Just beyond Rio de Ca' Foscari stands the magnificent 15C Ca' Foscari (151), which Henry James described as 'one of the noblest creations of the fifteenth century, a masterpiece of symmetry and majesty'. The *palazzo* is built on the site of an earlier palace of the Giustinian family, which in 1452 was purchased and demolished by Doge Francesco Foscari (1423– 57). The Doge then commissioned Bartolomeo Bon to build him the great edifice we see today, generally considered to be the most important extant example of a late-Gothic Venetian palace. The Doge ended his long and illustrious reign in 1457, when his enemies forced him to resign and retire here to Ca' Foscari, where he died three days later. Byron made the Doge's career the subject of his tragedy, *The Two Foscari*, which Verdi later adapted as the libretto for his opera of the same title. The palace was later used to house visiting heads of state when they came to Venice, the first and most notable occasion being when Henry of Valois stayed here in 1574, just before returning to France to be crowned as Henry III. The Commune of Venice acquired the palace in 1847, and it now houses the University Institute.

Adjacent to Ca' Foscari are the enormous Palazzi Giustinian (152), actually a pair of almost identical Gothic palaces side by side, begun in 1452 by Bartolomeo Bon. After the fall of the Republic the Palazzi Giustinian passed to a succession of owners and were eventually divided into a number of apartments. One of these apartments was rented by Richard Wagner for seven months in 1858, during which time he completed the first two acts of *Tristan und Isolde*.

Palazzi Giustinian was also the residence of William Dean Howells, who moved here from Palazzo Falier in the latter part of his stay in Venice.

Next is the 17C Palazzo Giustinian-Bernardo (153) and then, after Calle Bernardo, the 16C Palazzo Bernardo-Nani (154). We then come to Ca' Rezzonico (155), the magnificent palace that now houses the museum of 18C Venetian decorative arts. The palace was commissioned by Filippo Bon in 1667 and designed by Baldassare Longhena, but it was still incomplete at the time of the architect's death in 1682; it was completed for the Rezzonico family in 1756 by Giorgio Massari.

After Rio de San Barnaba we stop at Pontile Ca' Rezzonico. The two houses facing the ferry landing were originally a single structure, the 17C Palazzo Contarini-Michiel (156). The building with the garden beyond the landing-stage is the 19C Palazzetto di Madame Stern (157), erected on the site of the 15C Palazzo Michiel-Malpaga.

After Rio del Malpaga we pass a succession of three palaces, the first of which is Palazzo Moro (158), erected at the beginning of the 16C, its top floor added in the 19C. The second is the beautiful Palazzo Loredan dell'Ambasciatore (159), a late-Gothic palace erected c. 1450-70 and restored after a fire in 1891. The two shield-bearing knights on the facade are Lombardesque works of the late 15C. Two Doges were born here: Leonardo Loredan (1501–21) and Francesco Loredan (1752–62). Doge Francesco Loredan rented the palace in 1754 to the Austrian ambassador, Count Philip Orsini-Rosenburg, and then to his successor as envoy, Count Giacomo Durazzo, so that thereafter it was called 'dell'Ambasciatore'. The third palace is the Casa Mainelli (160), built in 1858 by the Venetian architect Lodovico Cadorin in the Lombardesque style of the early Renaissance.

After Rio de San Trovaso we pass two impressive palaces of the Contarini family: Palazzo Contarini Corfù (161) and Palazzo Contarini degli Scrigni (162). The first of these is a 15C Gothic palace whose interior was remodelled in the 17C by Francesco Smeraldi. The branch of the Contarini family who owned this palace took their second name from the fact that one of their ancestors was Venetian governor of Corfu. The second palace was built in 1609 by Vincenzo Scamozzi for a branch of the Contarini called 'degli scrigni', or 'of the coffers', because of the many treasure chests found in the family's villa on the Brenta. The palace was restored after a fire in 1891. Next is Palazzo Mocenigo-Gambara (163), erected in the mid 17C and enlarged in the 19C. Beyond that is Palazzo Querini (164), an 18C building that now serves as the British Consulate.

We now stop at Pontile Accademia, on Campo de la Carità just above the Accademia Bridge. At the back of the *campo* we see the former church and convent and *scuola* of Santa Maria della Carità, now the Accademia Galleries (165).

The first building beyond the bridge is the 17C Palazzo Brandolin-Rota (166). The palace was built in the late 17C for the Rota family, who were admitted to the Venetian nobility in 1685, and in 1750 it passed to the Brandolin. In the latter part of the 19C it served as a hotel, the Albergo dell'Universo, which numbered among its guests the poet Robert Browning. Next to it is the beautiful Palazzo Contarino dal Zaffo (167). The palace was erected at the end of the 15C, its design attributed to Giovanni Buora. In the latter part of the 16C it was acquired by the 'dal Zaffo' branch of the Contarini family. This name came from the fact that they were descendants of Giorgio Contarini, who in 1474 had been named by his cousin Queen Caterina Cornaro as Count of Zaffo, Venetian for Jaffa, a purely honorific title since the city was then in Muslim hands. During the latter part of the 18C the interior of the palace was decorated with frescoes by Giandomenico Tiepolo, some of which survive today. During the early years of the 20C the palace was owned by the Prince and Princesse de Polignac.

After this we pass a garden that occupies the site of Palazzo Paradiso, demolished after the Paradiso family became extinct in 1512. Beyond the garden is the 17C Palazzo Molin-Balbi-Valier (168). This is followed by Palazzo Loredan-Cini (169), dating from the mid 17C, its facade once decorated with frescoes attributed to Giuseppe Salviati, now vanished.

After Rio de San Vio and Campo San Vio we come to a succession of three *palazzi*. The first of these is the 16C Palazzo Barbarigo (170), which at the end of the 19C was acquired by the Compagnia Venezia e Murano, producers of fine glass and mosaics. The directors of the company commissioned Giulio Carlini to do the cartoons for the mosaics that we see on the canal-side facade of the palace; the two main scenes depict the Emperor Charles V in the studio of Titian and King Henry III of France visiting a glassworks in Murano. Next to it is Palazzo da Mula (171), a restored Gothic palace of the early 15C, with some architectural elements remaining from a 14C structure. Adjacent to this is the 18C Palazzo Centani (172). Then, after a small intervening house, we see the 17C Casa Biondetti (173). We then pass the former Palazzo Venier dei Leoni (174), now the Guggenheim Museum of Contemporary Art. The original palace was commissioned in the mid 18C by the Venier, a family who produced three Doges, but it was never completed, and in 1948 the site was purchased by Peggy Guggenheim for her museum.

After Rio de le Toresele we pass the 15C Gothic Palazzo Dario (175), renowned for its very beautiful facade, its marble revetment set with plaques and roundels of porphyry and verd-antique. The palace was built for Giovanni Dario, chancery secretary of the Republic, who in 1479 went to Istanbul to negotiate the treaty that ended the first war between Venice and the Ottoman Empire. The Republic rewarded him with a property near Padua, and Sultan Mehmet II showed his appreciation for Dario's efforts by presenting him with three robes of cloth of gold. Then in 1487 Dario commissioned this little palace, whose design is attributed to Pietro Lombardo; on the ground-floor facade is the dedicatory inscription in Latin: 'Giovanni Dario [dedicates his house] to the spirit of the city.'

Next is Palazzo Barbaro (176), another little Gothic palace of the 15C, once the residence of the famous actress Eleanora Duse. After Rio de le Fornace we pass the 19C Palazzetto Salviati (177), its facade decorated with mosaics produced by the glass company that owns it. Then, after an intervening house, we see Palazzo Benzon-Orio-Semitecolo (178), dating from the second half of the 14C.

After Calle del Tragheto San Gregorio we pass two houses before coming to the huge Palazzo Genovese (179), a neo-Gothic edifice built in 1892 on the site of one of the cloisters of the 15C church of San Gregorio. Beyond this is the former Abbazia di San Gregorio (180), the surviving cloister of the church, whose apse we see as we pass Rio de la Salute.

We now stop at Pontile Salute, under the great church of Santa Maria della Salute (181). This is the most magnificent sight on the Grand Canal, one of the defining views of Venice, with the great baroque church dominating the entrance to the Grand Canal, enthroned there, as Henry James wrote in his *Italian Hours*, 'like some great lady on the threshold of her salon'. 'She is more ample and serene, more seated at her door, than all the copyists have told us, with her domes and scrolls, her scalloped buttresses and statues forming a pompous crown, and her wide steps disposed on the ground like the train of a robe.'

The large building just beyond the church on Campo de la Salute is the Patriarchal Seminary (182). The long single-storey building beyond the Seminary is the Dogana da Mar (183), the Maritime Customs House in the days of the Republic. Beyond that is Punta de la Dogana, the promontory that divides the Grand Canal from the Giudecca Canal, with a tower surmounted by the gilded figure of Fortuna, the Italian goddess of Fortune, who here serves as the most charming of weathervanes. This is one of the most distinctive landmarks in Venice, whimsically described by Henry James in his *Italian Hours*:

The charming architectural promontory of the Dogana stretches out the most graceful of arms, balancing in its hand the gilded globe on which revolves the delightful satirical figure of a little weather-cock of a woman. This Fortune, or Navigation, or whatever she is called – she surely needs no name – catches the wind in the bit of drapery of which she has divested her rotary bronze loveliness.

The promontory is almost directly opposite Pontile San

Marco, where we finally complete our voyage up and down the Grand Canal. But the voyage invariably passes too quickly to examine the individual *palazzi* in detail, and although we will look at a number of them on our strolls through the city, there are many that can only be seen to full advantage from the Grand Canal. And so here one might consider investing in the luxury of a trip or two by gondola along the Grand Canal, particularly under a full moon, when the *palazzi* appear in their full romantic beauty. There are a number of gondola stations along the Grand Canal, and the largest of all is on the Bacino San Marco by the Molo, where gondolas are shown in the earliest depictions of Venice.

The gondola is first mentioned in 1094 in a decree of Doge Vitale Falier. The earliest depiction of gondolas is in Breydenbach's *Peregrinato ad Sanctum Sepulchrum* of 1480, which shows them as light lune-shaped skiffs with sharply upturned ends. They are represented in considerably greater detail in Carpaccio's *Miracle of the True Cross*, painted *c.* 1494, which gives a view of the Grand Canal looking from the Riva del Vin towards the Ponte de Rialto, in which some of the gondolas are shown with a rudimentary form of *felze*, the hood that later enclosed the passengers' seats like a miniature cabin, richly carved and painted and draped with sumptuous coverings. By the early 18C the gondola had developed essentially the form that it would have up into the first half of the 20C, when the *felze* began to disappear, so that today there are cabins on only a few private gondolas preserved in the *palazzi* and on those displayed in the Naval Museum. As early as 1723, Canaletto's paintings show the gondola much as it is today, except for the vanished *felze*, with the characteristic axe-like *ferro* with its teeth-like prongs at the prow and the gondolier poised on the rear deck as he plies his oar on the *furcola*, or fulcrum. Authorities disagree as to the function and significance of the *ferro*, some saying that it was originally used by the gondolier to gauge his way under low bridges on narrow canals, others that it is merely decorative; it is generally agreed that the six forward prongs stand for the six *sestieri* of Venice, with the one to the rear representing Giudecca. The final development of the gondola took place during the 1880s through the refinements of design introduced by Domenico Tramontin in his *squero*, or boatyard, on Rio de l'Avogaria. The gondolas of today are still made to his basic plan and dimensions, 11 m long and 1.4 m in width at the waist. The subtly skewed asymmetry of his design, in which the side where the gondolier stands is smaller in all of its dimensions than the other side, gives the boat greater speed and manoeuvrability and enables it to turn on its own vertical axis. By the end of the 16C there were ten thousand gondolas in Venice, but the establishment of the *vaporetto* service in the 1870s sharply reduced the number, so that today there are only some four hundred, with just three *squeri* making and repairing boats. Sumptuary laws were enacted during the 17–18C to control the extravagance of the nobles in adorning their gondolas, and eventually it was required that they all be painted black, which led Byron to remark that the *felze* looked 'just like a coffin clapt in a canoe'. Shelley wrote of the gondolas of Venice that 'I can only compare them to moths of which a coffin might have been the chrysalis.' And Thomas Mann, in *Death in Venice*, has the doomed Aschenbach shuddering at the sight of a passing gondola, 'with that peculiar blackness which is found elsewhere only in coffins – it suggests silent, criminal adventures in the rippling night, it suggests even more strongly death itself, the bier and the mournful funeral, and the last silent journey'.

The disappearance of the *felze* has made the gondola less sinister and mysterious and perhaps somewhat less romantic too, but with a musician and singer aboard on a moonlit night the experience can still be enchanting. (Verdi, when asked why he did not allow any outsiders to attend rehearsals of *Rigoletto* for its premier at La Fenice in 1876, replied that 'If I did, every gondolier on the Grand Canal would be singing my arias before opening night!')

Shelley's 'Julian and Maddalo', inspired by a trip to the Lido and back with Byron, evokes the romance of an evening's ride in a gondola across the lagoon:

> So o'er the lagoon
> We glided; and from that funereal bark
> I leaned, and saw the city, and could mark
> How from their many isles, in evening's gleam,
> Its temples and its palaces did seem
> Like fabrics of enchantment piled to heaven.

Byron writes of the gondola in a stanza from *Beppo*, which he wrote while living in the Palazzo Mocenigo on the Grand Canal:

> And up and down the long canals they go,
> And under the Rialto shoot along,
> By night and day, all paces, swift or slow,
> And round the theatres, a sable throng,
> They wait in their dusk livery of woe, –
> But not to them do woeful things belong,
> For sometimes they conceal a deal of fun,
> Like mourning coaches when the funeral's done.

Ezra Pound catches the romance of the gondola in one of his *Cantos*, written in nostalgic memory of the Venice he knew in his 'young youth':

> And at night they sang in the gondolas
> And in the *barche* with lanthorns;
> The prows rose silver on silver
>   taking light in the darkness.

Such is the poetry of the gondola and of the Grand Canal.

[6] Sestiere di San Marco

The first four chapters took us around Piazza San Marco and the monuments on its periphery. Now we will explore the rest of the Sestiere di San Marco.

SESTIERE DI SAN MARCO I (*Map Route 1*)

For the first stroll we will begin in Piazza San Marco at the clock tower, where the round arch leads to the market street known as Marzaria de l'Orologio.

Marzaria de l'Orologio is the first stretch of the ancient market street that leads from the north-east corner of the Piazza to the Rialto Bridge, changing its name several times *en route*. Originally known as the Merceria throughout its length, it was first paved in brick in the 13C and then repaved in stone in 1675. Since it is very narrow, and was used throughout the year by processions going to and from the Piazza, there were regulations forbidding all awnings, benches, barrows or projections of any kind exceeding 6 inches, and after 1291 one could ride through it on horseback only in the very early hours before the shops opened.

After passing under the clock tower we come after a few steps the first turning on the left, Sottoportego del Cappello. This is named after the Locanda del Cappello Nero, an inn that was located a short way along the Merceria as far back as 1341; Francesco dal Cappello was recorded as landlord in 1397. Over the round-arched entrance to the street there is a relief depicting Giustina Rossi, the heroine who helped put down the revolt of Bajamonte Tiepolo against Doge Pietro Gradenigo on 15 June 1310. Tiepolo and his followers had come along the Merceria to attack the Doge and his men, who were waiting for them in the Piazza. When Tiepolo's men paused under the archway the people in the surrounding houses began pelting them with stones and roof tiles. Giustina Rossi, hearing the commotion, opened her window, and knocked over a stone mortar, which landed on the head of Tiepolo's standard-bearer, killing him on the spot. This demoralized Tiepolo and his men, who soon retreated back along the Merceria in disarray. The Signoria expressed their gratitude to Giustina Rossi for her heroism and asked her if there was anything they could do for her in return. She replied with two requests: that she be allowed to display the banner of the Republic from her window on all feast-days, and that her landlords, the Procurators of San Marco, should refrain from raising the rent as long as she and her descendants lived in the house. A document in the Venetian archives records that one of her descendants, Nicolò Rossi, won an appeal against a rent increase imposed by the Procurators in 1468. A plaque on the ground under the archway marks the spot where Giustina Rossi's mortar killed Tiepolo's standard-bearer.

A few steps farther along the Merceria on the left is the Banca di Roma, which stands on the site of the Locanda del Cappello Nero. Opposite the bank we turn right on Calle Larga San Marco, a street joined to the Merceria in 1545 by demolishing an intervening house. The original name of the street was Corazzaria, the Street of the Cuirasses, from the armourers who had their shops in this area. We then turn left on Spaderia, the Street of the Sword-makers. The house at the entrance to the street on the right still bears the coat of arms of the guild of sword-makers, founded in the 13C, a shield with three swords surmounted by the Lion of St Mark.

At the far end of the Spaderia we come to Campiello San Zulian. This was a crossroads on the Merceria, as is evident from the names of the intersecting streets: there are branches of the Marzaria leading off in three different directions. On the facade of the house at the intersection of two branches of Marzaria San Zulian there is a relief of St George killing the dragon, with the date 1496. The relief denotes that this was once the property of the monastery of San Giorgio Maggiore, which owned all the houses on this street as far as Ponte Bareteri.

On the right side of the square we see the facade of the church of San Giuliano, known in Venetian dialect as San Zulian. According to tradition, San Giuliano was founded in 829. The present church is due to a complete rebuilding commissioned in 1553 by Tommaso Rangone, a physician and natural philosopher from Ravenna. Jacopo Sansovino was placed in charge of the reconstruction, but while he was erecting the new facade the rest of the building collapsed and he was forced to rebuild it from the foundations. Alessandro Vittoria was called in to collaborate on the project, which he completed in 1580, ten years after Sansovino's death. Above the architrave a great round arch frames a bronze statue of Rangone done by Sansovino in 1554. Inscriptions in Latin, Greek and Hebrew extol Rangone's accomplishments in science and philosophy and his generosity in founding the church.

The gilded wooden ceiling was decorated *c.* 1585; the central panel, *The Apotheosis of St Julian*, is by Palma il Giovane and assistants. On the first altar from the rear on the right there is a *Pietà* above Sts Roch, Mark and Jerome, done in 1584 by Paolo Veronese, whose assistants did the lower part of the painting. The *St Jerome* over the side door is by Leandro Bassano. The second altar on the right was dedicated by the Guild of Mercers. The altarpiece is *The Assumption* by Palma il Giovane; on the altar-front is a relief of the Nativity of the Virgin, by Alessandro Vittoria, who also did the statues of Daniel and St Catherine of Alexandria. The chapel to the right of the chancel has on its right wall a painting of *Sts John the Evangelist, Joseph and Anthony* by Palma il Giovane. On the high altar is a *Coronation of the Virgin and Saints* signed by Girolamo da Santacroce. On the side walls of the chancel there are two huge paintings by Antonio Zanchi, *A Miracle of St Julian* and *The Martyrdom of St Julian*. The Sacramental Chapel to the left of the chancel was designed by Giovanni Antonio Rusconi, with the Virgin and Mary Magdalene represented in terracotta statues painted to resemble bronze by Girolamo Campagna, who also did the relief of the Pietà. On the left wall is a *Last Supper*, attributed to Tintoretto. On the wall above the arch that frames the chapel is a *Resurrection* by Palma il Giovane.

We go out of the church by the side door on the left, which leads to Campiello San Zulian. In the centre of the *campiello* there is a handsome *vera da pozzo* dating from the 17C; it still retains its iron spout, inserted in the period 1882–4, when the public wells were used as storage tanks for the water piped into Venice by the aqueduct.

We leave the *campiello* by the alley at its far right-hand corner, after which we turn left into Sottoportego Primo Lucatello. This leads to Cortile Lucatello, where there is a *vera da pozzo* dating from the 14–15C. We leave the courtyard at its far end via Sottoportego Secondo Lucatello. At the end of the *sottoportego* we emerge on Rio dei Bareteri, turning left to reach the end of Marzaria San Zulian at Ponte dei Bareteri, the Bridge of the Cap-makers. The first bridge at this point was built in wood, *c.* 1200, and reconstructed in stone in 1508. The street that runs straight ahead from the bridge is Marzaria del Capitello, another branch of the Merceria. Until the 14C it was called Bareteria, because it was flanked by shops selling caps and hats. It takes its present name from the fact that it leads to a *capitello*, or tabernacle.

After crossing Ponte dei Bareteri we turn right on Sottoportego de le Acque, an arcaded *fondamenta* that runs along Rio dei Bareteri almost to the end of the canal. At No. 4939 we pass the former Casino or Ridotto of the Procuratoressa

Venier, a gambling club that was famous in the mid 18C. This and all other such clubs were closed by a decree of the Maggior Consiglio on 27 November 1774, for there was a limit to the debauchery that was tolerated in Venice even in its final decadence.

At the end of the *sottoportego* we turn left on Calle de le Acque. This street took its name from the fact that it was once flanked with *botteghe da acque*, or 'water shops', which served coffee and hot chocolate in addition to iced drinks of various types. Coronelli's guide to Venice, in the 1724 edition, mentions that the best *botteghe da acque* were on the Calle de le Acque near the Ponte dei Baretcri.

Calle de le Acque leads to Marzaria San Salvador, another branch of the Merceria. At the beginning of this street on the right is the 15C Palazzo Giustinian-Faccanon, whose beautiful canal-side Gothic facade can be seen by turning right at the corner and walking back for a few steps on Riva Tonda.

Continuing along the Marzaria San Salvador, notice that the houses along the left side of the street have their upper floors carried outwards on *barbacani*, or wooden corbels, a feature of the oldest dwellings in Venice. Just before the end of the street we pass on our left the side entrance to the church of San Salvador. At the end of the street we come to Campo San Salvador, where we turn left to approach the main entrance of the church.

According to tradition, the original church of San Salvador was founded in the 7C; it was rebuilt in the 12C by the canons of St Augustine, creating the edifice that is depicted in Barbari's view of 1500. The present church dates from another series of rebuilding projects beginning in 1507, with Giorgio Spavento designing the building and Tullio Lombardo supervising its construction, which Jacopo Sansovino completed, in 1530–34. The facade was rebuilt in 1649–63 to a design by Giuseppe Sardi, with Bernardo Falcone adding the sculptural decoration, which was completed by 1703. The Lombardesque side portal on Marzaria San Salvador was built by Sansovino in 1532.

On the right wall between the second and third altars is the tomb of Doge Francesco Venier (d. 1556), by Sansovino. The third altar is also by Sansovino; the altarpiece is Titian's famous *Annunciation*, *c.* 1560–65. On the end wall of the right transept is the tomb of Caterina Cornaro, Queen of Cyprus (d. 1510), who was reinterred here after having been buried in the church of the Santi Apostoli; her monument was created in 1580–84 by Bernardino Contino. On the right wall of the transept is a painting of *Sts Roch, Lorenzo Giustinian, Francis de Sales and Anna* by Girolamo Brusaferro. On the left side the altarpiece is *St Lorenzo Giustinian and Other Saints* by Francesco Fontebasso. The chapel to the right of the chancel is dedicated to St Theodore, the first patron saint of Venice, whose ashes are in an urn on the altar. On the right wall of the chapel is *The Martyrdom of St Theodore*, attributed to Paris Bordone.

The painting on the high altar is another masterpiece by Titian, *The Transfiguration*, done in the 1560s. Behind it is a Pala d'Oro depicting the Transfiguration, a 14C work that is exhibited only on 3–5 August and on high holy days. The first altar from the front on the left was dedicated by the Guild of Sausage-makers; it was made by Alessandro Vittoria, who also did the flanking statues of St Roch and St Sebastian; the altarpiece, depicting *St Anthony and Other Saints*, is by Palma il Giovane. The marble frame of the side door on the left and the gilded front of the organ above were done in 1530 by Sansovino. The doors of the organ are open to show the paintings on their inside surfaces, *The Transfiguration* and *The Resurrection*, by Francesco Vecellio, Titian's brother. On the second altar from the front there is a statue of St Jerome by Tommaso da Lugano. In the vault beyond is the tomb of Doge Lorenzo Priuli (d. 1559) and his brother Doge Girolamo Priuli (d. 1567) by Cesare Franco. On the last altar there is a painting of *St Nicholas, St Leonard and the Blessed Arcangelo Canetoli*; this was begun by Giambattista Piazzetta, and finished after his death in 1754 by his student Domenico Maggiotto.

The column in the centre of the *campo* commemorates the founding of the independent Republic of San Marco, proclaimed in Venice by Daniele Manin and his supporters on 22 March 1848. The column stands on the site of an ancient elm tree, which was used as a hitching-post for horses after the ordinance of 1291 forbade anyone to ride along the Merceria after the shops opened in the morning.

Facing the church, beside it to the right at the corner we see the former monastery of San Salvador, now the headquarters of the telephone company. The monastery was built in the first half of the 16C, and is attributed to Sansovino.

Across the street from the monastery on the right side of the square is the former Scuola di San Teodoro. This was the last of the six Scuole Grandi, or Great Guilds, to be established in Venice, and was founded in 1530. The members of these six guilds attended the Doge on all public occasions and were under the direct control of the Council of Ten. Besides the six Scuole Grandi there were numerous other guilds associated with the various trades of the city, the oldest of them dating back to the 12C. The guildhall of the Scuola di San Teodoro was built in 1655 through the generosity of Jacopo Galli, with Giuseppe Sardi designing the classical facade and Bernardo Falcone doing the sculptural decoration. The building is now used as an exhibition hall.

We now leave the square along the Marzarieta Due Aprile, the last stretch of the Merceria before the Rialto Bridge.

At the end of the street we come to Campo San Bartolomeo, one of the most popular meeting places in Venice. On the right side of the square, at No. 5308, is the handsome but somewhat dilapidated Palazzo Moro, dating from the early 14C. In the centre of the square there is a bronze statue of the great Venetian playwright Carlo Goldoni (1707–93), a work done by Antonio dal Zotto in 1883 and restored in 1985.

We leave the square along Salizzada del Fontego dei Tedeschi. The street is named after the Fontego dei Tedeschi, the Warehouse of the German Merchants, which now serves as the general post office. The entrance to the building is halfway along the street on the left.

The Fontego dei Tedeschi is first mentioned in 1228 as a commercial building leased by German merchants, who continued to do business there until 1812. The original structure was burnt down in 1478; rebuilding was begun in 1505 by Giorgio Spavento, to a design by Girolamo Tedesco, with the project being completed in 1508 by Antonio Scarpagnino. The interior is a great colonnaded square with a portico of five arches on each side, with three loggias of successively diminishing height; in the centre of the court is a 15C *vera da pozzo*. The facades along the Grand Canal and the main street were once decorated with frescoes by Titian and Giorgione, all of which have vanished except for some fragments preserved in the Ca d'Oro museum.

Returning to Campo San Bartolomeo, we now turn right on Salizzada Pio X, which leads from the square to the Rialto Bridge. On the left side of the street before the final approach to the bridge we come to the side entrance to the former church of San Bartolomeo.

According to tradition, a small church dedicated to San Dimitrio was erected on this site in the first half of the 9C. In the 12C the church was completely rebuilt and re-dedicated to St Bartholomew. From the early 13C onwards San Bartolomeo was used by the German merchants from the Fontego dei Tedeschi. The church was rebuilt once again in 1723, creating the building that we see today. The building was closed and deconsecrated in the 1980s, and it has recently reopened as an exhibition hall. All its paintings and other works have been removed except for the sculptures on the altars and on the choir loft at the rear. One fresco remains on the ceiling over the high altar, *St Bartholomew in Glory*, a work of Michelangelo Morleiter.

We leave by what was once the main entrance of the church, turning right on the narrow Calle dei Bombaseri.

This brings us past the campanile of San Bartolomeo, a distinctive structure with an onion dome, built by Giovanni Scalfarotto in 1747–54.

At the corner we turn right and then after a few steps left on to Salizzada Pio X, which brings us to the famous Rialto Bridge.

During the early years of the city there was only a *traghetto* here. In 1180 a bridge of boats was built by Nicolò Baratieri, the engineer who erected the two columns on the Piazzetta; this was called the 'Quartarolo', from the copper coin that was the toll for those crossing. In the mid 13C a wooden span was built on piles across the canal, but this was destroyed in 1310 by Bajamonte Tiepolo and his supporters to prevent the Doge's men from pursuing them after the failure of their revolt. The bridge was rebuilt, but then collapsed in 1444, overloaded by the weight of a crowd watching the wedding procession of the Marchese di Ferrara along the Grand Canal. It was replaced in 1458 by a larger wooden span with shops and a central drawbridge, depicted in Carpaccio's painting of *The Miracle of the Relic of the Holy Cross*, dated *c*. 1494. By 1524 a decision was made to replace the wooden span with a new bridge in stone, and the leading architects of the day submitted plans. The commission was finally awarded in 1588 to Antonio da Ponte, who with his nephew Antonio Contino completed the bridge in 1591, during the reign of Doge Pasquale Cicogna. The bridge spans the canal in a single arch 28 m long, with its crown 7.5 m above the *fondamente* on either side. The bridge is divided laterally into three parts, with two rows of arcaded shops connected by a large archway at the middle, dividing the wide central stairway from the two narrower side stairs, bordered on the sides by balustrades. Doge Cicogna's commemorative inscription and coat of arms can be seen on either side of the bridge at both ends. On the side towards San Marco there are reliefs of the Angel of the Annunciation and the Archangel Gabriel by Agostino Rubini; on the other side St Mark and St Theodore by Tiziano

Aspetti; and on the crown of the arch on either side a dove; all of the sculptures dating from the end of the 16C.

We now walk back from the bridge along the San Marco side of the Grand Canal. The first stretch of the canal-side walkway here is known as Pescaria San Bartolomeo, indicating that this was once the site of a fish market, long since transferred to Campo de la Pescaria on the other side of the Rialto Bridge. The canal-side walkway then becomes Riva del Ferro, which takes its name from the iron (*ferro*) that was unloaded here from barges that had come by river from Germany. Venetian merchants traded this iron in the Orient for silks and spices, which were then sold in Europe, Venice's principal exports.

After passing Calle Larga Mazzini we walk through Sottoportego Manin, which runs through the arcade of Palazzo Dolfin-Manin. The palace was commissioned in 1538 by Giovanni Dolfin; the architect was Jacopo Sansovino, who completed the building in 1540. The Dolfin family became extinct in 1602, after which the palace passed in turn to the Contarini and Pesaro before being purchased by Ludovico Manin, the last Doge of Venice, who died here in 1802.

We cross Rio de San Salvador on Ponte Manin, bringing us to Riva del Carbon, so called because the coal boats unloaded here, the earliest record of this name being in 1537. The first building after Rio de San Salvador is Palazzo Bembo, a 15C Gothic palace considerably altered in 1657–71. Seven branches of the Bembo family were listed in the Golden Book. Famous members of the family include Doge Giovanni Bembo (1615–18) and Cardinal Pietro Bembo, the historian and poet, who was born here in 1479. Another member of the family, Leo, was canonized, and two others, Antonio and Illuminata, were beatified.

We now turn left on Calle Bembo, passing along the side of Palazzo Bembo. At the first intersection the street changes its name to Calle dei Fabbri. This is named for the *fabbri*, or blacksmiths, who had their smithies along this street because of its proximity to the coal docks on Riva del Carbon. The guild of the blacksmiths was an old and important one, with their *scuola* near the church of San Moisè. At public processions they donned the ancient costumes that their predecessors wore in 1162, when they played an important part in the Venetian repulse of an attack on Grado by Ulrich, the German-born Patriarch of Aquileia, launched on the instigation of the Emperor Frederick Barbarossa. The Venetians captured the Patriarch along with 700 of his followers, releasing them only after Ulrich swore to give the Republic an annual tribute of a bull, a dozen pigs, a dozen loaves of bread and a barrel of wine. This tribute was to arrive in Venice each year on the Wednesday before Lent, and on the following day, Giovedi Grasso, 'Fat Thursday' the Venetians chased the animals around Piazza San Marco until they caught them, after which the bull and the pigs were killed by the smiths and their meat distributed to the needy, a practice that went on until the fall of the Republic.

We follow Calle dei Fabbri as far as Rio Terà de le Colonne. The street is named for the columns that support an arcade along its right side, forming a *sottoportego* under the adjoining houses. At the second corner on the right we turn in to Sottoportego dei Armeni, which leads into Calle dei Armeni. This street, along with another *sottoportego* of the same name that extends from it to Rio dei Ferali, are so called because they formed the bounds of the tiny Armenian quarter that existed here under the Republic. This quarter, mentioned as early as 1253, was inhabited by Armenian merchants who had come here from eastern Asia Minor, building a small *fontego* as their residence and warehouse on Rio dei Ferali. In 1496 the Armenians built a church on the bank of the canal and dedicated it to Santa Croce di Cristo, the Sacred Cross of Christ. The church was completely rebuilt in 1682–8, and was further renovated in 1703. Santa Croce is no longer open to the public, for the tiny Armenian community in Venice now attends services at the island monastery of San Lazzaro degli Armeni.

Continuing to the end of Calle dei Armeni, we turn right on Calle Fiubera, the Street of the Buckle-makers, whose shops are recorded as being located here as early as 1496. This takes us back to Calle dei Fabbri, where we turn left. We turn left at the next corner and then right a few steps farther on, as we come to the final stretch of Calle dei Fabbri. Then we cross Rio de le Procuratie on Ponte dei Dai, bringing us to Sottoportego dei Dai. The *sottoportego* and bridge are first mentioned on 10 June 1310, when some of Bajamonte Tiepolo's men fled this way after being routed by the Doge's men in the Piazza.

After passing through the *sottoportego* we emerge in Piazza San Marco, where this stroll comes to an end.

SESTIERE DI SAN MARCO II (*Map Route 2*)

The second of our four strolls through the Sestiere di San Marco begins in the north-west corner of Piazza San Marco. There we leave the square through Sottoportego dei Cavalletto, after which we cross Rio de le Procuratie on Ponte dei Cavalletto and continue ahead on the *calle* of the same name. The name comes from the Hotel Cavalletto, whose main entrance we pass on the left midway along the street. The original hotel on this site was founded in the 14C as the Albergo del Cavalletto, taking its name from the fact that guests kept their horses in a stable here when they came to Piazza San Marco.

Calle del Cavalletto leads into Campo San Gallo. As we enter the *campo* we see on our left the former church of San Gallo, erected in 1582 and altered to its present form in 1703. The church served as the chapel of an almshouse that had originally been a hostel for pilgrims to the Holy Land, known as the Ospizio Orseolo. This was founded in 977 by Pietro Orseolo I, the only Doge to be canonized as a saint; it originally stood in Piazza San Marco next to the campanile, but it was transferred here in 1582 to make way for the

Procuratie Nuove. The hostel was later converted into an alms-house for women, known as the Orsoline di San Gallo. The almshouse was partly annexed to the Albergo del Cavalletto in 1869, while the remainder of the building was demolished. In front of the church there is a 14C *vera da pozzo*.

At the far end of the square we turn left on Calle Tron, after which we cross Ponte Tron o la Piovola. As we do so we pass on our left the Banco Nazionali del Lavoro, which stands on the site of a mansion that in the early 19C was the residence of Francesconi, the proprietor of Caffè Florian in Piazza San Marco. The sculptor Antonio Canova, who was a close friend of Francesconi, died here in 1822.

After crossing the bridge we turn right on Fondamenta Goldoni, which takes us along Rio Orseolo. After a few steps we pass on our left Corte del Spiron d'Oro, named after a druggist's shop 'at the sign of the golden spur', mentioned in documents of the 17C. In the centre of the court there is a *vera da pozzo* dating from the 14–15C.

At the end of the *fondamenta* we cross Rio dei Fuseri on Ponte Goldoni, continuing ahead on Calle Goldoni as far as Campo San Luca. In the middle of the square there is a pedestal with a flag-pole, which Francesco Sansovino, in his 1581 guide to Venice, says was placed here to mark the geometrical centre of Venice. The pedestal bears the date 1310 and the coats of arms of the Scuola della Carità and the Scuola dei Pittori. This indicates that it was actually erected to commemorate the defeat of Bajamonte Tiepolo and his followers on 15 June 1310, in which the members of these two *scuole* played an important part.

We leave the square on Calle del Forno, the Street of the Bakery, one of the most common street names in Venice. At the first corner we turn right on Calle del Teatro o de la Comedia, and halfway down the block on the left we come to the Teatro Goldoni, one of the oldest theatres in Venice. The original theatre on this site, the Teatro San Salvatore, also known as the Teatro San Luca, was founded in the 17C by the Vendramin family. After some reconstruction in 1875 it was renamed in honour of Carlo Goldoni, whose works had been performed here as well as in the numerous other theatres in Venice at the time.

The alleyway to the left of the theatre leads into Corte del Teatro, surrounded by a number of picturesque old houses, with coats of arms and reliefs embedded in their walls. In the centre of the court there is a *vera da pozzo* dating from the 15C.

We leave the court at its far right-hand corner via Ramo del Carbon, which leads out to Riva del Carbon on the Grand Canal. Halfway along the alleyway becomes a *sottoportego*, at which point we see on the left a tabernacle with a relief of a saint holding the Christ Child. These tabernacles were usually placed in dark passages like this, with an oil lamp to light the way of passers-by and to discourage lurking thieves, who would be put off by the presence of a sacred image.

After emerging from the *sottoportego* we turn left on Riva del Carbon to walk for a short way along the Grand Canal. The second house on the left bears a plaque identifying the site of Palazzetto Dandolo, the birthplace of Doge Enrico Dandolo (1192–1205).

Adjacent to the Dandolo birthplace, at No. 4168, there is a 14C Gothic *palazzetto*. During the years 1551–6 this was the home of the notorious poet and playwright Pietro Aretino (1492–1566), who rented the house from Leonardo Dandolo. Aretino moved to Venice in 1527 after having been forced to leave Rome because of the outcry following the publication of his *Sonetti lussuriosi*, or 'Lewd Sonnets'. Here he entertained his many friends, who included Sansovino, Titian, Pietro Bembo, the humanist and poet who was made a cardinal by Pope Paul III, and Ludovico Ariosto, who in his great poem *Orlando Furioso* described Aretino as 'the Scourge of Princes'. Aretino's guests also included his many lovers, male and female, among whom were the most accomplished courtesans in Venice, who were thus known as Aretine.

After passing Calle del Carbon we come to Palazzo Piscopia o Loredan. The palace was built in the 13C for the Bocassi family of Parma in the Veneto-Byzantine style, with the two lower storeys surviving from the original structure. Doge Jacopo Contarini spent the last years of his life here as a guest of the Bocassi after his abdication on 5 March 1280. The building was purchased in 1867 by the Commune of Venice, and today it serves as the town-hall, along with the adjacent palace.

The neighbouring palace, Palazzo Farsetti-Dandolo, was erected in the Veneto-Byzantine style in the 12–13C; in the early 14C it was purchased by Andrea Dandolo, who served as Doge in 1343–54. The palace was purchased by the municipality in 1826; in 1874 it was restored and another floor was added in 1892, after which it was linked with the adjacent Palazzo Piscopia o Loredan to serve as the town-hall.

We now leave the Grand Canal along Calle Cavalli, which passes between Palazzo Farsetti-Dandolo and the 17C Palazzo Martinengo-Rava. At the end of the street we turn right into Campiello de la Chiesa, on the right side of which we pass the side entrance of the church of San Luca. On the left side of the square at its far end, at No. 4038, there is an interesting doorway dating from the 12C, with a triangular pediment decorated with a brickwork pattern, a relief of two kissing peacocks at its centre. This is the entrance to the 14C Palazzo Magno, whose Gothic facade can be seen on Rio de San Luca.

Ramo a Fianco la Chiesa leads to Rio de San Luca and Fondamenta de la Chiesa, where we see the main entrance of the church of San Luca.

The original church of San Luca was erected before 1072 by the Dandolo and Puzzamano families. The church was rebuilt in the 16C and repaired in 1832, after part of the facade collapsed.

On the first altar from the rear on the right there is a Gothic wood-carving showing the Virgin and Child worshipped by two sainted nuns, an early-15C work attributed to Michele da Firenze. The altarpiece in the side chapel to the right of the chancel is a *Virgin in Glory with Saints* by Palma il Giovane. The painting on the high altar was done in 1581 by Paolo Veronese, showing the Virgin in glory appearing to St Luke as he writes his Gospel. On the first altar from the front on the right is *A Miracle of St Lorenzo Giustinian* by Carl Loth. On the second altar is *Sts Cecilia, Margaret and Louis* (Louis IX of France) by Nicolò Renieri. In the corridor leading to the sacristy is the funerary monument of Carl Loth (d. 1698), by Heinrich Meyring.

Pietro Aretino was buried in San Luca in 1556, but his tomb was covered over in the 19C restoration. Lorenzetti, noting that Aretino is buried here, remarks of the 'Scourge of Princes' that he was 'a writer of brilliant mind but of debauched life'. Pompeo Molmenti writes of the last days of Aretino in the *palazzo* on Riva del Carbon:

Here he spent the remaining days of his life in low intrigues. Tradition has it that he found an ignoble end to an ignoble life; it is said that in a fit of immoderate laughter at some filthy joke he lost his balance, fell off his stool and cracked his skull; but as a matter of fact he died of apoplexy – the very death he himself desired, as he says in one of his letters to Bollani.

Beyond the church on Fondamenta de la Chiesa is the back entrance to the 16C Palazzo Grimani, now the Court of Appeal. On the far side of the bridge is the Cinema Rossini, the former Teatro Rossini. This was originally the Teatro San Benedetto, built in 1755 by the Grimani; from then until the opening of La Fenice in 1792 it was the largest and most popular theatre in Venice.

After crossing Ponte del Teatro we turn immediately right and then left into Sottoportego Muneghe (nuns), which leads to the *calle* of the same name. After turning right at the first corner we come to the intersection of Calle San Andrea and Ramo Contarini, where we turn right to enter the little

Corte San Andrea. Records show that the monks of San Andrea della Certosa were given a house here in 1272 to serve as their residence in Venice. A relief on the facade of the house to the left, No. 3981, shows San Andrea (St Andrew the Apostle) between the diminutive figures of two praying friars, with the coat of arms of the Minotto family and an inscription stating that it was built by the Prior Marco Minotto in 1356. In the middle of the court there is a *vera da pozzo* of the 14C, decorated with reliefs of rosettes and Gothic shields.

Returning to the intersection, we now walk along Calle San Andrea, turning right at the first corner on Salizzada del Teatro. This brings us into Campo San Beneto, where we see straight ahead the church of San Benedetto, known in Venetian dialect as San Beneto.

According to tradition, the church of San Benedetto was founded in the second half of the 11C, and in 1229 it was given to the monastery of Brondolo by Pope Gregory IX. The present structure dates from a reconstruction in 1619; unfortunately it is now closed.

The building to the left of the church is Palazzo Martinengo, whose main facade is on the Grand Canal. In the centre of the *campo* there is a *vera da pozzo* dating from the 14–15C.

As we face the church, on our left is Palazzo Pesaro, now the Fortuny Museum, whose main entrance is around to the left on the side street, Ramo Orfei. The palace was built by the Pesaro family in the 15C in the Venetian Gothic style. It is also known as Palazzo degli Orfei, from the fact that in the years 1786–92 it was the home of the famous Philharmonia Società l'Apollinea, known as the Orfei, which afterwards moved to the Teatro La Fenice. At the beginning of the 20C the palace was bought and restored by Mariano Fortuny y Madrazo, a Spanish painter, designer, craftsman and inventor. He reinvented the processes whereby the Venetians of the Renaissance wove cloth with threads of gold and silver, and reintroduced these fabrics into the world of high fashion and the decorative arts. Six years after his death in 1950 the palace was presented to the Commune of Venice by his widow, Madame Henriette Fortuny, and since then it has been a museum, used for art exhibitions and for a display of the fabrics, paintings and other examples of the versatile genius of Mariano Fortuny. Marcel Proust remarked of Fortuny's exotic gowns that they were 'faithfully antique but markedly original'. And in *La Prisonnière* he writes: 'The Fortuny gown which Albertine was wearing that evening seemed to me the tempting phantom of that invisible Venice.'

The exit to the museum leaves us out on Campo San Beneto. There we turn left and then left again on Calle Pesaro, which brings us to Ponte Michiel. Pausing on the bridge, we look back to the left to see the splendid canal-side facade of Palazzo Pesaro. On the right is the beautiful walled garden of Palazzo Benzon.

After crossing Ponte Michiel we continue ahead on Calle Pesaro and Ramo Michiel, after which we cross Ponte de l'Albero. We then turn right on Fondamenta de l'Albero, followed by a left into Corte de l'Albero. In the middle of the court there is a 14C *vera da pozzo* of white Verona marble. In the angle of the court on the right, at No. 3870, is Palazzo Sandi-Porto, built by Domenico Rossi in 1725 and decorated by Giambattista Tiepolo.

We leave Corte de l'Albero via Ramo Narisi, which takes us out to an angle of Rio de San Anzolo. There we turn right on Fondamenta Narisi, which takes us through a *sottoportego* to the foot of Ponte del Pestrin, the Bridge of the Milk-seller. We bypass the bridge and continue along the *fondamenta* to cross the canal on Ponte San Samuele. This brings us to Piscina San Samuele, where we see on our right, at Nos. 3395–7, Palazzo Pisani, a Gothic palace of the 15C.

Continuing along Piscina San Samuele, we soon pass on our left Palazzo Querini (No. 3431), a little Gothic palace of the 15C. A tablet with the Querini coat of arms bears an inscription recording that this was the home of the explorer Francesco Querini, who died in 1904 on the expedition to the North Pole led by the Duke of Abruzzi.

Near the end of Piscina San Samuele we turn left and ascend a short flight of steps to enter Campiello Novo o dei Morti. This little square takes its name from the fact that it was once the graveyard of the monastery of San Stefano. The graveyard was closed after the plague of 1630, and it was opened as a public square in 1838.

At the opposite end of the square we go down a short flight of steps and turn right on Calle del Pestrin. At the corner we see the church of San Stefano, which we will visit on our next stroll; there we turn left on Calle dei Frati, the Street of the Friars. We then cross Ponte dei Frati, built in 1455. The *calle* and the bridge take their name from the fact that they were used by the friars of San Stefano, whose monastery now houses the Ministry of Finance.

Campo San Anzolo takes its name from the ancient church of San Michele Arcangelo, which was suppressed by the French in 1810 and then demolished by the Austrians in 1837. The church, founded in 920 by the Morosini family, stood to the right of the bridge as one enters the *campo*. The church is shown in Barbari's view of 1500, along with the little oratory that still stands to the left of the bridge. This was founded in 920 by Giacomo Morosini and rebuilt in 1520. In 1372 the oratory was given to the Scuola dei Zoppi, the Confraternity of Cripples. The chapel has been restored and is occasionally open to the public; inside there is an *Assumption* by Palma il Giovane.

Ramo dei Frati leads behind the chapel to Calle Va in Campo, which borders the side of the square to the left of the bridge. This side of the *campo* is largely taken up with two palaces: the 17C Palazzo Pisani-Trevisan (No. 3831), and the 15C Palazzo Gritti (No. 3832). On the opposite side of the *campo* is the 15C Palazzo Duodo (No. 3584).

There are two 15C *vere da pozzo* in the *campo*, one opposite

Palazzo Pisani-Trevisan and the other by Palazzo Duodo. The first of them is decorated with reliefs of the Archangel Michael and the Virgin of the Annunciation, indicating that it was associated with the nearby oratory.

We leave the square via Calle del Spezier, another very common street name in Venice. The name comes from *spezie*, meaning spices or drugs, and the various streets were named for shops dealing in those commodities as well as chemists, confectioners and those selling sugar, wax candles, olive oil, perfumes and other such things. The *spezieri* all belonged to the same guild originally, but in later times the pharmacists formed their own confraternity, the Farmacisti.

At the first intersection we pass on the left Rio Terà de la Mandola and on the right Rio Terà dei Assassini. Before this canal was filled in it was crossed at this point by a bridge called Ponte dei Assassini, because of the numerous murders committed there in times past.

We continue along Calle de la Mandola, the Street of the Almond. This was named for a wine shop that sold a special brandy flavoured with almonds. On the next block the street changes its name to Calle de la Cortesia, which ends at Ponte Cortesia. Both names come from an inn named Albergo Cortesia, the Hotel of Courtesy, founded here in 1785.

Ponte de la Cortesia takes us across Rio de San Luca to Campo Daniele Manin, formerly Campo San Paternian. In the centre of the square there is a statue of Daniele Manin done by Luigi Borro in 1875. Manin's house is across the canal between Ponte Cortesia and Ponte San Paternian, marked by a plaque. The house to its right, at No. 4013 on Calle San Paternian, is the 16C Palazzo Pisani-Revedin.

The old name of the square came from the ancient church of San Paternian, which stood at the far end of the *campo* opposite the two bridges, on the present site of the Cassa di Risparmio di Venezia. The church was suppressed in 1810, and demolished in 1871.

We leave the square by the Calle de la Vida o de le

Locande, the Street of the Vine or of the Inns. A record of 1740 mentions three inns on this short *calle*: the Three Keys, the Three Roses, and the Three Faces. At the end of the block, where the *calle* turns left, we see the entrance to Palazzo Contarini del Bovolo (No. 4298), whose main facade is on Rio de San Luca. We approach the palace by turning right off the *calle* at the next corner on to Calle Contarini del Bovolo, which brings us into the *corte* of the same name. Here we see the spectacular spiral stairway which is the outstanding feature of the palace. The stairway is called *bovolo*, which in Venetian dialect is a small edible snail with a spiral shell. The palace was built in 1499 for Pietro Contarini by Giovanni Candi, a Venetian architect who began his career as a humble carpenter. Candi's crowning achievement is the beautiful stairway, with its interrupted series of arches, which makes six complete turns in ascending to the five arcaded loggias and the domed belvedere, a structure unique in Venice.

In the middle of the *corte* there is a 15C *vera da pozzo*. In the garden of the palace there is a collection of ten *vere da pozzo*, ranging from pre-Romanesque to Renaissance.

We return to the *calle* and turn right on Calle dei Fuseri, the Street of the Metal-workers, which in earlier times was notorious for the number of robberies and murders committed there. At the end of the street we cross the Rio dei Fuseri on the bridge of the same name. This brings us to Ramo dei Fuseri, where a plaque on the first building on the right, Palazzo Molin, records that Goethe stayed there in 1786.

At the end of Ramo dei Fuseri we turn left on to Frezzaria, an ancient market street that took its name from the fact that its shops were devoted principally to the sale of *frezze*, or arrows. During the 14C all Venetian males between the ages of fourteen and thirty-five were required to be proficient in the shooting of the crossbow, which they practised at ranges on the Lido, and at that time the shops selling arrows proliferated along this street.

At the end of the street, where Frezzaria turns right to meet its other branch, we continue straight ahead on Sottoportego del Spiron d'Oro, which brings us out on to Fondamenta Orseolo. There we turn right and walk along the canal to the Bacino Orseolo, a basin at the intersection of two canals, Rio Orseolo and Rio de le Procuratie. The basin was created in 1869 by widening the two canals at this point so as to allow gondolas to approach more closely to the Piazza San Marco. The *fondamenta* goes around the end of the basin to Sottoportego de l'Arco Celeste. The *sottoportego* took its name, The Celestial Arch, from a café with that sign that was situated here in the 18C. We pass through the *sottoportego* to emerge in the north-western corner of Piazza San Marco, where this stroll comes to an end.

SESTIERE DI SAN MARCO III (*Map Route 3*)

The third of our strolls through the Sestiere di San Marco begins on the Molo between the two columns. From there we walk westwards along the *fondamenta*, passing the Zecca and the Giardini Reali. At the far end of the garden we pass around a neoclassical pavilion of white Istrian stone, built as a coffee-house for the Austrians by Lorenzo Santi in 1815–17.

We now cross a bridge over Rio dei Gardinetti, formerly known as Rio Luna. The old name of the canal came from the ancient Albergo della Luna, whose site is now occupied by the Hotel Luna Baglioni, on Calle Larga de l'Ascension. Albergo della Luna was founded in the 12C by the Knights Templar as a hospice for pilgrims going to Jerusalem. The *calle* took its name from the ancient church of the Ascension, which stood on the west side of the street until it was demolished in 1810. The church was originally known as Santa Maria in Broglio, because it stood in the orchard (known as the Brolo) that later became Piazza San Marco.

After crossing the bridge we pass the building that serves as the headquarters for the Capitaneria di Porto. This is a 15C structure that has been frequently restored, most recently in 1992. The building once housed the Magistrato della Farina, the magistrates in charge of the cereal trade. In the first half of the 18C it became the Accademia di Pittura e di Scultura, the first art gallery in Venice, under the presidency of Giambattista Tiepolo. It continued to serve as an art gallery until 1807, when the works of art were moved to the church of Santa Maria della Carità, the present Accademia Galleries.

After passing Pontile San Marco we turn right on Calle Vallaresso. A short way along we pass on our right the well-known Harry's Bar. Farther down the *calle* on the left is the Teatro Ridotto. This is named for the Ridotto, a gambling-house opened in 1638 by Marco Dandolo in his palace. The present theatre occupies part of that palace, with its auditorium in the great andron of the *palazzo*. The Ridotto became a famous place of resort for both Venetian and foreign nobility, but the enormous sums of money that were squandered there led the Signoria to close it on 27 November 1774.

At the end of the *calle* we turn left into Calle Secondo de l'Ascension, which after the first corner becomes Salizzada San Moisè. After the first block we pass on our left the north side of the church of San Moisè, whose main entrance is in the *campo* of the same name.

According to tradition, the original church on this site was founded in the 8C and dedicated to San Vittore. Tradition goes on to say that a new church was built here in the 10C by a Moisè Venier, who dedicated it to San Moisè, St Moses. The present church dates from a complete rebuilding beginning in 1632. The facade, financed by a legacy from Vincenzo Fini, was completed in 1668 by Alessandro Tremignon, with the sculptural decoration under the direction of Heinrich Meyring. An obelisk over the central doorway supports a bust of Vincenzo Fini, while the busts of two other members of his family are over the side doors. The heavy and highly over-decorated facade has no known admirers; Ruskin condemned it 'as one of the basest examples of the basest school of the Renaissance'.

The painting in the centre of the ceiling is *The Vision of Moses*, attributed to Nicolò Bambini. The first altar from the rear on the right has a painting of *The Adoration of the Magi* by Giuseppe Diamantini. The altarpiece on the second altar is *The Discovery of the True Cross, with St Helena and other Saints* by Pietro Liberi.

The chapel to the right of the chancel has on its conch a fresco of *The Virgin in Glory and St Anthony of Padua* by Jacopo Guarana. The high altar, a heavy baroque work by Alessandro Tremignon, is surmounted by an extravagant sculpture representing Moses receiving the Ten Commandments, by Heinrich Meyring. On the right wall of the chancel is an outstanding painting of *The Plague of Serpents* by Giovanni Antonio Pellegrini; on the left wall is *Moses on Mount Sinai* by Girolamo Brusaferro. The chapel to the left of the chancel has on its right wall a painting of *The Last Supper*, attributed to Palma il Giovane; on the left wall is *The Washing of the Feet* by Jacopo Tintoretto. The altarpiece on the first altar from the front on the left side is *The Birth of the Virgin*, attributed to Maffeo da Verona. On the second altar is the *Virgin and Saints* by Antonio Molinari.

After leaving the church we cross the Ponte San Moisè. This brings us to Campiello Barozzi, where there is a gondola station at the foot of the bridge. The writer Frederick Rolfe, who called himself Baron Corvo, referred to this place as 'that dreadful little ditch of a canal by Sanmoisè which is lined on both sides with the gondole of the most disagreeable extortionate nasty-tempered gondolieri in Venice.'

In the centre of the *campiello* there is a *vera da pozzo* dating from the end of the 14C or the beginning of the 15C. The well-head was originally in Ca' Pesaro, and is decorated with a Norman shield bearing the arms of the Pesaro family.

We now continue straight ahead on Calle Larga XXII Marzo, which was extended to its present width in 1880. Halfway along the street on the left is Calle del Teatro San Moisè. This is named for the Teatro San Moisè, which was located in the little *corte* of the same name at the end of the *calle*. The first opera produced here, in 1610, was *Arianna*, with words by Ottavio Rinuccini and music by Claudio Monteverdi. A musical drama with puppets for actors was performed here in 1679.

Near the end of Calle Larga XXII Marzo we turn left into Calle dei Do Pozzi, which brings us into the *corte* of the same name. The *calle* and *corte*, as well as the hotel which is located here, are named for the two *vere da pozzo* in the centre of the court, both of them 14C.

Returning to the main street, we turn left at its end on Calle de le Ostreghe, which bends right to bring us to the *fondamenta* and bridge of the same name. *Ostrega* means 'oyster', and the *fondamenta* and bridge and the street on the other side of Rio de l'Alboro take their name from the fact that oysters were sold here in earlier times. After crossing the bridge we continue on Calle de le Ostreghe, which brings us into Campo Santa Maria Zobenigo, where there is a *vera da pozzo* in pink Verona marble dating from the 14C. The *campo* is named for the church at its far right side, also known as Santa Maria del Giglio, Our Lady of the Lily.

According to tradition, the church was founded in the 10C by a family known as Jubenico, corrupted in time to Zobenigo. The present church dates from a reconstruction in 1670–80 by Giuseppi Benoni, with the facade erected by Giuseppe Sardi and completed in 1683. The sponsor of the new church was Antonio Barbaro, Provveditore Generale of Dalmatia, who is represented in a statue by Giusto Le Court over the main doorway. The high pedestals that support the columns on the lower order of the facade have relief maps of the six Venetian fortresses where Barbaro and his brothers served the Republic; from left to right these are: Zara, Candia, Padua, Rome, Corfu and Spalato. The six pedestals on the upper range contain reliefs of Venetian warships. The absence of any Christian symbolism other than the two angels scandalized Ruskin, who remarked on the facade's 'manifestation of insolent atheism'.

On the ceiling there are three large paintings done in 1690–96 by Antonio Zanchi: *The Birth, The Assumption* and *The Coronation of the Virgin*. On the wall above the main entrance is a large painting of *The Last Supper* by Giulio del Moro, and on the sides four Sibyls by Giuseppe Salviati. The Stations of the Cross were painted in pairs in 1755–6 by seven artists; beginning at the front of the right aisle, these are (I and XIV) Francesco Zugno, (II and XIII) Giambattista Crosato, (III and XII) Domenico Maggiotto, (IV and XI) Francesco Fontebasso, (V and X) Giuseppi Angeli, (VI and IX) Gaspare Diziani, (VII and VIII) Jacopo Marieschi.

The Barbaro Chapel at the rear of the right aisle has an altarpiece depicting the *Martyrdom of St Eugene, with the Virgin and St Anthony of Padua*, by Carl Loth. Next is the Molin Chapel, which has in its vestibule a bust of Girolamo Molin by Alessandro Vittoria. The painting of the *Madonna and Child* on the ceiling in the rear of the chapel is attributed to Domenico Tintoretto. This part of the chapel serves as the treasury of the church, with cases displaying precious reliquaries. Around the walls above the cases are ten *Scenes from the Life of Christ* by Giovanni Antonio Pellegrini. At the centre of the rear wall there is a painting of the *Madonna and Child and the Young St John the Baptist*, attributed to Peter Paul Rubens. The second altar on the right has a statue of the Blessed Gregorio Barbarigo by Gian Maria Morleiter. Next is the Chapel of the Baptistery, and beyond that the Duodo Chapel, whose altarpiece is *The Visitation of St Elizabeth* by Palma il Giovane.

Above the entrance to the sacristy is *Supplicant Venice*, a painting by Antonio Zanchi. The most notable painting in the sacristy is on the wall to the right, *Abraham and Lot Dividing the World* by Antonio Zanchi. On the high altar there are statues of the *Angel and Virgin of the Annunciation* by Heinrich Meyring. At the centre of the wall behind the altar there is a painting of *The Birth of Christ and the Eternal Father* by Giuseppe Salviati. This is flanked by two paintings that originally formed the doors of the organ; these depict the four Evangelists, by Jacopo Tintoretto. Over the arch to the left of the chancel is *The Annunciation* by Antonio Zanchi.

The first altar from the front on the left has a painting of *The Saviour with Sts Francesco di Paola and Giustina*, attributed to Domenico Tintoretto. On the wall to the left of this is *The Assumption* by Antonio Zanchi. On the second altar there is a statue of *The Immaculate Conception* by Gian Maria Morleiter. The altarpiece on the third altar is *The Martyrdom of St Anthony Abbot* by Antonio Zanchi.

Returning to Campo Santa Maria Zobenigo, we continue past the church and cross Ponte de la Feltrina to Campiello de la Feltrina. At No. 2513 on the right we see Palazzo Malipiero, a 15C Gothic palace. We then cross Ponte Zaguri. This is named for Palazzo Zaguri, whose canal-side entrance is at No. 2631 on Fondamenta Corner Zaguri. We then enter Campo San Maurizio, where we see on our left at No. 2667A another facade of Palazzo Zaguri. The *campo* is named for the church of San Maurizio, whose neoclassical facade we now see on our right.

According to tradition, the original church of San Maurizio was founded in the 9C, although the earliest documented reference to it is dated 1088. The present church dates from a complete rebuilding that began in 1806; it was designed by Pietro Zaguri and constructed by Antonio Diedo and Giannantonio Selva, with the sculptural decoration by Giovanni Ferrari and Luigi Zandomeneghi. The interior was designed by Giannantonio Selva, who also built the high altar and its tabernacle.

The building in the north-west corner of the *campo*, at No. 2760, is Palazzo Bellavista, dating from the mid 16C. Plaques on the building record that the poet Giorgio Baffo (1694–1768) lived in the palace, and that in 1803–4 it was the home of Alessandro Manzoni, author of the great Italian novel *I promessi sposi*. The building on the same side of the square at No. 2758 is the 15C Palazzo Molin. In the *campo* there is a *vera da pozzo* dated 1521, with a relief of St Maurice.

At the south-west corner of the *campo* Calle del Dose da Ponte leads out to the Grand Canal. The *calle* is named after Doge (Dose, in the Venetian dialect) Nicolò da Ponte (1578–85), whose *palazzo* at No. 2746 was built by Giulio Cesare Lombardo.

We leave the *campo* at its north-west corner via Calle del Piovan, the Street of the Rector. Immediately beyond the church we pass on our right the Scuola degli Albanesi. This guild was founded towards the end of the 15C by the Albanian community in Venice, Christians who found refuge here when their homeland was overrun by the Turks.

On the next block the street changes its name to Calle del Spezier, which crosses Ponte del Santissimo. This brings us to Campo Francesco Morosini, also known as Campo Santo Stefano. The statue in the centre of the *campo* is a monument to Nicolò Tommaseo (1802–74), who, with Daniele Manin, led the 1848 Venetian uprising against Austrian rule. There are also two large *vere da pozzo* in the *campo*, both of them dated 1724.

Because of its large size and central location, Campo Santo Stefano was in times past the scene of numerous public entertainments, including bullfights. The last bullfight in Venice took place here in 1802, when the collapse of the grandstand killed a number of spectators, which led to the permanent banning of such spectacles.

The church of Santo Stefano is at the northern end of the *campo*. The monastery of Santo Stefano was founded in 1264 by the Hermits of St Augustine, who laid the foundation stone of the original church thirty years later. The church and monastery were completed by 1325. The church was rebuilt in a project that was completed in 1443. The main entrance, a splendid work of the early 15C, is by Bartolomeo Bon.

The interior is divided into a nave and side aisles by two colonnades of alternate columns of white Greek marble and pink Verona marble, with gilded capitals from which spring ogive arches. The ceiling is in the form of a ship's keel. There are three funerary monuments on the *controfacciata* and another nine elsewhere in the church. The finest of these is to the left of the main door, the tomb of Giacomo Surian of Rimini, done in 1488–93 by the workshop of Pietro Lombardo. Over the door is the equestrian monument of the *condottiere* Domenico Contarini (d. 1650). On the floor in the middle aisle is the splendid tombstone of Doge Francesco Morosini (d. 1694).

The first altar from the rear on the right has as its altarpiece the *Nativity of the Virgin*, an outstanding work by Nicolò Bambini. The painting on the second altar is *Sts Luigi Gonzaga, Anthony Abbot and Francesco Saverio* by Giuseppe Angeli; the two statuettes on the altar, representing St John the Baptist and a Virtue, are by Pietro Lombardo. The painting on the third altar is *Sts John Nepomucene and Lucy* by Jacopo Marieschi. On the fourth altar is *St Augustine Suppressing Heresy* by Giustino Menescardi.

There are three paintings by Jacopo Tintoretto in the sacristy: *Christ in the Garden, The Washing of the Feet* and *The Last Supper*, all dating from *c.* 1580. Above the door there are three large paintings by Gaspare Diziani: *The Adoration of the Magi, The Flight into Egypt* and *The Massacre of the Innocents*. The altarpiece is a *Crucifixion* by Giuseppi Angeli. Above the altar there is a large painting by Sante Peranda, *The Martyrdom of St Stephen*. Other works in the sacristy include a *Crucifixion* by Paolo Veneziano, *c.* 1348, an altarpiece with *St Clare of Montefalco, St Augustine and the Holy Trinity* by Pietro Liberi, one of *The Holy Family and St Catherine of Alexandria* by Palma il Vecchio and fragmentary paintings of St Peter and St Lawrence, part of a polyptych by Bartolomeo Vivarini.

The Chapel of the Sacrament to the right of the chancel was made in 1609 by Giulio del Moro. The high altar, framed in a great arch with bronzed wooden statues of St Mark and St Monica under smaller arches on the sides, is a work of Girolamo Campagna. In the apse behind the high altar is the choir, with thirty-six stalls in inlaid wood, begun in 1481 by

Leonardo Scalamanzio and completed and signed in 1488 by Marco Cozzi. The Chapel of St Michael to the left of the chancel has a baroque altar in black marble, appropriate for the funeral masses said here.

The first altar from the front on the left side was dedicated by the Guild of Ship-caulkers; the altarpiece is the *Virgin, St Mark and St Fosca* by Girolamo Brusaferro. The second altar has a *Martyrdom of St Stephen* by Antonio Foler. The third altar is dedicated to *St Nicholas of Tolentino*; the statue of the saint is by Pietro Lombardo, as are the statuettes of St Girolamo and St Paul the Hermit between the columns. The fourth altar was dedicated by the Guild of Shoemakers; the altarpiece is *Our Lady of Sorrows* by Teodoro Matteini. The fifth altar has a painting of the *Madonna of the Girdle and Saints* by Leonardo Corona. In front of the altar is the tombstone of the famous Venetian composer Giovanni Gabrieli (1557–1612).

Directly in front of the church on Campiello Santo Stefano is the former Scuola di Santo Stefano dei Lanieri (No. 3469). On the facade is a relief showing St Stephen being venerated by brethren of the guild.

We now walk back through Campo Santo Stefano. Midway along the *campo* on the right, at No. 2949, is the 16C Palazzo Barbaro. Beyond it is the huge Palazzo Loredan (No. 2945), which dates originally from the 15C. The palace was acquired by the Loredan family in 1536, at which time it was completely rebuilt in the Renaissance style by Scarpagnino. It now houses the Istituto Veneto di Scienze, Lettere e Arti. On the left side of the *campo*, at No. 2802, is the huge 18C Palazzo Morosini, partly obscured by the modern building in front of it. Beyond Palazzo Morosini we turn left into Campo Pisani, which is flanked to the left by Palazzo Pisani and to the right by a wing of Palazzo Barbaro, whose main facade is on the Grand Canal. Palazzo Pisani was begun in the second half of the 16C, but it was not finished until the first half of the 18C, completed by Girolamo Frigimelica.

At the southern end of Campo Santo Stefano we pass into Campiello San Vidal, named for the church on its right side. The original church on this site was founded by Doge Vitale Falier (1084–96), who dedicated it to his patron saint, St Vitale. The church was completely rebuilt through a bequest made in 1656 by Doge Carlo Contarini. Antonio Gaspari designed and built the new edifice in 1696–1700, and the facade was erected in the years 1706–14 by Andrea Tirali. San Vidal has been deconsecrated and now serves as an art gallery. The church still preserves its altarpieces, the most notable of which is the painting on the high altar, Carpaccio's *St Vitale on Horseback*.

We continue on to Campo San Vidal, which opens on to the Grand Canal at the Accademia Bridge. The *vera da pozzo* in the middle of the *campo* dates from the 16C.

We leave the *campo* via Ponte Giustinian, following a labyrinthian route that eventually takes us to Calle del Teatro. The *calle* take its name from the former Teatro San Samuel, which was opened by the Grimani family in 1665, and rebuilt in 1747 by Romualdo and Alessandro Mauri. The theatre continued to operate up until the end of the 19C, when it was closed and eventually demolished.

After a few steps along Calle del Teatro we turn right into Calle Malipiero. Giacomo Casanova was born in a house on this *calle* on 2 April 1725, though no plaque marks the site of his birthplace.

At the end of the *calle* we turn left on Salizzada Malipiero, which brings us out to the Grand Canal at Campo San Samuele. The *campo* is named for the former church at the rear of the square.

The original church of San Samuele dates from the 10–11C. In its present form it dates from a rebuilding in 1685, though its distinctive campanile of white Istrian stone dates to the 12C. The church now houses the International Centre for the Study of the Arts and Costumes. In the *campo* beside the church there is a 17C *vera da pozzo*.

The San Samuele quarter was in times past infamous for the immorality of its women. Late in the 14C a chronicler records that the married women of San Samuele 'ran away from their own homes to the parish priest with whom they committed adultery'. In 1468 a law prohibited 'such prostitutes, under the penalty of ten lire and twenty-five lashes, to live or even stop together with a man in the area from the end of the narrow street which leads to the church of San Samuele, as far as the grocer's shop in San Stefano'.

On the north side of the *campo* is the 18C Palazzo Grassi. The palace is open for occasional exhibitions, allowing one the opportunity to examine its splendid interior, decorated with frescoes by Michelangelo Morleiter and Fabio Canal.

We leave Campo San Samuele to the left of the church via Calle de le Carozze, the Street of the Carriage-makers. Although carriages were not used in Venice, they were made here for use on the mainland. At the end of the *calle* we come to Salizzada San Samuele. The corner building on the right at No. 3216 is the former Scuola dei Mureri, the Guild of Masons, whose emblems are displayed on the facade. The guild was founded in the 13C and its Scuola here was built in the 15C.

We continue along Salizzada San Samuele, and on the next block we see on our left Casa Veronese (No. 3338). A plaque records that this was the home of the painter Paolo Veronese, who died here in 1588.

At the end of Salizzada San Samuele we turn right on Crosera. On the right at No. 3127 we see the former Scuola dei Calegheri, the Guild of Shoemakers, identified by a 14C relief of a shoe and an inscription.

After the first intersection the street changes its name to Calle de le Boteghe. At the beginning of the *calle* we make a short detour by turning right into Sottoportego de le Muneghe, which leads to the *calle* of the same name. The left side of this *calle* is formed entirely by the facade of the former church and convent of Santi Rocco e Margarita, founded in 1488 and suppressed by the French in 1806.

1. The church of the Madonna della Salute beyond the Punta Dogana, the point where the Grand Canal meets the Giudecca Canal

2. The waterfront on the Bacino San Marco, with the campanile of the Basilica of San Marco to the left of the Doge's Palace

3. The Piazzetta and the two columns on the Molo, with Sansovino's Library on the right

4. The church of San Giorgio Maggiore

5. (*facing*) Piazza San Marco, with the Ala Napoleonica at the far end and the Procuratie Vecchie on the right

6. The Stairway of the Giants in the inner courtyard of the Doge's Palace

7. (*below left*) The Foscari Porch on the north side of the inner courtyard of the Doge's Palace, with the domes of the Basilica of San Marco behind

8. (*below right*) The Porta della Carta, the main entrance to the Doge's Palace, with a relief showing Doge Francesco Foscari kneeling before the Lion of St Mark

9. (*left*) The tetrarchs, a porphyry group beside the Basilica of San Marco, taken by the Venetians from Constantinople in 1204

10. (*right*) The Drunkenness of Noah, a relief on the corner of the Doge's Palace beside the Rio del Palazzo, with the Bridge of Sighs in the background

11. The Bridge of Sighs, with the Doge's Palace on the left and the Palace of the Prisons on the right

12. The waterfront along the Riva degli Schiavone, with the church of the Pietà on the right and, to the left in the rear, the leaning campanile of the church of San Giorgio dei Greci

13. The interior of the Basilica of San Marco, showing some of its famous mosaics

14. The Ponte de Rialto, the famous bridge across the Grand Canal

15. The Pescaria, or fish market, part of the ancient market quarter of the Rialto

16. The Palazzo Dario on the Grand Canal, a Renaissance palace noted for the beautiful stonework on its façade

We continue along Calle de le Boteghe to its end at the north-west corner of Campo Santo Stefano, from where we cross the square to go down Calle del Spezier. We retrace our steps along the *calle* as far as Campo San Maurizio, from where we follow a devious route to Campiello dei Calegheri. This is named for the *caligheri*, or shoemakers, who once had their shops here. In the *campiello* there is a *vera da pozzo* dating from the late 14C or early 15C.

We leave the *campiello* on Ramo Primo dei Calegheri, and eventually make our way to Calle de la Fenice. At the beginning of the *calle* we pass on our left Corte del Tagiapiera, where there is a *vera da pozzo* of the 16–17C. We then pass on our left Campiello Marinoni de la Fenice. The building on the left at No. 1929 was erected in 1869 from a plan by Giorgio Casarini; the cannon-balls set into the facade are missiles with which the Austrians bombarded Venice in 1849.

At the end of the *calle* we come to Campo San Fantin. This is named for the church of San Fantin, whose main entrance is on the eastern side of the *campo*, facing the Teatro La Fenice.

According to tradition, the church of San Fantin was founded in the 9C, though the earliest documented reference to it is dated 1134. In 1501 Cardinal Giovanni Battista Zeno made a bequest funding a complete rebuilding of San Fantin, whereupon the old church was demolished in 1506 and the cornerstone of the new one laid the following year. The new church was based on a design by Scarpagnino, who worked on the building until his death in 1549; Jacopo Sansovino was then placed in charge, completing the project in 1564.

Above the side door there is a large painting by Joseph Heintz the Younger, *Three Saints and a Parson Beseeching the Virgin to End the Plague of 1630*. On the wall beyond this is a painting of the *Deposition* by Palma il Giovane. On the altar to the right of the chancel there is a sacred icon of the 16C known as the Madonna della Grazia.

The splendid chancel was created by Sansovino in 1562–4;

the crucifix on the high altar dates from the 18C. On the left wall there is a large painting, *The Virgin in Glory, with Doge Alvise Mocenigo and the Signoria Giving Thanks for the Victory at Lepanto* by Palma il Giovane. Near the door there is a holy-water stoup made from an inverted 12C capital with Romanesque carvings.

We now cross the *campo* to the famous Teatro La Fenice, erected in 1790–92 by Giannantonio Selva. The theatre opened on Ascension Day 1792 with an opera called *I giuochi d'Agrigento*, written by Alessandro Pepoli and set to music by Giovanni Paisiello. The theatre was gutted by fire in December 1836, but it was rebuilt in two years by Tommaso Meduna and his brother Giovanni Battista. The operas that had their premier performance here in the 19C include Rossini's *Tancredi* (1813) and *Semiramide* (1823); Vincenzo Bellini's *I Capuletti e i Montecchi* (1830) and *Beatrice di Tenda* (1833); and Verdi's *Ernani* (1844), *Rigoletto* (1851), *La Traviata* (1853) and *Simon Boccanegra* (1857).

The cul-de-sac to the left of La Fenice is Corte San Gaetano, where at No. 1982 we see the 15C Palazzo Tiepolo. On the northern side of the *campo* is the former Scuola di San Fantin, a neoclassical edifice that now houses the Ateno Veneto, a scholarly academy. The Scuola was destroyed by fire in 1562 and rebuilt in 1592–1600 by Antonio Contino. The ground-floor hall is occasionally open for lectures. The thirteen panels of the ceiling have paintings by Palma il Giovane, and on the walls there are nine scenes of Christ's Passion, eight of them by Leonardo Corona and one by Baldassare d'Anna.

There are three *vere da pozzo* in Campo San Fantin. The well-head between the church and the Scuola dates from the late 14C or early 15C; the one in front of La Fenice is from the latter half of the 15C; while the third dates from the first half of the 18C.

We leave Campo San Fantin via Calle del Frutariol, the Street of the Fruiterers. Halfway along the *calle*, on the left at No. 1859, we pass the 15C Palazzo Giustinian. St Lorenzo

Giustinian, the first Patriarch of Venice, was born in this palace in 1381.

At the end of the *calle* we cross Rio dei Barcaroli on the bridge of the same name. The name comes from *barcaroli*, or boatmen, referring to the gondoliers who had their station farther down the canal. As we cross the bridge we see a plaque on the facade of the building on the right, Palazzo Basadonna, recording that Mozart and Goldoni stayed there during Carnival in 1771.

After crossing the bridge, we come to one of the branches of the Frezzaria, following it as it turns to the right. One block before the end of the Frezzaria we turn left on Bocca de Piazza, the Mouth of the Square, which brings us to the back of Ala Napoleonica at Calle Larga de l'Ascension. The splendid old building on the left side of Bocca de Piazza at No. 1241 is the former Albergo del Salvadego, a Venetian-Byzantine structure dating from the 14C.

Turning right on Calle Larga de l'Ascension, after a few steps we turn left into Sottoportego San Geminian. This brings us to the western end of Piazza San Marco, where our third stroll through the Sestiere di San Marco comes to an end.

SESTIERE DI SAN MARCO IV (*San Georgio*)

The Sestiere di San Marco also includes the isle of San Giorgio, whose beautiful sea-girt church is one of the principal adornments of the port of Venice. The No. 5 *vaporetto* goes out to San Giorgio from Pontile San Zaccaria, or in the reverse direction from the Zattere.

The island was originally known as Isola dei Cipressi, because of the groves of cypresses that grew there around the vegetable gardens and vineyards, all of which belonged to the Signoria. There was a church here as early as the 9C. Doge Tribuno Memmo granted the island to Giovanni Morosini in 982 for the establishment of a Benedictine monastery. The monastery was enriched by donations and revenues and given privileges by emperors, popes and Doges, most notably by Doge Sebastiano Ziani, who was buried here when he died in 1178. During the reign of Doge Ordelafo Falier (1102–18) the body of St Stephen, the protomartyr, was brought to Venice and enshrined in the monastery of San Giorgio. Thereafter the Doge and the Signoria came every year to the monastery on the feast-day of the saint, 26 December, followed by the entire population of the city, an event that continued as one of the most popular fêtes in Venice down to the end of the Republic. When the church and monastery were both destroyed by earthquake and fire in 1223 they were immediately thereafter rebuilt by Doge Pietro Ziani, who was buried here when he died in 1229. In 1433 the Signoria welcomed Cosimo I de' Medici to Venice during his brief exile, and in gratitude the Duke commissioned his architect Michelozzo to build a new and splendid library for the monastery. Around the middle of the 15C the monastery was rebuilt and enlarged by Giovanni Buora, who restored the Cloister of the Bay Trees. A second quadrangle, the Cloister of the Cypresses, was added to the monastery c. 1516–40 by Andrea Buora, son of Giovanni.

The most brilliant period in the history of the great Benedictine centre that had developed here began when Andrea Palladio was commissioned to enlarge and renovate the monastery and to build a new and grander church. The plan of the new church was produced by Palladio on 25 November 1565, and on 3 March of the following year the corner-stone of the building was laid. While working on the church Palladio also built the monastery's refectory, known as the Aula Palladiana. After Palladio died in 1580 work on the church continued for another thirty years, until in 1610 the facade begun by Simeone Sorella was completed. The years 1579–1614 saw the building of the new Cloister of the Cypresses; followed immediately by another period of construction directed by Baldassare Longhena, who built the apartments of the abbots, the Grand Staircase beside the Cloister of the Bay Trees, and a new library to replace that of Michelozzo.

In 1799–1800 the monastery housed the conclave of cardinals that elected Barnaba Chiaramonti as Pope Pius VII. The church and monastery were suppressed in 1806 by the French, who stripped the complex of its art treasures, most notably Veronese's great painting of *The Marriage Feast at Cana*, now in the Louvre. Although the church was reopened in 1808 the monastery was not reinstated, and in 1851 it was converted into a military barracks, resulting in the deterioration and radical alteration of its buildings. This period of depredation and neglect ended in 1951 with the establishment of the Giorgio Cini Foundation, founded by Count Vittorio Cini as a memorial to his son, who had died in an air crash in 1949. The State ceded the island to the Cini Foundation, which splendidly restored the monastery between 1951 and 1956, and turned the island into a cultural centre.

The Palladian facade of the church is in the form of a Greek temple front, with four colossal semi-columns on extremely high pediments flanking the central doorway. Niches between the columns on either side contain statues, with St Stephen on the left and St George on the right, both by Giulio del Moro. In each of the side sections there is a *naiskos* framing a sarcophagus, memorials to Doges Tribuno Memmo and Sebastiano Ziani. At the apex of the pediment there is a statue of the Saviour, flanked at the base by the figures of two angels, all done by Antonio Tarsia.

The plan of the interior is a Latin cross, with the two ends of the transept terminating in exedrae and a huge hemispherical dome with a lantern surmounting the crossing. The nave is separated from the side aisles by two colonnades of semi-columns and pilasters. Behind the square chancel there is a deep choir ending in a semicircular apse. Above the great entrance portal on the *controfacciata* wall is the funerary monument of Doge Leonardo Donà (d. 1612). The statues of the four Evangelists, in niches on either side, in stucco, are signed by Alessandro Vittorio and dated 1574.

All the side altars were probably designed by Palladio, though they were not completed until at least a decade after his death; their pediments are supported by alternating fluted and smooth columns of pink marble framing paintings and sculptures. On the first altar from the rear on the right the altarpiece is *The Nativity*, painted by Jacopo Bassano and probably finished by his son Francesco. On the second altar there is a painted wooden crucifix of the 15C, believed to be by a South Tyrolean master. On the third altar there are the relics of St Cosmas and St Damian; the altarpiece, *The Martyrdom of the Two Saints*, is from Jacopo Tintoretto's workshop. On the altar in the right transept there is a painting by Domenico Tintoretto representing St Benedict and other Benedictine saints. On the altar to the right of the chancel the altarpiece, *The Virgin Enthroned and Saints*, was painted in 1708 by Sebastiano Ricci.

The sumptuously decorated main altar, designed from a sketch by Antonio Vassilacchi, was built in 1591–3. The elaborate sculptural group on the altar represents the Holy Trinity, done by Girolamo Campagna after a sketch by Vassilacchi. On the side walls of the chancel there are two paintings done by Jacopo Tintoretto in 1594, the last year of his life; on the right is *The Last Supper* and on the left *The Fall of Manna*. The chancel is enclosed by four niches with statues in two orders; below are St Peter and St Paul, by Filippo Parodi; above are St Columbano and St Placido, by Giambattista Albanese. The balustrade of the choir is surmounted by two charming bronze statuettes done in 1593 by Nicolò Roccatagliata, with St Stephen on the left and St George on the right. The richly carved lectern in the centre of the choir is surmounted by a statuette of St George killing the dragon by Albert van der Brulle. Around the periphery of the choir are forty-eight stalls in two orders, carved with scenes from the life of St Benedict, done by Albert van der Brulle and Gaspare Gatti in 1594–98. Above, in six niches between the windows, there are statues of prophets by Filippo Catasio.

On the left is the entrance to the sacristy, whose periphery is lined with beautiful dossals of the 17C. The altarpiece is a painting of *The Purification of the Virgin* by Palma il Giovane; on either side there are statues of St Mark and St George, Lombardesque works dating from the beginning of the 16C. At the end of the corridor is the funerary monument of Doge Domenico Michiel (d. 1130).

Returning to the nave, we see on the altar to the left of the chancel a painting of *Christ Risen from the Sepulchre*; this was apparently begun in 1583 by Jacopo Tintoretto and finished in 1585 by his son Domenico. Above the side door is the funerary monument of Vincenzo Morisini (d. 1588); the portrait bust of the deceased, by Alessandro Vittoria, is flanked by those of his son and brother. On the altar in the left transept there is a painting of the *Martyrdom of St Stephen* by Jacopo Tintoretto in collaboration with his son Domenico and co-workers. On the first altar from the front on the left there is a painting of *St George Killing the Dragon* by Matteo Ponzone. The second altar has a marble group of the Virgin and Child, done in 1595 by Girolamo Campagna. On the third altar there is a painting of the *Martyrdom of St Lucy*, done in 1596 by Leandro Bassano.

An elevator in the far left-hand corner of the church takes one up to the observation deck of the campanile, from which one commands a panoramic view of the parts of Venice around the Bacino San Marco. One can also look down upon the two cloisters of the Benedictine monastery as well as the other buildings and gardens of the Giorgio Cini Foundation, which are not ordinarily open to the general public. The arcaded courtyard beside the front half of the church is the Cloister of the Bay Tree, while the other is the Cloister of the Cypresses. The structure that extends beyond the intersection of the two cloisters is the refectory, or Aula Palladiana, built by Palladio in 1559–63. At the far end of the Cloister of the Cypresses is the dormitory, known as the *manica lunga*, or 'long sleeve', extending behind the monastery and the apse of the church for 128 m to the *fondamenta* on the north side of the island. The *fondamenta* serves as the quay of a marina, protected by a breakwater. Both entrances to the haven are marked by little lighthouses dating from 1829, when the marina was built as a free port. One can walk along the *fondamenta* to the end of the marina, with a view across the Bacino San Marco to Riva degli Schiavone.

[7] Sestiere di Castello

We will now set out on the first of three strolls through the Sestiere di Castello, the easternmost of the six districts of Venice.

We begin on the Molo and walk past the southern facade of Palazzo Ducale. We then cross Rio de Palazzo on Ponte de la Paglia, the Bridge of Straw, taking us from the Sestiere San Marco into Castello. The bridge is so called because boats carrying straw used to tie up here. The bodies of those who drowned in the canals or the lagoon were laid out on the bridge for identification. This is one of the oldest bridges in Venice, first built in 1363 and reconstructed and enlarged to its present form in 1847. On the outer arch is the Tabernacolo della Fraglia del Traghetto, with a relief of the Madonna of the Gondoliers done in 1583.

Looking up the canal we see the famous Bridge of Sighs, a baroque structure built *c*. 1600 by Antonio Contino, decorated with a relief of a personification of Justice and the arms of Doge Marino Grimani, who commissioned its construction. Ponte de la Paglia brings us to Riva degli Schiavone, a broad promenade some 500 m in length along the Bacino San Marco. It is named for the Dalmatian mariners – *di Schiavonia*, or Slavs – who tied up their boats here. The *riva* was paved in 1324 and was enlarged to its present width in 1780.

We then pass the Palazzo delle Prigioni, whose front rooms were used as offices by the Signori di Notte al Criminale, magistrates responsible for policing the city, particularly at night. The narrow lane between the Palazzo delle Prigioni and the Hotel Danieli Excelsior is Calle dei Albanesi, the Street of the Albanians, whose quarter was near by. The equally narrow lane on the other side of the hotel, Calle de le Rasse, is named for the thick woollen cloth from Serbia known as *rascia*, which was sold here for the *felze* (cabins) of gondolas. Doge Vitale Michiel was assassinated near the entrance to Calle de le Rasse on 13 September 1102, while on his way from Palazzo Ducale to the church of San Zaccaria. The assassin was immediately hanged, and the Senate ordered the destruction of the houses at the entrance to the *calle*, where the Doge's murderer had concealed himself, decreeing that if rebuilt they should be of only a single storey. Consequently, no monumental buildings were ever built on that part of the Riva degli Schiavone during the subsequent history of the Republic and for a century and a half afterwards, until the erection in 1948 of the modern annexe of the Hotel Danieli, the Daniele Excelsior. The older part of the hotel occupies Palazzo Bernardo-Dandolo, a Gothic structure of the 15C. Among those who stayed at the Danieli in its early days were George Sand and Alfred de Musset, Charles Dickens, and the newly married John and Effie Ruskin. The Ruskins arrived in 1849 during an *acqua alta*, as he writes: 'The beginning of everything was in seeing the Gondola-beak come actually inside the door at Danieli's, when the tide was up, and the water two feet deep at the foot of the stairs.'

We cross Ponte del Vin, the Bridge of Wine. This was named for the boats that unloaded vats of wine on the quay here, from where they were carried up the first street to the left, Calle del Vin, into which we now turn. The *calle* takes us into the tiny Campiello del Vin, in the centre of which there is a *vera da pozzo* dating from the second half of the 14C. At the far end of the court we turn right and then left into Corte Nova, which takes us through a *sottoportego* out on to Calle San Provolo. There we turn right and in a few steps we come to a Gothic arch decorated with a beautiful relief in marble, showing the Virgin and Child between St John the Baptist and St Mark; this dates from the 15C and has been attributed to Bartolomeo Bon. The arch leads to Campo San Zaccaria and the beautiful church of San Zaccaria.

The present church of San Zaccaria is known as the *chiesa nuova*, while adjoining it to its right is its ancient predecessor, the *chiesa vecchia*. The original church was built by Doge Agnello Partecipazio (811–27); it was dedicated to St Zacharias, father of St John the Baptist, whose body was sent from Constantinople to Venice as a gesture of goodwill by the Byzantine Emperor Leo V (813–20). Its convent of Benedictine nuns is believed to have been founded at about the same time. Then a new church, the *chiesa nuova*, was built in a first stage of construction in 1444–65 by Antonio Gambello, whereupon the *chiesa vecchia* was turned over to the nuns of San Zaccaria, after being transformed in 1455–64. Work on the *chiesa nuova* was completed in 1483–1504 by Mauro Coducci, who was responsible for the facade. After the completion of the interior decoration, the present church was consecrated in 1543.

The lower level of the facade is in polychrome marble and the rest in white Istrian stone. The elaborately carved doorway with its round arch was done in 1483 by Giovanni Buora. The arch is surmounted by a statue of St Zacharias done *c.* 1580 by Alessandro Vittoria.

The central part of the nave is separated from the side aisles by two rows of three columns each. Next to the first columns from the rear on either side there are holy-water stoups with marble statuettes by Alessandro Vittoria, with St Zacharias on the left and St John the Baptist on the right.

At the rear of the right aisle high on the *controfacciata* wall there is a painting of *St Zacharias in the Temple*, by Nicolò Bambini. The altarpiece on the first altar is the *Madonna and Child in Glory with Five Saints* by Palma il Giovane. On the wall above is the *Annual Visit of the Doge to San Zaccaria* by Giovanni Antonio Zonca. On the second altar, designed in 1599 by Alessandro Vittoria, a sarcophagus supported by the figures of two angels contains the body of St Zacharias; below, another coffin contains the remains of St Athanasius. The altarpiece is *St Zacharias in Glory* by Palma il Giovane. Above there is a large painting by Giovanni Antonio Fumiani showing the Emperor Frederick III being escorted to the convent of San Zaccaria by Doge Pietro Orseolo II. To the left of the altar is *The Adoration of the Shepherds* by Antonio Balestra. In the third bay an ornate doorway frames in its upper part a painting of *Tobias Curing his Father* by Bernardo Strozzi; to the left is *The Presentation of Jesus in the Temple* by Andrea Celesti; the lunette above shows *Doge Pietro Lando Attending the Consecration of the Church of San Zaccaria* in 1543 by Daniel Heintz.

A fee is charged to visit the three chapels and the crypt, which are approached via the door in the third bay. The first of these is the large Chapel of St Athanasius. This was the central part of the *chiesa vecchia*, which in 1455–64 was transformed for the nuns of San Zaccaria, with the choir-stalls made by Francesco and Marco Cozzi; around 1595 it was rebuilt and converted into the Chapel of St Athanasius, with an altar designed by Alessandro Vittoria. The altarpiece is the *Birth of St John*, an early work by Jacopo Tintoretto. Other paintings in the chapel are by Palma il Vecchio, Palma il Giovane, Leandro Bassano, Anthony Van Dyck, Andrea Celesti, Antonio Vassilacchi, Michele Desubleo, Domenico Tintoretto and Giandomenico Tiepolo. A door in the far left corner leads into the little Cappella dell'Addolorata, which serves as a museum of the church's treasures. A stairway at the rear of the chapel leads down into the crypt, a 10C Romanesque colonnaded structure. Steps lead up from the left of Cappella dell'Addolorata into the Chapel of St Tarasius. This was originally the chancel and apse of the *chiesa vecchia*, reconstructed in its present form in 1440 by Antonio Gambello. Between the ribs of the Gothic apse there are frescoed figures of the Holy Father flanked by the Evangelists, St Zacharias and John the Baptist, done in 1442 by Andrea del

Castagno. On the altar and side walls there are three gilded Gothic polyptychs, all carved in 1443 by Ludovico da Forlì. The one on the altar has at its centre *The Virgin and Child Enthroned between St Blaise and St Martin*, signed in 1385 by Stefano da Sant'Agnese; the flanking panels show St Mark and St Elizabeth, done *c.* 1443 by Giovanni and Antonio da Murano, who also did the three orders of saints at the back above. On the wall to the left is the *Altarpiece of St Sabina*, and on the wall to the right is the *Altarpiece of Corpus Christi*, the paintings in both of which are signed by Giovanni and Antonio da Murano and dated 1443. In front of the altar there is a large fragment of the mosaic floor of the 12C church, and through a hole in the pavement at the rear of the chapel one can see a small piece of the mosaic pavement of the original 9C church.

We now return to the main body of the church, looking first at the high altar and its tabernacle, attributed to Alessandro Vittoria. Framed in the arches on the four sides of the tabernacle are scenes from the life of Christ by Palma il Giovane. The fresco in the conch of the apse shows *St Zacharias in Glory*, attributed to Giovanni Antonio Pellegrini.

We now return to the right side of the chancel to walk around the ambulatory behind the high altar. Just beyond the door of the Chapel of St Athanasius is a painting of *The Presentation of Jesus in the Temple* by Giovanni Segala. Beyond that towards the front of the nave are two large paintings; below, *The Communion of the Apostles* by a pupil of Bernardo Strozzi; above, *The Conversion of St Paul*, attributed to Giovanni Antonio Fumiani.

The outer periphery of the ambulatory opens into four radial chapels, the first of which has a painting of *St Peter and the Cock* by Francesco Santacroce. The second chapel contains the organ, built in 1790 by Gaetano Callido. The pavement of the ambulatory has a number of Lombardesque tombstones. At the end of the ambulatory we see the tombstone of the sculptor Alessandro Vittoria (1524–1608).

The first altar beyond the sacristy is adorned with the famous painting of the *Virgin and Child Enthroned, with Angel-musicians and Sts Peter, Catherine, Lucy and James*, signed by Giovanni Bellini and dated 1506. Above the altar there is a large painting showing Pope Benedict III taking refuge in the convent of San Zaccaria in 855, by Andrea Celesti. Between the first and second altars there are two paintings by Antonio Vassilacchi, *The Marriage of the Virgin Mary* and *The Presentation of the Virgin in the Temple*. The altarpiece on the second altar shows *The Saviour, St Cosmas and St Damian Healing a Sick Man, with St Zacharias and St John the Baptist* by Giuseppe Salviati. Above the altar there is *The Body of St Zacharias Arriving in Venice from Constantinople in 827* by Andrea Celesti. Beside the altar is *The Visitation*, by Antonio Molinari. On the *controfacciata* wall there is a *Nativity of St John the Baptist* by Andrea Celesti.

The northern side of the *campo* is formed by a 16C portico, now occupied by shops, that was formerly part of the convent of San Zaccaria, suppressed by the French in 1810. To the right of the church is the brick facade and arcade of the *chiesa vecchia*, with its 13C campanile in the Veneto-Byzantine style. The fenced-in garden in front of the arcade contains architectural fragments from the earlier structure of San Zaccaria, along with a *vera da pozzo* dating from the 13–14C. In the *campo* in front of the church there is a remarkable *vera da pozzo* dating from the end of the 15C, richly decorated with Lombardesque reliefs.

We leave the *campo* at its south-west corner, passing on our left the headquarters of the Carabinieri, which occupies part of the former convent of San Zaccaria. After passing through Sottoportego San Zaccaria we turn left on Riva degli Schiavone and continue along the waterfront. As we do so we pass the huge equestrian monument to King Victor Emmanuel II, done in 1887 by Ettore Ferrari.

We cross Rio dei Greci on Ponte de la Pietà. The bridge is named for the church of the Pietà, which we see just ahead on the Riva degli Schiavone. The canal takes its name from the church of San Giorgio dei Greci, whose perilously leaning campanile we see on the right side of the *rio* beyond the facades of Palazzo Gritti and Palazzo Cappello-Memmo. Palazzo Gritti, the farthest from the bridge, is a Gothic structure dating from the 15C, restored in 1931. Palazzo Cappello-Memmo, a Lombardesque edifice dating from the beginning of the 16C, is adorned with plaques of coloured marbles. These two palaces were for centuries part of La Pietà, one of Venice's four *ospedali maggiori*, or great hospitals. La Pietà was established as an orphanage for foundlings in 1346 by Fra Petruccio di Assisi. The orphanage provided a musical education for the orphan girls, who performed in the choir of the Pietà, while the boys were generally trained in trades and crafts. These choirs became very popular, and the orphanages of the four Great Hospitals competed in recruiting prominent musicians and composers to teach the girls; music was specially commissioned for their performances, which were an important source of revenue for the institutions. Antonio Vivaldi (1675–1741) was appointed violin teacher at the Pietà in 1703 and then *maestro dei concerti* in 1735. While he was at the orphanage Vivaldi was, from 1714 on, also producing operas at the Teatro Sant'Angelo. His output was phenomenal, including some 500 concertos, ninety sonatas, at least fifty operas and hundreds of other pieces.

The church of the Pietà, dedicated to Santa Maria della Visitazione, the Visitation of the Virgin, was a chapel within the orphanage. The great success of Vivaldi's performances led the orphanage to commission the present church, begun in 1745 on a design by Giorgio Massari and consecrated in 1760. The facade of the church was completed in 1906 according to Massari's original design.

The design of the nave was based to a large extent on its acoustic properties, with two galleries for the singers and musicians corbelled out on balconies midway along the sides, and a double gallery above the entrance, all of them with elaborate wrought-iron screens to shield the girls from public view. The ceiling panel above the entrance has a fresco symbolizing *Fortitude and Peace*, done by Giambattista Tiepolo in 1754–5, along with his two other frescoes in the church. One of these is the *Triumph of Faith*, which is in the central panel of the ceiling, showing the Virgin being crowned by the Eternal Father, surrounded by Angels and the heavenly court; the other is in the ceiling above the high altar, *The Cardinal Virtues*. The painting on the high altar is *The Visitation*, begun by Giambattista Piazzetta and completed after his death in 1754 by his pupil Giuseppe Angeli.

Just beyond the church, separated from it by Calle de la Pietà, is the Metropole Hotel, which stands on the site of the ancient orphanage of the Pietà. A short way down the *calle*, on the left beside the church, there is a tablet with an inscription condemning those who left foundlings here which they could afford to care for themselves.

After passing the hotel we cross Ponte del Sepolcro. The first building on the other side of the bridge is Palazzo Navagero, a Gothic palace erected in the mid 15C. This was the home of Andrea Navager, the historian, and his nephew Andrea Navager, the poet, who died here in 1529. The building beyond it is the former Aristide Cornoldi Barracks, now the headquarters of the military garrison of Venice. The handsome neoclassical doorway is a work of Alessandro Vittoria. The building was originally the convent of the church of San Sepolcro, the Holy Sepulchre. The convent was founded in 1409 as a hospice for pilgrims travelling to the Holy Land, and the church was erected in the 16C. San Sepolcro was suppressed by the French in 1808; the church was demolished and the convent converted into a military barracks. The church stood on the site of the ancient Palazzo Barbaro-Molin. A plaque records that the poet Petrarch lived here in 1362, when he came to Venice as ambassador of the princes of Milan.

We turn left from Riva degli Schiavoni into Calle del

Dose, passing on our right Calle de la Malvasia Vechia. At the end of Calle del Dose we enter Campo Bandiera e Moro o de la Bragora, in whose far right-hand corner we see the church of San Giovanni in Bragora. Antonio Vivaldi was born in a house on this *campo* on 4 March 1675.

According to tradition, the first church on this site was founded at the beginning of the 8C, though the earliest recorded reference to it is dated 1090. The church was rebuilt in the Gothic style in the last quarter of the 15C; its original campanile was demolished in 1826 and replaced by the present stump of a belfry.

On the *controfacciata* wall there is a painting of *Christ before Caiaphas* by Palma il Giovane. At the rear of the right aisle there are two paintings by Francesco Maggiotto, *Elijah and the Angel* and *The Sacrifice of Abraham*. The second chapel enshrines the remains of St John the Almsgiver; the altarpiece, by Jacopo Marieschi, depicts the transfer of the saint's body from Alexandria to Venice in 1247. To the right of the sacristy door there is a beautiful painting done in 1502 by Giambattista Cima da Conegliano, *The Emperor Constantine and His Mother St Helena*, with a predella showing the discovery of the True Cross. On the left there is a painting of *The Saviour with Sts Mark and John the Evangelist* by Alvise Vivarini.

The chancel, rebuilt in the years 1485–94 by Sebastiano Mariani, was decorated in 1593 by Alessandro Vittoria. On the wall behind the altar there is a superb painting of *The Baptism of Christ*, done in 1492–4 by Cima da Conegliano. On the wall of the chancel to the right is *The Last Supper* by Paris Bordone; above that is *Elijah and the Angel* by Francesco Maggiotto. On the left wall is *The Washing of the Feet* by Palma il Giovane; above is *The Sacrifice of Abraham* by Francesco Maggiotto. The chapel to the left of the chancel has on its right wall a painting of *Sts Andrew, Jerome and Martin* by Francesco Bissolo. On the left wall is a triptych of the *Madonna and Child between St Andrew and John the Baptist*, signed by Bartolomeo Vivarini and dated 1478.

On the wall of the nave in the left aisle are two paintings by Alvise Vivarini, a *Head of the Saviour* and *The Madonna Adoring the Child*. The first chapel has on its right wall a painting of *Christ and St Veronica*, a 16C work by the school of Titian. The altarpiece in the second chapel, *St Joseph and Five Saints*, is attributed to Domenico Maggiotto. The baptistery has a beautiful 15C octagonal font in pink Verona marble. Among those who were baptized here were Antonio Vivaldi and Pietro Barbo, the future Pope Paul II (1467–71).

The building to the left of the church is a small *scuola* of the 16C. In front of the church there is a *vera da pozzo* dating from the end of the 15C or the beginning of the 16C. On its side there is a relief of St John the Baptist, the patron saint of the church.

The handsome Gothic building on the northern side of the *campo* is the 15C Palazzo Gritti-Morosini-Badoer (No. 3608), now a hotel called La Residenza. The piano nobile has a balcony with a particularly beautiful five-light opening with pointed arches, the cusps of three of them surmounted by classical heads; above the central window there is a *patera* with a 10C Byzantine relief of a peacock. In front of the *palazzo* there is a *vera da pozzo* dating from the 14–15C.

We now retrace our steps to Calle del Dose and then turn left into Calle de la Malvasia Vechia. This brings us into Campiello del Piovan, a picturesque court with three *vere da pozzo*. Two of the well-heads are cylindrical in form and the third is a most unusual parallelopiped. The two cylindrical well-heads have identical inscriptions recording that they were restored in 1691 by the Provveditore di Comun; one of them dates from the 14–15C and the other from the 15–16C. The third one, which dates from the 16C, has on its sides carvings representing St John the Baptist and a Greek cross.

We leave the *campiello* at its far right-hand corner, where the Calle del Forno takes us back to the Riva degli Schiavone. There we turn left and continue in the same direction as before. After the next turning on the left, Calle del Cagnoleto, we pass the Hotel Gabrielli, housed in the 14C Palazzo Gabrielli. In the courtyard there is a *vera da pozzo* of the late 14C, with well-preserved carvings of the Gabrielli coat of arms and a figure of the archangel Gabriel, the family's patron saint.

We now cross Ponte de la Ca' di Dio, which brings us to the *riva* of the same name. The name comes from that of the large building on the left, the former Ospizio e Oratorio della Ca' di Dio, founded in the 13C as a hostel for pilgrims going to the Holy Land. The building now serves as a *casa di riposo*, or old people's home. Above the main doorway there is a fragmentary statuette of the Virgin with Child.

Just beyond the *casa di riposo* we turn left into Calle del Forno. Near the end of the *calle* we turn left again into Ramo Primo de la Pegola, the Street of Pitch, so-called because of the shops of ship-caulkers that were situated here. At the end of the alley we come to Rio de la Ca' di Dio and turn right on Fondamenta del Piovan o Erizzo. A short way along we pass on our right Calle del Piovan, where in a lunette over the gate at the end there is a 16C relief showing St Martin dividing his cloak with a poor man.

We then turn left and cross the canal on Ponte Erizzo. The bridge is named for the handsome palace on the far side of the canal just to the right. Palazzo Erizzo dates from the early 16C, and has both Gothic and Renaissance elements in its design, the former evident in its ogival arches. This was the birthplace of Doge Francesco Erizzo (1631–46).

From here we make our way to the church of Sant'Antonin, which stands on the *campo* of the same name facing Rio de la Pietà. According to tradition, the original church of Sant'-Antonin, dedicated to St Anthony Abbot, was founded in the 6-7C. The church in its present form dates from a rebuilding in the second half of the 17C, perhaps by Baldassare Longhena. It is now closed for restoration. The building on the north side of the *campo* is the *canonica* of Sant'Antonin (No. 3493), with a relief of St Paul and the date 1519.

We now walk north along the canal on Fondamenta dei Furlani, which at its end brings us to the Scuola di San Giorgio degli Schiavoni.

The Dalmatians in Venice founded their confraternity in 1461 under the protection of their patron saints, Sts George, Tryphon and Jerome. At the beginning of the 16C they built their Scuola here, with a neoclassical facade designed by Giovanni de Zan. Over the entrance is a relief of St George and the Dragon, done in 1552 by Pietro da Salò; above is a mid-14C relief of St John the Baptist and St Catherine.

The hall on the ground floor has paintings done for the Scuola by Carpaccio, most of them in the years 1502–9, along with one work each by Palma il Giovane and Antonio Vassilacchi, which were added later. The paintings represent episodes from the life of the three patron saints of the Dalmatians, along with scenes from the life of Christ. The second painting in this series, Carpaccio's *Triumph of St George*, was considered by Ruskin to be one of the supreme masterpieces of Venetian art. The upper floor is the former hostel of the Scuola, with paintings attributed to Andrea Vicentino and followers of Antonio Vivarini.

The street to the right of the Scuola is a cul-de-sac called Calle San Giovanni di Malta. This leads to the church and former monastery of San Giovanni di Malta. The original church of San Giovanni del Tempio (of the Temple) was built in the 11–12C by the Knights Templar of St John. The foundation included a monastery and a hospice, dedicated to St Catherine, built to house pilgrims to the Holy Land. After the dissolution of the Knights Templar in 1312 the church passed to the Knights of St John of Rhodes, later known as the Knights of Malta. The present church dates from a total rebuilding completed in 1565. The church and monastery were closed and despoiled by the French at the beginning of the 19C. But then in 1839 the Knights of Malta regained possession and the church was reopened.

Now we find our way to the church of San Lorenzo,

whose unadorned brick facade looks across its *campo* to the canal of the same name.

According to tradition, the original church of San Lorenzo was founded in the 6–7C, while its Benedictine convent was established in 863 by Orso Partecipazio, who was elected Doge the following year. The present church dates from a complete reconstruction in 1592–1602 by Simeone Sorella. The church was badly damaged during the First World War, after which it was stripped of its works of art and closed; since then the convent has been converted into a hospital. Marco Polo (1255–1324), the famous Venetian traveller, was buried here, but his sarcophagus was lost during the rebuilding of the church. In front of the church there is a *vera da pozzo* dated by an inscription to 1747.

We cross the canal on the Ponte San Lorenzo. This is depicted in Gentile Bellini's painting of *The Miracle of the Cross on the Bridge of San Lorenzo*, done in 1500 and now in the Accademia Galleries. We then turn left on the Fondamenta San Lorenzo. The first large building on the right is Palazzo Ziani (No. 5053), now the headquarters of the Questura, the security police. Doge Pietro Ziani retired to an earlier *palazzo* of the same name on this site after his abdication in 1229, dying there a few days later. Farther along we come to Ponte Lion, which takes its name from Palazzo Lion, the building just north of the bridge on the opposite side of the canal. The noble Lion family lived here from 1570 until the extinction of this branch in 1761. After passing Ponte Lion we see on the other side of the canal Palazzo Maruzzi-Pellegrini, a late Renaissance palace. Just beyond that is the 15C Palazzo Zorzi-Liassidi. We then turn left to cross Rio Ponte dei Greci, after which we turn immediately right on the *fondamenta* on the other side. This brings us to the courtyard of the Greek Orthodox church of San Giorgio dei Greci.

The Greeks in Venice founded a *scuola* in 1498, and in 1511 they were permitted to erect the present church, dedicated to St George. The church is built in the style of the late

Renaissance, with a neoclassical facade showing the strong influence of Sansovino. The first architect was Sante Lombardo, who worked on the building from 1539 until his death in 1547; he was succeeded by Giannantonio Chiona, who completed the structure in 1573. The campanile was erected by Simeone Sorella in 1587–92. In 1577 one of the priests of San Giorgio, Gabriel Seviros, was appointed Metropolitan of Philadelphia, an ancient see in Asia Minor which was transferred *de facto* to Venice. Seviros founded a convent at San Giorgio in 1599 and in 1610 he obtained a grant to establish the Flanginian College, the neoclassical building to the left of the church, which was completed *c.* 1680 to a design by Baldassare Longhena. Longhena also designed the palace to the left of the college, which originally housed the Greek Scuola of St Nicholas.

The interior of San Giorgio, which is preceded by a small narthex, is a domed basilica without side aisles, with the nave separated from the sanctuary by the iconostasis. Except for one mosaic by Giannantonio Marini, the early works of art in the church are all by Greek artists. There are forty-six paintings on the iconostasis alone, eighteen of them done in 1574–7 by Michael Damascinos, the most renowned artist of the Veneto-Cretan School. The funerary monument on the right side of the nave is that of the Metropolitan Gabriel Seviros (1577–1616) by Baldassare Longhena.

There are 16C *vere da pozzo* in the courtyards on either side of the church. The one on the right has reliefs of St Nicholas and St George, while the one on the left has a coat of arms and the figure of St George, who on both well-heads is shown killing a dragon.

The Flanginian College now houses the Hellenic Institute of Byzantine and Post-Byzantine Studies. It also has a museum with 104 Byzantine and post-Byzantine icons ranging in date from the 14–17C.

We now retrace our steps across Ponte dei Greci, after which we turn left and then right along Fondamenta de l'Osmarin. This takes us along Rio de San Provolo, passing on our right Ponte del Diavolo, the Devil's Bridge, a name of obscure origin. Just beyond the bridge on the opposite side is the 15C Palazzo Priuli. We then pass on our right Ponte dei Carmini, after which we veer left from the canal into Calle San Provolo. After passing through a *sottoportego* we enter Campo San Provolo, where there is a 14C *vera da pozzo*. The *campo* is named for the ancient church of San Provolo, destroyed in the 19C.

We then turn right and cross Ponte San Provolo, after which we continue along Salizzada San Provolo into Campo Santi Filippo e Giacomo, where there is a 16C *vera da pozzo*. The *campo* is named for the ancient church of Santi Filippo e Giacomo, demolished in the 19C. The house at No. 4358 was the home of Antonio Vivaldi in the years 1719–30.

We continue straight ahead on Rughetta San Apollonia, at the end of which we turn left on the *fondamenta* of the same name. The last building on the side of the *fondamenta*, now the Jesurum lace gallery, stands on the site of the church of Santi Filippo e Giacomo. At the end of the *fondamenta* is the entrance to the former Benedictine monastery of Santa Scolastica, now the Museum of Diocesan and Sacred Art.

The monastery, which was also dedicated to Santa Apollonia, was founded in the 12–13C. It preserves the only Romanesque cloister in Venice, with a 13C *vera da pozzo* in the centre. Around the courtyard there are arrayed a number of sculptural and architectural fragments, most of them from former Venetian churches.

We walk back along the *fondamenta* and turn left to cross Ponte de la Canonica, after which we turn right on the *fondamenta* of the same name. At the end of the *fondamenta* we pause for a moment at the foot of Ponte Cappello to look across the canal at the 16C Palazzo Trevisan-Cappello, now the Pauly glass works. We then turn left on Calle de la Canonica. This takes us into Piazzetta dei Leoni, where we complete our first stroll through Castello.

SESTIERE DI CASTELLO II (*Map Route 5*)

We begin the second of our strolls through the Sestiere di Castello on Riva de la Ca' di Dio, the turning-point of our last walk.

The large building that takes up the eastern half of the *riva* is the former military bakery and bread stores of the Republic, erected in 1392 and rebuilt in 1473. Set into the crenellated walls of the building there are a number of coats of arms of magistrates of the Republic and reliefs of allegorical figures, dating from the 16–17C.

We now cross Ponte de l'Arsenal, which brings us to Riva San Biagio and the *campo* of the same name. The name comes from the former church of San Biagio, which is at the far end of the *campo*; perpendicular to it is the Museo Storico Navale. According to tradition, the church of San Biagio was founded in the 11C. The church in its present state dates from a complete rebuilding in 1749–54 by Francesco Bognolo; it has recently been restored and is now open as part of the Naval Museum. On the left side of the nave there is a funerary monument to Angelo Emo (d. 1792), the last admiral of the Venetian Navy, who in 1784–6 led a victorious campaign against the Bey of Tunis.

The Museo Storico Navale has exhibits associated with the maritime activities of the Venetian Republic and of modern Italy. The museum has a vast collection of ship models, dating from antiquity to modern times. An extension to the museum has been opened in the Officini Remi, the large 16C building on Fondamenta de l'Arsenal.

We continue to the end of Riva San Biagio, crossing Ponte de la Veneta Marina. This brings us to Riva dei Sette Martiri, laid out in 1937 on the site of ship-building yards dating back to the time of the Republic. Just beyond the bridge the promenade is joined by Rio Terà Garibaldi, a wide avenue created by Napoleon in 1807 by filling in a canal. The building at the acute angle between Garibaldi and the seaside promenade has a plaque placed there in 1881, stating that the famous navigators John Cabot and his son Sebastian lived in Castello during their stay in Venice.

We continue along Riva dei Sette Martiri, passing a public garden, after which we come to an ancient apartment house known as Casa della Marinarezza, distinguished by the two great round archways that pass through its facade. The complex consists of three parallel blocks on three storeys, a total of fifty-five contiguous houses, its three sections separated by two *corti* that pass through the archways. These three blocks were erected by the Procuratia di Citra in 1335 as public housing, the dwellings being awarded to sailors who had distinguished themselves in the cause of the Republic, and they can be seen in Barbari's view of 1500. The block with the two archways overlooking the Bacino San Marco was added in 1645–61. About 80 m farther along we pass Villino Canonica, a little neo-Renaissance palace erected in 1911 for the sculptor Pietro Canonica.

We now cross Ponte San Domenego, which brings us to Riva dei Partigiani. Looking back and to the left we see Viale Garibaldi, a public park that extends to the end of Rio Terà Garibaldi, also created by Napoleon in 1807. At the same time he had the Giardini Pubblici made, extending along Riva dei Partigiani for 300 m from Rio de San Isepo. During the making of the gardens two ancient churches were demolished, San Nicolò di Bari and Sant'Antonio, both of which appear in Barbari's view of 1500.

At the eastern end of the Giardini Pubblici we come to the gardens of the Venice Biennale, the site of the International Exhibition of Modern Art. Within the park are the pavilions of twenty-six nations as well as that of Venice itself, the largest being the Palazzo d'Italia.

Continuing along Riva dei Partigiani, we now cross Ponte dei Giardini on the bridge of the same name. This brings us to Isola Sant'Elena, almost all of which is on former marshes and meadows filled in during the 19–20C. After crossing the bridge we turn right on the seaside promenade, and then left along the west bank of Rio de Sant'Elena. We turn right to cross Ponte Sant'Elena, from where we continue straight ahead to the church of Sant'Elena.

The church was founded in 1175, along with a hospice for pilgrims bound for the Holy Land. In 1211 it was used to enshrine the body of St Helena, mother of Constantine the Great, which the Venetians had removed from Constantinople. A bull of Pope Gregory XII in 1407 called for the creation of a monastery for Benedictine Olivetan monks at Sant'Elena, which led to the reconstruction of the church complex, completed in 1439 by Giacomo Celega, with the assistance of Bartolomeo Tesenato. Another period of reconstruction and renovation intervened before the reconsecration of the church in 1515. The campanile was erected in 1558, but this was demolished when the church and monastery were suppressed by the French in 1807. After renovation the church was reconsecrated in 1929, with the present campanile being completed in 1958 by Ferdinando Forlati. The lunette above the splendid 15C doorway contains a statue group showing the Admiral Vittore Cappello (d. 1467) kneeling before St Helena, with his sarcophagus in the background, done c. 1476 by Antonio Rizzo. To the left of the church is the cloister of the former monastery.

The large chapel of St Helena, a late Gothic structure of the 15C, opens into the rear of the right aisle. This was commissioned by Alessandro Borromeo as a funerary chapel for his family, several of whose tombs can be seen there, along with a modern sarcophagus containing the remains of St Helena. In the chapel there is a painting of *The Annunciation, with Donors*, attributed to Marco Vecellio. Farther along the right aisle is the Giustinian Chapel, built in 1460 by Domenico di Giovanni, and now used as the sacristy. To the left of the chancel is the late-15C Chapel of St Francesca Romana. On the walls of the chapel there are six tablets painted by Antonio da Firenze, along with a depiction of St Helena at the foot of the Cross by Paolo Piazza.

We now make our way back across Isola Sant'Elena to Ponte del Paludo, and from there to Campo San Isepo. This is one of two contiguous *campi* of the same name, on the first of which there is an hexagonal *vera da pozzo* dated 1571, with reliefs of Sts Joseph, Augustine and Anthony Abbot. In the second *campo* we come to the church of San Isepo or Giuseppe (Joseph), which is on the right beside the canal of the same name. The church and its convent were founded in 1512 by a decree of the Venetian Senate. The church was completed in the latter half of the 16C, with a neoclassical facade. Over the doorway there is a relief of the Adoration of the Magi by Giulio del Moro.

On the first altar from the rear on the right there is a panel of *The Archangel Michael Fighting with the Devil*, attributed to the workshop of Jacopo Tintoretto. On the second altar is *The Eternal Father with Saints*, attributed to Sante Peranda. The altarpiece on the high altar is *The Adoration of the Shepherds*, done by Veronese in 1570–75. On the wall to the left is the funerary monument of the Procurator Girolamo Grimani (d. 1570), father of Doge Marino Grimani, by Alessandro Vittoria. On the left wall of the nave is the monument of Doge Marino Grimani (d. 1605) and his wife Morosina Morosini, with marble figures and bronze reliefs by Girolamo Campagna.

At the Ponte de San Isepo we cross over and turn right on Fondamenta San Isepo, and then at the first corner left on Calle del Magazen. This is one of the most common street names in Venice, deriving from *magazen*, a wine shop where the customers could pawn their possessions, receiving two thirds of the payment in cash and the other third in rot-gut wine to be consumed on the premises. The proprietors of these taverns, the *magazenieri*, had their own *scuola* in the church of San Salvador.

On the next block, after crossing Seco Marina, the street becomes Calle Giambattisto Tiepolo, which ends at Campiello Correr on Rio de Sant'Ana. Here we turn right and walk along Fondamenta Sant'Ana. Just before reaching the end of the *fondamenta* we pass on our right the former church of Sant'Anna, founded along with its convent in 1240. The church in its present form is the result of a rebuilding in 1634 by Bernardino Contino. The church and convent were suppressed by the French in 1807. The convent now houses an infirmary.

At the end of the *fondamenta* we cross the Canal de San Piero on Ponte de Quintavale, which brings us to the Isola de San Piero. The bridge and the *calle* on the other side are named for the Quintavale, a family whose origins go back to the earliest recorded references to the Isola da San Piero, an island known originally as Olivolo, later to be called Castello because of a fortress erected there in the 9C.

At the end of the *calle* we turn left on Fondamenta Quintavale, after which we turn right on Calle drio el Campaniel, pausing to examine the tabernacle at the corner to the left. The tabernacle has a beautiful relief in marble dating from the first half of the 15C, showing the Virgin enthroned with Child presenting the keys to St Peter, with a half-figure of the Saviour above the cornice embowered in Gothic foliage.

We follow the *calle* as it veers round to the left and brings us to Campo San Piero. There we find ourselves under the campanile of San Pietro, with the church itself at the rear of the *campo* facing the canal. According to tradition, the first church on this site was an early Christian basilica dedicated to St Sergius and St Bacchus. In the first half of the 9C this was replaced by a new church dedicated to St Peter, which became the seat of the Bishop of Castello. By the middle of the 9C an episcopal palace with a baptistery had been constructed to the right of the church. The Bishop of Castello was originally under the jurisdiction of the Patriarch of Grado. But then in 1451 the bishoprics of Grado and Castello were combined by Pope Nicholas V. The Pope then appointed the Bishop of Castello, the aged Lorenzo Giustinian (canonized in 1609), as the first Patriarch of Venice. San Pietro di

Castello thus became the cathedral of Venice, a status that it retained until 1807, when the patriarchate was transferred to the Basilica of San Marco. Erection of the campanile began in 1463, to be completed in 1482 by Mauro Coducci. Then in 1558 Andrea Palladio was commissioned to rebuild the church by the Patriarch Antonio Diedo, whose death the following year interrupted the project. The facade was completed in 1594–6 by Francesco Smeraldi, and the interior in 1619–21 by Giovanni Grapiglia, both of whom kept to Palladio's original design.

The marble seat between the second and third altars on the right is known as the Throne of St Peter, and is said to have come from Antioch during the Crusades; its back is made from a Muslim tombstone inscribed in Cufic letters with a quotation from the Koran. The chapel to the right of the chancel has on its right wall a painting of *The Plague of Serpents*, by Pietro Liberi; on the left wall is *The Adoration of the Magi* by Pietro Ricchi. The high altar in the chancel was commissioned by the Senate in 1649; it was designed by Baldassare Longhena and built by Clemente Moli, who did the figure of San Lorenzo Giustinian on the saint's sarcophagus.

The fresco on the conch and vault of the apse is *San Lorenzo in Glory* by Girolamo Pellegrini. On the right wall is a painting of *San Lorenzo Imploring God to Save Venice from the Plague in 1477* by Antonio Bellucci; on the left wall is *San Lorenzo Giving Alms to the Poor* by Gregorio Lazzarini. The chapel to the left of the chancel has a large wooden cross with the figures in beaten copper of the Virgin, St John and an angel, dating from the 14C.

In the left arm of the transept is a chapel dedicated to Cardinal Francesco Vendramin (d. 1619), built in 1645 to a design by Baldassare Longhena. The altarpiece depicts *The Virgin and Child, with Repenting Souls* by Luca Giordano. On the wall of the left aisle beyond the transept there is a painting of *Sts John the Evangelist, Peter and Paul* by Veronese. Beneath

147

this is the entrance to the Landro Chapel, built in 1425, with a mosaic altarpiece depicting Ognissanti, All the Saints, signed by Arminio Zuccato and dated 1570, perhaps from a cartoon by Jacopo Tintoretto. On the first altar from the front there is a statue representing the Immaculate Conception by Gian Maria Morleiter. On the second altar there is a painting of *The Martyrdom of St John the Evangelist* attributed to Alessandro Varottari.

The former Patriarchal Palace is the huge structure to the right of the church, with the coat of arms of the Patriarch Lorenzo Priuli (d. 1601) above the entrance. The house adjacent to the palace on the right, at No. 69, is the former Scuola del Santissimo Sacramento, originally an oratory dedicated to St John the Evangelist. The door still has its marble frame and elaborately carved architrave. Set into the wall of the house are several reliefs and statuettes dating from the 15C.

The Campo San Piero was the scene of an ancient Venetian festival that took place annually on 31 January, when betrothed couples came to the cathedral to celebrate their marriages, the girls carrying their dowries in small chests called *arcili*. During the festival in 944 Istrian pirates raided the island and made off with all the brides, after which they stopped in Caorle to divide up the loot. The pursuing Venetians, led by Doge Pietro Candiano III, caught the pirates there and killed them, returning in triumph with the brides and their dowries. This incident, known as '*il ratto delle spose*', the 'rape of the brides', was thenceforth commemorated in a re-enactment of the event called the 'Festa delle Marie', which was celebrated at San Pietro until 1397.

We now recross the canal on Ponte San Piero. On the other side of the bridge we continue straight ahead on Calle Larga de Castelo, at the end of which we turn right on Salizzada Streta, followed by a left at the first corner on Ramo San Daniel. This brings us to Rio de San Daniel, which we cross on Ponte San Daniel. The isolated little *campo* of the same name at the junction of Rio de San Daniel and

Rio de le Vergini is the site of the former church of San Daniele, founded in 820 and first referred to in 1046. The church was demolished in 1839 and its monastery now serves as a military hospital.

Rio de le Vergini is named for the ancient church of Santa Maria delle Vergini, demolished in 1869. The church stood on the north bank of the canal opposite the *campo*. Set into the crenellated wall of the Arsenal we see all that is left of the church, a 15C lunette with a relief of the Virgin and Child flanked by St Mark and St Augustine.

We now return to Salizzada Streta, where there are a number of picturesque old houses; the one at No. 101 dated by an inscription to 1565, and the one at Nos. 105–8 a late-Gothic *palazzetto* of the 15C. At the end of the street we enter Campo Ruga San Lorenzo Giustiniani, in the centre of which there is a 15C *vera da pozzo*. On the left side of the *campo* near the far corner, at No. 327, there is a *palazzetto* of the 17C.

At the far end of the *campo* we turn right on Calle Ruga. At the canal we turn left on Fondamenta del Rielo and then right on to Ponte Rielo. After crossing the bridge we turn left on Fondamenta del Forner and then right on Calle San Gioachin, which turns to the left at the end of the block. At the corner we see on the right, at No. 450, a Gothic portal surmounted by a relief showing the Madonna and Child flanked by St Peter and St Paul, dating from the 14C. This was the entrance to the former Ospizio dei Santi Pietro e Paolo, founded in the 11C as a hospice for pilgrims to the Holy Land, along with an oratory dedicated to St Joachim.

At the end of the *calle* we come to Ponte San Gioachin, on the other side of which we see a relief of the Madonna and Child over the doorway at No. 993. This led to Ospizio Foscolo, founded by a bequest of Lucia Foscolo on 6 October 1418 as a refuge for indigent widows.

We turn right on Fondamenta San Gioachin, crossing Rio de la Tana on Ponte Novo, after which we walk along the last stretch of Rio de Sant'Ana on the walkway known as Fondamentina. Across the canal to our left we see, at No. 1132, a 15C *palazzetto* that has recently been restored, with a number of Veneto-Byzantine *paterae* of the 12C set into its facade. We then come to the inner end of Rio Terà Garibaldi, where a market is held every weekday, with boats bringing fish and vegetables to it along Rio de Sant'Ana.

Before continuing down Garibaldi we will first make a brief diversion, turning right through a *sottoportego* into Calle Loredan. This takes us to Fondamenta de la Tana, on the canal of the same name, which extends along the wall of the largest single building in the Arsenal. This is the Corderie ('rope-works') della Tana, a vast hall 316 m long divided into three aisles. The Corderie was first erected in 1303 and was rebuilt by Antonio da Ponte in 1579–85.

Turning left on Fondamenta de la Tana, we see on the wall of the first building an old plaque inscribed with regulations concerning the minimum size of the various fish that could be sold in the local market.

We now turn left on Calle Friziera, which brings us back to Rio Terà Garibaldi, where we turn right. As we do so we pass on our left Viale Garibaldi, which leads to Pontile Giardini on the Bacino San Marco. Inside the gate there is a huge bronze monument to Giuseppe Garibaldi, done in 1885 by Augusto Benvenuti. The gateway and monument are on the site of the ancient church and monastery of San Domenico, destroyed when the park was laid out in 1810. The name of the complex is perpetuated in that of the first street on the left beyond the park, Calle San Domenigo. Halfway down the *calle*, a *sottoportego* on the right leads into Corte San Domenigo. A plaque records that the painter Giambattista Tiepolo was born in a house on this *corte* in 1696.

The first house on the left after the park, at No. 1310, has on its facade a Gothic archway with a 14C relief showing Sts Domenic, John the Evangelist and Peter Martyr. This was the entrance to the Conservatorio delle Zitelle, a music school for girls founded in 1312, along with the adjacent church and monastery of San Domenico.

Almost directly across the street is the church of San Francesco di Paola. The history of this site dates back to 1291, when Bartolomeo Querini, the Bishop of Castello, made a bequest to build a hospice for the old and infirm, to which an oratory was added. Then in 1580 the complex was taken over by the Fathers of the Minimi order, who eight years later rebuilt the hospice as a monastery and erected a new church, which they dedicated to San Francesco di Paola. The monastery was suppressed by the French in 1806 and in 1855 it was demolished.

The paintings in the panels of the ceiling, *Scenes from the Life of Christ* and *Doctors of the Church*, were done in 1603 by Giovanni Contarini. On the second altar from the rear on the right there is a painting of *The Virgin and St John the Evangelist*, attributed to Palma il Giovane. On the fourth altar the *St Francesco di Paola* is by Alvise dal Friso. The altarpiece in the chapel to the right of the chancel is an *Annunciation* by Palma il Giovane. The fresco on the vault of the chancel shows *St Francesco di Paola in Glory* by Michele Schiavone. On the high altar there are two marble statues, on the left, St Mark by Gregorio Morleiter; on the right, St Bartholomew by Alvise Tagliapietra.

The altarpiece on the first altar from the front on the left is *The Martyrdom of St Bartholomew* by Jacopo Marieschi. On the last altar on that side are four portraits of saints attributed to Palma il Giovane. Above, on the cornice around the walls, there are nine 18C paintings depicting scenes from the life of St Francesco di Paola; one of these, *The Saint Crossing the Strait of Messina on his Cloak*, is attributed to Giandomenico Tiepolo.

We continue along Garibaldi, as a spendid view opens up of the Bacino San Marco with the church of the Salute in the background. The *calli* on either side are among the oldest in Venice, all of them appearing in Barbari's view of 1500.

On the right, Calle dei Preti is flanked at its far end by terraced houses of the 15C, their top floors added in the 17C. On the right again, Corte Nova is also flanked by ancient terraced houses, with two *vere da pozzo* of the 14C along its central axis. On the left side of Garibaldi, at No. 1581, is the 16C Palazzo Marcora, which in 1538 was bequeathed to the Scuola di San Rocco.

We now turn right off Garibaldi on the narrow Calle del Forno. This brings us back to Rio de la Tana, which we cross here on an iron bridge of the same name. Continuing straight ahead for a few steps on Ramo de la Tana, we then turn left into Campo de la Tana, a long and broad street that on its right is bordered by one of the ancient buildings of the Arsenal. This is the Fonderie, or foundry, first erected in 1390 and rebuilt in the 16C and again in the 18C. Farther along on the left, at No. 2157, is the former Casa dei Visdomini della Tana, the house of the magistrate in charge of the Corderie della Tana, with the coat of arms of Doge Pasquale Cicogna and the date 1589. In the centre of the *campo* there is a richly decorated *vera da pozzo* of the 15C.

At the end of the street we come to Rio de l'Arsenal, where we turn right on the *fondamenta* of the same name, approaching the great gateway of the Arsenal. The large building on the right is the Officina Remi, where oars were made for the Venetian navy and wood stored; it is now a part of the Museo Storico Navale. This was erected in 1546, and its great hall was used for a time as the meeting place of the Maggior Consiglio after the Palazzo Ducale was badly damaged by fire in 1577.

The last stretch of the *fondamenta* beyond the bridge was the site of the little 16C church of the Madonna dell'Arsenale, demolished by the French in 1808. On the facade of the building by the bridge there is a large relief with a lion passant between coats of arms and trophies. There is also a plaque commemorating the outbreak of the Venetian revolt against the Austrians, which began here on 22 March 1848 when the workers in the Arsenal rioted and killed their Austrian supervisor.

We now cross the canal on the wooden Ponte de l'Arsenal to Campo de l'Arsenal. This brings us to the great gateway of the Arsenal, the former shipyard of the Venetian Republic.

The word 'arsenal' comes from the Arabic *darshane*, or 'workshop', usually meaning a shipyard. According to tradition, the Venetian Arsenal was founded in 1104 on what were then two islets, subsequently expanded to the vast area we see today, which almost cuts off the eastern part of Castello from the part to the west of Rio de l'Arsenal. The western part of the Arsenal is known as Darsena Vecchia and the much larger eastern part is Darsena Nuova, which, when it was added in 1303-25, more than quadrupled the area of the shipyard. The Arsenal comprises an area of 46 hectares (115 acres); at its peak it was staffed by an average of 2,000 workers – the *arsenalotti* – and as many as 3,000 in times of emergency. In the middle of the 16C, when Venice was fighting for its existence against the Turks, the Republic often fitted out fleets of over one hundred galleys, keeping another hundred warships in reserve in the Arsenal. When King Henry III of France visited Venice in 1574 he was taken to the Arsenal one morning to watch the keel of a galley being laid, and that evening when he returned he was amazed to see the ship being launched, fully rigged and equipped and ready to set sail. The Arsenal was still operating at the end of the Republic and for 120 years afterwards, but after the First World War its role was greatly diminished; today its shipbuilding activities have virtually ceased and it is little more than a naval training centre.

The great archway at the land entrance to the Arsenal was erected in 1460; it is attributed to Luciana di Martino de Laurana, who constructed it on a classical model that marks the beginning of the Renaissance style in Venetian architecture. Above the entablature a large *aedicula* frames a high relief of the Lion of St Mark, attributed to Bartolomeo Bon;

the two Nikes were added after the victory at Lepanto in 1571, and then in 1578 a statue of St Giustina by Girolamo Campagna was added at the peak of the pediment, since it was on her feast-day that the battle was fought. The pair of crenellated towers at the water entrance on the canal were rebuilt in 1574, enlargements of the original ones that appear in Barbari's view of 1500. Then in 1682 a terrace was built around the archway of the land-gate and eight statues of allegorical figures were erected on the balustrade. The two large lions that flank the gateway were sent back from Athens in 1687 by Francesco Morosini. The two smaller lions to the right of the gateway were put in place in 1716; the larger one is from the Lion Terrace on Delos, a work of the 6C BC. On the defence wall of the Arsenal to the right of the gateway there is a bronze bust of Dante Alighieri, a modern work by Giulio Monteverde. Beneath the bust and on another plaque to the left of the gateway there is a quote from Canto XXI of Dante's *Inferno*, where the poet compares the crowded darkness of hell's depths to the scene he witnessed at the Arsenal in 1300.

The Arsenal is a military zone, and visitors are permitted only as far as the vestibule inside the gateway, where high on the wall to the left there is a relief of the Madonna and Child by Sansovino.

We leave the *campo* on Fondamenta de Fazza l'Arsenal, which leads along Rio de l'Arsenal to Campo San Martin. On the left is the church of San Martino, picturesquely situated at the junction of four canals, crossed by two bridges.

According to tradition, San Martino was founded in the 7–8C. The church was rebuilt in its present form in 1540 by Jacopo Sansovino. To the right of the doorway, which is the original by Sansovino, there is a *bocca di leone*, or 'lion's mouth', a slot for inserting denunciations of those guilty of blasphemy and other sins. On the right side of the facade there is a relief of the Madonna and Child dated 1362.

The flat ceiling is decorated with architectural perspectives by Domenico Bruni; the central fresco shows *St Martin in Glory* by Jacopo Guarana. On the parapet of the organ and choral gallery over the entrance there is a *Last Supper*, signed by Girolamo da Santacroce and dated 1549. Over the side door is the funerary monument of Doge Francesco Erizzo (d. 1646), by Mattia Carnero. On the wall by the third altar there is a small painting of *The Resurrection*, signed by Girolamo da Santacroce. The frescoes in the chancel are by Fabio Canal: on the vault, *The Glory of the Sacrament*; on the walls, *The Sacrifices of Abraham and Melchizedek*. In the back choir there are two paintings by Palma il Giovane, *The Flagellation* and *The Road to Calvary*. On the left side by the pulpit there is a Lombardesque altar supported by the figures of four angels, created by Tullio Lombardo *c.* 1484

The little building beside the church to the right, at No. 2426, is the former Scuola di San Martino, founded in the 16C by the Guild of Ship-caulkers. On the facade is a 15C relief showing St Martin on horseback dividing his cloak with a poor man. This is the traditional image of St Martin, and on his feast-day it appears on large cookies that are given as presents to children.

We now cross the canal on Ponte dei Panini and continue straight ahead on the *fondamenta* of the same name, which takes us along the west bank of Rio de le Gorne. This brings us to Campo de le Gorne, which has a 14C well-head in the centre. On the crenellated wall of the Arsenal to the right there is a large relief of the Lion of St Mark.

We turn sharp left in the *campo* and enter Calle del Bastion, whose name suggests that it marks part of the ancient defence wall that extended from Castello to the Bacino San Marco. After passing on its left Piscina San Martin the street changes its name to Calle de le Muneghete. On the right, at No. 2616, we pass the former Convento delle Muneghette, founded by an order of secular nuns in the 12–13C and reconstructed by Baldassare Longhena in 1681.

At the end of Calle de le Muneghete we come to Campo

dei Do Pozzi, the Square of the Two Well-heads. Despite its name, there is only one *vera da pozzo* in the *campo*, dating from the early 16C. But a relief on one of the six panels shows a pair of well-heads in perspective, indicating that there were in fact two of them in the *campo* originally. There are also reliefs on two of the other panels, one of them showing St Martin and the other three half-length figures of angels representing the Holy Trinity. These reliefs symbolized the nearby churches of San Martino and Santa Ternità, the Holy Trinity, the latter demolished in the 19C. On the right side of the *campo*, at No. 2611, there is a Gothic *palazzetto* with pointed arches dating from the 14C. Opposite, at Nos. 2684–9, is Palazzo Malipiero, which appears to date from the 16C.

We leave the *campo* at its far left corner via Calle Magno. At the first crossing we pass on our right Sottoportego de l'Anzolo, where over the lintel there is a relief of an Angel of Benediction, a beautiful sculpture of the early Renaissance, along with the coat of arms of the Rizzo family, bearing the bristling figure of a porcupine. A short way farther along the *calle* we pass on our right Palazzo Magno (No. 2693), a splendid Gothic palace dating from the second half of the 14C.

At the end of the *calle* we turn left on Calle Donà, after which we cross Rio de Santa Ternità on Ponte de la Scoazzera. As we do so we see to our right, on the east bank of the canal at its end, the 17C Palazzo Celsi-Donà. After crossing the bridge we come to Campo a Fianco la Chiesa and then to Campo Santa Ternità, which opens on to Rio de San Francesco de la Vigna. The *campo* is named for the church of Santa Ternità, founded during the reign of Doge Pietro Centranico (1026–32) and demolished in 1832. On the western side of the *campo* there is a *vera da pozzo* dated 1526, with reliefs representing St John the Baptist and St Francis of Assisi. On the left side of the *campo* a private bridge leads to a *palazzetto* of the late 16C or early 17C; behind it and to the right is the contiguous south-east wing of the enormous Palazzo Sagredo, dating from the end of the 15C.

We now cross Rio de San Francesco on Ponte del Suffragio, after which we turn right on Fondamenta del Cristo and then left into Campo de la Celestia. The *campo* is named for the former church of Santa Maria Celeste, known as the Celestia, which, with its convent, occupied the entire right side of the square. The church was erected in the late 11C and the convent was founded in 1237. The church and convent were both suppressed by the French in 1810. The church was demolished later in the 19C, while the convent was converted to secular use; today it houses part of the historic archives of Venice and also the university's Faculty of Chemical Engineering.

At the far end of the *campo* we turn left into Calle del Cimitero, the Street of the Cemetery. The *calle* took its name from the burial-ground of the church of San Francesco della Vigna. This graveyard was closed by Napoleon in 1807 along with all the other local burial-grounds in Venice, with the deceased being re-interred on the Isola di San Michele.

At the end of the *calle* we turn left and then right to enter Campo de la Confraternita, which is bounded on its north side by the church of San Francesco della Vigna. Over the side entrance to the church there is a relief of the Virgin and the Angel of the Annunciation, a 16C work attributed to Guglielmo Bergamasco. The building on the east side of the *campo* is the former Scuola di San Pasquale Baylon, created in 1603.

The *campo* is bounded on its south side by the former Convento delle Pizzochere. This was founded in 1471 as a convent school for poor girls, which was closed by the French in 1810. In 1838 it was purchased by the Franciscans, who joined it by an arcade to the building at the far end of the *campo*, the Palazzo Nunziatoro, where they were then living. This palace was built in 1525 for Doge Andrea Gritti; it was purchased by the Republic and presented to Pope Pius

IV in 1564 as a residence for the Apostolic Nuncio. Then in 1836 it was acquired by the Franciscans, who lived there and in the adjacent Convento delle Pizzochere until 1866, when both buildings were taken over by the Italian government for use as a military tribunal.

At the far end of the *campo* we turn right into Campo San Francesco de la Vigna, where we come to the main entrance of the church.

The church and its monastery was founded by the Franciscans in 1253. The land on which the church was built had been a *vigna*, or vineyard, and so it came to be called San Francesco della Vigna. The church in its present form dates from a rebuilding in 1534 by Jacopo Sansovino, with a new facade added in 1568–72 to a design by Palladio. The campanile was erected in 1571–81 by Bernardino Ongarin.

The interior of the entrance is flanked by colossal bronze statues of Moses and St Paul, both by Tiziano Aspetti. On either side there are holy-water stoups with bronze statuettes signed by Alessandro Vittoria; on the left is St Francis and on the right St John the Baptist. On the wall to the right of the door there is a 13C relief of the Virgin and Child; on the left is a painting of *Sts Jerome, Bernardino of Siena and Louis of Toulouse*, attributed to Antonio Vivarini. The altarpiece in the first chapel on the right is *St John the Baptist and Other Saints* by Giuseppe Salviati; on the right wall is a *Last Supper* by Girolamo da Santacroce; on the left is *The Resurrection*, dated 1516, by the school of Giorgione. The third chapel contains the tombs of Doges Francesco Contarini (d. 1624) and Alvise Contarini (d. 1684); the altarpiece is *The Virgin and Child with Saints* by Palma il Giovane. The altarpiece of the fourth chapel is *The Resurrection*, attributed to Veronese. On the altar in the right transept there is a beautiful painting of the *Virgin and Child Enthroned*, signed by Antonio da Negroponte and dated 1470.

The high altar, dating from c. 1543, is surmounted by a ciborium carried on four pairs of columns, with statues of St

Bernardino and St Francis over the side doors. On the left wall of the chancel is the tomb of Doge Andrea Gritti (d. 1538). On the walls of the choir are paintings by Andrea Vicentino, Francesco Maggiotto, Gregorio Lazzarini, Domenico Tintoretto, Pietro di Mera and Sante Peranda, and two by Palma il Giovane.

The splendid chapel to the left of the chancel was dedicated to the Giustinian family in a bequest made in 1478 by Girolamo Badoer. On the altar there is a marble triptych showing St Jerome between four saints and, above, the Virgin and Child by a Lombard master of the late 15C. The reliefs on the altar are attributed to Bartolomeo Bellano and to Pietro Lombardo and his sons Tullio and Antonio.

Over the side door in the left transept is the funerary monument of Doge Marcantonio Trevisan (d. 1554). The door leads to Cappella Santa, the left side of which looks out on to the 15C cloister. The altarpiece is a beautiful painting of the *Virgin and Child with Saints and Donor*, signed by Giovanni Bellini and dated 1507.

The first chapel from the front on the left, dedicated by the Giustinian family, has on its altar a painting of the *Madonna and Child Enthroned with Sts John, Joseph, Catherine and Anthony Abbot*, done in 1551 by Veronese. The altarpiece in the second chapel, dedicated by the Dandolo family, is a depiction of the *Madonna and Child with St Bernard and St Anthony Abbot* by Giuseppe Salviati, who also did the frescoes. The third chapel contains the funerary monuments of Doge Nicolò Sagredo (d. 1676) and his brother the Patriarch Alvise Sagredo (d. 1688); the monochrome frescoes were done in 1743 by Giambattista Tiepolo, representing the Evangelists in the spandrels of the vault and Virtues in the two roundels on the walls. On the altar of the fourth chapel are statues of Sts Anthony Abbot, Sebastian and Roch, done in 1565 by Alessandro Vittoria. The fifth chapel contains the tomb of Giovanni Grimani, Patriarch of Aquileia (d. mid 16C); the altarpiece is *The Epiphany*, done in 1564 by Federico Zuccari. In niches flanking the altar there are bronze statues of Justice and Temperance, signed by Tiziano Aspetti and dated 1592.

After leaving the church we cross Campo de la Confraternita and pass through the arcade on its south side, which brings us to Campiello de la Chiesa, on Rio de San Francesco. In the *campiello* there is a *vera da pozzo* inscribed with the date 1596; this probably records a repair, since the Gothic form of the well-head dates it to the 14–15C.

We now cross the canal on Ponte de San Francesco. To the right of the bridge on the other side is Palazzo Contarini della Porta di Ferro, 'of the iron door', so called because its door was once covered with wrought-iron decorations, destroyed in 1839. We continue straight ahead from the bridge on Ramo al Ponte San Francesco, turning right at the first corner on Salizzada Santa Giustina. At the corner on the right we see a figure of the Madonna and Child dated 1716. The corner house opposite on Calle del Murion, at No. 2951, was in times past a hospice for impoverished women, founded in the 14C. Later it became a night refuge, the first in Venice.

A short way along Salizzada Santa Giustina on the left we pass Calle dei Bombardieri, the Street of the Bombardiers. This is named for the Confraternita dei Bombardieri, founded in 1500 by artillerymen in the Venetian army, with its *scuola* at the church of Santa Maria Formosa. The confraternity owned six small houses on the *calle*, which are still identifiable by the numbers I–VI, three of them bearing figures of St Barbara, patron saint of the gunners.

Continuing along Salizzada Santa Giustina, halfway down the block on the right, at No. 2926, is the land-entrance of Palazzo Contarini della Porta di Ferro. The entrance has a marble arch in the Veneto-Byzantine style, with a 14C relief of an angel and coats of arms. Doges Franceso Contarini (1623–4) and Alvise Contarini (1676–84) belonged to this branch of the family, which became extinct in 1799.

At the end of Salizzada Santa Giustina we turn right on Calle del Fontego. On the left side of the *calle* is Palazzo da

Riva (No. 2856), rebuilt in 1712 on the site of an earlier palace of the Valier family. On the right is the 15C Palazzo Morosini (No. 2845). This was the birthplace of Marcantonio Morosini, who in 1499 deposed Ludovico Sforza, Duke of Milan, and captured Cremona for the Republic. At the end of the *calle* is Ponte del Fontego, which takes us back across Rio de San Francesco to Campo Santa Giustina, at the junction of four canals.

The *campo* takes its name from the former church of Santa Giustina, which stands on the northern side of the square. According to tradition, the church was founded in the 7C, though the first documented references to it are from the 12C. The church was rebuilt in the early 16C, and then in 1640 a new facade was added by Baldassare Longhena. The church and its convent were suppressed by the French in 1810. Later in the 19C a large part of the convent was demolished, along with the campanile; then in 1844 the church was converted into a military school. The church and what remains of the convent now house the Liceo Scientifico G. B. Benedetti. The former church still retains its neoclassical Longhena facade, though shorn of the uppermost part above the architrave.

A private bridge crosses Rio de San Francesco from Campo Santa Giustina to the 17C Palazzo Gradenigo. Another private bridge crosses Rio de Santa Giustina from the *campo* to Ca' Zon, built in 1400.

We now cross Rio de Santa Giustina on the bridge of the same name, continuing straight ahead on Calle Zon. At the end of the *calle* on the right we come to Campo Santa Giustina detto (called) de Barbaria. The last part of the name is believed to derive from the wood-shavings, known in Venetian dialect as *barbaria*, or 'beards', that were planed from the boards in the lumberyard here. On the left side of the square as we enter is the little Oratorio della Madonna Addolorata, Our Lady of Sorrows, built in 1829 by a confraternity of the same name.

At the north-west corner of the *campo* Calle de le Capucine leads all the way out to the Fondamente Nove, the seaside promenade that extends along a long stretch of the northern shore of Venice. Near the end of the *calle* we pass on our left the church of Santa Maria del Pianto. The church is dedicated to Santa Maria del Pianto dei Sette Dolori, the Weeping Madonna of the Seven Sorrows. The church and its Capuchin monastery were founded in 1649, and consecrated in 1687. The complex was suppressed in 1810. The monastery now serves as an orphanage, but the church remains closed.

We retrace our steps along Calle de le Capucine to Campo Santa Giustina detto de Barbaria, where we turn right on Calle del Cafetier. This is another of the common street-names of Venice, called after a café that once did business on the *calle*. On the left, at No. 6480, is the 15C Palazzo Bragadin. Over the entrance there is a medallion bust of the heroic General Marcantonio Bragadin (d. 1571). On the wall there is a relief of Daniel in the Lion's Den, believed to be from the demolished church of San Daniele.

We now turn left into Calle Muazzo. At the end of the *calle* we pass through a *sottoportego* to Ponte Muazzo, which crosses Rio de San Giovanni Laterano. The *sottoportego* has taken us through the 16C Case Muazzo, which we now see on the left as we cross the bridge, and beyond them Palazzo Bragadin. On the opposite side of the canal to the left of the bridge is the 15C Palazzo Cappello. After crossing the bridge we continue on Campiello and Ramo Cappello. This brings us to Rio de la Tetta, where we turn right on Fondamenta Seconda San Giovanni Laterano.

Here we see on our right the former convent of San Giovanni in Laterano. The convent was founded in 1504 on the grounds of an oratory belonging to the church of San Giovanni in Laterano in Rome. The complex was rebuilt after a fire in 1573, and then in the second half of the century the convent was reconstructed in its present form, along with the oratory. The complex was suppressed by the French in

1806 and the oratory was partly demolished, while the convent was converted to secular use.

On the other side of the canal we see the 16C Palazzo Dolfin and beyond it the 15C Palazzo Gabrielli. At the end of the *calle* we come again to Rio de San Giovanni Laterano, where a private bridge crosses to Palazzo Morosini, dating from the end of the 15C or the beginning of the 16C. We turn left on Fondamenta San Giovanni Laterano, and then at its end left on Calle Tetta. This takes us across Rio de la Tetta to the *fondamenta* of the same name, which takes us to Ponte Cavagnis, where we turn left to cross Rio de San Severo. This brings us to Fondamenta Cavagnis, where on our left we see a little church of the Evangelican Waldensians. We turn right on the *fondamenta* and then left into Calle de la Madoneta, which turns right at the end of the block. This brings us to Calle Larga San Lorenzo, where we turn right; then at the end we come to Rio de San Severo and on our left the *fondamenta* of the same name. On our right at the corner is Palazzo Donà-Ottoboni, which belonged to the Dona family until 1582 and in the following century was acquired by the Ottoboni. Marco Ottoboni was living here when he became Patriarch of Venice in 1639. His son Pietro, born here in 1610, was elected pope in 1679 as Alexander VIII.

On the other side of the canal, at its junction with Rio de Santa Maria Formosa, is the 16C Palazzo Grimani, its rusticated entrance attributed to Michele Sanmichele. The palace was noted for its frescoes and the collection of ancient sculptures kept here by the Grimani, including the colossal statue of Agrippa now in the courtyard of the Archaeological Museum. King Henry III of France came to the palace to see this collection during his visit to Venice in 1574.

We now turn left on Fondamenta San Severo, passing on our left at the first corner Borgoloco San Lorenzo, where there are two *vere da pozzo* dating from the 13C. We then pass on our right Ponte Novo. Looking across the canal, we see one block beyond the bridge the 15C Palazzo Zorzi-Bon, and beyond that the contiguous Palazzo Zorzi, built at the beginning of the 16C to a design by Mauro Coducci.

At the end of the *fondamenta* we come to Campo San Severo. The *campo* is named for the ancient church of San Severo, demolished in 1839. At the far end of the *campo* is the 15C Palazzo Priuli.

At the end of the *campo* we turn left on Calle dei Preti and then right on Calle Diavolo, which brings us along the east side of Palazzo Priuli to Ponte Diavolo, where we cross Rio de San Provolo. We then turn right on Fondamenta de l'Osmarin, at the end of which we veer half-left on Calle San Provolo and continue on through Campo San Provolo. We then turn right on Calle San Provolo, and then at Ponte San Provolo we turn left through a *sottoportego* into Fondamenta del Vin on the canal of the same name. At the end of the *calle* we turn left and then right into Campiello del Vin, at the end of which we follow the *calle* of the same name out to Riva degli Schiavoni, ending the second of our three strolls through Castello.

SESTIERE DI CASTELLO III (*Map Route 6*)

We begin the third and last of our strolls through Castello in the Piazzetta dei Leoni. From there we walk along Calle de la Canonica to the first corner and turn left on the *ramo* of the same name, crossing Calle Larga San Marco and continuing in the same direction on Calle de l'Anzolo. At the first corner we turn right on Ramo de l'Anzolo, which brings us to Ponte del Remedio and Rio de Palazzo, which is here the boundary between the San Marco and Castello districts.

The palace to the left of the bridge on the far side is Palazzo Soranzo, which is at the junction of Rio del Palazzo and Rio del Mondo Novo. According to Pietro Gradenigo, writing in the 18C, the latter canal and the bridge that crosses it to a *calle* of the same name were named for a tavern called the Mondo Novo, which continues to operate as a trattoria on Salizzada San Lio. Palazzo Soranzo, which dates from the 13–14C, is also called Casa dell'Angelo, because of the relief of the angel on its facade. According to Pietro Gradenigo, the angel was placed there in 1522 as a talisman, after a priest had driven from the house a devil in the form of a pet monkey belonging to the owner.

After crossing the bridge we continue straight ahead on Calle del Remedio, which ends at the *fondamenta* of the same name on Rio de San Zaninovo. Here we turn right on the *fondamenta*, continuing at its end through Sottoportego de la Stua. This brings us into Campo San Zaninovo, where on the left we see the church.

San Zaninovo is Venetian dialect for San Giovanni Nuovo. The actual name of the church is San Giovanni in Oleo – St John in Oil – dedicated to St John the Evangelist, who was martyred in a cauldron of boiling oil. The church was founded in 968; in its present form it dates to a complete rebuilding of 1751–62 to a design by Matteo Lucchesi. The church has now been converted into an art gallery. On the altar is *The Martyrdom of St John the Evangelist in a Cauldron of Boiling Oil* by Francesco Maggiotto. On either side are chiaroscuros by Fabio Canal, depicting the sacrifices of Melchizedek and Isaac.

We leave the *campo* via Sottoportego de la Stua and retrace our steps along Fondamenta del Remedio. At the end of the *fondamenta* we turn right on Ponte Pasqualigo, which is a double bridge, first crossing Rio de San Zaninovo and then bending left to go over Rio de Santa Maria Formosa. This brings us to Campo Querini Stampalia, which is at the junction of Rio de Santa Maria Formosa and Rio del Mondo Novo. The *campiello* takes its name from Palazzo Querini Stampalia, the beautiful palace on the other side of Rio de Santa Maria Formosa, approached by a private bridge just to the left of Ponte Querini.

The *palazzo* was built in 1528 by the Querini. This branch of the family were from the early 14C until 1537 lords of the Aegean isle of Astipalia, known to the Venetians as Stampalia, so that they called themselves the Querini Stampalia. They accumulated an outstanding collection of paintings and other works of art, along with an important library. The last male of the line, Giovanni Querini Stampalia, died in 1869 after having bequeathed all of his possessions to the foundation that has converted the palace into a library and museum.

The Querini Stampalia Library, which is on the first piano nobile of the palace, contains about 300,000 books, 1,638 volumes of manuscripts dating back to the 16C, 99 incunabula (books printed before 1501), 450 old maps and 2,600 prints. The picture gallery is on the second piano nobile, and there is also an exhibition gallery on the ground floor. The picture gallery begins in the Portego, or Great Hall; this and the other rooms and corridors of the gallery, twenty in all, are decorated with stucco and frescoes, with period furniture and objects of art, almost all of the 18C. In Room 1 there is a remarkable series of genre paintings by Gabriele Bella comprising sixty-nine *Scenes of Venetian Public Life*. Among the art works exhibited in the other rooms there are paintings by Giovanni Bellini, Paris Bordone, Palma il Vecchio, Palma il Giovane, Luca Giordano, Giambattista Tiepolo, Sebastiano Bombelli, Gregorio Lazzarini, Antonio Zanchi, Vincenzo Catena, Pietro Vecchia, Sebastiano Ricci, Pietro Longhi, Alessandro Longhi, Nicolò Bambini, Girolamo Forabosco, Bernardo Strozzi and Francesco Maffei. The genre paintings by Pietro Longhi are particularly delightful, evoking the spirit of Venice in the last half-century of the Republic.

The baroque palace to the right of Palazzo Querini Stampalia, between the two public bridges, is the 17C Palazzo Avogadro.

We leave Campiello Querini Stampalia via an alley at its north-east corner, taking us into Campiello Santa Maria Formosa. From there we pass through a sottoportego into Campo Santa Maria Formosa, named for the church whose apse we now pass on the left. Behind the apse there is a *vera da pozzo* with an inscription recording that it was built in

1512; one of the reliefs on its panels shows the Madonna della Misericordia, Our Lady of Mercy. There is another *vera da pozzo* in the centre of the *campo*, dating from the mid 18C.

We now walk around the apse of Santa Maria Formosa and its side entrance on the *campo* to approach the main entrance of the church, which faces Rio de Mondo Novo.

According to tradition, the church was founded in the 7C by St Magnus, Bishop of Oderzo. The saint was inspired by the Virgin, who appeared to him in the guise of a buxom maiden, of the type known in Italian as *formosa*, and so the church came to be called Santa Maria Formosa. The earliest recorded reference to the church is from 1060. The church was rebuilt in a project that began in 1492 under Mauro Coducci, who worked on it until his death in 1504. The present facade facing the canal was completed in 1542, while the one on the *campo* was not finished until 1604. The campanile was rebuilt in the baroque style in 1678–88 by Francesco Zucconi. The main facade facing the canal was commissioned by the Cappello family. The figure standing on the sarcophagus over the main doorway is that of Captain Vincenzo Cappello (d. 1541), by Pietro da Salò.

The first chapel from the rear on the right has on its altar a beautiful triptych, *The Madonna della Misericordia, The Birth of the Virgin* and *The Meeting of St Joachim and St Anna*, signed by Bartolomeo Vivarini and dated 1473. The altarpiece in the second chapel is *The Pietà and St Francis* by Palma il Giovane. Passing into the right transept, we see on the wall to the right *The Last Supper* by Leandro Bassano. The chapel on the left was dedicated by the Guild of Bombardiers to St Barbara, their patron saint. The altarpiece is a polyptych done *c.* 1509 by Palma il Vecchio, showing St Barbara between St Sebastian and St Anthony Abbot, with St Vincent Ferrer and St John the Baptist in the upper panel and a Pietà above.

The high altar in the chancel, with its ciborium carried on four columns of verd-antique, was erected in 1592 by Francesco Smeraldi. Behind the altar is *The Allegory of the*

Foundation of the Church of Santa Maria Formosa by Giulia Lama; on the ceiling above is *The Return of the Brides Captured by the Istrian Pirates*, attributed to Antonio Molinari. The chapel to the left of the chancel was dedicated by the Scuola dei Casselleri, the Guild of the Coffer-makers – they made the chests known as *arcili*, used by brides for their dowries. The chapel to the right of the chancel was dedicated by the Querini family in 1592; the three statues – representing Sts Francis, Lawrence and Sebastian – are attributed to Girolamo Campagna. The chapel in the north transept is dedicated to the Holy Sacrament, with statues of the Redeemer and two adoring angels attributed to Giulio del Moro. The second altar from the front on the left was dedicated by the Guild of Fruit-sellers to their patron saint, St Jehosophat; the altarpiece shows *The Saviour Showing the Blessed Heart to Saints* by Lattanzio Querena.

The building perpendicular to the main facade of the church on its right-hand side, beside Ponte de le Bande, was formerly the Scuola dei Bombardieri (No. 5266). The small building between the main facade of the church and the campanile is the former Scuola della Purificazione (No. 5264); on its facade there is a relief of the Madonna and Child dating from the 15C. The Scuola was founded by the Guild of the Casselleri and was rebuilt in the late 16C.

The Guild of the Casselleri had the privilege of receiving the Doge when he visited their Scuola on the annual Festa delle Marie, celebrated each year on 2 February, the feast-day of the Purification of the Virgin. The origin of this custom dated back to 944, when Doge Pietro Candiano III asked the Guild of the Casselleri what he could give them as a reward for their heroism in rescuing the captured brides (see p.148). Pompeo Molmenti writes of this in his monumental work on Venetian life:

Tradition says that the guild of cofferers took the largest part in the victory and asked for no other reward than that the Doge, on the

Festa delle Marie, should visit the church of Santa Maria Formosa, their parish. The Doge, joking with the frank simplicity of those times, said, 'But what if it is raining, or what if I am athirst?' And the cofferers at once replied, 'We'll give you hats for your heads, and drink to quench your thirst!' The bargain was kept on both sides, and as long as the Republic lasted not a single year passed without the procession of the Doge to Santa Maria Formosa, where he was met by the parish priest, who presented him with gilded straw hats, flasks of malmsey and oranges.

The arch at the base of the campanile has a relief of the most grotesque of all of the city's many *antidiavoli*, also called *mascherone*, monstrous talismanic heads that were purported to drive away the devil. This particular *mascherone* outraged Ruskin:

A head – huge, inhuman, and monstrous – leering in bestial degradation, too foul to be either pictured or described, or to be beheld for more than an instant: yet let it be endured for that instant; for in that head is embodied the type of the evil spirit to which Venice was abandoned in the fourth period of her decline; and it is as well that we should see and feel the full horror of it on this spot . . .

We now walk around the campanile and cross the *campo* to the sottoportego opposite the apse of the church, leading into Calle Secondo dei Orbi. The house on the *campo* just to the left of the *sottoportego* is Palazzo Vitturi (No. 5246), which dates from the second half of the 13C, with windows, capitals, crosses and *paterae* in the Veneto-Byzantine style.

By way of Calle dei Orbi we eventually come to the church of Santa Maria dei Dereletti, known as the Ospedaletto.

The Ospedaletto owes its diminutive suffix to the fact that it is part of the smallest of the four great Venetian hospitals established for the care of *dereletti*, or homeless poor, particularly for orphans and foundlings. The hospital was founded in

February 1528, together with a chapel. As at the Pietà, the schooling of the girls in particular included training in music, and the choir of the Ospedaletto became one of the most renowned in Venice. This influenced the design of the new and larger church which was erected to replace the original chapel. The new church was begun in 1575 to a plan by Palladio. Work proceeded slowly because of a shortage of funds, but then in 1662 a large bequest by Bartolomeo Carnioni brought about a renewal of the project, including an enlargement of the entire institution, with Antonio Sardi and his son Giuseppe responsible for the hospice, and Baldassare Longhena for the facade of the church, which he completed in 1668–74.

The church is entered through the lobby of the hospice, which is now a *casa di riposo* (No. 6691). The rectangular nave has three altars on either side, all of them designed by Longhena. The high altar was built by Antonio Sardi and his son Giuseppe in 1659–65; the ciborium was done in 1668 to a design by Longhena, flanked by two adoring angels carved by Tommaso Ruer. The paintings include works by Giambattista Tiepolo and Palma il Giovane. The hospice is famous for its 17C spiral staircase and its elegant Sala di Musica, adorned with frescoes done in 1776 by Jacopo Guarana.

A few steps to the east of the *casa di riposo* we see a closed-off *sottoportego* that leads into a cul-de-sac called Corte de la Teraza. This is the outer courtyard of what was once Palazzo Magno, dating from the end of the 15C, approached by an outside staircase with three ascending arches decorated with delicate mouldings in a floral pattern. In the courtyard there is an octagonal *vera da pozzo* dating from the late 15C.

We now retrace our steps along Barbaria de le Tole, which beyond the Ospedaletto becomes Salizzada San Zanipolo. This brings us past the south side of the great church of Santi Giovanni e Paolo, known in Venetian as San Zanipolo. The *salizzada* then widens into the L-shaped Campo Santi Giovanni e Paolo, where the main facade of the church overlooks

Rio dei Mendicanti. As we pass the side of the church we come to a particularly beautiful *vera da pozzo*, decorated with reliefs of putti, festoons and 'horse-head' shields, its rim carved with floral designs. The well-head is dated to the early 16C; it originally stood in Palazzo Corner Ca' Grande and was placed here in 1823.

As we approach the front of the *campo* we come to the famous bronze equestrian statue of Bartolomeo Colleoni (d. 1475) of Bergamo, who served the Venetian Republic as a *condottieri*. The monument was begun in 1481 by the Florentine sculptor Andrea del Verrocchio, and after his death in 1488 the work was completed by Alessandro Leopardi.

We now walk over to the front of the *campo* to approach the main entrance to the church of Santi Giovanni e Paolo.

The plot of land on which the church stands was given to the Dominicans in 1234 by Doge Giacomo Tiepolo. The church was dedicated to St John and St Paul, two brothers who had been martyred in Rome in the third century. The original architects were the Dominican fathers Bonviso da Bologna and Nicolò da Imola. The work proceeded slowly, with the apse and cross-vault completed only in 1368, and the church was not consecrated until 1430.

The facade of the church is in the Gothic style; the three tabernacles that crown the pediment contain statues of St Dominic flanked by St Thomas Aquinas on the left and St Peter Martyr on the right. The Gothic porch was designed by Bartolomeo Bon, completed after his death in 1464 by Maestro Domenico and Maestro Luca. The portal is flanked by 13C figures of the Virgin and the Angel of the Annunciation. The porch is flanked by two pairs of sarcophagi, the one just to the left of the door being that of Doge Giacomo Tiepolo (d. 1249) and his son Doge Lorenzo Tiepolo (d. 1275).

The plan of the interior is a Latin cross, with a dome over the crossing, the nave separated from the side aisles by five huge columns on either side supporting a Gothic arcade. On the *controfacciata* wall we see the funerary monuments of three

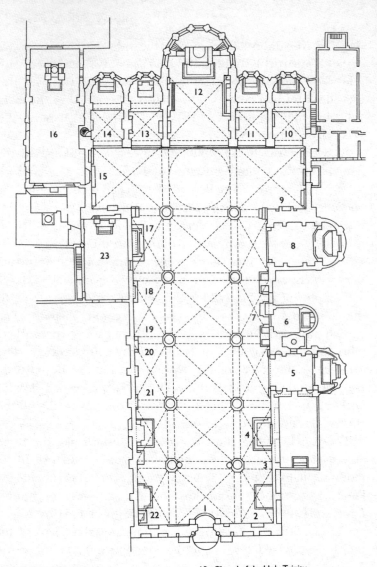

1. Tomb of Alvise Mocenigo I
2. Tomb of Pietro Mocenigo
3. Monument to Marcantonio Bragadin
4. Polyptych by Giovanni Bellini
5. Chapel of the Blessed Giacomo Salomoni
6. Chapel of the Madonna of Peace
7. Valier Mausoleum
8. Chapel of St Dominic, ceiling by G.B. Piazzetta
9. Gothic window
10. Chapel of the Crucifixion
11. Chapel of the Magdalene
12. High Altar, monuments to the Doges M. Morosini,
    L. Loredan, M. Corner and A. Vendramin

13. Chapel of the Holy Trinity
14. Chapel of St Pius V
15. Monuments to A. Venier and Sebastiano Venier
16. Chapel of the Rosary, with paintings by Veronese
17. Panels by Vivarini
18–21. Monuments to the Doges P. Malipiero, M. Steno,
    T. Mocenigo and Nicolò Marcello
22. Monument to Doge G. Mocenigo and to B. Bragadin
23. Sacristy

Santi Giovanni e Paolo

Doges of the Mocenigo family. In the centre is the tomb of Doge Alvise Mocenigo I (d. 1577) and his wife Loredano Marcello, by Giovanni Girolamo Grapiglia, with sculptures attributed to Girolamo Campagna; on the right that of Doge Giovanni Mocenigo (d. 1485), by Tullio Lombardo; on the left that of Doge Pietro Mocenigo (d. 1476), by Pietro Lombardo. At the beginning of the right-hand aisle is the sarcophagus of Doge Raniero Zen (d. 1268).

In the first bay of the right aisle is the funerary monument of Marcantonio Bragadin, attributed to Vincenzo Scamozzi, with a bust of the deceased by Tiziano Aspetti. Bragadin's bust surmounts an urn that stands in front of a lead coffin containing his meagre remains, the skin that was flayed from him by the Turks in 1571 after he surrendered the Venetian fortress at Famagusta in Cyprus. The second altar is dedicated to St Vincent Ferrer, who is depicted in the central panel of a magnificent polyptych by Giovanni Bellini dated c. 1465. The third bay opens into the Chapel of the Blessed Giacomo Salamoni, whose remains are contained in a reliquary on the altar.

The fourth bay contains the huge Valier Mausoleum, designed in the baroque style in 1708 by Andrea Tirali. The statue in the centre represents Doge Bertucci Valier (d. 1658), flanked on the left by his son, Doge Silvestro Valier (d. 1700), and on the right by the Dogaressa Elisabetha Querini (d. 1708). The archway on the right at the base of the monument opens into the Chapel of the Madonna della Pace, so called from the sacred Byzantine icon of the *Virgin and Child* on the altar. The chapel was originally dedicated to St Hyacinth, who is depicted in a painting on the left wall by Leandro Bassano. On the right wall is *The Flagellation* by Antonio Vassilacchi and on the ceiling is *The Eternal Father* by Palma il Giovane.

The fifth bay opens into the Chapel of St Dominic, designed in 1690 by Andrea Tirali; in the vault there is a painting of *St Dominic in Glory*, done in 1727 by Giambattista

Piazzetta, who also did the four roundels depicting the Cardinal Virtues. On the walls there are six reliefs in bronze illustrating periods in the life of St Dominic by Giuseppe Mazza, as well as one carved in wood by Giovanni Battista Meduna. The fresco in the apse of the chapel shows *St Dominic among the Saints around the Virgin* by Girolamo Brusaferro.

We now enter the right transept, where we see the great Gothic window with stained glass made in Murano in the second half of the 15C from cartoons by Bartolomeo Vivarini, Girolamo Mocetto and Cima da Conegliano. Below the window is a memorial to Captain Dionigi Naldi da Brisighella (d. 1510), with a statuette of the deceased by Lorenzo Bregno. The memorial is flanked by two Renaissance altars; the altarpiece on the one to the right, *St Antonino of Florence Enthroned*, was done by Lorenzo Lotto in 1542. On the right-hand wall of the transept is a beautiful painting of *Christ Bearing the Cross*, done in 1474 by Alvise Vivarini. Beside it is *The Coronation of the Virgin*, attributed to Cima da Conigliano.

The first of the two apsidal chapels to the right of the chancel was dedicated by the Confraternity of St Jerome, who looked after those who were condemned to death. The black marble altar is a work of Alessandro Vittoria, who also made the bronze group of the Grieving Madonna and St John the Baptist. On the right is the memorial of Edward Winsor, an English baron who died in Venice in 1574, attributed to Alessandro Vittoria.

At the centre of the apse is the baroque high altar, attributed to Baldassare Longhena. On the right-hand wall just inside the pilaster is the funerary monument of Doge Michele Morosini (d. 1382), by an unknown master of the Tuscan school at the beginning of the 15C. Next to this is the monument of Doge Leonardo Loredan (d. 1521), by Giovanni Grapiglia; the statue of the Doge is by Girolamo Campagna. Doge Francesco Loredan (d. 1762) is buried in the tomb at the foot of the monument. On the left-hand wall of the chancel just inside the pilaster is the monument of Doge Marco Corner (d. 1368). Next to it is the monument of Doge Andrea Vendramin (d. 1478) by Tullio Lombardo. The second chapel to the left of the chancel has on its left wall the monument of Doge Giovanni Dolfin (d. 1361).

Beneath the large clock in the end wall of the left transept is the monument of Doge Antonio Venier (d. 1400), attributed to the Dalle Masegne. To the right of the doorway leading to the Chapel of the Rosary is a bronze statue, by Antonio dal Zotto, of Doge Sebastiano Venier (d. 1578), who commanded the Venetian contingent at the battle of Lepanto. The Chapel of the Rosary opens off the end of the transept; this is also known as the Lepanto Chapel, because it was dedicated to the Madonna of the Rosary in thanksgiving after the victory at Lepanto. The gilded ceiling encloses four large paintings that are considered to be among the finest works of Paolo Veronese: *The Adoration of the Shepherds*, *The Assumption*, *The Annunciation* and, above the altar, *The Adoration of the Magi*. On the back wall there is another version of *The Adoration of the Shepherds*, also by Veronese.

On the wall of the first bay from the front in the left aisle there are three panels, from a polyptych, depicting Sts Lawrence, Augustine and Dominic, signed by Bartolomeo Vivarini and dated 1499.

Just beyond the door of the sacristy, now closed for restoration, we come to the first of a succession of funerary monuments, that of Doge Pasquale Malipiero (d. 1462) by Pietro Lombardo. Next is the monument of Senator Giambattista Bonzio (d. 1518), attributed to Giovanni Maria Mosca; at either side of the double arch below are statues of St Thomas Aquinas and St Peter Martyr attributed to Antonio Lombardo. Beyond this is the tomb of Doge Michele Steno (d. 1413). Within the arcade to the left of this is the tomb of Alvise Trevisan (d. 1528) by Giovanni Maria Mosca. Above is the gilded wood equestrian monument of Captain Pompeo

Giustiniani (d. 1616), known as Ironfist, a work of Francesco Terilli. Beneath the monument there are three historical tablets, the central one noting that Doge Giovanni Dandolo (d. 1289) is buried in the adjoining cloister. Next is the monument of Doge Tommaso Mocenigo (d. 1423), signed by Pietro Lamberti. Following this is the monument of Doge Nicolò Marcello (d. 1474) by Pietro Lombardo. The coat of arms and the tablet to the left of the monument commemorate Doge Marino Zorzi (d. 1312), who is also buried in the adjoining cloister. In the last bay is a Renaissance altar done in 1524 by Guglielmo Bergamasco. On the altar is a statuette of St Jerome, carved in 1576 by Alessandro Vittoria, who also did the relief of the Virgin Received into Heaven.

The northern side of the *campo* is taken up by the former Scuola di San Marco, whose Renaissance facade in polychrome marble makes a striking contrast with the red-brick Gothic front of Santi Giovanni e Paolo.

The Scuola di San Marco was one of the six Scuole Grandi of Venice, built in 1260 by a powerful confraternity that included many of the leading dignitaries of the Republic. The building was taken over in 1437 by the Dominicans, who enlarged it and converted it into a monastery. The original structure was badly damaged by fire in 1485, after which the Dominicans commissioned a new building, designed by Pietro Lombardo; the construction was supervised by Giovanni Buora in 1486–90, and from 1490 to 1495 by Mauro Coducci, who completed the project. The building was greatly enlarged to the rear by Jacopo Sansovino between 1533 and 1546, and a hospice dedicated to St Lazarus added in the 17C. After the suppression of the monastery in 1807 the complex was converted into a public hospital, the Ospedale Civile.

The main facade of the building remains essentially as it was designed by Pietro Lombardo, with the lunettes added by Mauro Coducci. The monumental main entrance, its pedestals decorated with reliefs of dancing children, is by Giovanni Buora; the painted relief in the lunette of the upper arch shows St Mark venerated by the Brothers, and the statue above represents Charity, both works dated *c.* 1445 and attributed to Bartolomeo Bon. The four relief panels below are by the Lombardo school; these are two lions, symbols of the Scuola di San Marco, flanking the main entrance, and, to the right, on either side of the smaller door, two episodes from the life of St Mark, the Baptism and the Healing of St Ananius.

Here we make a detour along Fondamenta dei Mendicanti, which extends along the side of the hospital all the way out to Fondamente Nove. Some 200 m along the *fondamenta* we come to the church of San Lazzaro dei Mendicanti. The name Mendicanti comes from that of the mendicant friars who founded the Hospice of St Lazarus in 1601. This was one of the four Ospedali Maggiori of Venice; like the other three, it was famous for its music school, where Vivaldi's father taught violin between 1689 and 1693. The cloisters of the hospice and the core of the church were designed by Vincenzo Scamozzi and completed in 1631. The church was consecrated in 1636, though its canal-side facade, designed by Giuseppe Sardi, was not finished until 1673. The main door is rarely open, and those who enter the church generally do so from inside the grounds of the hospital. The most notable paintings in the church are *Christ on the Cross, with the Virgin and St John*, which is almost certainly by Veronese; and *St Ursula and the Eleven Thousand Virgins* by Jacopo Tintoretto.

We now retrace our steps along Fondamenta dei Mendicanti, passing on the other side of the canal a picturesque old *squero* that still makes and repairs gondolas. As we re-enter Campo Santi Giovanni e Paolo we pass on our right Ponte Cavallo, which crosses Rio dei Mendicanti into the Sestiere di Cannaregio. The house just to the right on the other side of the bridge has a fine relief of the Annunciation dating from the mid 17C, attributed to either Melchiore Barthel or Giusto Le Court.

We walk diagonally across the *campo* and enter Calle

Brassana, from where we follow a tortuous route back to Campo Santa Maria Formosa. Turning right and walking along the east side of the *campo*, the first building we pass, at No. 6129, has on its facade a plaque noting that this was the home of Doge Sebastiano Venier, the hero of Lepanto. Just beyond this, at No. 6126, we pass the first section of the 14C Palazzo Donà, whose other section, entered at No. 6121, continues along the remainder of the east side of the *campo* and the street beyond, Ramo Borgoloco. The entrance to the first section of the palace has a Gothic doorway with two putti supporting a coat of arms, with a pretty relief in the lunette dating from the 15C. At the north end of the *campo*, just to the left of the beginning of Ramo Borgoloco, is the splendid Palazzo Ruzzini-Priuli (No. 5866). The palace was built in 1580 by Bartolomeo Monopola for the Ruzzini family, first mentioned in a Venetian document dated 994. The family produced one Doge, Carlo Ruzzini (1732–35), who owned the *palazzo* but did not live there.

We pass between Palazzo Ruzzini-Priuli and Palazzo Donà and cross Rio del Pestrin on Ponte Borgoloco. The *palazzetto* just to the left of the bridge on its far side dates from the late 16C or early 17C. As we continue straight ahead on Ramo Borgoloco we pass the left side of the *palazzetto*, which is corbelled out over the sidewalk on *barbacani*.

At the end of the *ramo* we come to the court known as Borgoloco Pompeo Molmenti, named for the distinguished historian of Venice. We continue through the left side of the court to enter Calle de Borgoloco, which leads to Rio del Piombo and Ponte Marcello. Just before reaching the bridge we pass on our right the land-entrance to the 14C Palazzo Marcello-Pindemonte-Papadopoli, which has canal-side facades on both Rio del Piombo and Rio Santa Marina. Doge Nicolò Marcello was born here in 1397. This palace later passed to the Pindemonte, a noble family from Verona, who rebuilt it in 1630–35, with a new facade on Rio Santa Marina attributed to Baldassare Longhena. In 1808 it was purchased and redecorated by the Counts Papadopoli-Aldobrandini.

We cross Ponte Marcello, and then we continue straight ahead on Calle Marcello into Campo Santa Marina. This pretty *campo* is named for the demolished church of Santa Marina, which actually stood in the *campiello* of that name, approached via the street that leads off from the north-western corner of the square to Rio Santa Marina. The church was founded in the second half of the 11C. Doge Michele Steno (d. 1413) and Doge Nicolò Marcello (d. 1474) were both buried in Santa Marina, but when the church was suppressed in 1818 their funerary monuments were removed to Santi Giovanni e Paolo. After the suppression of the church it served for a time as a wine shop, until it was finally demolished in 1820. The Venetian historian Emanuele Cicogna, writing in the 1820s, recalls the blasphemous attitude of the waiters in the church-turned-wine shop, who would call out to the tavern-keeper: 'A jug in the chapel of the Madonna; another jug at the altar of the Holy Sacrament!'

There are two *vere da pozzo* in the *campo* and a third in the *campiello*, all of them dating from the 14–15C. One of the well-heads in the *campo* has a relief of St Marina. On the northern side of the *campo* is the 15C Palazzo Dolfin (No. 6073).

We leave Campo Santa Marina via its south-west corner, where we turn left and then almost immediately right through a *sottoportego* into Calle Scaleta. Then at the first corner we turn left through another *sottoportego*, which brings us into Corte Spechiera, where there is a 15C *vera da pozzo*. We leave the court through a *sottoportego* at its far end, after which we turn left and then immediately right into Calle del Pistor. This brings us to Ponte del Pistor, where looking along the *fondamenta* to the right we see the canal-side facade of Palazzo Cavazza, a Gothic palace built in 1461. Crossing the bridge to the beginning of Calle Carminati, the first building that we pass on the left is the 16C Palazzo Carminati (No. 5663), with the family coat of arms on the facade. At the end of the *calle* we come to Campo San Lio, where there is a *vera da pozzo* dated by an inscription to 1572. On the left side of the *campo* we come to the church of San Lio.

The original church on this site was founded in the 9C by the Badoer family, who dedicated it to St Catherine. Then in 1054 it was rebuilt and re-dedicated to the canonized Pope Leo IX (1049–54), who had espoused the cause of Venice in the disputes between the Patriarchs of Grado and Aquileia. At the beginning of the 16C the church was reconstructed by Pietro Lombardo and his son Tullio. It was rebuilt again in a project that was completed in 1619, and in the middle of that century its campanile was demolished. The church was restored in 1783, producing the plain and unadorned facade we see today, with only the classical doorway remaining from the early-16C structure.

The fresco on the ceiling shows *St Leo (Pope Leo IX) in Glory* and *The Exaltation of the Cross*, painted in 1783 by Giandomenico Tiepolo, who also did the monochrome panels depicting angels and the Cardinal Virtues. To the right of the chancel is the Cappella Gussoni, created at the beginning of the 16C by Pietro and Tullio Lombardo. The altarpiece on the high altar is *The Dead Christ Sustained by Angels* by Palma il Giovane. On the left wall of the chancel there is a large *Crucifixion* by Pietro Vecchia; the fresco on the ceiling is *Elijah and the Angel*, attributed to Pietro Moro. On the first altar from the front on the left there is a painting of *The Coronation of the Virgin*, a work dating from the second half of the 16C that shows traces of Titian's hand. On the second altar from the front on the left side there is a depiction of the Apostle James, done by Titian in the 1540s. On the ceiling there are monochrome frescoes by Giandomenico Tiepolo, depicting *St Leo in Glory* and the *Exaltation of the Cross*.

We leave the *campo* at its south-western corner via Calle de la Fava. At the end of the *calle* we turn right and then immediately left to enter Campo de la Fava, which opens on to the Rio de la Fava and the bridge of the same name, dominated on its east side by the church of the Fava. Fava means 'broad bean', and the *calle, campo,* canal, bridge and church take their names from the fact that sacks of dried beans were unloaded here from barges in times past.

The actual name of the church is Santa Maria della Consolazione, founded at the end of the 15C as an oratory. At the beginning of the 18C the oratory was demolished, and plans for a new and larger church were drawn up by Antonio Gaspari. The church was completed in 1750, the final phase of the construction being directed by Giorgio Massari.

Between the pillars on the sides of the nave there are eight niches with statues of the Evangelists and saints by Giuseppe Bernardi, called il Torretto. The altarpiece on the first altar from the rear on the right shows the *Virgin and Child with St Anne and St Joachim,* done in 1732 by Giambattista Tiepolo. On the second altar is *The Visitation* by Jacopo Amigoni. On the third altar is *The Virgin and Child with Blessed Gregorio Barbarigo,* done in 1762 by Giambettino Cignaroli. The high altar in the chancel is flanked by statues of two adoring angels, by Gian Maria Morleiter. On the first altar from the front on the left is a *Crucifixion* attributed to Gregorio Lazzarini. On the second altar there is an outstanding painting showing *The Virgin and Child in Prayer with St Philip Neri* by Giambattista Piazzetta. The altarpiece on the third altar is *The Virgin and Child with St Frances of Sales* by Jacopo Amigoni.

We leave the *campo* at its south-east corner via Calle drio la Fava, which turns to the right and then left to bring us to Ramo Licini. There on the right we pass the entrance to Corte Rubbi, where there is a 14C *vera da pozzo*. At the far end of the *ramo* we enter Corte Licini, which we cross to pass through a *sottoportego* of the same name. Following this we turn left into Calle de le Malvasia, at the end of which we veer left and then turn right into Corte Perina. On the house at No. 5485 there is a plaque recording that this was the home of the painter Antonio Canal, known as il Canaletto (1697–1768). In the centre of the court there is an elegant *vera da pozzo* dating from the early 15C.

We leave the court at its north-west corner via Calle de l'Oratorio, after which we turn right on Calle dei Preti, turning right again at its end on to Calle del Cafetier. At the end of the *calle* we emerge on Salizzada San Lio, just opposite the apse of the church of San Lio. Just behind the church, at Nos. 5662–72, we see one of the oldest houses in Venice, dating from the 13C, with a Gothic arch at the centre of the building leading to its entrance on Calle de le Vele.

We now turn right on Salizzada San Lio, which we follow as far as the fourth corner on the left after Calle de le Vele; there we turn left under a Gothic archway into Calle del Paradiso, which ends at a bridge of the same name over Rio del Mondo Novo. The *calle* and bridge take their name from that of the surrounding neighbourhood, which in times past was known as Paradiso, so called because of the splendid illuminations that the locals created after sunset on Good Fridays to celebrate the coming of Easter. This is one of the oldest byways of Venice, with all the houses along it on both sides corbelled out on *barbacani* and framed at both ends in Gothic arches. An inscription records that the houses were built in 1407 for the abbot of the monastery of Santa Maria della Pomposa near Ravenna.

At the end of the *calle* we cross the canal on Ponte del Paradiso and come to Fondamenta del Dose, where we turn back to look at the beautiful Gothic archway above the alleyway. The archway dates from the beginning of the 15C; in the lunette there is a relief of the Madonna della Misericordia, flanked by the coats of arms of the Foscari and Mocenigo families. To the right of the archway is Casa Foscari-Mocenigo, a 13C Gothic palace, with its piano nobile adorned with a Veneto-Byzantine triforium, or three-light window, to which a fourth opening in the Byzantine style has been added.

The house on the *fondamenta* at No. 5879 has over its doorway a relief with the turbaned head of an old man, presumably a Turk. Antonio Vivaldi lived in this house from 1722 until 1730.

We now cross Rio del Pestrin on Ponte dei Preti, where we turn right on the *fondamenta* of the same name along Rio del Mondo Novo. At the end of the *fondamenta* we pass Ponte del Mondo Novo and turn left to enter Campo Santa Maria Formosa once again. We walk around the church and veer right across the *campo* to its south-eastern corner, where we cross Rio de Santa Maria Formosa on Ponte Ruga Giuffa. The splendid palace to the right of the bridge on its far side is Palazzo Malipiero-Trevisan, dating from the first half of the 16C.

After crossing the bridge we continue straight ahead on Ruga Giuffa, at the end of which we turn right and almost immediately left into Calle Rota. At the end of the first stretch of the *calle*, where it turns to the left, we pass on our left Corte Rota, where there is a *vera da pozzo* of the 13–14C. We follow Calle Rota as it bends right and then almost immediately left to go through a *sottoportego*. A few steps farther along we cross Rio de San Provolo on Ponte dei Carmini, after which we turn right on Fondamenta de l'Osmarin and then veer left into Calle San Provolo. This brings us through a *sottoportego* into Campo San Provolo, at the far end of which we veer left across Calle San Provolo and pass through another *sottoportego* into Corte Nova. At the end of the *corte* we turn right and then left into Campiello del Vin, at the end of which we continue on into Calle del Vin. This brings us out on to Riva degli Schiavone, where we end our third and last stroll through Castello.

[8] Sestiere di Cannaregio

The name of this area, the north-western part of Venice, was originally *regione delle canne*, the district of bamboo, or the cane break, after the thicket of overgrown marshes on which it was first built up, a primitive landscape that one can still see on the undeveloped islets of the lagoon.

SESTIERE DI CANNAREGIO I (*Map Route 7*)

We begin our first stroll – of three – on the San Marco side of the Rialto Bridge, from where we walk north for a short way on Fondamenta Tragheto del Buso. This takes its name from an ancient *traghetto* station that took passengers across the Grand Canal just above the bridge. Thomas Coryat mentions this *traghetto* in his description of Venice, writing that 'the boatmen that attend at this ferry are the most vicious and licentious varlets about all the City'.

At the end of the *fondamenta* we turn right on Calle del Fontego dei Tedeschi, at the end of which we then turn left on the *salizzada* of the same name. At the end of the block we come to Rio del Fontego dei Tedeschi, which here forms the boundary between the *sestieri* of San Marco and Cannaregio.

We cross the canal on Ponte de l'Olio, the Bridge of Oil, so called because shipments of olive oil were once unloaded and stored at warehouses here. After crossing the bridge we continue straight ahead on Salizzada San Giovanni Grisostomo. Then at the corner on the right beyond Corte Civran we come to the church of San Giovanni Crisostomo.

The original church on this site was founded in the 11C and dedicated to St John Chrysostom. This was destroyed by fire in 1475 and replaced by a new church erected in 1497–1504 by Mauro Coducci.

The first altar from the rear on the right side has a beautiful painting, *Sts Jerome, Christopher and Louis of Toulouse*, signed by Giovanni Bellini and dated 1513. The altarpiece on the second altar is *The Transit of St Joseph* by Carl Loth. On the high altar in the chancel there is an outstanding painting of *Sts John the Baptist, Liberale, Mary Magdalene and Catherine*, done *c.* 1509 by Sebastiano del Piombo. The chapel to the left of the chancel has on its altar a painting of *The Crucifixion and Saints* by Bartolomeo Letterini. The first altar from the front on the left has a superb marble relief showing the Coronation of the Virgin among the Apostles, signed by Tullio Lombardo and dated 1500–1502. On the last altar there is a painting of St Anthony of Padua by a follower of Alvise Vivarini.

We continue along the *salizzada*, passing on our right Campo San Giovanni Grisostomo, in which there is a *vera da pozzo* of the late 15C, decorated at its corners with four lion heads.

At the far end of the *campo* we make a short detour to the left on Corte de la Stua, which at its end opens on the right into Corte del Remer; from there a *sottoportego* leads to Campiello del Remer, a court on the Grand Canal. The *corte* and *campiello* are courtyards of Palazzo Lion-Morosini, a Veneto-Byzantine palace of the 13C. There is an outside Gothic stairway of the palace in Corte de Remer; in the centre of the courtyard there is a 13C *vera da pozzo* in pink Verona marble.

Returning to the *salizzada*, we follow it along its last stretch to Ponte San Giovanni Grisostomo, which we cross to Campiello Flaminio Corner. We turn left from the *campiello* into Calle Dolfin and then right into Campiello Riccardo Selvatico, at the end of which we continue straight ahead on the second stretch of Calle Dolfin. Calle Dolfin ends at Rio dei Santi Apostoli, where we see an ancient stela with an inscription on both sides. On the landward side it states that no one shall sell bread who is not a member of the Arte di Pistori, the Guild of Bakers, while on the other side it warns gondoliers not to transport loaves that are not made by members of the guild.

Here we turn left into the arcaded Sottoportego Falier, which takes us along the canal to Ponte dei Santi Apostoli. There we make a brief excursion into the alleyway to the left of the bridge, which leads into Corte Leon Bianco. This is the courtyard of Ca' Da Mosto, an ancient Veneto-Byzantine palace whose main facade is on the Grand Canal. The most famous of the family who originally dwelt here was Captain Alvise da Mosto, who in 1465 was the first European to sail around Cape Verde in Africa. From the latter part of the 16C until the late 18C the *palazzo* served as a luxurious hostelry known as the Albergo del Leon Bianco. Among the royal guests who stayed there were the Emperor Joseph II, in 1769 and 1775, and the Russian Grand Duke Paul Petrovich and his wife, the future Tsar and Tsarina of Russia, who in 1782 registered under the pseudonyms of 'the Count and Countess of the North'.

We now cross Ponte dei Santi Apostoli, pausing on the bridge to look back on the historic building under which we passed in Sottoportego Falier. This is Palazzo Falier, a Gothic palace dating from the second half of the 13C. This was the home of Marin Falier up until the time of his election as Doge in mid-September 1354, the third and last of his family to hold that office. Marin Falier's reign lasted less than a year; he was deposed on 16 April 1355, immediately after the failure of his insane plot to extinguish the nobility of Venice, and on the following day he was beheaded, after which his palace was confiscated by the Republic. The Veneto-Byzantine windows at the centre of the facade date from the 13–14C, as do the four panels of Byzantine reliefs.

On the other side of the bridge we come to Campo dei

Santi Apostoli, where there is a 17C *vera da pozzo*. On the north side of the *campo* is the church of the Santi Apostoli, whose main facade is on the west side of the square just before the beginning of Strada Nova.

Santi Apostoli was founded in the 9C. The church was radically rebuilt *c.* 1570–75, probably by Alessandro Vittoria, and half a century later the campanile was reconstructed by Andrea Tirali.

The frescoes on the ceiling were done in 1748 by Fabio Canal; in the great central panel are *The Communion of the Apostles* and *The Exaltation of the Host*, with the Evangelists in the four ovals. At the rear of the nave on either side of the door are two holy-water stoups with statuettes by Giacomo Piazzetta, one of St Peter and the other of St John the Baptist. Off the right side of the nave is the large domed Cappella Corner, built at the end of the 15C by Mauro Coducci for Queen Caterina Cornaro of Cyprus, who was buried here in 1510, to be reinterred in the church of San Salvatore *c.* 1580. On the walls are two Lombardesque tombs made for relatives of the queen: her father Marco Corner (d. 1511) and her brother Giorgio Corner (d. 1540). On the altar is *The Communion of St Lucy* by Giambattista Tiepolo, 1746-8

On the second altar is *The Birth of the Virgin*, by Giovanni Contarini. The chapel to the right of the chancel is decorated with the remnants of 14C frescoes in the Byzantine style, depicting *The Descent from the Cross* and *Mourning for Christ in the Sepulchre*; on the altar there is a relief of St Sebastian by Tullio Lombardo.

On the right wall of the chancel is a huge painting of *The Last Supper*, done in 1583 by Cima da Conegliano; on the left wall is *The Fall of Manna*, from the workshop of Paolo Veronese. The altarpiece in the chapel to the left of the chancel is *The Guardian Angel* by Francesco Maffei, commissioned by a donor in thanksgiving for having been rescued in a shipwreck. On the third altar from the front on the left is a painting of *The Virgin and Child with Sts Joseph, John the Baptist and Anthony* by Gaspare Diziani. On the fourth altar there is a depiction of *St Catherine and Three Saints* by Domenico Maggiotto.

The handsome building on the canal beside the bridge is the former Scuola dell'Angelo Custode (No. 4443), begun in 1713 by Andrea Tirali. The marble group of the Guardian Angel over the entrance is by Heinrich Meyring. When the Fontego dei Tedesci was suppressed in 1812 the German Protestants began to use this building for their religious services; now it serves as an Evangelical Lutheran church. The church has two paintings from the Fontego dei Tedeschi: *The Madonna in Glory with the Archangel Michael* by Sebastiano Ricci and *Christ in Benediction*, in the manner of Titian.

We now walk around behind the church into Campiello drio la Chiesa, where there is a *vera da pozzo* of the 14–15C. At the far end of the *campiello* we turn right into Calle del Manganer, and at its end we turn right and then immediately left into Campiello de la Cason. Doge Agnello Partecipazio (811–27) lived in a palace on this *campiello* before the completion of the first Palazzo Ducale.

We leave the *campiello* at its north-east corner through a *sottoportego* that leads into Calle del Volto o de la Cason, after which we turn left on Calle del Tragheto. At the first corner on the left, the house at No. 4571 is supposed to occupy part of the site of the ancient Palazzo Partecipazio. In 1661 it became the home of the painter Pietro Muttoni, known as della Vecchia, and later it housed a little theatre.

After crossing Rio Terà Santi Apostoli we continue straight ahead on Calle Larga dei Proverbi, the Wide Street of the Proverbs. The *calle* takes its name from a proverb that was inscribed on the cornice of a now-vanished house along the street: '*Chi semina spine non vadi descalzo*', 'The man who casts thorns should not go barefoot'.

Just beyond the first turning on the left, the house at No. 4564 has a fine brick doorway dating from the 13C; beside it there is a *patera* of the 11C that may once have served as the grille of a circular window.

At the end of the *calle* we turn left on Salizzada del Pistor, where the first two buildings on the left are *palazzi* of the early 16C. This brings us into the extension of the *campo* in front of Santi Apostoli, where on the right we see the 16C Palazzo Corner (No. 4438).

We now turn right to start down Strada Nova, a broad avenue created in 1868–71. At the beginning of the avenue we pass on our left the garden of Palazzo Mangilli-Valmarana-Smith (No. 4392), whose main facade is on the Grand Canal. During the second quarter of the 18C the palace was acquired by Joseph Smith (1682–1774), an Englishman who had lived in Venice since he was eighteen and who in 1744 was appointed as George III's consular representative with the Republic. In 1743 Smith commissioned the engraver Antonio Visentini to design a new facade for the *palazzo*, a project that was not completed until 1751. Smith acted as agent for several artists, including Canaletto, Rosalba Carriera, Francesco Zuccarelli and the brothers Marco and Sebastiano Ricci. His collection of Canaletto's works alone included fifty paintings and 140 drawings, most of which were acquired by George III when financial pressures forced Smith to sell off his collection, including his books, which formed the nucleus of the King's Library.

Continuing along Strada Nova we come to Campo Santa Sofia, which opens out to the Grand Canal. Opposite the *campo* on the right is the church of Santa Sofia, its facade obscured by the houses in front of it.

According to tradition, the church was founded towards the end of the 9C, though the earliest reference to it is dated 1020. In its present form it dates from a rebuilding in the late 17C by Antonio Gaspari. The church was suppressed in 1810, but reopened in 1836.

The four statues flanking the entrance and the chancel represent Sts Luke, Andrew, Cosmas and Damian; they date from the second half of the 15C and are in the style of Antonio Rizzo. The altarpiece on the high altar is *The*

Baptism of Christ by Daniel Heintz; on the walls of the chancel are two paintings by the school of Bassano: *Christ Mocked* and *The Adoration of the Magi.* In the sacristy there is a fragmentary 15C Gothic sculpture of the Virgin, possibly by Bartolomeo Bon.

In the middle of Campo Santa Sofia there is a *vera da pozzo* with an inscription dating it to 1785. At the end of the *campo* on the Grand Canal is the station of the Santa Sofia *traghetto.* This is one of the oldest *traghetto* stations in Venice, its guild of gondoliers founded in the 12C.

One block beyond Santa Sofia we turn right off Strada Nova on Calle Priuli. The Scuola dei Pittori, or Guild of Painters, built their guildhall at the entrance to this *calle* in 1572, but now all that remains is the coat of arms of the confraternity on the pillar at the right of the entrance. The *calle* bends right and then left before bringing us into Campiello Priuli. There on the left we pass the entrance to Palazzo Priuli (No. 4011), built in 1572.

We now cross Ponte Priuli and then turn right on Fondamenta Priuli, which after one block crosses Rio de la Guerra and goes on into an arcaded *sottoportego* in front of an ancient Gothic palace. This is Palazzo Benedetti, one of the oldest palaces in Venice. The noble family who built it ended with Vincenzo Benedetti, who was murdered in the palace by thieves one night in 1658.

At the end of the *sottoportego* we turn left into Ruga Do Pozzi, the Street of Two Wells. The street is named for the two *vere da pozzo* that stand along its central axis, both of them dating from the second half of the 18C. At the end of the street we cross Ponte Sant'Andrea, after which we continue straight ahead on Calle Zanardi. At Nos. 4132–3 we pass an elegant gateway marking the entrance to Palazzo Zanardi. The palace was built by a *cittadini* family named Rizzo, from whom it was purchased in the second quarter of the 17C by Zan Andrea Zanardi, a shop-boy who became wealthy by selling a type of spice cake eaten at the festival of the Ascension. Zan Andrea's sons contributed 100,000 ducats to the Republic in 1653 in order to have the family admitted to the nobility.

At the end of Calle Zanardi we cross Ponte Santa Caterina, after which we turn left on Fondamenta de Santa Caterina. Midway along the *fondamenta* we pass on the right the former church and convent of Santa Caterina (No. 4941), which now houses a school. The convent was founded in the 11–12C. The present church dates from a rebuilding in the mid 15C.

At the end of the *fondamenta* we turn right on Calle Longa Santa Caterina, which takes us along the western side of the cloister and then on to Fondamente Nove. Here we turn left and make a short excursion to the end of the *fondamenta*, where we pause for a moment to take in the view, which opens up to the west and south across the large rectangular bay called Sacca de la Misericordia. Directly across the bay, on its north-western corner, we see Casino degli Spiriti, the House of Spirits, completely isolated by its surrounding gardens at the edge of the lagoon. The Casino was part of the 16C Palazzo Contarini del Zaffo, designed as a pleasure-dome for entertainments at the palace, the *'spiriti'* meaning high-spirited guests, not ghosts, though in the nearly two centuries since the fall of the Republic the lonely building has acquired the reputation of being haunted.

We now retrace our steps along Fondamente Nove, a walkway laid out along the northern lagoon shore of the city in 1589. From here we have a view north across the lagoon to Isola di San Michele, the cemetery-isle of Venice, and beyond that to the island of Murano.

We turn right off the *fondamenta* on to Calle Marco Foscarini, at the far end of which we pass through Campiello Sant'Antonio before turning left on Fondamenta Zen. This brings us past the Palazzi Zen (Nos. 4922–5), three contiguous Renaissance palaces built in the first half of the 16C by Francesco Zen (d. 1538), a nobleman who studied architecture as a hobby.

At the next corner we turn left into Campo del Gesuiti, named for the beautiful church at the far end of its right side. The rest of the right side of the *campo* between Rio de Santa Caterina and the church is formed by the facade of the Caserma Manin, a former military barracks that was originally the convent of the Gesuiti. The left side of the *campo* is defined first by the western side of the Palazzi Zen, then beyond that by the Oratorio dei Crociferi, and then opposite the church by several buildings that once served as guildhalls. Before we go on to look at these buildings in more detail we will first walk over to Ponte dei Gesuiti, which crosses the canal of the same name at the southern end of the *campo*. The building just to the left of the bridge on the other side of the canal has on its facade a large relief of the Madonna della Misericordia. The six lion heads under the Madonna are part of the coat of arms of Tommaso Carazza, whose bequest in 1495 provided the funds for building this and the other houses that extend along the south bank of the canal.

In the middle of the *campo* by the bridge there is a *vera da pozzo* dated by an inscription to 1527, with a relief representing St Francis.

On the left side of the *campo* a *sottoportego* passes between the Palazzi Zen and the Oratorio dei Crociferi, leading us into Corte de le Candele. In the centre of the court there is a *vera da pozzo* of pink Verona marble dating from *c.* 1500.

Returning to the *campo*, we now go on to look at the Oratorio dei Crociferi, the Oratory of the Cross-bearers, founded *c.* 1150. The Crociferi, who received great support from Doge Raniero Zen (1253–68), also built a hospice on the other side of the *campo*. The oratory was renovated in the late 16C through the support of Doge Pasquale Cicogna (1585–95), who commissioned Palma il Giovane to adorn it with a series of paintings illustrating the history of the Crociferi. The building was restored after the *acqua alta* of 1966 and reopened in 1985. The cycle of paintings in the oratory were done by Palma il Giovane in the years 1583–92. The paintings on the walls show the foundation of the Order of the Crociferi and incidents involving its patrons, Doges Raniero Zen and Pasquale Cicogna. Over the two doors are *The Flagellation* and *The Deposition*. The central panel in the ceiling is *The Assumption*.

We now cross the *campo* to the church of the Gesuiti. The first church on this site was built in the 12C by the Confraternity of the Crociferi, who dedicated it to Santa Maria Assunta, the Assumption of the Virgin. The church and convent were rebuilt after fires in 1214 and 1514. After the suppression of the Crociferi the complex was taken over in 1657 by the Jesuits, who soon afterwards enlarged the convent and, between 1715 and 1728, the church, which by then was known as the Gesuiti, with funds for its new facade provided by the Manin family. The new church was designed by Domenico Rossi, assisted by Fra Giuseppe Pozzo, while the facade was created by Giovanni Battista Fattoretto. The convent was closed when the Jesuits were suppressed in 1807, after which it was converted into a barracks. The Jesuits were allowed to return to Venice in 1844, when they again took over the Gesuiti, which in their absence had been kept functioning by the priests of the church of Santi Apostoli.

The facade of the church is in two orders, the lower one accentuated by a colonnade of lofty columns flanking the entrance, the upper one in the form of a classical Greek temple front. The pediment is surmounted by statues of the Virgin and Angel of the Assumption by Giuseppe Torretti; the figures of the Twelve Apostles and Angels over the columns and in niches are by a number of other sculptors.

The interior decoration is in inlaid marbles of green and white, creating an impression of rich tapestries, while the ceiling is adorned with golden and white stuccoes by Abbondio Stazio surrounding frescoes by Francesco Fontebasso and Louis Dorigny. On the *controfacciata* wall is Sansovino's funerary monument of three Procurators of the Da Lezze family, Priamo (d. 1557), Giovanni (d. 1580), and Andrea (d. 1604).

The first altar from the rear on the right has a painting of *The Guardian Angels*, done in 1619 by Palma il Giovane.

The huge baroque altar in the chancel, commissioned by the Manin family, was designed by Fra Giuseppe Pozzo; the baldachin, supported on ten twisted columns of verd-antique, inspired by Bernini, covers a tabernacle encrusted with lapis lazuli. Above the baldachin there is a marble group of the Eternal Father and the Saviour seated on a globe, by Giuseppe Torretti, who also did the statues of the archangels at the corners of the crossing.

The chapel to the left of the chancel contains the funerary monument of Doge Pasquale Cicogna (d. 1595), by Girolamo Campagna and his workshop. In the sacristy there are sixteen paintings by Palma il Giovane, five of which comprise a Eucharist Cycle and the others illustrating the *History of the Cross* and the *Order of the Crociferi*.

The altar in the left transept, dedicated by the Zen family, is adorned with a painting of *The Assumption*, done in 1554–5 by Tintoretto. The altarpiece on the last altar on the left side is the *Martyrdom of St Lawrence*, done in 1558–9 by Titian.

Opposite the church stood the Scuola dei Botteri, or Guild of Cask-makers, demolished in 1847; a plaque marking the site is on the facade of the building at No. 4902. Four other guilds were located to the south of the church, with entrances in the facade of the former convent of Santa Maria Assunta.

We now continue north past the church on Salizzada dei Spechieri. The street takes its name from the Spechieri, or Makers of Looking-glasses, who had their *scuola* and oratory here. At the end of the *salizzada* we come again to Fondamente Nove, where we turn right and soon come to Ponte Donà and cross the Rio dei Gesuiti. This brings us to the Pontile Fondamente Nove, which is in front of Palazzo Donà delle Rose (No. 5038). The cornerstone of this palace was laid on 24 March 1610 by Doge Leonardo Donà (1606–12), who lived here with his brother Nicolò. The design of the palace is attributed to Paolo Sarpi, but apparently the two brothers argued violently over the details of its construction, for Doge Leonardo is said to have had the stroke that killed him in 1612 while arguing with Nicolò over a proposed alteration of the plan.

We turn right at the next corner on Calle de le Tre Crose, which brings us to Calle Larga dei Boteri. Opposite and to the left, at No. 5113, is the entrance to Casa Tiziano, Titian's house. Titian lived here from 1531 until his death on 27 August 1576, entertaining, on one occasion, Henry III of France accompanied by the Dukes of Ferrara, Mantua and Urbino, as well as a circle of friends that included Pietro Aretino, Jacopo Sansovino and the famous Florentine humanist Francesco Priscianese. At that time Fondamente Nove and the houses along it had not yet been built, and so from his garden Titian had a view of the lagoon and on a clear day he could see the mountains of his native Cadore. Priscianese writes of an evening at Casa Tizianio when the lagoon below them was set with thousands of little gondolas 'adorned with the most beautiful women, and abounding with diverse harmonies and the music of voices and instruments'.

We now make our way by the most direct route to Ponte dei Sartori, which crosses Rio del Gozzi. There we turn left to look back at the 16C Palazzo Seriman, whose walled garden extends along the north bank of Rio del Gozzi as far as Rio del Gesuiti.

From Ponte dei Sartori we make a detour along the *fondamenta* of the same name, which ends just beyond Calle dei Sartori. This name comes from the Scuola dei Sartori, the Guild of Tailors, who at the beginning of the 16C owned seventeen houses on this little island, which is bounded by four canals. The guild had a hospice on the *fondamenta* at No. 4838, where the facade is adorned with a relief, dated 1511, showing the Virgin enthroned between the patron saints of the guild, St Barbara and St Omobon, the latter holding a huge pair of scissors.

We then retrace our steps and cross Ponte dei Sartori, after which we continue straight ahead on Salizzada dei Spezier. At the end of the street we turn left on Rio Terà Barba Frutariol, which brings us to Ponte Giustinian. As we approach the bridge we pass the entrance to the 16C Palazzo Giustinian-Jagher (No. 4760), whose main facade is on the canal.

After crossing the bridge we pass through a *sottoportego*, a *corte*, and then a second *sottoportego* to enter Calle de la Madona, which brings us to the *campiello* of the same name. A plaque on the house to the right, at Nos. 5432–3, records that this was the home of the painter Francesco Guardi (1712–93).

At the end of the *campiello* we turn right on Calle Morandi and then left on Calle Varisco, which brings us into a little *campiello* at the end of Calle Pestrin. In the *campiello* there is a pretty *vera da pozzo* dated 1712. The well-head was probably once a holy-water stoup in the chapel of a palace, and is the only one of its kind in Venice.

We leave the *campiello* through Sottoportego Algarotti and pass into Campiello Stella. There we turn right to cut across Campiello Widmann, which we leave at its far right end via the *calle* of the same name. The *campiello* and *calle* take their name from Palazzo Widmann, which forms the right-hand side of both as we pass through to Rio de Ca' Widmann and Ponte Widmann. From Ponte Widmann we turn back to look at the main facade of the palace, which is just to the left of the bridge. The palace was built by Baldassare Longhena *c.* 1625–30 for Paolo Sarti, a wealthy merchant of the *cittadini* class. Soon afterwards it was acquired by the Widmann family, from Carinthia, who had been created Counts of Ortenburg and Sommeregg, and who were admitted to the Venetian nobility in 1646.

We retrace our steps from the bridge and turn right into Sottoportego Widmann, after which we pass the 17C Ca' Paolina, which has a Veneto-Byzantine style cornice of the 11C, with numerous *paterae* of the same period set into its facade. We continue on through Sottoportego Magazen, a canal-side arcade that brings us to Calle Piovan. There we turn right on to Ponte Piovan, which crosses Rio de Ca' Widmann at its intersection with Rio dei Miracoli. The latter canal is named for the church of the Miracoli, which we now see ahead and to the left on a little island surrounded by four canals. We continue straight ahead on Fondamenta Piovan to Campo Santa Maria Nova. The *campo* is named for the former church of Santa Maria Nova, founded in the second half of the 10C. The church was suppressed by the French in 1808 and then demolished in 1852.

We now walk to the far right-hand corner of the *campo* to Ramo del Campaniel, after which we turn left on Calle del Campaniel and then at its end right on Campo San Canzian. There on our right we come to the main entrance of the church of San Canzian.

According to tradition, the original church on this site was founded in 864 by refugees from Aquileia, though the earliest reference to it is dated 1040. The church was dedicated to Sts Canziano, Canzio and Canzionello, Christians martyred at Aquileia in 304, but in common Venetian usage all three have been combined as San Canzian. The church in its present form dates from a rebuilding in 1705–6 by Antonio Gaspari; this was done through a legacy by Michele Tommasi, whose bust is set above the main entrance.

The altarpieces of the two altars on the right side are by Bartolomeo Letterini: on the first from the rear is *The Mourning Angel and Saints*, on the second *The Virgin and Child Adored by St John Nepomucene and Other Saints*. The chapel to the right of the chancel is dedicated to St Massimo, whose sarcophagus and statue are on the altar, both done in 1639 by Clemente Moli. On the side walls of the chancel there are two paintings by Domenico Zanchi; on the right *The Pool at Bethesda* and on the left *The Miracle of the Loaves and Fishes*. The altarpiece in the chapel to the left of the chancel is *The Virgin and St Philip Neri*, by Nicolò Renieri. On the first altar from the front on the left is a depiction of *The Immaculate*

Conception and Saints by Bartolomeo Letterini. The altarpiece on the third altar is *The Assumption* by Giuseppe Angeli; on either side are paintings of *St Massimo* and *St Canziano* by Giovanni Contarini.

After leaving the church by the main door we turn right into Campo San Canzian, where there is a 15C *vera da pozzo*. The *campo* opens on to Rio dei Santi Apostoli, here crossed by Ponte San Canzian. This was the site of the ancient *traghetto* station to Murano, moved to Pontile Fondamente Nove in 1589.

We now retrace our steps to the church and continue on into Campiello Bruno Crovato, where there is a *vera da pozzo* dating from the second half of the 16C. We then turn right into Campiello Santa Maria Nova, at the centre of which there is a *vera da pozzo* dated 1527. At the far end of the *campo* we see the entrance to the 15C Palazzo Bembo-Boldu (No. 6000). A niche on the facade contains a statue of a bearded man representing Saturn as the symbol of Time, holding in his hands a solar disc. The statue was installed in the 16C by Senator Giammateo Bembo, a renowned scholar.

At the far end of the *campiello* we turn left into Calle dei Miracoli, which at its end brings us to the canal and bridge of the same name. There we cross to the little Campo dei Miracoli, where we finally come to the church of Santa Maria dei Miracoli.

The church had its origin in a miraculous icon of the Virgin, which in 1408 was enshrined by Francesco Amadi in what is now Campo dei Miracoli. The numerous miracles attributed to the icon led to the collection of sufficient funds to build a church dedicated to the Madonna. The present church was erected in 1481–9 to a design by Pietro Lombardo, who with his sons and the workers in his workshop adorned both the exterior and interior with superb marbles and carvings that make its facade one of the most beautiful in Venice.

The interior consists of a single barrel-vaulted nave extended in a rectangular apse surmounted by the hemispherical inner dome. The chancel is raised on a high flight of steps over an arcaded crypt approached by doorways on either side, with an ornate balustrade above flanking the stairway and creating galleries on the sides. The interior walls are revetted with even more sumptuous marbles than the exterior. The nave is preceded by a *barco* (singing gallery) supported by ornately carved pillars. The carved and gilded wooden ceiling of the *barco* is divided into square compartments decorated with paintings, the most notable of which depicts the *Virgin and Child* by Palma il Giovane. The wooden vault of the nave, also carved and gilded, has fifty compartments with portraits of prophets and patriarchs, mostly by Pier Maria Pennacchi. Along the sides there extends a very elaborate frieze. On the balustrades of the galleries flanking the stairway leading up to the chancel there are statuettes representing the Virgin and Angel of the Annunciation, the Archangel Gabriel, St Francis and St Clare, all of them works of Tullio Lombardo. Flanking the altar are bronze statuettes of St Peter and St Anthony Abbot by Alessandro Vittoria. On the altar is a painting of the *Madonna and Child*, by Nicolò di Pietro. At the base of the great arch that frames the apse there are extraordinary reliefs depicting putti and mermaids, attributed to Antonio Lombardo.

After leaving the church we bear left across the *campo* to reach the western end of Calle Caselli, where at the inner corner on the right we see the romantic courtyard of Ca' Amadi (Nos. 6076–86), a Gothic building dating from *c.* 1400. We then turn left into Calle Caselli, which leads to Fondamenta de le Erbe on the west bank of Rio de la Panada. Looking to the left, we see at the northern end of the *fondamenta* the beautiful gateway of Palazzo Soranzo-Von Axel, built in 1473–9.

We now make our way by the most direct route through a corner of Castello to Ponte Marco Polo, where we cross Rio de San Lio to re-enter Cannaregio. To the right of the bridge, on the Castello side of the canal, the second building is

Palazzo Bragadin-Carabba, a Gothic palace rebuilt in the early 16C by Michele Sanmicheli. Across from Palazzo Bragadin-Carabba, at the intersection of Rio de San Lio and Rio de San Giovanni Grisostomo, we see the huge rear facade of the former Teatro Malibran. Set into the side wall of the Teatro Malibran we see a neoclassical entrance that was once part of the Case dei Polo, the ancient complex of houses built by the family of Marco Polo, the famous Venetian traveller. Marco Polo was born here in 1255, and after his epic journey into Asia, which began in 1271, he lived in Case dei Polo until his death in 1324.

After crossing the bridge we pass through a *sottoportego* into Corte Seconda del Milion, where there is a 15C *vera da pozzo*. This and the courtyard beyond, Corte Prima del Milion, take their name from Marco Polo, who was known in his time as 'Marco Millions', from the stories of the fabulous riches that he had acquired on his Asian journey. On the right side of the courtyard we see two circular arches springing from a pair of piers, their surfaces decorated with reliefs in the Veneto-Byzantine style of the 11–12C, also part of Case dei Polo. Passing under the ancient archway, we turn left into Calle del Teatro, which brings us to the *corte* of the same name, where we see the main facade of what was once the Teatro Malibran. The original theatre here was opened in 1678 by Giovanni Grimaldi as the Teatro San Giovanni Crisostomo.

From here, we retrace our steps to Corte Seconda del Milion, turning right into the other *sottoportego* to pass into Corte Prima del Milion, another courtyard of the Case dei Polo. At the far end of the *corte* we pass through another *sottoportego* that brings us to the side of the church of San Giovanni Crisostomo. There we turn left into Calle del Cagnoletto, and at its end left again into Calle Morosini. Halfway along the *calle* we pause to look through a gateway on the right into Corte Amadi, where there is a 15C *vera da pozzo*. This is the courtyard of Casa Amadi, a 15C Gothic palace where the suite of Frederick III were housed when the Emperor visited

Venice in 1452. At the end of the *calle* we turn right and then left through a *sottoportego* that takes us into Corte Morosini, where there is a 14C *vera da pozzo*. This is the courtyard of the Case dei Morosini, first mentioned in 1369. Here we have come to one of the oldest byways in Venice, with hardly a trace of the modern world in sight except the television aerials on the ancient rooftops.

We now return to the church of San Giovanni Crisostomo, where this itinerary comes to an end.

SESTIERE DI CANNAREGIO II (*Map Route 8*)

The second of our itineraries through Cannaregio begins at Pontile Ca' d'Oro. At the left of the *vaporetto* station as we land is the beautiful Ca' d'Oro, the House of Gold, a name that originated in the gilded stonework of the palace's facade on the Grand Canal.

The first building on the site was a Veneto-Byzantine *palazzo* owned by the Zen family, which shortly before 1412 was acquired by Marino Contarini, Procurator of San Marco. Contarini soon afterwards demolished the Zen *palazzo* and began preparations for building a new palace. Work began in 1420 under the direction of the stonemason Matteo de Raverti and his team of Lombard craftsmen, who built the great entrance on what is now Calle Ca' d'Oro, the outdoor stairway and the windows facing the inner courtyard, and the loggias on the Grand Canal. In 1425 the project was placed under the direction of Giovanni Bon and his son Bartolomeo, who with their Venetian artisans created on the main facade the multi-light apertures with their elaborate tracery, as well as the other carvings and sculptured decorations there and in the interior, using remains from the earlier Veneto-Byzantine *palazzo* whenever possible. Then in 1431 the facade was decorated by the Flemish artist Jean Charlier, who highlighted the natural hues of the polychrome marble, tinting it in ultramarine, black, white and gold on all parts that stood out in high relief. After the death of Marino Contarini in 1441, the palace passed to his son Pietro, and when he died in 1464 his heirs altered the interior layout of the building, beginning the deterioration of the structure. Then in 1518 the palace passed from the Contarini, and over the course of the next 376 years it was held in turn by at least a dozen different owners, until finally in 1894 it was bought by Baron Giorgio Franchetti. Immediately after acquiring Ca' d'Oro Franchetti began restoring the palace in order to recreate its original appearance, both internally and externally, his purpose being to convert it into a gallery for his extraordinary art collection. Franchetti died in 1922, after bequeathing Ca' d'Oro to the state, which continued the restoration with the aim of recreating the palace as a monument of Gothic architecture in Venice, as well as a museum to house not only Franchetti's collection but also works of art from the Archaeological Museum, the Correr Museum and the Accademia Galleries, and from other sources. Ca' d'Oro and the Giorgio Franchetti Gallery were opened to the public as a museum in 1984.

On each of the three floors there is a great central hall, with rooms opening off it on either side; in front of this on the ground floor is the water-entrance, while on the first and second floors there are loggias overlooking the Grand Canal. On the ground floor there is also an entrance off Calle Ca' d'Oro opening into a courtyard with an outside stairway leading up to the first piano nobile. In the courtyard there is a magnificent *vera da pozzo* in pink Verona marble, carved in 1427 by Bartolomeo Bon.

The works of art in the galleries of the first and second floors comprise mostly paintings, statues and reliefs, including polyptychs, *paterae*, bronzes, medallions and the panels known as *formelle*, along with tapestries, frescoes, Venetian porcelain and majolica pieces. The paintings include works by Antonio Vivarini, Andrea Mantegna, Michele Giambono, Lazzarro Bastiani, Benedetto Rusconi, Vittore Carpaccio, Giovanni Agostino da Lodi, Marco Palmezzano, Biagio d'Antonio, Carlo Braccesco, Luca Signorelli, Giovanni Boccati, Titian (*Venus at the Mirror*), Paris Bordone, Anthony Van Dyck, Jan Steen, Adriaen Van Ostade, Gabriel Metsu, Jan Fyt, Francesco Guardi and Claes Berchem. There are also fragmentary frescoes by Pordenone, Domenico Campagnolo, Titian and Giorgione. The sculptures and reliefs include works by Domenico da Tolmezzo, Pisanello, the Maestro of the Barbarigo Altar, Giovanni Maria Mosca, Andrea Briosco, Tullio Lombardo, Gian Cristoforo Romano, Jacopo Sansovino, Alessandro Vittoria, Lorenzo Bernini and Giacomo Piazzetta.

After leaving the museum we make our way northwards across Cannaregio to Campo de la Misericordia, where on our right we see the former Scuola Nuova della Misericordia, one of the six Scuole Grandi of Venice. The present building, a huge basilica-like edifice that extends all the way back to Rio de la Sensa, was begun in 1532 by Jacopo Sansovino to replace an older and smaller guildhall of the confraternity. The building was dedicated in 1583 by Doge Nicolò da Ponte. The Scuola was suppressed in 1806 by the French, and subsequently the building was used for a variety of purposes; it is currently undergoing restoration.

The walkways that lead off from the two sides of the *campo* are both known as Fondamenta de la Misericordia. We take the one that leads along the west bank of Canale de la Misericordia beside the Scuola. Looking to the right across the canal, we see on the opposite bank Palazzo Pesaro-Papafava, a Gothic palace mentioned as early as 1372.

At the end of the *fondamenta* we cross Rio de la Sensa on Ponte de l'Abazia. This brings us to Campo de l'Abazia, where on our left we see the former Scuola Vecchia della Misericordia and straight ahead the church of Santa Maria Valverde, better known as the Misericordia.

The church was founded in 936, along with its abbey, and dedicated to the Blessed Virgin. It was known as Santa Maria di Valverde for the wooded islet on which it stood. At the beginning of the 13C the church was rebuilt on a larger scale, appearing in Barbari's view of 1500 much as it is today. The principal difference is the facade of the church, rebuilt in 1651–9 by Clemente Moli, the funds having been provided through the generosity of Gaspare Moro. The church was closed in 1868, whereupon its many works of art were dispersed. In the great arch over the door there is a portrait-bust of Gaspare Moro by Clemente Moli, who also did the allegorical figures that flank the doorway and the statue of the Virgin on the peak of the pediment. On the facade to the right there is a 14C relief of the Virgin and Child.

The most renowned prior of the Misericordia was Girolamo Savina, author of a noted chronicle, who was murdered while saying Mass on 9 June 1611 by a priest who put poison into his communion wine. The abbey was in ruinous condition in the last days of the Republic, and it was demolished early in the 19C.

The Scuola Vecchia della Misericordia was built in the first half of the 15C, with the Bon family probably serving as architects. The Confraternity of the Misericordia was housed here until 1583, when it moved to the new building now known as the Scuola Nuova della Misericordia. The old guildhall was then given over to the Scuola dei Tessitori di Seta, the Guild of Silk-weavers, who remained there until the end of the Republic. One can still see the outline of the Gothic arch that surmounted the doorway, framing in its lunette a large relief of the Madonna della Misericordia. The arch was demolished in 1612, after which the relief and other sculptures from the Scuola were removed to London, and they are now in the Victoria and Albert Museum.

In the centre of Campo de l'Abazia there is a superb *vera da pozzo* dating from the second half of the 14C. On three faces of the well-head the same relief is repeated, in which two genuflecting angels hold between them the emblem of the Scuola, with the initials SMV (Santa Maria Valverde) surmounted by a crown.

We leave the *campo* via Sottoportego de l'Abazia, an arcaded passage that was opened in 1503 through the south side of the Scuola along Rio de la Sensa. This brings us to Fondamenta de l'Abazia, where after the first building on the right we come to Corte Nova. The Abbey and Scuola of the Misericordia had a hospice on this court for their indigent brothers. The entrance to the hospice, at No. 3568, has an inscription recording that the building was erected in 1505. Above the gateway there is a late-14C relief of the Madonna della Misericordia.

We continue along the *fondamenta* until we turn right into Corte Vechia, after which we cross Ponte de la Sacca. We then turn left on Fondamenta Gaspare Contarini, at the beginning of which we pass an enormous palace whose grounds extend all the way out to the lagoon on the north shore of Cannaregio. This is the Palazzo Contarini dal Zaffo, whose Casino degli Spiriti we saw from the western end of Fondamente Nove on our last itinerary. The palace was built in the early 16C for Gaspare Contarini (1483–1542), a renowned scholar and diplomat who in 1535 was made a cardinal by Pope Paul III. Just beyond the Contarini palace is the 17C Palazzo Minelli-Spada.

Farther along the *fondamenta*, as we approach Ponte Madona de l'Orto, we see on the other side of the canal Palazzo Mastelli. The palace dates from the 15C, with restorations in the following century, as evidenced by its elegant six-light Gothic window over a three-light Renaissance opening. Set into its facade are fragments of friezes, Byzantine *pateṛae* of the 13C, and the remains of a Roman altar serving as a column by a corner window. These and other architectural fragments indicate that the palace was built on the site of an earlier Veneto-Byzantine *palazzo*. The palace is also called Camello, because of the quaint relief on the right side of its facade, where a turbaned figure in Arab dress leads a heavily laden camel. Four other similar figures set into the facades of houses in the nearby Campo and Fondamenta dei Mori are undoubtedly associated with this relief, all of them probably part of the original sculptural decoration of Palazzo Mastelli. The turbaned figures are known as the 'Mori', or Moors; legend has it that they were Greek brothers, perhaps ancestors of the Mastelli, who went off to the East in the early 16C to make their fortunes, returning with spices and other goods of the Orient loaded on their camels.

Continuing along the *fondamenta*, we pass the bridge and immediately come to Campo de la Madona de l'Orto. There at the back of the *campo* on our right we see the Gothic facade of Madonna dell'Orto, one of the most beautiful churches in Venice.

The church and its monastery were founded in the second half of the 14C by Fra Marco Tiberio de' Tiberi of Parma, General of the Order of the Umiliati. The complex was originally dedicated to St Christopher, patron saint of the gondoliers who operated the nearby *traghetto* to Murano. Soon after the founding of the church miracles began to be attributed to an unfinished statue of the Madonna and Child in the nearby garden of the sculptor Giovanni de Sanctis. The statue was purchased from de Sanctis by the Confraternity of St Christopher, and on 18 June 1377 it was placed on the high altar of the church. Thenceforth the church was called Madonna dell'Orto, Our Lady of the Garden.

A lengthy project of reconstruction began in 1399 and continued until 1473, by which time a new facade had been erected and the interior of the church completely redecorated. A new and larger monastery was also built during this period. In 1787 the monastery was suppressed because only four monks remained, whereupon the Republic turned over the church to secular priests. By 1841 the fabric of the church had deteriorated to the point that it had to be closed, and then after a clumsy project of restoration it was reopened in 1868 as a parish church. New restorations were carried out in 1930–31, after which the church was given over to the Congregation of St Joseph. The church was badly damaged during the great *acqua alta* of 4 November 1966. Afterwards it underwent a thorough programme of repair and restoration under the auspices of the Venice in Peril Fund.

The sloping lateral cornices of the Gothic facade are surmounted by a false gallery, the only example in Venice. The statues in the niches of the gallery represent the twelve Apostles, done by the Dalle Masegne family. The handsome entrance was designed in 1460 by Bartolomeo Bon; it was not completed until 1483, two decades after the architect's death. At the crown of the ogive arch over the doorway there is a statue of St Christopher attributed to Nicolò di Giovanni. Above the columns there are statues of the Virgin and the Angel of the Annunciation, done *c*. 1470–80 by the school of Antonio Rizzo.

The interior plan is that of a basilica, with the central nave separated from the side aisles by two rows of five columns each, with pointed arches springing between them, their intrados decorated with figures of saints, painted in the early 15C. On the first altar from the rear on the right there is a superb painting of *St John the Baptist, with Sts Peter, Mark, Jerome and Paul*, done in 1494–5 by Cima da Conegliano. On the wall beyond the fourth altar on the right is the very beautiful *Presentation of the Virgin in the Temple*, painted by Jacopo Tintoretto in 1552 on the outer surface of the organ shutters.

We now enter the Chapel of St Maurus. Next to the altar is the large unfinished statue of the Madonna and Child for which the church is named, a crude work by Giovanni de Sanctis. Around the walls there are twenty-eight paintings of saints and beatified Venetians, commissioned in 1622 by the Patriarch Giovanni Tiepolo; they are by a number of artists, most notably Palma il Giovane, who did the portrait of the Blessed Giuliana di Collalto.

The chapel to the right of the chancel was originally dedicated by the Bonetti family, but in the 19C it was renamed for Jacopo Tintoretto (d. 1594), whose ashes were interred here along with those of his son Domenico and his daughter Marietta. The altarpiece is a painting of *St Ambrose and St Jerome* by Girolamo da Santacroce.

On the side walls of the chancel are two colossal paintings done *c.* 1560 by Jacopo Tintoretto; on the left is *The Making of the Golden Calf*, one of his most famous works; on the right is *The Last Judgement*. Behind the high altar in the chancel are eight paintings, with three in the lower zone between the pilasters and five above in the lunettes of the ribs in the conch. In the centre of the lower zone is *The Annunciation* by Palma il Giovane; this is flanked by two paintings by Jacopo Tintoretto: on the left *St Peter's Vision of the Cross*; on the right *The Beheading of St Christopher*. Above the central painting is an allegorical representation of Faith attributed to Pietro Ricchi; this is flanked by four paintings by Jacopo Tintoretto, representing *Temperance, Justice, Prudence* and *Fortitude*. The chapel to the left of the chancel has on its right wall a painting of *The Crucifixion* by Palma il Giovane.

The first altar from the front on the right side was dedicated by the Renier family, three of whom have funerary monuments here. The altarpiece is *George Killing the Dragon, between St Jerome and St Tryphon* by Matteo Ponzone, who also did the painting of *The Flagellation* on the small altar below the funerary monuments of Alvise Renier (d. 1560) and Federico Renier (d. 1560). On the wall, the painting of *God the Father* is by Domenico Tintoretto.

Next is the Contarini Chapel, containing funerary monuments of six members of the family, with portrait busts of two of the deceased by Alessandro Vittoria and one by Heinrich Meyring. The altarpiece, *St Agnes Reviving the Son of a Roman Prefect*, was done by Jacopo Tintoretto *c.* 1570–75. On the outer wall of the chapel is a *Madonna and Child, with St Catherine and St Sebastian* by the school of Titian.

We then come to the Morosini Chapel, commissioned through a bequest by Marco Morosini (d. 1441), and built in 1442–5 by Giovanni Bon and his son Bartolomeo. The altarpiece is a *Nativity* by Domenico Tintoretto, who also did the painting of the *Angels Bearing Censers*. Following this is the Vendramin Chapel, whose beautiful altar is adorned with intarsia decorations and columns of green Genoa marble. The altarpiece is a painting of *The Dead Christ, the Virgin and St Giovanni di Matha* by Bartolomeo Letterini. On the wall is a painting of *St Vincent, with St Dominic, Pope Eugene IV, St Lorenzo Giustinian and St Helena*, by Palma il Vecchio.

Last is the Valier Chapel, built in 1526 through a bequest of Vincenzo Valier (d. 1520), who is buried here. The altarpiece was a beautiful *Madonna and Child*, done *c.* 1480 by Giovanni Bellini; this was stolen on 1 March 1993 and has not been recovered.

The building perpendicular to the church on its left is the former Scuola of Santa Maria dei Mercanti. This was originally the Scuola of St Christopher, which in 1571–2 was totally rebuilt except for its outer walls by Andrea Palladio, a project commissioned by the Scuola of Santa Maria dei Mercanti, who had established themselves here in 1570. Above the door on the *campo* there is a 14C relief of the Madonna della Misericordia, flanked by St Mark and St Francis of Assisi. The main entrance on the *fondamenta* is a handsome Palladian portal.

We now make an excursion westwards along Fondamenta Madona de l'Orto, which comes to an end at Rio dei Zecchini. Just beyond Ponte Loredan we pass on our right Corte del Cavallo, the Court of the Horse. This takes its name from the equestrian statue of Colleoni, which was created in his studio here in 1481–8 by the Florentine sculptor Verrocchio. The painter Paris Bordone (1500–71) lived in Corte del Cavallo for the last thirty years of his life. He died here on 19 January 1571, and was buried in the nearby church of San Marziale.

The last building on the *fondamenta* is the 15C Palazzo Benzi-Zecchini (No. 3458), which now serves as a hospital. In the lobby there is a magnificent 15C *vera da pozzo* in pink Verona marble.

We then retrace our steps to Ponte Madona de l'Orto. After crossing the bridge we come to Calle dei Mori, which at its far end widens into Campo dei Mori. On the left side of the *calle*, at No. 3381, we pass a private *corte* that leads to the entrance of Palazzo Mastelli. On the right side of the *calle* at No. 3370 is the former Scuola dei Forneri, the Guild of Bakers, which was established here in 1445. In the *campo* there is a *vera da pozzo* dating from the late 17C or early 18C.

Set into the facade of the building on the left side of Campo dei Mori we see the three figures of the so-called Moors for which it is named, with a fourth one around the corner on Fondamenta dei Mori. Three of the figures are wearing turbans, while the one at the corner, who has on a kind of skullcap, with his stone nose replaced by one in iron, is carrying on his shoulders a corded bale with the inscription RIOBA. The 15C Gothic house at No. 3399 on Fondamenta dei Mori is known as Casa Tintoretto. This was Jacopo Tintoretto's home for the last seventeen years of his life; he died here on 31 May 1594.

We now walk westwards on Fondamenta dei Mori, crossing Ponte Brazzo and then continuing in the same direction on Fondamenta de la Sensa. On the third block beyond the bridge we pass Palazzo Arrigoni (No. 3336), a 15C Gothic palace. Near the end of the next block, at No. 3319, we see a Gothic house of the 15C; just beyond, at No. 3318, there is a late 17C *palazzetto*.

After crossing Ponte Reaso, we come to Ponte de la Malvasia, where we turn right on Calle del Capitelo. At the end of the *calle* we cross Ponte Sant'Alvise, and come to the church of Sant'Alvise, which stands at the right side of the *campo* facing the canal.

Sant'Alvise is Venetian dialect for St Louis, Bishop of Toulouse. According to tradition, the church and its convent were founded in 1388 by a pious patrician lady named Antonina Venier. The church was rebuilt in the 15C. The lunette of the Gothic arch above the doorway contains a statue of Sant'Alvise dating from the 15C.

On the right wall under the *barco* is a painting by Pietro Vecchia, comprising the two pieces of the cartoon for the mosaic over the last doorway on the right of the Basilica of San Marco, depicting *The Stealing of St Mark's Body from Alexandria*. The other painting there is *The Redeemer with St Peter and St Paul* by Antonio Zanchi. Beyond this on the right wall is a painting of *St Alvise Consecrated as Bishop of Toulouse*, from the workshop of Veronese. In the central niche of the altar on the right side of the church there is a 16C carving of Sant'Alvise in polychrome wood; on either side are statues of St John the Baptist and St Anthony, attributed to Girolamo Campagna. On the wall beside the altar is *The Last Supper*, attributed to Girolamo da Santacroce. Beyond this are two large paintings done by Giambattista Tiepolo in 1738–40: *The Flagellation* and *The Crowning with Thorns*.

There is another painting by Tiepolo on the right wall of the chancel, *The Road to Calvary*, done *c.* 1740. On the left wall is *Christ in the Garden* by Angelo Trevisani. The altar on the left side of the church is adorned with marble and sculptures, most notably three marble statues attributed to Gian Maria Morleiter, with the Virgin and Child flanked by St Dominic and St Theresa. Over the baptistery there is a portrait of Father Filippo, signed by Jacobello del Fiore and dated 1420.

The little building to the left of the church on the *campo* is the former Scuola di Sant'Alvise, built in 1402 and restored in 1608. Membership in this confraternity was restricted to those who were of what was called the class of the *cittadini originali*, that is families that had been classified as *cittadini* since the founding of the Republic.

We now walk westwards from Campo Sant'Alvise along Fondamenta dei Reformati. After passing two *calli* we see a fragmentary Renaissance entrance (No. 3150) dating from the beginning of the 16C. This is all that remains of the ancient Palazzo Donà, demolished in 1823.

Here we come to Ponte San Bonaventura, named for the

little church just beyond it on the *fondamenta*. The church and its adjacent monastery were built in 1620 by the Franciscan order of the Reformati. The church and monastery were suppressed in 1823. The former monastery, whose canal-side facade extends along the remaining stretch of the *fondamenta*, was reopened in 1859 under the patronage of the Countess Paolina Giustinian-Recanti to house an order of barefoot Carmelite nuns. The church serves as the chapel of the convent.

We now cross Ponte San Bonaventura and continue straight ahead on Calle di Reformati, which brings us to Rio de la Sensa. There we turn left on Fondamenta de la Sensa and walk as far as Ponte Turlona, where we pause to look at the splendid old palace on our left just beyond the bridge, at No. 3218. This is the Palazzo Michiel, which dates from the early 16C. King Henry III of France was a guest here in 1574.

We cross this bridge and continue straight ahead on Calle Turlona, which brings us to Rio de San Girolamo and Fondamenta dei Ormesini. The *fondamenta* took its name from the shops along the canal here that made garments of *ormesini*, or ermine, much used by the Venetian nobility for their robes.

Turning right on the *fondamenta*, we cross Ponte de le Torete and then turn left on Ponte de San Girolamo, after which we turn right on Fondamenta San Girolamo. This soon brings us past the church of San Girolamo, whose former monastery stands beside it to the south.

The monastery of San Girolamo was founded in 1375 by Augustinian monks from Treviso, along with a small oratory. At the end of that century work began on the enlargement of the monastery and the erection of a church, which was completed in 1425. The church in its present form dates from a rebuilding by Domenico Rossi in the first half of the 18C. The church and monastery were both suppressed in 1807. From 1840 until 1855 the church was used as a steam mill for a sugar factory, with the chimney protruding from the top of its campanile. The church is currently under restoration.

We continue along the *fondamenta* as far as the next bridge, the wooden Ponte de le Capuzine, which we cross to the *fondamenta* of the same name. The name comes from the little church just to the left of the bridge, the Chiesa delle Cappuccine. This was originally the oratory of a monastery founded by the Franciscans in 1612. Two years later construction began on the present church, dedicated to the Virgin and St Francis, which was consecrated in 1623. Over the doorway there is a small carving of the Madonna and Child dating from the end of the 16C, possibly a work of Girolamo Campagna. The large building to the right of the church is Palazzo Grimani, dating from the end of the 16C.

We now walk eastwards along Fondamenta de le Capuzine, which after crossing Ponte de la Toreta becomes Fondamenta dei Ormesini. We continue along the *fondamenta* as far as Ponte de Gheto Novo, where we turn right and cross Rio de San Girolamo once again. This brings us to the spacious Campo de Gheto Novo, the centre of what was once the Jewish ghetto of Venice.

The former Venetian ghetto comprises three areas: Ghetto Nuovo, Ghetto Vecchio and Ghetto Nuovissimo, the 'old', 'new' and 'newest' ghettos. The latter two areas are linked to the first by bridges across Rio del Gheto, with Ghetto Vecchio to the south-west of Ghetto Nuovo and Ghetto Nuovissimo to its east. The name comes from the Venetian *geto*, or 'foundry', and Ghetto Vecchio took its name from the fact that the original foundries for casting metal and making cannon for the Republic were located there until the beginning of the 16C.

Jewish merchants are recorded as doing business on the Rialto as early as the 10C. But Jews were not permitted to live in Venice until 1385, when the Senate for the first time granted a *condetta*, or residence permit, to Jewish money-lenders who wanted to carry on their business while living in the city centre. However, the Senate revoked the *condetta* in 1394, restricting Jewish merchants to a maximum stay of two weeks in Venice at any one time. Large numbers of Jews were forced to take refuge in Venice in 1509, when the Veneto was overrun by the marauding troops of the League of Cambrai. In 1516 the Senate accepted a proposal by the scholar Zaccaria Dolfin to deal with the problem of housing the Jewish refugees, deciding that they should live across from the old foundries, the Ghetto Vecchio, on the island known as Ghetto Nuovo. During the course of three days, beginning on 29 March 1516, representatives of the Senate escorted some seven hundred Jews into the existing houses around what is now Campo Gheto Novo, thus establishing the first ghetto in Europe. Three bridges linked the ghetto to the adjacent isles of Cannaregio, and guards were stationed at the gates that gave access to these from within the Jewish compound. These gates were closed an hour after sunset in summer and two hours after in winter, and they were not opened till dawn, with all Jews required to be inside the ghetto during those hours, and during the day forced to wear their distinctive badges when they went elsewhere in the city.

When the ghetto was first created most of its residents were Ashkenazim from Germany, along with some Italian Jews from the south. As time went on they were joined by Sephardim from Spain, Portugal and the Ottoman Empire. In the spring of 1541 the Levantine Jews received permission from the Senate to move from the crowded confines of the Ghetto Nuovo into more spacious accommodation in the Ghetto Vecchio. Then in 1633 the Senate approved a request by the Levantine and Ponentine Jews, those from Spain and Portugal, to move across into what then became known as the Ghetto Nuovissimo. These two successive expansions required the blocking off of all the streets that led into the two new quarters of the ghetto from outside, leaving one new gateway into the Ghetto Vecchio and another into Ghetto Nuovissimo. This established the bounds of the Venetian ghetto down to the end of the Republic, during which time the Jewish population there averaged about 2,000, declining from a peak of 4,500 in the mid 17C. Soon after the French occupied Venice they revoked all anti-Jewish laws, and three Jews from the ghetto were elected to the democratic city council. Then on 10 July 1797 the gates of the ghetto were demolished, 'with music and dancing by Jews along with Christians', as reported in the *Gazzetta Veneta Urbana*.

Today the Jewish population of the former ghetto is only a small fraction of what it was in the mid 17C. But the ancient traditions of the neighbourhood have been preserved, particularly through the restoration of the old synagogues and the creation of a museum. The Jewish Museum is located on the eastern side of the *campo* at No. 2902B. It is housed in the old Scuola Grande Tedesca, the synagogue of the Ashkenazim from Germany, founded in 1528. This synagogue has been superbly restored, as have the other two synagogues in the Ghetto Nuovo and the two in the Ghetto Vecchio. Admission to the museum entitles one to a guided tour of all five synagogues. The exhibits in the museum consist of objects used in these synagogues and in Jewish homes in the ghetto during the days of the Republic.

One of the other two synagogues in the Ghetto Nuovo is the Scuola Canton, which is located in the south-east corner of the *campo*. This synagogue was founded in 1531–2 by a group of Ashkenazim from Germany who belonged to an extended family known as the Cantoni. The other synagogue, the Scuola Italiana, is on the southern side of the *campo*; this was founded in 1575 by Jews from southern Italy.

There are three *vere da pozzo* of the 15C in Campo de Gheto Novo; each of them has a relief of a Gothic shield with three lions passant.

A short *calle* at the south-western corner of the *campo* leads to Ponte di Gheto Vechio, where we cross Rio del Gheto. There we continue straight ahead on the *calle* called Gheto Vechio. This brings us to Campiello de le Scuole, which takes its name from the fact that two *scuole*, or synagogues, are located there. One of these is the Scuola Levantina, the handsome building on the north side of the *campiello*, erected in 1538 and transformed in 1654, probably by Baldassare Longhena. The Scuola Levantina was founded in 1538 by Sephardim from the Ottoman Empire, who formed the Levantine 'nation' in the Ghetto Vecchio. From 1836 onwards this building also housed the Scuola Luzzatta, which moved there from its original location in Campo Gheto Novo. On the south side of the *campiello* is the Scuola Spagnola, established in 1573 by Sephardic Jews from Spain, who together with the Sephardim from Portugal formed the Ponentine 'nation', that is, those from 'the West'. Before the building of these *scuole* the square here was known as Campiello del Pozzo. This name came from the 16C *vera da pozzo* in the centre of the *campiello*.

The *calle* called Gheto Vechio leads out to Fondamenta de Cannaregio. On the right side of the *calle* there is a tablet set into the wall; this bears an inscription recording a decree of the Venetian Senate, dated 20 September 1704, forbidding Christians to enter the ghetto.

We now retrace our steps to Campo de Gheto Novo, walking diagonally across to the *sottoportego* on its eastern side. Here there were several pawnshops where the Ashkenazim did business for nearly three centuries, lending money to Venetians who left personal belongings as collateral. This leads to Rio del Gheto and Ponte di Gheto Novissimo, where we turn back to look at the houses on the west bank of the canal, tenements seven and eight storeys high, evidence of the crowded conditions in the Ghetto Nuovo in the 17C.

After crossing the bridge we continue straight ahead on Calle Gheto Novissimo to the first corner on the left. There we turn left through a *sottoportego* into the second branch of Calle Gheto Novissimo, which comes to a T-junction at Calle del Porton, where we turn right. This is the heart of the Ghetto Nuovissimo, which extended eastwards for only a short distance from Rio del Gheto. At No. 1469 on Calle del Porton is Palazzo Casselli, the only palace in the ghetto. This belonged to the Casselli in the 17C and later it passed to the Treves, both of them wealthy Sephardic families.

At the end of Calle del Porton we turn left on to Calle dei Ormesini. At the end of the *calle* we come to Ponte dei Ormesini, which we cross to leave the ghetto.

On the other side of the bridge we turn right on Fondamenta dei Ormesini. Some 60 m along the *fondamenta* we pass on our right Ponte Ca' Loredan, and then after another 60 m we go through a short *sottoportego* and pass Ponte de l'Aseo. Across the canal, just before the bridge, we see Palazzo Loredan-Gheltof, a 15C Gothic palace.

A few steps beyond the *sottoportego* we cross Ponte dei Lustraferi. The name comes from the *lustraferri*, or polishers of metal, who had their shops here in times past, their speciality being the polishing of *ferri*, the metal prows of gondolas.

After another 60 m we pass Ponte dei Servi, a private bridge leading to the former monastery of Santa Maria dei Servi. After passing Calle Longo we see Palazzo Grimani-Longo (No. 2591), a 15C Gothic palace. At the second turning beyond the palace we come to Calle Larga, where on the house on the right, at No. 2554, we see this old inscription: 'Bestemmie non più, a date gloria o Dio', 'Swear no more and give glory to God'. This was posted by the magistrates who dealt with profanity and blasphemy, the only such notice that has survived in the city.

Continuing along the *fondamenta*, we pass on our right Rio del Grimani and then Ponte San Marziale. As we approach the end of the *fondamenta* we pass on our left the splendid Palazzo Da Lezze-Antonelli, designed by Baldassare Longhena and completed in 1654.

At the end of the *fondamenta* we come again to Campo de la Misericordia. From the *campo* we cross over the junction of the three canals on Ponte de la Misericordia, continuing ahead on the short *ramo* of the same name and then turning right on Fondamenta San Felice. As we do so we pass Ponte Chiodo, a private bridge without a balustrade, the only one of its type remaining in the city. We follow the *fondamenta* for almost its entire length along Rio de San Felice, passing on our left Ponte Racheta and then Rio Priuli. We then pass on our left the 17C Palazzo Priuli-Scarpa.

We now cross the canal on Ponte Umberto Belli. We then continue straight ahead on Calle San Felice, turning right at its end into Corte dei Pali già Testori, which opens out on to Strada Nova. At the outer end of the court there is a *vera da pozzo* dating from the second quarter of the 19C, one of the very few public well-heads to be built in Venice after the fall of the Republic.

We now turn left on Strada Nova and then at the next corner right on Calle Ca' d'Oro. This brings us back to our starting-point, the Pontile Ca' d'Oro, where we conclude our second stroll through Cannaregio.

SESTIERE DI CANNAREGIO III (*Map Route 9*)

We begin our third and last stroll through Cannaregio at Pontile Ca' d'Oro, where we began and ended our previous itinerary. From there we walk out to the end of Calle Ca' d'Oro and turn left on the Strada Nova, which after 80 m brings us to Rio San Felice and the bridge of the same name. As we cross the bridge we see on our right the church of San Felice, whose main facade is on the canal, with a side entrance on Campo San Felice.

According to tradition, the church of San Felice was founded in the 10C. The church in its present form dates from a rebuilding that began in 1531, to a design influenced by Mauro Coducci. Above the main entrance there is a statue of an angel, dating from the 14C.

A radical reconstruction of the interior in 1810 resulted in the removal of the richly decorated altars of the 16C church and their replacement by inferior modern works. Over the entrance there is a bronze group of the Madonna and Child with St Peter and St John the Baptist, by Giulio del Moro, who also did the statues of Hope and Charity in niches on either side of the high altar. On the third altar from the rear on the right there is a painting of *St Demetrius and a Donor of the Ghisi Family*, done in 1574 by Jacopo Tintoretto. Over the sacristy door there is a plaque honouring Pope Clement XIII, who as Carlo Rezzonico was baptized here on 29 March 1693.

Leaving the church by the side door, we turn right on Campo San Felice. One block farther along we come to Rio de Noal and the broad Ponte Pasqualigo, which brings us to the next stretch of Strada Nova. At the first corner beyond the bridge we veer half left into Calle de Noal, from where we make our way by a short but tortuous route to the main entrance of the church of the Maddalena on Campo Madalena.

The first church on this site, dedicated to St Mary Magdalene, was founded in 1220 by the Baffo family. The present church was built in 1760–89 to plans by Tommaso Temanzo. The most striking feature of the facade is the huge porch that frames the main doorway, designed in the form of a Greek temple front with four Ionic columns supporting an architrave and pediment. The building is circular in plan on the exterior, inspired by the ancient Pantheon in Rome, while in the interior it forms a hexagon, with the nave covered by a hemispherical dome. The church is presently closed for restoration.

Just to the right of the church there a Gothic gateway with a pointed arch dating from the 15C, all that remains of the ancient Palazzo Magno. At the centre of the *campo* there is a superb *vera da pozzo* in the Lombardesque style, dating from the late 15C or early 16C.

We now walk back along Fondamenta de la Madalena, looking to our left across the canal to see Palazzo Correr, a 15C Gothic palace partially rebuilt in the 18C. We continue along the canal side through the arcaded Sottoportego de la Colonete and then along the *fondamenta* of the same name. At the end of the *fondamenta* we turn left to cross the canal on Ponte Correr, continuing straight ahead on the *calle* of the same name. At the end of the *calle* we emerge once again on Strada Nova, where we turn right. On our left is the side wall of the church of Santa Fosca, which we will visit presently. After a few steps we come on our right, at No. 2233A, to the famous Farmacia Santa Fosca. This is the oldest pharmacy in Venice, its walnut furnishings and beamed ceiling remaining from the 17C, with 18C majolica vases from the Veneto.

We cross over Strada Nova into Campiello de la Chiesa, walking behind the apse of Santa Fosca. On our right are the gardens of Palazzo Donà-Giovanelli, whose main facade is on Rio de Santa Fosca. In the *campiello* there is a 17C *vera da pozzo* of pink Verona marble.

At the far end of the *campiello* we cross Rio de Santa Fosca on Ponte Vendramin. Directly across the bridge is the 16C Palazzo Vendramin, with a splendid Renaissance entrance at its centre. At the other side of the bridge we turn right on Fondamenta del Forner, from where we can see on the other side of the canal the north facade of the 15C Palazzo Donà-Giovanelli, restored by Jacopo Sansovino in 1550. Frederick II, Emperor of the West, was a guest in the palace when he visited Venice in 1709.

Retracing our steps, we now continue past Ponte Vendramin to the next bridge, Ponte Santa Fosca, where we turn right on Calle Zancani. At the end of the *calle* we cross Ponte Zancani, which brings us to the *campo* and church of San Marziale.

According to tradition, the church was founded in the 9C and dedicated to San Marcilliano, who in Venetian dialect became San Marziale. The church was then rebuilt to house an icon of the Virgin and Child that came miraculously from Rimini to Venice by boat in 1286. The new church was consecrated in 1333; the present edifice dates from a reconstruction in the years 1693–1721.

The paintings on the ceiling were done between 1700 and

1705 by Sebastiano Ricci; in the central panel is *The Holy Father in Glory*; in the other three are *St Marziale in Glory* and two scenes depicting the miraculous icon of the Virgin and its arrival from Rimini in 1286. The painting on the second altar shows *St Marziale between St Peter and St Paul*, done by Jacopo Tintoretto in 1548–9. The altarpiece on the third altar depicts *The Saviour between St Nicholas and St Clare*, signed by Antonio Zanchi and dated 1712. On the pilasters flanking the chancel there are two paintings by Domenico Tintoretto, *The Virgin* and *The Angel of the Annunciation*, which originally formed the doors on the organ. On the high altar there is a colossal marble group in the baroque style representing *Christ on the World with Angels and Saints Below*, with the statues attributed to Tommaso Ruer. On the right wall of the chancel is *The Crucifixion* by Passignano; on the left is *The Resurrection* by Antonio Vassilacchi; both paintings are signed and dated 1586.

The altarpiece in the sacristy is Titian's celebrated painting of *The Archangel Raphael and Tobias*, done *c*. 1530.

The altarpiece on the first altar from the front on the left is *The Transit of St Joseph* by Antonio Balestra. On the second altar from the front on the left there is a statue in gilded and polychrome wood of the Virgin and Child, dating from the end of the 14C.

After leaving the church we turn left and retrace our steps to Campo San Marziale. As we do so we pass on the right side of the *campo* an ancient house with an inscription recording that it was built in 1324 and restored in 1505. This is the former Confraternity of the Blessed Virgin of the Visitation. In the *campo* there is a 15C *vera da pozzo*, one of its sides bearing a relief representing San Marziale.

Retracing our steps through Campo San Marziale, we turn right before the bridge on to Fondamenta Moro, at the end of which we cross Ponte Moro. We then turn left on Fondamenta Grimani followed by a right on to Fondamenta Daniele Canal, passing at Nos. 2381–3 the remains of the 16C Palazzo

Grimani. This brings us to the site of the former church and monastery of Santa Maria dei Servi.

The monastery was founded by the Servite Order in 1318 and work on the church began in 1330, though it was not consecrated until 1491. The church and monastery were suppressed in 1812 and almost entirely demolished. Then in 1862 Canon Daniele Canal purchased the site and its surviving buildings, founding there a charitable institution for girls now known as the Istituto Canal Marovich ai Servi. The church has now been rebuilt and serves as the chapel of the institute. All that remains of the original monastery is the 15C Gothic entrance.

We now retrace our steps along Fondamenta Daniele Canal, continuing straight ahead to cross Ponte Diedo, bringing us to the *fondamenta* of the same name. The name comes from Palazzo Diedo, whose entrance is at No. 2386. The palace was built for the Diedo in the 16C from a design by Andrea Tirali.

We now turn right on Ponte Santa Fosca, which brings us across to the *campo* of the same name. There on the left we see the main entrance of the church of Santa Fosca.

The *campo* is dominated by a large bronze statue of Fra Paolo Sarpi, done in 1892 by Emilio Marsili. Pietro Sarpi (1552–1625), known as Fra Paolo when he entered the Servite Order, distinguished himself as a scientist and mathematician as well as a theologian and polemicist. He is credited with discovering the circulation of the blood a quarter of a century before Harvey, and Galileo acknowledged his help in inventing the telescope. Sarpi, who had served as court theologian to the Duke of Mantua, returned to Venice in 1575 when he was appointed Provincial of the Servite Order, at just twenty-three years of age. Sarpi won renown during the controversy between Venice and Pope Paul V, who on 17 April 1606 put the city under an interdiction and excommunicated everyone in the Republic, the reason being the refusal of the government to allow the Papacy to interfere in matters that it considered to be its own concern. Sarpi defended the Republic with such eloquence and courage that he became a hero, particularly after surviving an assassination attempt on 25 October 1607, in which he said sardonically that he 'recognized the Roman style'. Despite the severity of his wounds Sarpi lived on until 1625, when he was buried with great honours at the Servite monastery.

The church of Santa Fosca was founded in the 10C. The church in its present form dates from a rebuilding in the years 1730–41.

Above the main entrance there is a painting of *The Baptism of Jesus* by Giambattista Mariotti. On the first altar to the right is a painting of *St Joseph in Glory*, signed by Pier Antonio Novelli and dated 1760. At the end of the right wall is *Christ Sustained by Angels* by Carl Loth. Behind the high altar in the chancel there are two paintings by Filippo Bianchi: above, *The Trinity*; below, *Five Saints and the Parish Priest Fra Melchiori*. On the right wall of the chancel is a depiction of *Eleazer and Rebecca* by Carl Loth; on the left wall is *The Holy Family* by Domenico Tintoretto. On the left wall over the pulpit is *The Baptism of St Fosca* by the school of Bassano.

The handsome Gothic building directly across from Campo Santa Fosca is Palazzo Correr, whose facade on Rio de la Madalena we saw earlier on this itinerary. Walking westwards on Salizzada Santa Fosca, we pass Palazzo Correr and then cross Ponte San Antonio. This brings us to Rio Terà de la Madalena, a street created in 1389 by filling in a canal, apparently the earliest such project in Venice. Near the beginning of the street on the right, at No. 2343, is Palazzo Donà delle Rose, a Gothic palace reconstructed at the end of the 17C, a work attributed to Domenico Rossi. Francesco Donà was living in the palace here when he was elected Doge in 1545. A few steps farther along on the left, at No. 2083, we see the arms of the Donà delle Rose on the facade of an earlier palace that belonged to the family. Then on the right, with its entrance at No. 2347, we pass the 15C Palazzo Contin.

We continue along the street as far as the last turning on the right before the next bridge, where a *sottoportego* leads into Corte Volto Santo, the Court of the Holy Face. This takes its name from the relief of a crowned and bearded head representing Christ the King, which appears in a tondo on the 15C *vera da pozzo* in the centre of the court, as well as on another relief on the inner lintel of the *sottoportego*. This was the emblem of the Scuola dei Lucchesi, the Guild of Silk-weavers, who in 1398 built a guildhall and hospice here, both of which were destroyed by fire in 1789.

We now cross Ponte de l'Anconeta, continuing straight ahead on Calle de l'Anconeta into the *campiello* of the same name. On the right, at Nos. 1944–5, is the former Teatro Italia, a neo-Gothic building dating from the beginning of the 20C. At the far end of the *campiello* we turn left into the tiny Campiello del Boter, where a little shrine on the right side of the alley at the end marks the site of an ancient oratory of the Madonna. This oratory enshrined a sacred *anconetta*, or 'little icon', which was removed in 1895, though its memory is preserved in the names of the *ponte* and *calle* and *campiello* that we have just passed.

We continue through Corte del Pegoloto and turn right on Calle del Cristo, at the end of which we turn left on Rio Terà del Cristo. At the end of the street we come on our right to the former Scuola del Cristo. This was built in 1644 for the Confraternity of Christ Crucified, whose duty it was to bury those who died by drowning.

We now turn left into Rio Terà drio la Chiesa, passing on our right Campiello drio Ca' Memo, where there is an hexagonal *vera da pozzo* dated 1710. A few steps farther along we come on our right to a side entrance of the church of San Marcuola.

The church was founded in the 9–10C and dedicated to St Ermagora and St Fortunato, whose names were combined in the Venetian dialect as San Marcuola. The church was rebuilt after a fire and reconsecrated in 1343, appearing in Barbari's view of 1500, where it is shown with its main axis perpendicular to the Grand Canal, with its apse to the north. It was rebuilt again in the years 1728–36 by Antonio Gaspari and Giorgio Massari, who reoriented the church so that its main axis was parallel to the Grand Canal, with its apse to the east.

The interior is rectangular in plan, with pairs of altars at each of the four corners. All eight of the altars have statues rather than paintings as altarpieces, all of them by Gian Maria Morleiter and his assistants. The painting on the ceiling of the nave depicts *St Ermagora and St Fortunato in Glory* by Francesco Migliori. Around each of the pulpits on the side walls there are groups of paintings; on the right these include works by Francesco Vecellio, Alvise dal Friso, Carl Loth and a late follower of Titian; and on the left by Francesco Migliori, Alessandro Varottari and the workshop of Veronese.

The tabernacle on the high altar is flanked by statues of St Ermagora and St Fortunato, both attributed to Gian Maria Morleiter. The altarpiece is *The Assumption*, by Francesco Migliori, who also did the painting on the ceiling of the chancel, *The Fall of Manna*. On the left wall of the chancel there is a painting of *The Last Supper*, done in 1547 by the youthful Jacopo Tintoretto.

We leave by the door on the right side of the nave, which takes us out to Campo San Marcuola on the Grand Canal. In the centre of the *campo* there is a monumental *vera da pozzo* in the baroque style, dated by an inscription to 1713.

We now walk around the apse of the church on Campiello de la Chiesa, turning left at its end on Rio Terà drio la Chiesa. We then continue straight ahead on Calle Cristo o Piscina, and at its end we turn right on Calle del Magazen. This brings us out on to Rio Terà San Leonardo, where we turn left. As we do so we see immediately across the street to the right Casa Zecchin (No. 1373), a Gothic structure of the 15C. Walking westwards on Rio Terà San Leonardo, we soon come on our left to Campo San Leonardo and the church of the same name.

The church of San Leonardo was founded in the 11C. The church in its present form dates from a rebuilding in the second half of the 18C, when it acquired its present neoclassical facade in the form of a Greek temple front. It was suppressed by the French in the first decade of the 19C. San Leonardo now serves as the local civic centre and is used for occasional exhibitions.

In the centre of the *campo* there is a cylindrical *vera da pozzo*, dated 1518.

We now continue along Rio Terà San Leonardo to the Canal de Cannaregio and Ponte de le Guglie, the Bridge of the Obelisks, so called because of the four obelisks that decorate it. This is one of the oldest bridges in the city, originally known as Ponte de Cannaregio; it was first erected in wood in 1285, redone in stone in 1580, restored in 1641 and 1776, and rebuilt in its present form in 1823.

The Canal de Cannaregio has *fondamente* along both of its banks. We will take advantage of this by walking up one side and down the other, crossing near its far end at Ponte dei Tre Archi, the only bridge over this wide waterway other than Ponte de le Guglie.

We turn right from the foot of Ponte de le Guglie on to Fondamenta de Cannaregio, after which we pass in succession three *sottoporteghi*, the third of which leads in to Ghetto Vecchio. Then, after passing Calle del Forno, we come to Palazzo Nani (No. 1105), a handsome Renaissance palace dating from the mid 16C. About 250 m farther along we come to Palazzo Surian-Bellotto (No. 968). This was built for the Surian family towards the end of the 17C, probably from a design by Giuseppe Sardi. The French ambassador Montaigu resided here in 1743, one of his secretaries being Jean-Jacques Rousseau. The palace was also occupied for several years by a series of English ambassadors.

We continue along the *fondamenta*, coming to Ponte dei Tre Archi, the Bridge of Three Arches, built in its present form in 1688 by Andrea Tirali and restored in 1794 and again in 1980.

Continuing along Fondamenta de Cannaregio, we see at No. 923 the 16C Palazzo Roma. Near the end of the *fondamenta* we come to the church and hospice of Santa Maria dei Penitenti. The Hospice was founded in 1703 by Maria Elisabetta Rossi as a home for 'fallen women'. The church was built in the years 1730–38 by Giorgio Massari.

We now return to Ponte dei Tre Archi and cross to the west bank of the canal. On the other side of the bridge we continue straight ahead into Campo San Giobbe, which leads to the church of the same name.

The church originated in a small oratory of San Giobbe (St Job) attached to a hospice, founded in 1378 by Giovanni Contarini as a refuge for the poor and homeless. St Bernardino of Siena preached here in 1463 at the request of Doge Cristoforo Moro (1462–71), who provided money to build a new and larger church and a monastery. The church, designed by Antonio Gambello, was completed in 1470 by Pietro Lombardo, who created here one of the first Renaissance edifices in Venice. The beautiful Renaissance entrance was built and decorated by Pietro Lombardo and his assistants; the relief in the lunette above the door shows St Job and St Francis of Assisi; the three statues above represent Sts Bernardino, Alvise and Anthony.

The painting on the first altar from the rear on the right depicts *Saints and Monks* by Antonio Zanchi. On the second altar is a portrait of *St Job* by Lattanzio Querena. The altarpiece on the third altar is *The Madonna in Glory, with Saints* by Paris Bordone. Beyond the third altar is the funerary monument of Count Argerson, ambassador of Louis XIV to Venice. The fourth altar, dedicated by the Boatmen's Guild of Mestre and Marghera, has as its altarpiece a painting of Sts Peter, Andrew and Nicholas, signed by Paris Bordone.

At the front of the nave on the right is the large Contarini Chapel, part of the original 14C Gothic oratory, now serving as the ante-sacristy. The altarpiece is a *Nativity*, done *c.* 1540 by Gian Girolamo Savoldo. Going on into the sacristy, we see at its far end the Da Mula Chapel; the altarpiece is a triptych of *The Annunciation with St Anthony of Padua and the Archangel Gabriel*, done *c.* 1445 by Alvise Vivarini.

The chancel is framed in a splendid triumphal arch built *c.* 1471 for Doge Cristoforo Moro by Pietro Lombardo, who also did the statues of the Angel and Virgin of the Annunciation above the pilasters and the reliefs of the Evangelists in the pendentives of the dome. The grave of the Doge (d. 1471) and his wife is marked by a Lombardesque tombstone in the chancel. The stalls in the deep choir behind the altar date from the 16C. The chapel to the right of the chancel was built in 1506 for the Correr family; the altarpiece is a painting of St Joseph by Giuseppe Angeli. The chapel to the left of the chancel, built in 1502 for the Marin family has on its altar a statue of St Francis attributed to Lorenzo Bregno.

On the left side of the nave there are five chapels, the most interesting being the fourth and fifth. The fourth chapel was built early in the 16C for the Martini family, silk-weavers from Lucca; it is a rare Venetian example of Tuscan workmanship, attributed to Antonio Rossellino, who did the statuette of St John the Baptist in the centre of the marble reredos. The domed vault is revetted in glazed terracotta by the Della Robbia family, with the Redeemer at the centre and the four Evangelists in roundels at the corners. The last chapel, dedicated to St Luke, was made for the Grimani family at the beginning of the 16C, and is decorated with reliefs in the Lombardesque style. The statue of St Luke in the central niche was done by Lorenzo Bregno.

We go back to Ponte dei Tre Archi, turning right on Fondamenta San Giobbe. Just beyond the bridge we pass the site of an ancient oratory of the Virgin, founded in 1512 to replace the one incorporated in the original church of San Giobbe. At Nos. 581–613 we pass the Comun Contarini, formerly the Ospizio Contarini. This was founded in 1378 by Zuan Contarini, a priest and nobleman, as a hospice for poor people from the parish of San Geremia.

About 80 m farther along we come to Calle Busello. The house just before the *calle* is the ancient Palazzo Bussello, which towards the end of the 16C belonged to Piero Bussello, a rich merchant in sugar and drugs, whose beautiful garden here was mentioned by Francesco Sansovino in his 1581 guide to Venice. The house just beyond Calle Bussello is the 15C Palazzo Cendon. Fifty metres farther along we come to the 15C Palazzo Testa (No. 468). The palace was built by the Testa, a *cittadini* family; it too is mentioned by Francesco Sansovino, who writes of 'the noble garden of Francesco Testa'. A hundred metres farther along, at No. 349, we pass the entrance to Palazzo Savorgnan, a monumental edifice with a large coat of arms and reliefs of helmets set into its facade. The palace was begun in 1699 from a design by Giuseppe Sardi, with its wings added in 1765. Its first owners were descended from Federigo Savorgnan, who was admitted to the Venetian nobility in 1385, the first outsider ever to be made a patrician. This palace, which was also noted for its beautiful garden, was acquired in 1859 by the Duke of Modena.

Then, after a pretty 16–17C *palazzo* at No. 346, we come to Palazzo Venier-Priuli-Manfrin (Nos. 342–3). The coat of arms and inscription on the facade record that the palace was built by the Priuli in 1520. In 1787 the palace was purchased by Count Girolamo Manfrin.

The *fondamenta* finally brings us back to Ponte de le Guglie, where we cross the beginning of Salizzada San Geremia and continue straight ahead on Fondamenta de Ca' Labia. This brings us past the main facade of Palazzo Labia, which is on the west bank of the Cannaregio Canal near its confluence with the Grand Canal. The end of the palace facing the Grand Canal abuts the campanile of the church of San Geremia, whose west entrance, set in a grandiose neoclassical facade, is just beyond on the *fondamenta*, where there is a superb view from the junction of the Cannaregio Canal and the Grand Canal. At the end of the *fondamenta* there is an eroded statue of St John Nepomucene, done in the mid 18C by Giovanni Marchiori.

We now retrace our steps along the *fondamenta* to Salizzada San Geremia, where we turn left and at the end of the street enter Campo San Geremia. There at the far end of the *campo* we see the north entrance to the church of San Geremia, and on the left side of the square the rear facade of Palazzo Labia.

The church of San Geremia was founded in the 11C and rebuilt in the second half of the 13C. The church in its present form dates from a rebuilding by Carlo Corbellini in 1753–60. The only element of the original church that remains is the 13C campanile.

The interior plan is a Greek cross with semi-domes at the end of each arm and a great oval dome at the crossing. The paintings in the church include four canvases by Palma il Giovane and individual works by Bernardino Lucadello, Francesco Maggiotto, Giovanni Marchiori, Giovanni Ferrari, Antonio Marinetti, Francesco Fontebasso, Agostino Ugolino, the school of Piazzetta, and one attributed to Giambattista Mengardi.

The left transept contains the Cappella di Santa Lucia, built in 1863 to enshrine the body of the martyr of Syracuse after the demolition of her church to make way for the railway station. A door to the right leads to a small room used to display church treasures and other works of art.

The facade of Palazzo Labia on the *campo* is less elaborate than the main one on the Cannaregio Canal. The main facade was built in the Longhena style by Andrea Cominelli towards the end of the 17C. The facade on Campo San Geremia, done in a simpler style, was completed *c.* 1750 by either Alessandro Tremignon or his son Paolo. The Labia were a family of extremely wealthy merchants who originated in Spain, and bought their way into the Venetian nobility in 1646. The great hall of the palace preserves frescoes done in 1747–50 by Giambattista Tiepolo and Girolamo Mengozzi-Colonna, depicting *Episodes from the Life of Cleopatra*.

There are four *vere da pozzo* in Campo San Geremia. The oldest of these is the one beside the church to the right of the north entrance; this is made of pink Verona marble and is cylindrical in form, dating from the 12–13C. Two of the others date from the 14–15C and one dates from the first quarter of the 16C.

We now leave Campo San Geremia and begin walking along Rio Terà Lista di Spagna, which was laid out on a canal filled in during the 18C. On the left at No. 233 there is a Gothic doorway of the 15C, once the entrance to Palazzo Morosini della Tressa, or 'of the bar', because of the device on the family coat of arms, which is displayed over the door. On the right at No. 168 is Palazzo Renier-Zeno, built in 1613. In the 18C the palace became the Spanish Embassy, giving its name to Rio Terà Lista di Spagna. At the end of the 18C it was acquired by the Manin family. Then in 1857 it became the Manin Orphanage, created through a bequest by Lodovico Manin, the last Doge of Venice. Today the palace is the regional headquarters for the Veneto.

After passing on our left Rio Terà del Sabioni we come to the 15C Palazzo Lezze (No. 134). Then on our left, at No. 122, we pass the entrance to the restored 15C Palazzo Calbo-Crotta.

The Fondamenta and Ponte dei Scalzi at the approach to the railway station are named for the church of the Scalzi, or Barefoot Carmelites, which overlooks the Grand Canal just beyond the bridge.

The Barefoot Carmelite friars first came to Venice in 1633, and in 1645 they bought this plot of land on which to build a monastery and church. In 1646 they commissioned Baldassare Longhena to design the church, which was dedicated to Santa Maria di Nazareth. The facade was erected in 1672–80 by Giuseppe Sardi. The statues between the columns flanking the central doorway are attributed to Bernardo Falcone, as are the figures of the Virgin and Child in the niche above.

The first chapel from the rear on the right has on its altar a statue by Bernardo Falcone of St John of the Cross. The altarpiece in the second chapel is a statue of the Ecstasy of St Theresa, done in 1697 by Heinrich Meyring. On the walls of the chapel there are two paintings by Nicolò Bambini depicting *Miracles of St Theresa*. The third chapel has over its altar a statue of St John the Baptist by Melchiore Barthel.

The baroque high altar is surmounted by an extraordinarily elaborate baldachin supported by spiral columns. The arch of the baldachin is surmounted by a statue of the Saviour flanked by two recumbent sibyls, by Giovanni Marchiori, who also did the flanking statues of St Theresa and St John of the Cross.

The first chapel from the front on the left has on its altar a statue of St Sebastian, signed by Bernardo Falcone and dated 1669. Over the altar of the second chapel there is a group in high relief of the Virgin and Child with St Joseph in Glory, by Giuseppe Torretti. Buried in the chapel is Lodovico Manin, the last Doge of Venice, who died on 23 October 1802. The third chapel has on its altar a large marble crucifix and on its altar-front a relief of Christ falling under the Cross, both attributed to Gian Maria Morleiter. On the vault of the chapel there is a fresco depicting *Christ's Agony in the Garden* by Giambattista Tiepolo.

At this point we end the third and last of our strolls through Cannaregio, having thus explored all three of the *sestiere* on the San Marco side of the Grand Canal.

[9] Sestiere di Dorsoduro

The Sestiere di Dorsoduro is the largest of the three 'sixths' on 'the other side' of the Grand Canal, and includes within its bounds the island of Giudecca. The name of the *sestiere* is believed to stem from its *dossi*, or ridges of firm earth that rose up above the tidal marshes east and south of the Rialtine islands when the city was first being settled and developed.

SESTIERE DI DORSODURO I (*Map Route 10*)

Our first stroll through Dorsoduro will begin at Campo de la Carità, at the foot of Ponte de l'Accademia. The present wooden bridge dates from 1932, replacing the original iron span erected in 1854 by the Austrians. Directly in front of us is the former church of Santa Maria della Carità, Our Lady of Charity, with its main facade facing to the right. At the back of the *campo* to the right is the main facade of the former Scuola della Carità, now the Accademia Galleries.

The first church and convent on this site were founded in 1134 by friars of the Canonici Lateranesi Order of Ravenna. Then in 1260 the complex became the home of the Scuola Grande di Santa Maria della Carità, a lay confraternity dedicated to helping the poor. The confraternity built a guildhall beside the convent in 1344, and in the next eight years Bartolomeo Bon erected for them a new and larger church beside the cloister. The convent buildings were transformed in 1552 to a design by Andrea Palladio, who built a magnificent portico and loggia along the eastern side of the complex.

The church was suppressed in 1807, after which the entire complex was remodelled by Giannantonio Selva to house the Venetian Academy. The reconstruction was completed in 1810, and in 1817 the Pinacoteca, or picture gallery, was opened to the public. Since then the complex has been redesigned and altered several times, creating the Accademia Galleries.

Room I is the former chapter house of the Scuola della Carità. This great hall was built in 1461–84, its superb gilded ceiling ascribed to the woodcarver Marco Cozzi. The central panel has a painting of *God the Father* by Alvise Vivarini, while the four corners have depictions of the prophets by Domenico Campagnola.

This room is the first of twenty-five exhibition areas, which are arrayed around the contiguous structures of the Scuola, convent and church, with Room XII along the only remaining wing of the great Palladian cloister, Room XXIII in the upper part of the church, and Room XXIV in the former hospice of the Scuola. The arrangement of the paintings in the various galleries is as follows: I, primitives (early Venetian painters); II, large 15C altar frontals; III, Giovanni Bellini; IV, Mantegna, Piero della Francesca, Cosmè Tura; V, Giorgione; VI, Paris Bordone, Bonifacio Veronese (Bonifacio de' Pitati), Jacopo Tintoretto; VII, Lorenzo Lotto; VIII, Romanino and Jacopo Palma il Vecchio; IX, followers of Titian; X, Titian, Paolo Veronese, Jacopo Tintoretto; XI, Paolo Veronese, Jacopo Tintoretto, Giambattista Tiepolo, Bernardo Strozzi; XII, Marco Ricci, Francesco Zuccarelli, Giuseppe Zais; XIII, Jacopo Bassano and portraits by Jacopo Tintoretto; XIV, pictures of the 17C; XV, Giovanni Antonio Pellegrini, Giambattista Tiepolo, Francesco Solimena; XVI, early works by Giambattista Tiepolo; XVIa, Alessandro Longhi, Giambattista Piazzetta, Fra Galgario; XVII, Canaletto, Francesco Guardi, Giambattista Tiepolo, Pietro Longhi, Rosalba Carriera; XVIII, paintings by applicants for Academy membership; XIX, Bartolomeo Montagna, Giovanni

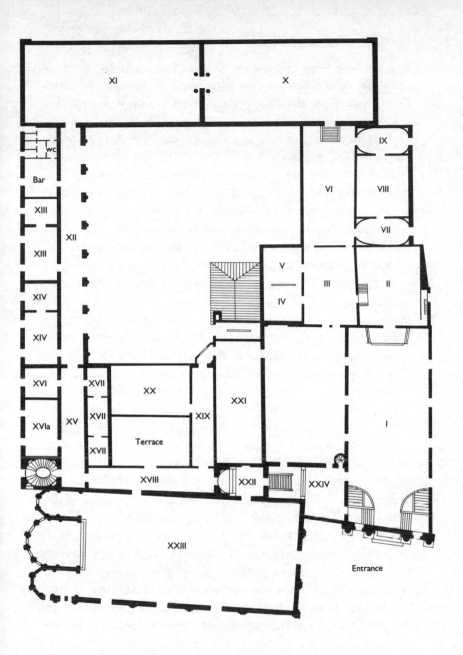

The Accademia

Agostino da Lodi, Boccaccio Boccaccino; XX, Miracles of the Relic of the Holy Cross from the Scuola of St John the Evangelist; XXI, the St Ursula Cycle by Vittore Carpaccio; XXII, neoclassical landscape settings; XXIII, 15C works of the Venetian School; XXIV, Titian, Antonio Vivarini, Giovanni d'Alemagna.

After crossing the *campo,* we turn right on Rio Terà Antonio Foscarini, created in 1863 by filling in Rio Sant' Agnese, which extended from the Grand Canal to the Giudecca Canal. At the second corner on the left we turn into Calle Nova Sant'Agnese, which, after the first intersection on the right, becomes Piscina del Forner.

At the end of Piscina del Forner on the left is the entrance to Palazzo Cini-Valmarana (No. 864), built in 1600. The palace now houses the Vittore Cini collection of Tuscan paintings and decorative arts, which is open to the public during the summer. These works were collected by Vittorio Cini (1884–1977), patron of the arts and philanthropist, whose estate is now administered by the Cini Foundation.

We now cross Ponte San Vio to the *campo* of the same name, which opens out to the Grand Canal. The name comes from the ancient church of San Vio – dedicated to St Vito and St Modesto – which was demolished in 1813. Fragments of the church were used in the construction of a chapel dedicated to St Vito and St Modesto which was erected at the back of the *campo* in 1865 to a design by Giovanni Pividor; this is now a private house and is not open to the public.

On the south-east side of the *campo* is the Anglican church of St George, erected in 1926 to a design by Luigi Marangoni, with sculptural decoration by Napoleone Martinuzzi. In the *campo* there is a *vera da pozzo* dating from the first decade of the 16C. The side of the well-head has two reliefs representing saints, undoubtedly St Vito and St Modesto.

We leave the *campo* on Calle de la Chiesa. At the end of the block we pass on our right Ponte del Formager which crosses Rio de le Toresele at a bend in the canal. We continue straight ahead on Fondamenta Venier dei Leoni, which takes us along the north bank of Rio de le Toresele. Halfway along the *fondamenta*, at No. 707, we pass on our left a 13C Veneto-Byzantine archway. At the end of the *fondamenta* we turn left into Calle San Cristofolo, which at a bend to the right halfway along its length brings us to the entrance of the former Palazzo Venier dei Leoni, now the Guggenheim Museum of Contemporary Art.

The palace was designed for the Venier family in 1749 by Lorenzo Boschetti, whose plans called for a huge edifice that would stretch back from the Grand Canal to Rio de le Toresele. However, a shortage of funds interrupted the project after the erection of the ground-floor wing on the Grand Canal, and the rest of the site remained a garden. It seems that the family kept one or more lions caged in the garden, and so the unfinished palace came to be known as the Palazzo Venier dei Leoni. The palace was eventually demolished except for the ground floor facade on the Grand Canal. In 1948 the site was purchased by Peggy Guggenheim, who held an exhibition of her collection of modern sculpture in the garden of the palace in 1949. By that time work had already commenced on the modern building that today houses the museum behind the facade of Palazzo Venier dei Leoni.

We continue along the second stretch of Calle San Cristofolo. At the end of the *calle* we cross Ponte Cristofolo to Campo Barbaro, whose left side is formed by the garden wall of Palazzo Dario. A plaque on the garden wall in the *campo* records that the French writer Henri de Régnier lived in the palace between 1899 and 1901, noting appreciatively that he wrote *venezianamente*, or 'in the Venetian manner'. This is evident in his description of the evening view from Palazzo Dario, as he writes in his *Esquisses Vénitiennes*:

As I write these words, the evening light thickens over the Grand Canal, the bells sound under a grey November sky. From my table at the window I see the gondolas glide over the water with their black Harlequins at the stern. Here and there a light goes up in the facade of a palace.

We now cross Ponte San Gregorio, continuing straight ahead on Calle del Bastion and then on Calle San Gregorio. This brings us into Campo San Gregorio, named for the church at its far end.

The church of San Gregorio was founded in the 9C. In 989 it was given to the Benedictines of Sant'Ilario, who founded an abbey here in 1160. The church was rebuilt in 1445–61 by Antonio da Cremonase, who added the present Gothic facade and the triple apse at the rear. Then in 1806 both the church and monastery were suppressed by the French. The church now serves as a laboratory for the Directorate of Fine Arts and Historic Monuments. The building to the right of the church is its former *canonica*. Built into its facade to the left of its doorway is a Gothic arch, all that remains of a 14C funerary monument. In front of the church there is a superb *vera da pozzo* of the 15C.

Leaving the *campo* at its far corner on the left, we follow Calle de l'Abazia and then the *sottoportego* of the same name, with the church on our right and on our left Abbazia di San Gregorio, the surviving cloister of the Gothic abbey. At the end of the *sottoportego* we emerge at Rio de la Salute and Ponte de l'Abazia. There we are confronted with the magnificent church of the Madonna della Salute, standing on a high platform above its *campo* near the eastern end of the Grand Canal.

The Salute is built on the site of the Ospizia della Trinità, founded in the 11–12C. This was demolished in 1630 to make way for the Salute, which was built as a plea to the Virgin to deliver Venice from the terrible plague which struck the city that year. A competition was held and fifteen architects submitted their designs for the church, with that of Baldassare Longhena being chosen as the winner. The cornerstone of the church of Santa Maria della Salute, Our Lady of Salvation, was laid on 1 April 1631. On 28 November of that year Doge Francesco Erizzo was able to announce that the plague had ended, whereupon he led a procession of thanksgiving to the site of the Salute on a bridge of boats across the Grand Canal, initiating an annual festival that continues to the present day. Construction of the church was not completed until 1681, the year before Longhena died. The sculptural decoration of both the exterior and interior continued for another six years, completed in time for the consecration of the church on 9 November 1687.

The church has a centralized octagonal plan, whose internal arrangements are reflected in its external appearance. The central space is defined by eight enormous piers that support the octagonal drum of the main dome. A great arch frames the chancel, which is surmounted by a lower dome, with semicircular exedrae on either side covered by semi-domes. Around the central octagonal space is the ambulatory, from which six radial chapels open up in the projected spaces between each pair of side piers. Each of the chapels projects from the periphery of the building in a tympanum with a semicircular window, above which is the roof of the ambulatory and the sides of the octagonal drum of the dome, each with two windows. From each corner of the dome there project two spiral volutes, sixteen in all, highly decorative elements that also serve as buttresses for the central dome. The smaller dome over the chancel is flanked to its rear by twin bell-towers with loggias, each of them surmounted by a little cupola. The central entrance is flanked by four colossal Corinthianesque semi-columns on high pedestals; above them is the architrave, surmounted over the two inner columns by a triangular pediment. The sculptural decoration, including the statues and reliefs on the main facade and the numerous figures on the other sides and on the volutes, is attributed to Francesco Cavrioli, Giusto Le Court, Michele Ungaro and Tommaso Ruer. The statue surmounting the lantern of the main dome represents the Madonna as Admiral of the Sea.

The three chapels on the right side of the nave have altarpieces by Luca Giordano; starting from the rear, these are *The Presentation of the Virgin, The Assumption* and *The Birth of the Virgin*. On the second altar there is a statue of St Girolamo Miani by Gian Maria Morleiter.

The high altar in the chancel, designed by Longhena, is surmounted by a vault carried on four enormous Corinthian columns from the Roman theatre at Pola. The sculptural group above the high altar is by Giusto Le Court; at the centre are the Virgin and Child in glory with Venice kneeling before them pleading for protection from the plague, which is represented by the figure of an old hag fleeing from the scene. The altarpiece is a sacred Byzantine icon of the Virgin and Child, brought from Crete in 1669 by Francesco Morosini. Behind the high altar the 17C monks' choir extends around the periphery of the apse. The paintings in the three central panels of the ceiling are by Giuseppe Salviati, depicting *The Prophet Elijah Fed by an Angel, The Fall of Manna* and *The Prophet Habakkuk Comforts Daniel in the Lion's Den*.

A door on the left side of the apse leads into the sacristy. On the end wall over the altar there is a painting done in 1512 by Titian, showing *St Mark Enthroned, with Sts Sebastian, Roch, Cosmas and Damian*. Flanking the altar are eight roundels by Titian with heads of the Evangelists and Fathers of the Church, done *c.* 1540–49 for the monastery of Santo Spirito in Isola. The exquisite tapestry on the altar-front dates from the 15C; it is decorated with a scene showing the Descent of the Holy Ghost among the Apostles, based on a cartoon by Mantegna. On the wall opposite the entrance is a large canvas depicting *The Marriage at Cana*, a masterpiece signed by Jacopo Tintoretto and dated 1551. On the ceiling there are three panels that were done by Titian for Santo Spirito *c.* 1540–49: *The Sacrifice of Abraham, David Killing Goliath* and *Cain and Abel*. Other paintings in the sacristy include five by Giuseppe Salviati, two by Palma il Giovane, one each by Pier Maria Pennacchi, Girolamo da Treviso and Alessandro

Varottari, as well as two attributed to Pietro Liberi and one to Marco Basaiti.

Returning to the nave, the altarpiece in the first chapel from the front on the left is *The Descent of the Holy Spirit*, done by Titian *c*. 1555 for Santo Spirito. The altarpieces in the second and third chapels are by Pietro Liberi: *Venice Pleading with St Anthony to Relieve Her from the Plague* and *The Annunciation*.

The building to the left of the church is the Patriarchal Seminary. This was built in 1669–71 by Baldassare Longhena as a monastery for the Somaschi Fathers; the order was suppressed by the French in 1810, and seven years later, through a decree by Francis I of Austria, the building became the Patriarchal Seminary. Under the direction of its canon, Father Moschini, the seminary began to collect paintings and other works of art removed from the suppressed churches and seminaries of Venice. These were augmented by the acquisition of the art collection of Federico Manfredini (1743–1829) of Rovigo. These works can be seen by special appointment.

On the wall joining the seminary to the church of the Salute there are five statues, all taken from the demolished church of the Virgin in Castello; one of these, the Saviour, is by Giulio del Moro, and the other four are by Orazio Marinali. Directly in front of the seminary there is a *vera da pozzo* dating from the second half of the 15C.

We now walk out along Fondamenta de la Dogana a la Salute. This takes us past the Dogana da Mar, the Republic's maritime customs house, built in 1677 by Giuseppe Benoni. The Doric facade that extends from the end of the customs house out to Punta Dogana is also by Benoni, and was built in 1676–82. At the apex of the Doric facade there is a little tower surmounted by a monument designed by Bernardo Falcone: two Atlantes in bronze support a golden globe on which the gilded bronze figure of Fortune stands poised with a weather-vane.

Continuing around the point, we soon cross Rio de la

Salute on Ponte de l'Umiltà. The bridge is named for the former church of Santa Maria dell'Umiltà, Our Lady of Humility, which stood in what is now the sports field of the seminary. The church was built in 1578–89; it was suppressed by the French in 1805 and demolished in 1824.

On the other side of the bridge is the beginning of Fondamenta Zattere, which extends from there along almost the entire shore of Dorsoduro on the Giudecca Canal. This canalside promenade was known in earlier times as 'la Carbonaria', from the coal that was unloaded there; it was paved in 1519, and since then it has been called the Zattere, from the *zatte*, or rafts, that were floated down the rivers of the Veneto into the lagoon and tied up there, after which they were disassembled and their logs used as lumber.

A short way along the Zattere we turn right into Calle del Squero. At the end of the *calle* we turn left into Rio Terà del Catacumeni, laid out on a canal filled in during the 18C. The street is named for the building that takes up its entire left side, the former Hospice of the Catacumeni. This was built soon after the battle of Lepanto in 1571 to house Muslim prisoners-of-war and slaves who chose to become Christians. The hospice was completely rebuilt in 1727 by Giorgio Massari, who also erected here an oratory dedicated to St John the Baptist.

We now turn left on Rio Terà ai Saloni. Halfway down the street on the right, at Nos. 70–72, we see Palazzetto Costantini, a quaint little Gothic palace of the early 15C. The arcaded *sottoportego*, with its wooden architrave under the piano nobile of the palace, dates from the 14C.

At the end of the street we turn right on Fondamenta Zattere, passing the huge single-storey building that formerly served as the Magazzini del Sale, the salt warehouse. The original warehouse was built in 1340 around Punta Dogana, with the present building here on the Zattere being erected in 1830 by Alvise Pigazzi.

At Rio de le Fornace, we turn right on Fondamenta Ca'

Balà. After walking by the canal-side facade of the Magazzini del Sale, we pass on our left Ponte de Mezo, the Middle Bridge. A few steps beyond the bridge we turn into an unnamed alleyway, where halfway along on the right we see a plaque identifying the house in which the poet Ezra Pound spent the last decade of his life.

Sixty metres farther along, at No. 222, we see a 16C house with a seven-part mullioned window, with a balcony over its round-arched entrance. Then, just after passing Rio Terà del Spezier, we see at No. 212 another 16C house with mullioned windows.

At the end of the *fondamenta* we turn left to cross the canal on Ponte San Gregorio. We then turn left again to walk back along the west bank of the canal on Fondamenta Soranzo de la Fornace. At the end of the *fondamenta* we turn right on Calle de la Crea, passing on our left at the corner a house with an ornate entrance and a statue of the Madonna and Child at the corner of an upper terrace garden. At the end of the *calle* we turn left into Campiello allo Spirito Santo, which we cross diagonally to enter Calle Larga de la Chiesa. This brings us once again out to Fondamenta Zattere, where on our right we come to Spirito Santo, the church of the Holy Ghost.

The church and its monastery were founded in 1483 and rebuilt early in the 16C. The complex was suppressed in 1806, but the church was reopened a few years later. The facade is in the Lombardesque style of the early 16C, while the interior is largely due to reconstruction and redecoration in the following two centuries. Almost the whole of the *controfacciata* wall is taken up with the elaborate funerary monument of the Paruta family, attributed to Baldassare Longhena. The third altar from the front on the left has a painting of *The Marriage of the Virgin* by Palma il Giovane. The paintings on the other altars are by Nicolò Renieri, Giovanni Buonconsiglio, Antonio Marinetti and Fra Felice Cignaroli.

Beside the church to the right is the former Scuola dello

Spirito Santo, founded in 1506 and suppressed three centuries later.

A short distance farther along the Zattere we come to the huge three-storeyed building that formerly served as the Ospedale degli Incurabili, the Hospital for Incurables. This was founded in 1522 by St Gaetano of Thiene, whose work was carried on by St Girolamo Miani, with St Ignatius Loyola also serving in the hospital in its early years. The patients were initially lepers and syphilitics, but later it was converted into an orphanage, which, like other such institutions in Venice, became renowned for its musical performances. The present building was constructed in the years 1527–91. The hospital was suppressed by the French in 1807; since then it has been used for a variety of purposes, and now serves as a home for juvenile delinquents.

After passing the main facade of the Ospedale we turn right on Campiello drio agli Incurabili. At the rear of the *campiello* there is an ornate entrance surmounted by a coat of arms, with an inscription noting that it belonged to the Procurates de Ultra, dated 1613. The house at No. 560 was once the residence of the historian Horatio Brown, who moved to Venice in 1874. As Brown wrote of the atmosphere here in his day: 'And on the Zattere the air is laden with the perfume of honeysuckle and other creepers that trail over the wall of Princess Dolgorouki's garden.'

We continue through the rear of the *campiello* on Calle degli Incurabili, which takes us along the eastern side of the Ospedale. After passing through a *sottoportego* we turn right and then find ourselves in a labyrinth of narrow *calli* and tiny *campielli* behind the Ospedale, with old houses dating back to the 16C and two *vere da pozzo* of the 15–16C. Bearing ahead and to the right through a *campiello*, and then a *ramo*, another *campiello* and a *calle*, all named Incurabili, we eventually turn right on Calle del Navaro and then continue straight ahead on Rio Terà San Vio. At the eastern end of Rio Terà San Vio we turn left on Calle Molin o de Case Rote, which takes us through two *sottoporteghi* before emerging on the final right-angle bend of Rio de le Toresele before it joins the Grand Canal. There we turn left on Fondamenta Ospedaleto, where at No. 372 we pass a 17C *palazzo* with a walled garden to its right. Beyond that is Corte del Sabion, in which there is a *vera da pozzo* of the 15C. At the end of the *fondamenta* we turn right to cross Ponte del Formager, after which we turn left into Calle de la Chiesa.

This brings us back into Campo San Vio, where we turn left on Fondamenta de Ca' Bragadin, following the east bank of Rio de San Vio. The *fondamenta* is named for a *palazzo* of the Bragadin family, which was destroyed by fire in the 18C. At No. 605, there is a small three-storeyed house with a central wrought-iron balcony, built in the 18C for the Scuola di San Rocco. At No. 587 we see Ospizio Pizzochere di Sant'Agnese, a hospice founded in 1432 and recently restored.

Continuing to the end of the *fondamenta*, we turn right to cross the canal on Ponte de la Calcine, bringing us to the little *campiello* of the same name. The bridge and *campiello* take their name from the fact that stores of lime (*calcine*) used to be unloaded there. On the landward side of the *campo* stands the Pensione Calcina, which has on its main facade a plaque recording that John Ruskin lived here in 1877. Ruskin lived on the ground floor, as he indicates in a letter: 'I look along the water instead of down on it and get perfectly picturesque views of boats instead of mast-head ones, and I think I shall be comfy.'

At the back of the *campiello* we enter Calle del Pistor, which after passing through a *sottoportego* takes us out on to the broader Calle Antonio da Ponte, named after the renowned Venetian architect. We turn left here and then a short way along we turn right into Piscina Sant'Agnese. About 50 m along this street we come to a *vera da pozzo* of the late 17C or early 18C. A short way farther along we see on our left, at Nos. 830–33, an 18C house with a niche on its facade containing a statue of the Madonna. The handsome building just beyond this, at No. 834, is Palazzetto Sant'Agnese, a 15C Gothic palace.

At the end of the street we turn left on Calle Nova Sant'Agnese. Then at the next corner we turn left again, on the broad and tree-shaded Rio Terà Antonio Foscarini, the former Rio de Sant'Agnese. On the left, at Nos. 880–81, is the site of the ancient Palazzo Contarini, partly demolished and altered in 1863 when the canal was filled in. This *palazzo* was the residence of Senator Antonio Foscarini, for whom the street is named. Foscarini was executed for treason on 20 April 1622, in a sensational case involving Lady Arundel. Four months later the Council of Ten discovered that Foscarini was innocent, whereupon they executed the person who had falsely accused him and reburied the Senator with the highest honours.

Just beyond Calle Larga Pisani we see on our right, at No. 979A, the ancient Palazzo Pisani. This palace originally belonged to Doge Agostino Barbarigo (1486–1501), who bequeathed it to Bartolomeo Pisani. Then at the end of the street we come on our left to the church of Sant'Agnese, which stands with its side on the *campo* of the same name.

The church of Sant'Agnese was founded in the 10–11C and rebuilt in the early 14C. It was suppressed by the French in 1810, after which it was stripped of its furnishings and works of art. The church was reopened in 1872 by the Cavanis Fathers and has been restored in recent years. The only notable art work remaining in the church is a painting of *The Guardian Angel* by Lattanzio Querena.

In the centre of the *campo* beside the church there is an hexagonal *vera da pozzo* dated 1520. On one side of the wellhead there is a relief of a robed female figure, undoubtedly representing Sant'Agnese.

We leave the *campo* midway along its southern side via Sottoportego Trevisan, which is named for the building that forms its left side, the 15C Palazzo Trevisan, now the Swiss Consulate. At the end of the *sottoportego* we turn right on the

Zattere, passing at the end of the block Rio Terà Gesuati. This brings us to the church of the Gesuati.

The church takes its name from the order of the Poor Gesuati, founded in Venice in 1392. The Gesuati first established themselves at the church of Sant'Agnese; then, with funds from a bequest, they built a church and monastery here in 1494–1524. The church was dedicated to San Girolamo, but to the Venetians it came to be known after its founders as the Gesuati. After the suppression of the Gesuati in 1688 the Dominicans took possession of the church. Then in 1724 the Dominicans under Fra Paolo commissioned Giorgio Massari to build the present church, dedicated to Santa Maria del Rosario.

Between the columns of the classical facade there are four niches in two rows containing statues representing Virtues. On the right side of the church, in Rio Terà Gesuati, there is a relief showing the Dead Christ Supported by Two Angels, a 15C work of the Paduan school.

The rectangular nave is flanked by four pairs of columns on each side. Between the columns there are reliefs of biblical scenes and statues of saints and Old Testament figures, all by Gian Maria Morleiter. In the ceiling there are frescoes painted by Tiepolo in 1737–9; in the centre is *The Institution of the Rosary*; in the other parts are scenes involving St Dominic and St Augustine.

The first chapel from the rear on the right side has a painting of *The Virgin and Sts Catherine of Siena, Rose of Lima and Agnes*, done by Giambattista Tiepolo *c*. 1740. In the second chapel the marble altarpiece representing Angels in Glory, by Gian Maria Morleiter, frames a portrait of St Dominic, done in 1743 by Giambattista Piazzetta. The altarpiece in the third chapel is a painting of *Sts Vincent Ferrer, Hyacinth and Louis Bertrand*, done by Piazzetta *c*. 1739. The high altar is surmounted by an elaborate ciborium carried on marble columns, with a tabernacle encrusted with lapis lazuli. Behind the altar is a painting of *The Virgin and Child*, signed by Matteo Ingoli and dated 1630.

247

The first chapel from the front on the left has as its altarpiece a painting of *The Crucifixion*, a superb work done by Jacopo Tintoretto in the years 1555–60. The altarpiece in the third chapel is a painting of *St Pope Pius V between St Thomas Aquinas and St Peter Martyr*, done by Sebastiano Ricci in 1733.

The building to the left of the church is the former monastery of the Gesuati, dedicated to Santa Maria della Visitazione, Our Lady of the Visitation. This is now used as a craft school for orphaned boys.

Immediately beyond the monastery is the little church of Santa Maria della Visitazione. The church, which was attached to the monastery of the Gesuati, was built in 1494–1524, and is attributed to either Mauro Coducci or Tullio Lombardo. The church was suppressed at the beginning of the 19C and stripped of its furnishings and works of art. It was re-opened in 1825, restored in 1884 and again in 1947–8. The interior retains its original coffered ceiling forming a frieze around the walls, with fifty-eight compartments each containing a portrait of a saint or prophet, with a medallion of *The Visitation* in the centre; these are Tuscan works of the 16C and are attributed to Pier Paolo Agabiti.

Continuing along the Zattere, the building beyond the church is the 15C Palazzo Cavanis (No. 920). The second building beyond that is the 16C Palazzo Moro (Nos. 926–8), which stands at the junction of Rio de San Trovaso and the Giudecca Canal. At the corner beneath it is a 15C portico with a wooden architrave supported by stone columns.

We now turn right on Fondamenta Nani to walk along the east bank of Rio de San Trovaso, which 40 m beyond the bridge is joined on the left by Rio dei Ognissanti. Just beyond the junction of the two canals we see the oldest *squero* in Venice, a picturesque boatyard dating from the 17C. Since 1884 the *squero* has been operated by three generations of the Tramontin family, who still make and repair gondolas.

Just beyond the *squero* on the west bank of the canal is the

church of San Trovaso, which we will visit presently. Opposite the side facade of the church we pass on our right Palazzo
Nani-Barbarigo (Nos. 960–61). The palace was built in the
latter part of the 15C for the Barbarigo family, and in the
following century the interior was restored by Alessandro
Vittoria. The palace was the birthplace of two Doges: Marco
Barbarigo (1485–6) and Agostino Barbarigo (1486–1501). It
now houses a branch of the University of Venice.

After passing Calle Larga Nani we come to Ponte San
Trovaso. The building facing the bridge on our right, with its
entrance at No. 993, is the 17C Palazzo Gritti. As we approach
the next bridge, Ponte de le Maravegie, we pass on our right
the 17C Palazzo Basadonna-Giustinian-Priuli (No. 1012). The
palace was restored in 1983 and now houses a secondary
school for students studying art.

We turn left on to Ponte de le Maravegie, pausing on
the bridge to look at the *palazzo* just to the right on the west
bank of the canal, at No. 1071 on Fondamenta Bollani. This is
Palazzo Alessandra Maraviglia, dating from the 16C. The
palace is named for the heroine Alessandra Maraviglia, wife
of Pietro Albino, the last Venetian Grand Chancellor of
Cyprus. When Nicosia was captured by the Turks in 1570,
she set fire to the ship that was to take her and the other
captives to Istanbul, blowing it up along with the Turkish
vessels around it.

After crossing the bridge we turn left on Fondamenta
Sangiantoffetti. The first building that we pass is Palazzo
Bollani (No. 1073), now the Liceo Marco Polo. The palace
was built in 1709 for the Bollani family, who lived here until
1820. At No. 1075 we pass Palazzo Marcello-Sangiantoffetti.
The palace was built in the mid 16C for the Marcello family,
who commissioned Jacopo Tintoretto to decorate its facade
with frescoes, now nearly vanished. The palace now houses
another branch of the University of Venice.

Continuing along the *fondamenta*, we pass Ponte San Trovaso once again and then come to Campo San Trovaso. The

campo extends around the campanile and side facade of the church of San Trovaso to its main facade on Rio dei Ognissanti. On the part of the *campo* beside the church along Rio de San Trovaso there are two *vere da pozzo*. The first that we come to is a cylindrical well-head dating from the second half of the 14C, its sides decorated with reliefs of a Gothic shield and a Maltese cross. The well-head was the scene of a macabre incident that took place in June 1779, when the headless and dismembered corpse of a murdered man was found in the well, followed within a few hours by the discovery of other parts of his body in a well elsewhere in the city. The murderers turned out to be the man's wife and her lover, who were duly executed for the crime.

The second *vera da pozzo* beside the church dates from the 15C; on one of its sides there is a relief of a Gothic shield with the arms of the Giustinian family, a double-headed eagle. The house to the left of the side facade of the church is the *canonica* of San Trovaso; on its wall there is a Byzantine relief of St Peter dating from the 13C.

There is another *vera da pozzo* in the *campo* in front of the main facade of the church on Rio dei Ognissanti. This dates from the 16C, with an inscription on one panel recording that it was repaired in 1723 by the Provveditore Flaminio Corner. On another panel there is a relief of a robed figure with a halo around his head. This is presumably either St Gervasio or St Protasio, the two saints to whom the church is dedicated, their names being combined in Venetian dialect as San Trovaso.

San Trovaso was founded in the first half of the 9C, and was rebuilt after being destroyed by fire in 1105. This building collapsed on 11 September 1583, and in the following year work began on the present church, which was consecrated in 1657.

The second altar from the rear on the right has a painting of *St Costanzo of Ancone* by Gaspare Diziani. The altarpiece on the third altar depicts *St Francesco di Paola with Faith,*

Charity and a Donor by Alvise dal Friso. The transept on the right contains the Clary Chapel; the parapet of the altar is decorated with a relief of angels carved by a 15C sculptor known as the Master of San Trovaso. Over the side door is a painting of *The Marriage at Cana* by Andrea Vicentino.

The chapel to the right of the chancel has as its altarpiece a painting of *Christ on the Cross, with the Three Maries* by Domenico Tintoretto; on the left wall is *St Crisogono on Horseback* by Michele Giambono. On the walls of the chancel there are two large paintings by Jacopo Tintoretto and his assistants: on the left, *The Expulsion of Joachim from the Temple*; on the right, *The Adoration of the Magi*. In the chapel to the left of the chancel the altarpiece is *The Temptation of St Anthony* by Jacopo Tintoretto.

The left transept contains the Cappella del Sacramento, built in 1566, with a tabernacle in the style of Alessandro Vittoria; on the wall to the right is *The Last Supper* by Jacopo Tintoretto. The little chapel on the side has on its altar *The Deposition and the Three Maries* by Palma il Giovane. The first chapel from the front on the left has on its altar *The Birth of the Virgin*, signed by Palma il Giovane, who also did the altarpiece in the second chapel, *The Virgin in Glory with Saints*. The altarpiece in the third chapel is *The Coronation of the Virgin, and Saints* by Pietro Malombra.

We now cross Ponte de la Scoazera and make our way out to the Zattere on the west side of Ponte Longo. There we turn right to begin the last stretch of our itinerary, which will take us to the western end of the Zattere.

The first building of note that we come to on this western stretch of the Zattere is Palazzo Michiel-Clary (No. 1397), built in 1580, which now serves as the French Consulate. The building at No. 1402 is the 16C Palazzo Giustinian-Recanati. This branch of the Giustinian family has lived here since 1784, with an important art collection that includes works by Canaletto and Tiepolo. The building at No. 1404 is Palazzo Lippomano. The palace was built no later than 1661 by the

Lippomano family, Greeks from Euboea who were admitted to the Venetian nobility in 1381. At No. 1411 we come to Palazzo Molin, a 15C Gothic palace now used by the Adriatica Steamship Company. The building at Nos. 1416–17 is Palazzo Zorzi, built in 1614. The building at No. 1473 is the former Scuola dei Luganegheri, the Guild of Sausage-makers. This house was acquired by the guild in 1681; on the facade there is a statue of St Anthony Abbot, the patron saint of the guild.

Near the end of the Zattere we come to Pontile San Basegio, where we turn right on Calle del Vento, the Street of the Wind. At the end of Calle del Vento we enter Campo San Basegio, which on its left side opens on to Rio de San Basegio. The *campo* and canal, as well as the bridge that crosses it here, take their name from the ancient church of San Basegio (St Basil). San Basegio was founded in the 9C, suppressed by the French in 1810 and demolished in 1824.

The house on the south side of the *campo*, with its entrance at No. 1520, is the 16C Palazzo Molin, which extends all the way back to Fondamenta Zattere. The house on the north side of the *campo* at No. 1527A is the former Scuola degli Acquaroli, a guild of boatmen who transported water from the mainland for sale in Venice. In the centre of the *campo* there is a *vera da pozzo* dated 1558, with a relief representing St Basil, to whom the former church was dedicated.

We now retrace our steps along Calle del Vento, turning right on Fondamenta Molin, where Ponte Molin crosses to the Stazione Marittima. This brings one out on to what was originally the Santa Marta peninsula, the south-westernmost promontory of Venice. It is named for the 15C church of Santa Marta, now deconsecrated and abandoned, which still stands at the far end of the docks. Santa Marta was once famous for the festival that was celebrated here annually on the feast-day of the saint, 29 July, when everyone in Venice would come out to the peninsula after sunset in illuminated boats, and after a service in the church the rest of the evening would be spent in feasting with music and song.

After looking at the church, we continue along the road for another 150 m until it rounds the point and comes to Pontile Santa Marta on the Canale de la Scomenzera. There we can board the No. 5 *vaporetto*, which in one direction goes to Piazzale Roma and the other back to San Marco via the Giudecca Canal.

SESTIERE DI DORSODURO II (*Map Route 11*)

Our next itinerary will take us to the Giudecca, which is a part of Dorsoduro, though separated from the rest of the *sestiere* by the wide Giudecca Canal. We will begin our stroll at Pontile Zitelle, the easternmost stop of the No. 5 *vaporetto* on the Giudecca.

The Giudecca consists of a dozen small interconnected isles. In the early days of the Republic it was called Spinalonga and only later did it become known as the Giudecca. The Giudecca was in times past renowned for the beautiful gardens laid out by the nobles on their estates, all of which have now vanished.

As we land at Pontile Zitelle, we see just to the left of the landing one of the three principal monuments on the Giudecca. This is the church of Santa Maria della Presentazione, Our Lady of the Presentation, better known as Le Zittele, or the Virgins, since its convent ran a hospice for girls of destitute families, who were trained as lacemakers as well as in music. The church was designed by Palladio *c.* 1570, and built in 1582–6 by Jacopo Bozzetto. The classical Palladian facade is flanked by the two wings of the convent-hospice, which extends around behind the church, with its cloister to the rear of the apse.

On the altar to the right there is a painting by Palma il Giovane of *The Agony in the Garden*, with portraits of the donors, Pasquale and Elisabetta Foppa, whose tomb is in front of the altar. The painting on the high altar is *The Presentation of the Virgin in the Temple* by Francesco Bassano.

On the altar to the left the altarpiece depicts the *Virgin, St Francis and the Donor* by Antonio Vassilacchi.

East of the church the canal-side promenade is known as Fondamenta San Giovanni, which ends at the quay of the Guardia Finanza. The *fondamenta* is named for the former church and monastery of San Giovanni Battista, founded in 1340; the complex was suppressed by the French and demolished early in the 19C.

The building just to the east of the church at Nos. 25–6 is a remnant of the ancient Ca' Mosto. The building next to that, with its entrance at Nos. 20–21, is Palazzo Mocenigo, erected in the late 16C through a bequest from Doge Alvise Mocenigo (d. 1577). The following building, at Nos. 11–13, is a 15C Gothic palace. The building beyond that, with its entrance at No. 10, stands on part of the site of the ancient Palazzo Nani-Barbarigo. A plaque on the building records that it was the site of the Accademia Filosofia, founded in 1484 by Ermolao Barbaro.

We now start strolling westwards from the church of the Zitelle. The second building to the west of the church is the Casa da Maria (No. 43). This pseudo-Gothic structure was designed for his own use by the Bolognese painter Mario de Maria, who built it in the years 1910–13. The building to the west of that is the 17C Palazzo Minelli (No. 50).

About 150 m past Pontile Zitelle the canal-side promenade is called Fondamenta de la Croce. This is named for Santa Croce, the church of the Holy Cross, which we see about 100 m in from the *fondamenta*. The church and its monastery were founded in the 13C. The church was rebuilt in the second half of the 15C by an architect known as Maestro Pellegrini, while the facade, which is in the Tuscan style, was erected in 1505–15. The complex was suppressed at the beginning of the 19C; the church has recently been restored, but it remains closed.

We now cross Ponte de la Croce to Fondamenta San Giacomo, which after about 50 m brings us to the church of the Redentore.

The church was founded by a decree of the Signoria in

1576, when the end of a terrible epidemic led the Senate to commission the erection of a new church dedicated in thanksgiving to the Redentore, or Redeemer. The building was begun in 1577 to a design by Andrea Palladio, and completed in 1592 by Antonio da Ponte. Thenceforth the Doge and the Signoria led a procession there on the eve of the third Sunday in July, the feast-day of the Redentore, crossing the Giudecca Canal on a pontoon bridge to the church for a thanksgiving service and a joyous celebration afterwards, beginning an annual festival that continues to the present day.

The church stands on a rusticated pediment, approached by a flight of fifteen steps. The central part of the facade is in the form of a classical Greek temple front, with pairs of colossal semi-columns and pilasters flanking the entrance. Niches on either side of the doorway contain statues of St Mark and St Francis attributed to Girolamo Campagna; above the side angles of the lower segmental wings there are statues of St Lorenzo Giustinian and St Anthony of Padua.

There are two large lunettes on the *controfacciata* wall. One shows *The Virgin Presenting Jesus to the Blessed Capuchin Felice* by Pietro Vecchia. The upper one depicts *The Virgin among Saints Supplicated by the Doge and the Signoria to Free Venice from the Plague*, a monochrome by Paolo Piazza.

The first chapel from the rear on the right has on its altar a painting of *The Nativity* by Francesco Bassano. The altarpiece in the second chapel is *The Baptism of Christ*, begun by Veronese and completed by his 'heirs', who have signed the work and dated it 1588, the year of the master's death. The altarpiece in the third chapel is *The Flagellation*, attributed to Tintoretto, but probably a product of his workshop.

The high altar in the chancel, its sumptuous tabernacle decorated with bronzes, was made in 1679 by Giuseppe Mazza. On the parapet the carvings of the Way to Calvary and the Deposition are attributed to Tommaso Ruer. The three statues, representing St Francis, St Mark and the Crucifixion, were done by Girolamo Campagna.

The sacristy is approached from the rear of the chancel. The paintings here include: *The Madonna Adoring the Child, with Two Angel-musicians*, done in 1490 by Alvise Vivarini; *The Baptism of Jesus*, painted in 1560 by Paolo Veronese; *The Madonna and Child with Saints*, by Palma il Giovane; and four tablets of a Eucharist cycle, by Francesco Bassano.

A door leads from the monks' choir to the lay choir. The paintings here include *The Resurrection* by Francesco Bassano and *Christ before Pilate* by Leandro Bassano.

The altarpiece in the first chapel from the front on the left is a *Deposition*, by Palma il Giovane. On the altar of the second chapel is *The Resurrection*, signed by Francesco Bassano. The altarpiece in the third chapel is *The Ascension*, attributed to Jacopo Tintoretto, who probably designed the painting and had it carried out by his workshop.

Continuing westwards along the *fondamenta*, some 70 m beyond the Redentore we come to Campiello San Giacomo. This is the site of the former church of San Giacomo, founded in 1343. The church was suppressed by the French and then demolished in 1837.

The *palazzo* at Nos. 218–24 is the ancient house of the Visconti of Milan, known as Casa Bianca, which later passed to the Foscolo family. The house dates from the end of the 15C, its Renaissance facade including an elegant doorway and a fine row of windows.

At the end of this stretch of the *fondamenta* we come to Ponte Longo and the broad canal of the same name. Here we turn left to make a detour on Fondamenta del Ponte Longo, which extends along the eastern bank of the canal nearly to its end. Halfway along the canal it is joined on its western side by Rio de la Palada, which at the junction is crossed by Ponte Sant'Angelo. The bridge takes its name from the former church of Sant'Angelo, which stood on the west bank of Rio del Ponte Longo at the point where it joins the lagoon south of the Giudecca. The church, which was dedicated to St Angelo of Concordia, was founded in 1555, along with a small monastery. The complex was demolished in 1943 to make way for the Junghans watch and clock factory.

We now return to cross Ponte Longo. About 100 m from the bridge we pause at the entrance to Sottoportego de l'Ospedaleto. A tablet on the house at No. 322 records that this was the site of the Ospedale di San Pietro, founded in 1316 by Pietro Brustolato and restored in 1568.

We then continue walking westwards along the *fondamenta*, which, 60 m farther along, crosses Ponte Piccolo. The first house along the *fondamenta* on the other side, at No. 430, has set into its wall a relief with a pilgrim's cross flanked by the letters SR, the emblem of the Confraternity of San Rocco, founded in 1478. In the first turning on the left, Calle dei Spini, there is a late-15C *vera da pozzo* in pink Verona marble bearing this same symbol.

Ninety metres farther along the *fondamenta* we turn left into Calle del Forno. This takes us into Corte dei Cordami, surrounded by terraced houses of the 17C, each with a tall chimney. In the middle of the *corte* there is a *vera da pozzo* dating from the first half of the 16C.

We leave the *corte* at its north-west corner on Calle dei Nicoli, at the end of which we pass through a *sottoportego* to re-emerge on the *fondamenta*. There we turn left and continue just past Calle Longa de l'Accademia dei Nobili. The *calle* takes its name from the *palazzetto* at Nos. 607–8, the Accademia dei Nobili, erected in 1619 as a meeting-place for the nobility, the only such edifice that has survived in Venice.

A hundred metres farther along we come to the church of Sant'Eufemia, whose main facade faces the side canal of the same name.

The church was founded during the reign of Doge Orso Partecipazio I (864–81); it was dedicated to four women martyrs: Sts Euphemia, Dorothy, Tecla and Erasma, but in time it came to be called by the name of only the first of these saints. The church was reconsecrated in 1371 after being rebuilt; it was renovated in the second half of the 16C and again in the mid 18C. These building programmes are recorded on the wall of the Doric arcade that flanks the side of the church on the *campiello*, a portico erected in 1596 by Michele Sanmicheli. In a niche under the portico there is a relief of a bishop-saint, a Gothic carving of the 15C. On the facade above the end of the portico there is a relief of the Crucifixion and Donors, a work in the Byzantine style dating from the 14C. Over the doorway of the church there is a relief of the Madonna and Child between St Euphemia and St Roch, done by the Bregno family at the beginning of the 16C.

Despite its later restorations, the church still retains its original form of a Veneto-Byzantine basilica, divided into a central nave and side aisles by two colonnades, some of whose columns and capitals date from the 11C. The frescoes on the ceiling of the nave and side aisles were done in 1764 by Giambattista Canal, depicting *St Euphemia in Glory* and scenes from her life. The altarpiece on the first altar from the rear on the right is part of a triptych depicting *St Roch and the Angel*, with a lunette of the *Virgin and Child*, signed by Bartolomeo Vivarini and dated 1480.

The chapel to the right of the chancel has on its altar an urn containing the remains of the Blessed Giuliana da Collalto (d. 1262). On the left wall of the chancel there is a painting of *The Last Supper* signed by Alvise dal Friso. On the second altar there is a marble statue of the Virgin holding the dead Christ by Gian Maria Morleiter.

We now cross Ponte Sant'Eufemia to make a detour along Fondamenta San Biagio, the last stretch of the canal-side promenade on the Giudecca. The building at No. 760, which has its main facade on Rio de Sant'Eufemia, is a factory dating from the end of the 18C, restored in 1970 and now divided into private apartments. The building at Nos. 761–77 is the 18C Palazzo Emo; No. 786 is the 15C Palazzo Maffetti; No. 788 is the Palazzo Vendramin, built for Doge Andrea Vendramin (1476–8) and reconstructed in the mid 16C, probably to a design by Jacopo Sansovino; and No. 795 is the 15C Palazzo Foscari. The remaining buildings along the *fondamenta* are part of the former Magazzini Vendramin, a vast warehouse for salt and coal used from *c.* 1400 up until the end of the 19C.

At the end of the *fondamenta* we look across Rio de San Biagio to the neglected Mulino Stucky, an enormous flour-mill erected in 1896 for the industrialist Giovanni Stucky. The mill ceased production in 1954 and since then it has been abandoned.

Rio de San Biagio is named for an ancient church that stood at what is now the north-west corner of Mulino Stucky. The church, dedicated to St Biagio and St Cataldo, was founded in the 10C. In 1222 a Benedictine convent was founded next to the church by the Blessed Giuliana da Collalto. The complex was suppressed in 1810 by the French and then demolished in 1882.

We now retrace our steps to Campiello Sant'Eufemia, where we turn right on Fondamenta del Rio de Sant'Eufemia. At the end of the *fondamenta* we come to Campo San Cosmo, which is at the junction of Rio de Sant'Eufemia and Rio de la Convertite.

At the far side of the *campo* we see the former church of Santi Cosmo e Damiano, founded in 1481. The church was rebuilt in its present form in the mid 16C, its facade attributed to Guglielmo Bergamasco. The church and its convent, which stands to its east, were suppressed in 1810. The church has been restored in recent years, but it remains closed to the public.

Ponte Lagoscuro leads across from the *campo* to Fondamenta de le Convertite, which extends along the south bank of the canal of the same name. A hundred metres along the *fondamenta*, just after passing Ponte de le Case Nove, we come to the church of the Convertite, dedicated to St Mary Magdalene. This is part of a complex, founded in 1534, that included the church, a convent and a hospice for reformed prostitutes. The church came to be called 'delle Convertite', since the purpose of its hospice was to convert fallen women to a more godly way of life. But not long after its founding the Convertite acquired a notorious reputation through the activities of its rector, Fra Giovan Pietro Leon, who for nearly twenty years used the convent as his private harem. He was finally denounced to the Council of Ten in 1561, after which he was beheaded and his remains burned.

The Convertite complex was suppressed by the French in the first decade of the 19C; since 1957 it has served as a women's penitentiary.

There is nothing else of interest to see on the Giudecca beyond this point, and so we will retrace our steps to Pontile Sant'Eufemia, where we can take a *vaporetto* to the Zattere or San Marco.

SESTIERE DI DORSODURO III (*Map Route 12*)

Our third and last itinerary through Dorsoduro will begin at the foot of Ponte de l'Accademia in Campo de la Carità.

We leave the *campo* via Calle Gambara, from where we make our way by the most direct route to Campo San Barnaba. There we come to the church of San Barnaba, whose classical facade dominates the right side of the *campo*.

San Barnaba was founded in the 9C. The church in its present form dates from a rebuilding in 1749–76 by Lorenzo Boschetti. The main facade is in the form of a Greek temple front, its monumental entrance flanked by four colossal semi-columns supporting an architrave surmounted by a pediment.

The ceiling is decorated with a fresco depicting *St Barnabas in Glory*, and another in the vault of the chancel represents *Faith*, both attributed to Costantino Cedini. On the side walls of the chancel there are paintings of *The Way to Calvary* and *The Last Supper*, both by Palma il Giovane. The paintings on the other altars are by Antonio Foler, Francesco Beccaruzzi, Giuseppe Gobbis and Damiano Mazza, with one attributed to Giovanni of Asola and his

son Bernardino. *The Holy Family*, attributed to \
being restored.

In the centre of the *campo* there is a *vera da pozzo*
from the first quarter of the 16C; on its sides there are re
representing St Barnabas and St Anthony of Padua.

Campo San Barnaba gave its name to the Barnabotti,
impoverished nobles who were attracted to this parish because
of the lower rents here. The Barnabotti still kept their hereditary seats in the Maggior Consiglio, where their votes were
for sale to the highest bidder.

Campo San Barnaba is enlivened by one of the oldest
markets in Venice, in which vegetables are sold from barges
tied up along Fondamenta Gherardini at the foot of Ponte dei
Pugni, the Bridge of Fisticuffs. The bridge takes its name
from the traditional brawls that took place there between the
two factions of working-class Venetians, the Castellani and
the Nicoletti, the former coming from the parish of San
Pietro in Castello and the latter from San Nicolò dei Mendicoli in Dorsoduro. At times of festivals the two factions met
in force on the bridge, which then had no balustrades, punch-
ing their opponents, beating them with clubs and throwing
them into the canal. The battles eventually became so bloody
that the fight on the bridge was banned and was replaced by
more civilized competitions in the Piazza San Marco. Today
the battles between the Castellani and the Nicoletti on Ponte
dei Pugni are commemorated by the imprint of two opposing
pairs of footprints in white stone on the paving of the bridge.

We leave the *campo* at its north-east corner via Ponte San
Barnaba, after which we turn right on Fondamenta Ca'
Rezzonico. This takes us along the north bank of Rio San
Barnaba to Ca' Rezzonico.

Around 1667 the Procurator Filippo Bon commissioned
Baldassare Longhena to rebuild two of his houses on this site
and convert them into a single palace. By the time of Longhena's death in 1682 the new palace was complete only up to
the height of the piano nobile. No further work was done

until 1745, when the heirs of Filippo Bon commissioned Giorgio Massari to construct the next two floors. But in 1751 financial difficulties forced the Bon family to sell the partially completed palace to Gian Battista Rezzonico. Rezzonico retained the services of Massari, who completed the palace in 1756. The fortunes of the Rezzonico reached a peak in 1758, when Gian Battista's younger brother Carlo was elected Pope as Clement III. During the following half century the Rezzonico family amassed an extraordinary collection of paintings, furniture and other works of art to adorn the palace, which was generally considered to be one of the most splendid in Venice in the last decades of the Republic. The family became extinct after the death of Abbondio Rezzonico in 1810, after which the palace passed to a succession of owners. In 1889 Ca' Rezzonico was purchased by the wealthy American wife of Robert ('Pen') Barrett Browning, son of the poet Robert Browning, who died here on 12 December of that year. A plaque on the facade of the palace where Rio de San Barnaba joins the Grand Canal commemorates the poet's death, quoting a line from one of his poems as an epitaph: 'Open my heart and you will see / Graved inside of it "Italy".'

The palace was acquired by the Commune of Venice in June 1934. After renovations the building was opened to the public on 25 April 1936 as a museum of Venetian decorative arts of the 18C, the palace's own treasures having been augmented with paintings, sculpture and furniture from other *palazzi* in Venice of the same period.

The ceilings of the various rooms in the palace are decorated with frescoes and the illusory architectural perspectives known as quadratures. The frescoes and other ceiling paintings, some done originally for Ca' Rezzonico and some for other *palazzi*, are by Giambattista Tiepolo, Giandomenico Tiepolo, Jacopo Guarana and other leading artists of the 18C. One of the galleries is devoted entirely to an extraordinary series of frescoes that Giandomenico Tiepolo painted in the years

1797–1804 in the family's little villa at Zianingo, near Mirano.

The framed paintings in the palace include the only views by Canaletto in the public collections of Venice: *View of Rio dei Mendicanti* and *The Grand Canal from Ca' Balbi towards the Rialto.* There is also a masterpiece by Giambattista Piazzetta, *The Death of Darius.* There are two famous works by Francesco Guardi, *The Nuns' Parlatory at San Zaccaria* and *The Foyer,* and a series of delightful genre paintings by Pietro Longhi. The other paintings include works by Alessandro Longhi, Francesco Zugno, Rosalba Carriera, Luca Carlevaris, Gregorio Lazzarini, Bernardo Strozzi and Francesco Zuccarelli; as well as sculptures by Alessandro Vittoria, Giorgio Massari, Giusto Le Court and Andrea Brustolon, whose superb furniture and other objects of art made for Palazzo Venier at San Vio are displayed in the Ballroom and the Sala del Brustolon. The third floor has a collection of Venetian costumes; a room fitted out as an old-fashioned chemist's shop; a marionette theatre; a collection of 18C Venetian china; a collection of chinoiserie; and a number of paintings, sketches and sculptures, including terracotta models for statues. The marionettes, which belong to the Correr Museum, represent the characters of the old *commedia dell'arte* and the Italian maskers illustrated in a painting, *The Three Maskers,* by Marco Marcola.

After leaving the museum we retrace our steps along Fondamenta Ca' Rezzonico as far as the second turning, just before Ponte San Barnaba, where we turn right into a *sottoportego* that leads into Calle Padroco. At the far end of the *calle* we pass through another *sottoportego* and then turn right on Calle del Fabro.

At the next corner, where Calle del Capeler leads to the left, we take a brief detour by continuing straight ahead on Calle Bernardo, followed by a left into Campiello Bernardo. In the centre of the *campiello* there is a very interesting *vera da pozzo* dating from the second half of the 14C or the beginning

263

of the 15C. On the sides of the well-head there are reliefs of a Gothic shield, a Gothic rosette and a seated Lion of St Mark, the latter being the only emblem of the kind that has survived in Venice, all of the others having been effaced in 1797 by the French as symbols of the Venetian Republic.

After our detour we return to the last corner we passed and there turn right on Calle del Capeler. At the end of the *calle* we come to Campiello dei Squelini, which we cross to enter Calle de Ca' Foscari. At the end of the *calle* we come to Ponte de Ca' Foscari. The bridge takes its name from the magnificent Ca' Foscari, whose entrance is on the right at No. 3246, a Gothic archway surmounted by the Foscari coat of arms supported by putti.

The garden to the left at the far side of the bridge is on the site of the ancient Palazzo Renier. The building to the left of the garden on the canal is the 17C Palazzo Secco Dolfin, whose rooms were once decorated with frescoes by Giambattista Tiepolo.

After crossing the bridge we continue in the same direction on Calle Larga Foscari, at the end of which we turn left on Crosera. On the corner at our left, at No. 3855, there is a small 14C house with a three-light mullioned window surmounted by Venetian Gothic arches. About 40 m along Crosera we see on the left, at Nos. 3820–21, a house with a 15C Gothic arch over its doorway.

We now turn left on Calle San Pantalon. At the end of the *calle*, where it widens and veers left to enter Campo San Pantalon, we turn left into Campiello de Ca' Angaran. The *campiello* takes its name from Ca' Angaran, a pair of 18C houses at Nos. 3717–18, built by the Angaran family of Piacenza; on the facade there is an interesting marble medallion with the figure of a Byzantine emperor, a work from Constantinople dating from the 10C. We continue on through Sottoportego de la Paruta into the little *corte* of the same name, where at Nos. 3721–5 we see the 18C Palazzetto Paruta.

We retrace our steps to the entrance of Campiello de Ca' Angaran and then bear left into Campo San Pantalon, which is at the junction of Rio de Ca' Foscari and Rio de San Pantalon. On our right we see the unadorned brick facade of the church of San Pantalon, which faces across the *campo* to Rio de Ca' Foscari.

According to tradition, the church was founded in the 9C, although the earliest documented reference to it is dated 1101. It was dedicated to Sts Pantaleon and Giuliana, but in common usage it came to be called San Pantalon. The church was rebuilt in the 13C and reconsecrated in 1305; this structure appears in Barbari's view of 1500, which shows its main facade facing Rio de San Pantalon. The church was totally rebuilt by Francesco Comino in 1668–86, when its axes were rotated ninety degrees to its present orientation.

The vaulted ceiling of the nave is decorated with frescoes done in 1680–1704 by Giovanni Antonio Fumiani, who was buried here when he died in 1710. Fumiani's vast and skilful composition is without parallel in Venice, the largest single work of Venetian art in the 17C. The main scenes are *The Martyrdom and Glorification of St Pantaleon*, the entire composition surrounded by the depiction of a huge portico in perspective. Fumiani also did several of the frescoes on the ceilings, walls and external spandrels of the six side chapels as well as other paintings in the church.

The second chapel from the rear on the right is dedicated to St Pantaleon; at its rear, which coincides with the apse of the 13C church, there is a painting of St Pantaleon healing a child, one of the last works of Veronese. On the walls of the chapel are two paintings by Palma il Giovane: *The Decapitation of St Pantaleon* and a *Miracle of the Saint*. The third chapel was dedicated to St Bernardino by the Guild of Wool-workers. The altarpiece is *St Bernardino Receiving the Symbol of Christ* by Paolo Veronese. On the left wall there is a painting of St Bernardino founding a hospital in Siena, from the workshop of Veronese.

The elaborately decorated high altar in the chancel was

built in 1668–71 to a design by Giuseppe Sardi; it is adorned with rich marbles, bronzes and four statues by Tommaso Ruer: Sts Peter, Paul, John the Baptist and John the Evangelist. To the left of the chancel is the Cappella del Santo Chiodo, the Chapel of the Sacred Nail, so called because it contains a reliquary with one of the nails supposedly used in the Crucifixion enshrined in a little Gothic altar made in the first half of the 15C. On the right wall of the chapel is a painting of *The Coronation of the Virgin*, signed by Giovanni d'Alemagna and Antonio Vivarini and dated 1444. On the left wall is a 13C triptych by the school of Paolo Veneziano; in the centre are the *Virgin and Child*, on the left *The Annunciation* and *The Nativity*, and on the right *The Presentation* and *The Death of the Virgin*.

The other paintings in the church include works by Antonio Balestra, Gregorio Lazzarini, Pietro Longhi, Alessandro Longhi, Angelo Trevisani, Giovanni Fazioli, Nicola Baldissini, Jacopo Guarana, Vicenzo Guarana, Pasquale Manfredi, Giovanni Segala, Luca Carlevaris, Alessandro Varottari, Louis Chéron, Antonio Molinari, Alessandro Tonioli and Nicolò Bambini.

After leaving the church we see on the left side of the *campo*, at Nos. 3707–8, Palazzo Signolo-Loredan, dating from the 16C. In the wall of the adjacent house there is a plaque with an inscription stating the minimum size of the fish to be sold in the local market. Directly across the canal we see a Gothic *palazzetto* of the 14C known as Casa Greci.

We now cross Ponte Santa Margarita; this brings us to Campiello del Tragheto, from where Calle de la Chiesa leads into Campo Santa Margarita. The *calle* passes in front of the former church of Santa Margherita, whose truncated campanile is to the left on the corner where the street enters the *campo*.

The church was founded in 853, during the reign of Doge Pietro Tradonico. In its present form it dates from a rebuilding in the first half of the 17C by Giovanni Battista Lambranzi. The church was suppressed in 1808, when the upper part of its campanile was demolished. Since then it has been used in

turn as an evangelical church and as a cinema, but now it has
been abandoned. A number of grotesque sculptural fragments
are embedded in the campanile.

Entering the *campo* and turning immediately left, we see an
attractive 18C house at Nos. 3429–30. On the top floor of the
house there is a niche containing a 15C statue of St Margaret
standing serenely on the back of a crocodile-like dragon.

Campo Santa Margarita is one of the largest *campi* in
Venice, its original site augmented by the filling in of a canal
on its southern side, where it is bordered by the area known
as Rio Terà and the two side streets called Rio Terà Canal
and Rio Terà de la Scoazzera. The original limit of the *campo*
to the south is marked by the isolated building between the
rest of the square and Rio Terà at No. 3020A. This is the
former Scuola dei Varoteri, the Guild of Tanners, built in
1725. The foundation of the guildhall is recorded by an
inscription under the large marble tabernacle framing a relief
of the Virgin sheltering the kneeling brethren of the Scuola,
dated 1501. On the facade of the building there is an inscription regulating the size of the fish sold in the local market.
The fish market still operates in front of the guildhall, and
there is also a vegetable market on the north-west side of the
campo, which together with its cafés and restaurants makes
this one of the liveliest and most colourful squares in Venice.

Directly across from the guildhall, on the south-western side
of the *campo* we see the picturesque Gothic house known as Casa
Foscolo-Corner (Nos. 2930–35). This was originally a Veneto-
Byzantine house of the 12–13C, rebuilt at the end of the 14C or
the beginning of the 15C. The main entrance of the building is
carved in pink Verona marble, with decorative brickwork in the
Byzantine style in the lunette of the arch above the lintel. To the
right of Casa Foscolo-Corner is Calle del Sangue, the Street of
Blood, so named not because of any bloody murder committed
there, as one might imagine, but after a wine shop opened in 1731
by Giacomo Sangue. Beyond Calle del Sangue, at Nos. 2945–62,
there are a pair of 14C houses bisected by Sottoportego de l'Uva.

There are two *vere da pozzo* in the *campo*, one towards the church and the other near the Scuola dei Varoteri. Both are hexagonal structures dated 1530, with the one nearest the Scuola bearing an inscription recording that it was restored in 1726.

We continue through the south-western corner of the *campo*, where it narrows into Rio Terà. On our left, at Nos. 3034–5, we pass an 18C house with a pedimented attic. A plaque records that this stands on the site of an almshouse for women founded in 1482 with a bequest from Madalena Scrovegni, and that it was rebuilt in 1762.

At the end of Rio Terà we see in front of us the side entrance of the church of the Carmini, and then at the end of the street on our right we come to the entrance of the former Scuola Grande dei Carmini.

The Confraternity of Santa Maria del Carmelo, Our Lady of Carmel, was founded in 1597. In 1627 the brethren of the Confraternity commissioned Franco Cantello to design the Scuola. Construction was interrupted by the plague in 1629, and it was finally consecrated in 1638, though still unfinished. The facade, designed by Baldassare Longhena, was erected in 1668–70. Then in 1739 the brethren commissioned Giambattista Tiepolo to do the great series of paintings on the ceiling of the upper hall of the Scuola, which he completed in 1743. The Scuola was suppressed by the French in the first decade of the 19C; it was reinstated in 1840 through the intervention of Ferdinand I of Austria, and since then the building and its works of art have been preserved and eventually opened to the public as a museum.

The rectangular building is divided on each floor into two parts; on the ground floor on the right is the reception hall, and on the left is the grand staircase, the sacristy and smaller rooms; on the first floor on the right is the Assembly Hall, while on the left is the Sala dell'Albergo and the Archive Room. The Assembly Hall has a superb ceiling and wooden panelling around the walls. Above the panelling there are monochrome paintings by Nicolò Bambini, who also did the allegorical figures beside the staircase and around the arcades. On the altar there is a painting of *The Assumption* by Sante Piatti, who also did the frescoes in the roundels of the barrel-vaulted stairway, with stucco decorations by Abbondio Stazio. The Upper Hall is famous for its painted ceiling by Tiepolo; in the centre is the *Madonna of Carmel in Glory Giving the Scapula to St Simon Stock*. The other paintings in the room are by Antonio Zanchi, Gregorio Lazzarini and Bernardo Falcone, who did the *Madonna of Carmel* on the altar. In the Archive Room the painting in the centre of the ceiling is the *Virgin Appearing to St Simon Stock* by Giustino Menescardi, who also did the figures of the sibyls in the other compartments. The other paintings in the room are by Menescardi, Gaetano Zompini and Piazzetta, who did the huge canvas of *Judith and Holofernes* beside the door to the next room. In the Sala dell'Albergo the painting in the centre of the ceiling is *The Assumption*, by Alessandro Varottari, while the four Evangelists and prophets along the sides are by Menescardi, as is the depiction of *The Circumcision* on one of the walls. The other paintings on the walls are by Antonio Balestra, except for *The Nativity*, which is by one of his followers.

After leaving the Scuola we turn right on Corte de la Scuola to enter Campo dei Carmini, which opens on to Rio dei Carmini, with the bridge of the same name just to the left. On our left is the main entrance to the church of Santa Maria del Carmelo, better known as the Carmini.

The Carmini was founded in 1286 by the Carmelite fathers and consecrated in 1348. The church was rebuilt at the beginning of the 16C and a new facade was erected in 1507–14, perhaps by Sebastiano Mariani, who probably also did the five statues on the tripartite crowning of the main facade. The side entrance on Calle de la Scuola preserves the Gothic facade of the 14C church, including remains of the cornice decorated with palmettes in the Veneto-Byzantine style, along with Byzantine *paterae* dating from the 11–12C.

The interior preserves its original 14C Gothic construction except for the chancel and its two flanking chapels, created in the early 16C by Sebastiano Mariani. At the end of the 16C and the beginning of the 17C the interior was adorned with numerous paintings and rich carvings in gilded wood. Among these are the gilded statues of twelve saints and prophets above the capitals of the colonnades flanking the central aisle; and over the cornice the series of twenty-four large paintings in the intercolumniations of the central aisle, depicting scenes from the history of the Carmelite Order. On the second altar from the rear on the right there is a beautiful painting of *The Nativity*, signed by Cima da Conegliano and dated 1509. The altarpiece on the third altar is *The Virgin of Carmel*, a work of the school of Titian, attributed to Pace Pace. On the ceiling there is a fresco depicting *Two Angels in Flight* by Sebastiano Ricci.

We now enter the sacristy, whose 15C ceiling has been restored, along with a fresco of *The Virgin and Angel of the Annunciation*. Over the entrance is a small lunette depicting *The Triumph of the Carmelites*, attributed to Giovanni Battista Lambranzi; over the Gothic arch of the little chapel is *The Annunciation* by Palma il Giovane.

The last bay of the nave is occupied by the two 16C singing galleries decorated with eight paintings by Andrea Schiavone and one by Marco Vicentino. The chapel to the right of the chancel has on its altar a painting of *The Holy Father and Elijah in the Desert* by Gaspare Diziani; to the left there is a bronze relief of *The Deposition* done *c.* 1474 by Francesco di Giorgio Martini, who also did the portrait busts of Federico da Montefeltro and Battista Sforza, Duke and Duchess of Urbino. The high altar in the chancel, built in 1507, is flanked by the statues of two adoring angels, by Giulio del Moro. The large paintings on the side walls of the chancel are, on the right, *The Miracle of the Loaves* by Palma il Giovane and *St Helena Discovering the True Cross* by Gaspare Diziani; on the left, *The Fall of Manna* by Marco Vicentino and *The Plague of Serpents* by Diziani. The altarpiece in the chapel to the left of the chancel is *St Anne, the Virgin, St Joachim and St Peter* by Diziani.

The first altar from the front on the left has a painting of *St Albert Blessing with the Cross* by Pietro Liberi. The altarpiece on the third altar is *St Anthony of Padua* by Lattanzio Querena. On the fourth altar is a beautiful painting of *St Nicholas in Glory*, done in 1529 by Lorenzo Lotto. The altarpiece on the last altar is *The Holy Trinity, St Maria Maddalena de' Pazzi and St Louis Gonzaga* by Bernardino Prudenti. At the rear end of the nave is a large painting of *St Liberale Curing the Sick*, done in 1638 by Alessandro Varottari.

On the right side of the *campo*, at No. 2615, we see a modern house that stands on the site of a palace built in the 15C by the Civran family. On the facade of the house overlooking the canal there is a statue of a page supporting a shield with the Civran coat of arms, done in the 15C by the workshop of Antonio Rizzo. This statue is a vestige of the original Palazzo Civran, referred to by Venetians as Casa d'Otello, for it was said to be the house of Shakespeare's Othello.

Across the canal at the foot of Ponte dei Carmini is Palazzo Foscarini, a handsome building dating from the 17C. This was the home of Doge Marco Foscarini (1762–3), a distinguished scholar, whose library was carried off by the Austrians in 1799 and is now in Vienna.

We now turn left from the *campo* on to Fondamenta del Soccorso. Some 60 m along the *fondamenta* we come to the beginning of the huge Palazzo Zenobio (No. 2597). The palace was built at the end of the 17C for the Zenobio family by Antonio Gaspari. Since 1850 the palace has housed the Armenian College of the Mechitarist Fathers. Permission can be obtained to visit the palace, the most splendid rooms of which are the *portego* and the ballroom, connected by a graceful archway; these were designed by Antonio Gaspari and decorated with frescoes by Louis Daubigny, as well as landscapes by Luca Carlevaris.

We continue along the *fondamenta* as far as the next bridge, Ponte del Soccorso, where we see immediately to our left the facade of a small oratory, the Oratorio del Soccorso. It was founded in 1580 by Veronica Franco, the famous courtesan and poetess, who built it as a hospice for reformed prostitutes. At the height of her career Veronica spent a night with Henry III of France when he visited Venice in 1574, later recalling her royal lover in one of her sonnets: '*In armi e in pace a mille provo esperto . . .*'

We now cross Rio dei Carmini on Ponte del Soccorso and turn left on Fondamenta Briati. About 60 m along we come to a beautiful Gothic palace at the junction of Rio de San Sebastian with Rio de l'Anzolo Rafael. This is Palazzo Ariani, built in the second half of the 14C, and recently very well restored as a school. This is one of the earliest and most pleasing examples of a Venetian Gothic palace, noted for its superb pointed-arch windows and their elaborate traceries.

On the other side of the canal we see the main facade of the church of Angelo Raffaele. Directly opposite the church we pass the 16C Palazzo Minotto (No. 2365). We then turn left to cross Ponte de l'Anzolo, after which we turn left again and walk back to the church.

The church is one of the oldest in Venice, with tradition dating its founding to 640. It was dedicated to the Archangel Raphael, which in Venetian dialect became Anzolo Rafael. The church in its present form dates from a reconstruction by Francesco Contino in 1618, with the main facade added in 1735. Over the main doorway in a niche is a statue of the Archangel Raphael with Tobias, a work from the beginning of the 16C attributed to Sebastiano da Lugano.

On the wall over the entrance is the organ, built in 1743–9 by the brothers Antonio and Tommaso Amigoni. On the parapet of the organ there are five paintings, *Scenes from the Life of Tobias*, done in 1750–53 by Giovanni Antonio Guardi. On either side of the organ there are depictions of *The Last Supper*, the one on the right attributed to Bonifacio de' Pitati and that on the left to the workshop of Veronese. The altarpiece in the first chapel from the rear on the right is *St Liberale and Other Saints* by Francesco Fontebasso. The altarpiece in the second chapel is *The Assumption*, a late-18C work derived from Titian's masterpiece at the Frari; on the left wall is *The Stigmata of St Francis* by Palma il Giovane. On the back wall of the chancel is a painting of *The Archangel Raphael with Tobias* by Michelangelo Morleiter. The paintings on the walls of the chancel are, to the right, *The Plague of Serpents* by Antonio Vassilacchi and, to the left, *Christ and the Centurion* by Alvise dal Friso. The altarpiece in the second chapel from the front on the left shows *St Anthony of Padua Preaching to the Crowd from a Tree* by Bonifacio de' Pitati. On the ceiling is a fresco depicting *The Archangel Michael Driving away Lucifer* by Gaspare Diziani.

We now retrace our steps across Ponte de l'Anzolo, after which we turn left on Fondamenta Barbarigo. At the end of the *fondamenta* we turn right into Campiello de l'Oratorio. At the far end of the *campiello* we bear left to pass the campanile of the church of San Nicolò dei Mendicoli. We then pass on our right the main façade of the church and its ancient porch, now no longer used, after which we turn right into Campo San Nicolò, passing on our left a little column surmounted by the figure of a lion. This brings us to the side of the church and its present entrance, which faces across the *campo* to Ponte San Nicolò and Rio de le Terese.

The name 'dei Mendicoli', or 'of the Beggars', stems from the fact that this parish was originally inhabited by the poorest class of people, mostly fishermen and their families. Originally an island, known because of its 'beggarly' inhabitants as Mendigola, it was apparently one of the first parts of Venice to be settled, because of its proximity to the mainland. According to tradition, the first church on this site was founded in the 7C and dedicated to St Lawrence. Recent restorations have revealed the foundations of this 7C church; the dig also showed that late in the 8C the building acquired a

Greek-cross plan, with galleries and rich frescoed decoration. The original church was destroyed by fire in 1105, to be replaced by the present Veneto-Byzantine edifice, which in the late 12C was re-dedicated to St Nicholas of Myra. The church of San Nicolò was restored in 1361–4, as recorded by inscriptions on two of the columns in the nave. The building was renovated internally and remodelled in 1553–80. The last major structural changes in the church were made in 1750–60, when a new facade was erected around the entrance facing Rio de le Terese. The building was restored in 1971–7 by the Venice in Peril Fund.

This restoration opened up the 15C porch with its arcade of pillars on the front facade, where traces of the original 12C building survive. The campanile is another survivor of the 12C building phase. The present entrance is in the form of a classical Greek temple front. The statue above the doorway represents the Immaculate Virgin Mary, and those on either side are St Anthony of Padua and St John Nepomucene, all by Giovanni Marchiori.

The interior retains its original 12C basilical plan, with the central nave divided from the side aisles by two colonnades of six columns each, all with large 14C capitals. Along both sides of the central aisle, above the capitals, are 16C statues of the twelve Apostles. Above these, on the architrave, are twelve paintings depicting *Scenes from the Life of Christ*; seven of these are by Alvise dal Friso, four by the workshop of Veronese and one by Palma il Giovane. The panels of the ceiling are decorated with frescoes; the roundels in the centre show *St Nicholas in Glory* by Francesco Montemezzano, while the side panels depict *Episodes in the Life of St Nicholas* by Leonardo Corona.

Above the doorway in the *controfacciata* wall is the late-16C organ, its balcony supported on corbels; the parapet is decorated with three small paintings depicting *Miracles of St Martha* by Carlo Caliari. The second chapel from the rear on the right is dedicated to St Nicetas, whose remains are enshrined in an ornate sarcophagus on the altar. On the front of the sarcophagus there are three tablets with paintings of *Scenes from the Life of St Nicetas*, by Andrea Schiavone.

The nave is separated from the chancel by a three-arched iconostasis surmounted by five statues in polychrome and gilded wood dated *c.* 1585, probably by a follower of Girolamo Campagna; over the central arch is Christ on the Cross, flanked by the Virgin and St John the Baptist and with two angels at the sides. Above the arch of the apse there are frescoes depicting *The Holy Father in Glory* and *The Annunciation* by Alvise dal Friso. Behind the high altar in a niche is a gilded wooden statue of St Nicholas blessing, carved by the workshop of the Bon family in the mid 15C. The chapel to the left of the chancel has a fine altar in the style of Sansovino, with a 15C marble ciborium.

The building to the left of the church in the *campo* is the 14C *canonica*. The small statue of the lion on the little column in the *campo* dates from the 18C. In the middle of the *campo* there is a cylindrical *vera da pozzo* in pink Verona marble dating from the 17–18C.

The *campo* was the gathering place for the Nicoletti, the fishermen of the Mendigola, whose traditional rivals were the Castellani, the men from the parish of San Pietro di Castello. Before the founding of Venice the people of Mendigola governed themselves under an elected official called the Gastaldo. After the establishment of the Republic Mendigola retained some semblance of local autonomy, and the Gastaldo came to be known as the 'Doge of the Nicoletti'. After his election the Gastaldo, wearing his scarlet robe of office, was rowed by the Nicoletti to the Palazzo Ducale, where the Doge welcomed him with a fraternal embrace. He also accompanied the Doge on the state barge, the Bucintoro, which was rowed by the Castellani. This gave rise to the traditional insult with which the Nicoletti taunted the Castellani during their brawls: 'You row for the Doge, we row with the Doge!'

We now cross the canal on Ponte San Nicolò, turning right on Fondamenta de le Terese. This brings us to the church of Santa Teresa, whose plain facade is flanked by the wings of its former convent.

The church and convent were built in the second half of the 17C by Andrea Cominelli for the Sisters of St Theresa, and the complex was consecrated in 1688. The convent is no longer functioning and the church is closed for restoration.

Across the canal from the church, on Fondamenta Tron, we see a row of contiguous houses, with seven tall chimneys marking the division between the separate dwellings. These were designed as dwellings for workers in the last century of the Republic.

Continuing along the *fondamenta* we come to Ospizio Zuane Contarini (No. 2209), a Gothic building at the back of a walled garden. The building was erected in the 14C as a hospice for the poor, serving much the same purpose today as an almshouse.

At the end of the *fondamenta* we continue straight ahead on Ponte de le Terese, which crosses Rio de l'Arzere at its junction with Rio de le Terese. We turn right on the *fondamenta* on the other side and continue straight ahead on Corte Maggiore, a wide street that leads back to Ponte de la Piovan. Halfway along the street we come to a *vera da pozzo* dating from the second half of the 14C.

At the end of Corte Maggiore we cross Ponte de la Piovan and turn left on Fondamenta de la Pescaria. We walk along the *fondamenta* as far as Ponte de l'Anzolo and the church of Angelo Raffaele, where we turn right on Salizzada de la Chiesa. This brings us along the side of the church, after which we turn left behind its apse into Campo de l'Anzolo Rafael, where there is a *vera da pozzo* dated by an inscription to 1349.

Beyond the apse of the church the square is divided by an intruding building into two parts, with Campazzo San Sebastian to the right and to the left Campo drio il Cimitero, named for the ancient cemetery once located here beside the church. In the middle of the *campo* there is a *vera da pozzo* dating from the first decade of the 16C. One of the panels on its sides has a relief of the Archangel Raphael with Tobias, while another has the figure of St Nicetas.

Bearing right, we pass through Campazzo San Sebastian into Campo San Sebastian. This brings us alongside the church of San Sebastiano, which faces the canal and bridge of the same name.

The first church on this site was an oratory of Santa Maria Assunta, founded in the mid 14C. During the years 1455–68 the oratory was replaced by a larger church dedicated to St Sebastian. The present church and its monastery were built for the Girolamini Fathers in 1505–45, to a design by Scarpagnino. The church is at present closed for restoration, but if the door is open one can step inside to look at the interior, particularly the great cycle of paintings done by Paolo Veronese in 1555–70. When Veronese died in 1588 he was buried in San Sebastian; his tombstone is in the floor near the organ.

We now cross the canal on Ponte San Sebastian, turning right on Fondamenta San Basegio. Then at the next corner we turn left into Calle de la Chiesa, which at its end takes us to Ponte Sartorio. To our left, on the west bank of Rio de l'Avogaria, we see the third of the three surviving *squeri* in Venice that still make and repair gondolas. It was in this *squero* that the present design of the gondola was perfected in the 1880s.

After crossing the bridge we continue straight ahead on the *fondamenta* to the church of Ognissanti (All Saints), whose side entrance is on the *campo* beside the canal.

The church was founded in 1472 by nuns of the Cistercian Order, along with a convent and hospice. A new and larger church was completed in 1580 and consecrated six years later. The complex was suppressed in 1806 by the French, who stripped the church of its works of art. Then in 1810 the complex was reopened to house the nuns from the suppressed Capuchin convent in Castello, who brought with them some of the paintings that now adorn the church.

On the wall over the doorway is a nuns' choir, in the gallery of which there is a *Deposition* by Palma il Giovane. The painting on the second altar to the right, *St Clare*, is attributed to Gregorio Lazzarini. The vaults of the chancel and side chapels are decorated with frescoes painted in 1673 by Agostino Letterini. At the rear there is *The Archangel Michael* by Andrea Vicentino.

After leaving the church we continue along Fondamenta Ognissanti as far as the next canal, Rio de le Romite. There we turn left on Fondamenta de le Romite, which about 100 m along brings us to the church of the Eremite. The church and convent of the Eremite, dedicated to Jesus, Mary and Joseph, were built in 1693 by Giovanni Battista Lambranzi for the Augustinian friars. The church is now the chapel of the Istituto Magisteriale Maria Immacolata.

We now cross the canal on Ponte de le Romite, turning left on Fondamenta di Borgo. At the end of the *fondamenta* we cross Rio del Malaga on Ponte de le Turchette, continuing straight ahead on the *calle* of the same name. At the end of the *calle* we turn right on Calle Longa, which takes us to Campo San Barnaba. There we continue in the same direction on Calle del Tragheto, which at its end brings us to the Grand Canal at Fondamenta del Tragheto. There on our left is Pontile San Barnaba, where we end the third and last of our strolls through Dorsoduro.

[10] Sestiere di San Polo

SESTIERE DI SAN POLO I (*Map Route 13*)

We now start out on the first of our two strolls through the Sestiere di San Polo, beginning at Pontile San Tomà.

We leave the *vaporetto* station via Calle del Tragheto Vechio, at the end of which we pass on our right the 14C campanile of the church of San Tomà. We turn left on Calle del Campaniel, and then right on Fondamenta del Forner. After about 50 m we see across the canal on our left Palazzo Corner dalla Frescada, a 15C Gothic palace that was built by the Corner family and later passed to the Loredan. Doge Pietro Loredan (1567–70) was born here.

We now turn right on Calle del Cristo, and at the next corner we turn right again on Calle del Mandoler, which brings us into Campo San Tomà. This is named for the church of San Tomà, whose classical facade we see at the far end of the *campo*.

The building directly to our left, at No. 2857, is the former Scuola dei Calegheri, the Guild of Shoemakers, which is now used as an art gallery. An inscription on the doorway records that the building was erected in 1478; there are reliefs of three shoes on the lintel. In the lunette above the doorway there is a late-15C relief by Pietro Lombardo showing *St Mark Healing the Cobbler Ananius*. Ananius was subsequently baptized and became Bishop of Alexandria, and after his canonization he became the patron saint of shoemakers. On the facade above, between the two windows, there is a mid-14C relief of the Madonna della Misericordia.

We now cross the *campo* to look at the church of San

Tomà. The church, dedicated to St Thomas the Apostle, was founded in the 10C and reconstructed in 1395 and again in 1652. A new facade in the classical style was erected in 1742 by Francesco Bognolo. The church was closed for restoration in 1984 and has not yet reopened.

In the centre of the *campo* in front of the church there is a *vera da pozzo* dated 1520. There is another *vera da pozzo* to the right of the church in Campiello del Piovan, dating from the 14C. On the side facade of the church facing the *campiello* there is a fragmentary sarcophagus of the Priuli family, dated 1370.

Returning to the *campo*, we now turn right into Campiello San Tomà. There, on the left side of the church, we see a marble relief of the Madonna della Misericordia, dating from the 15C.

We now cross the *campiello* and turn right on Fondamenta San Tomà. After a few steps we then turn left to cross Ponte San Tomà. On the far side of the canal we see to the left of the bridge Palazzo Bosso, a 15C Gothic palace, with decorative fragments in the Veneto-Byzantine style of the 13C, including a sculptured frieze, cornice and *paterae*.

On the far side of the bridge we come on the right to Palazzo Centani, a handsome Gothic palace of the 15C. On the canal-side facade of the house there is a plaque recording that this was the birthplace of the Venetian playwright Carlo Goldoni, who writes thus of the *palazzo* in his *Memoirs*: 'I was born in Venice in the year 1707, in a large and beautiful house between the bridges of Nomboli and Donna Oresta, at the corner of the street Ca' Centani, in the parish of San Tomà.'

Palazzo Centani has been restored and is now open to the public as a museum, the Casa Goldoni, whose entrance is on the right side of Calle dei Nomboli at No. 2793. We enter through a picturesque courtyard with a 15C well-head, ascending by an outside staircase. The museum, which also houses the Institute of Theatrical Studies, has memorabilia of Goldoni's life and career and theatrical costumes used in his plays.

After leaving Casa Goldoni we continue along Calle dei Nomboli as far as Rio Terà dei Nomboli, where we turn left. At the first corner we turn right into Calle dei Saoneri, the Street of the Soap-makers. We then turn left into a *sottoportego* that takes us into Corte del Luganegher and on to Calle Morolin. On the right side of the *calle* we pass the 16C Palazzo Moro-Lin. At the end of the block we follow Calle Morolin as it turns left, and at the next corner we turn right on Calle Secondo del Saoneri. At the end of the *calle* we turn left on Rio Terà, and then at the next corner we turn right on Calle del Tagiapiera. On the facade of the house on the corner to the right there is a statuette of the Madonna, who is holding the Christ Child and trampling on Satan.

Calle del Tagiapiera brings us into Campiello de Ca' Zen. On our right, at No. 2580, is the entrance to Palazzo Zen, erected in the 14C and then in the 17C rebuilt to a plan by Baldassare Longhena. In the centre of the *campiello* there is a 14C *vera da pozzo* of pink Verona marble.

We leave the *campiello* through a *sottoportego* that takes us to Rio dei Frari. There we turn right on Fondamenta dei Frari, and after a few steps we come to the bridge of the same name. This was built in 1428 to give access to the great church of Santa Maria Gloriosa dei Frari, whose main facade faces the bridge on the right side of Campo dei Frari.

The church is named for the Franciscan friars, who first made their appearance in Venice in 1220, six years before the saint's death. In 1236 Doge Giacomo Tiepolo gave the friars a plot of land behind San Stin 'on which, with alms received, they built a church and monastery in honour of Holy Mary'. On 3 April 1250 the papal legate Cardinal Ubaldi laid the foundation stone of a second and larger church, dedicating it to Santa Maria Gloriosa. Around 1333 the friars began building a new and much larger church, the present edifice. The first part of the new building to be erected was its apse, which together with the transept and the campanile was completed by 1382. The choir and high altar were completed in 1468, and on 13 February 1469 the altar was consecrated in the presence of the Emperor Frederick III, with the basilica itself being dedicated on 27 May 1492.

The main facade of the church is in the late Gothic style. The main entrance, surmounted by a pointed arch, has recessed mouldings with engaged columns flanked by two vertebrate columns extending well above the doorway. At the crown of the arch there is a statue of Christ Risen by Alessandro Vittoria; on top of the side column to the left are the Madonna and Child, attributed to either Bartolomeo Bon or Pietro Lamberti, and atop the left column is St Anthony, by the Bon school.

There are four other entrances, all on the north side of the church. These are all surmounted by 14–15C reliefs and statuettes, two of which are by the Dalle Masegne family and one attributed to Bartolomeo Bon.

The campanile is the highest in Venice after that of San Marco, rising to a height of 70 m. It was begun in 1361 by Jacopo Celega il Vecchio and completed in 1396 by his son Pier Paolo.

The interior plan is a Latin cross, with the central area of the nave separated from the side aisles by twelve enormous columns in two rows. The columns support an arcade of ogive arches, with transverse arches separating the groined vaults of the successive bays in all three aisles. Between the fourth and fifth columns from the rear is the entrance to the monks' choir, extending as far as the transept, the only one in Venice that is still in its original position in the nave.

The *controfacciata* wall at the rear of the church has three funerary monuments, that of Pietro Bernardo, on the right, done by Tullio Lombardo and his sons Girolamo and Lorenzo. The first altar on the right, dedicated to St Anthony, was built in 1663 by Giuseppe Sardi to a design by Baldassare Longhena; the sculptural decoration was done by Giusto Le Court and Bernard Falcone.

In the second bay on the right is the funerary monument of

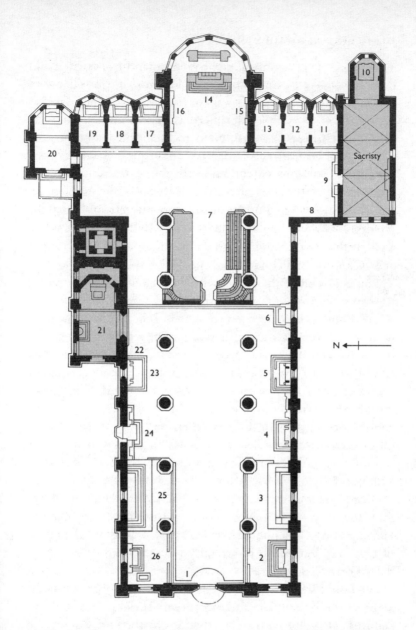

1. Monument to Pietro Bernardo
2. Altar of St Anthony
3. Monument to Titian
4. Altar of the Purification
5. Altar of St Joseph of Copertino
6. Altar of St Catherine of Alexandria
7. Monks' choir
8. Marcello monument
9. Monument of Benedetto Pesaro
10. Bellini triptych
11. Bernardo Chapel
12. Chapel of the Holy Sacrament
13. Chapel of St John the Baptist
14. Titian, *Assumption*
15. Monument to Doge Foscari
16. Monument to Doge Tron
17. Chapel of the Franciscans
18. Chapel of St Michael
19. Chapel of the Milanese
20. Chapel of St Mark
21. Chapel of St Peter
22. Monument of Jacopo Pesaro
23. Titian, *Ca' Pesaro Madonna*
24. Monument to Doge Giovanni Pesaro
25. Monument to Canova
26. Altar of the Crucifixion

Santa Maria Gloriosa dei Frari

Titian (d. 1576), commissioned by Ferdinand I of Austria and built in 1842–53 by Luigi and Pietro Zandomeneghi, followers of Canova. Next is the altar of the Zeno-Venier family, dedicated in 1517; the altarpiece is *The Purification of the Virgin* by Giuseppe Salviati. Next to this is the monument of Almerigo d'Este, Prince of Modena (d. 1666). Beyond this is the altar of the Zane family, completed in 1564 by Alessandro Vittoria. On the altar is a statue of St Jerome, signed by Alessandro Vittoria. On the pilaster to the left of this is the sarcophagus of Jacopo Barbaro (d. 1511). Beyond this is the altar of the Pesaro family, with a painting of *The Martyrdom of St Catherine* by Palma il Giovane.

The back end of the choir, with an arch above its entrance, is almost entirely of Istrian stone, its facade divided into panels framing busts of the prophets in relief. Above the arch there is a bronze Crucifix, a work of the Donatello school; this is flanked by twelve marble statues, with the Madonna and St John the Baptist on the sides of the arch, and on either side of them St Anthony and St Francis and eight Apostles, all works of Pietro Lombardo and his followers. The choir consists of 124 stalls in three tiers, all carved by Marco Cozzi of Vicenza, who completed the work in 1468. On the outer side of the choir, facing the aisles, there is a series of seven paintings by Andrea Vicentino.

Along the wall of the right aisle beside the choir there are four funerary monuments, those of Bishop Marco Zen (d. 1641), Bishop Giuseppe Bottari (d. 1708), Benedetto Brugnolo of Legnano, lecturer in philosophy (d. 1505) and Abbot Luigi dalla Torre (d. 1549).

We now enter the right arm of the transept, where immediately to the right is the monument of Admiral Jacopo Marcello (d. 1488) by Pietro Lombardo. On the end wall of the transept we see on the right side a terracotta monument to the Blessed Pacifico, done in 1437, probably by Giovanni Rosso. At the centre of the wall, surrounding the entrance to the sacristy, is the monument of Admiral Benedetto Pesaro

(d. 1503) by Lorenzo Bregno and Bartolomeo Sinibaldi. To the left of the door is the equestrian monument of Baron Paolo Savelli (d. 1405).

The apse at the rear of the sacristy contains the Pesaro Chapel, added in 1487. The altarpiece is a superb triptych done in 1488 by Giovanni Bellini; in the centre are the Madonna and Child, serenaded by angel-musicians; on the left are St Nicholas of Bari and St Peter; on the right St Mark and St Benedict. On the back wall of the sacristy there is a painting by Paolo Veneziano, originally in a lunette over the sarcophagus of Doge Francesco Dandolo (1329–39); this depicts the *Doge and Dogaressa being Presented to the Madonna and Child by St Anthony and St Elizabeth.*

The apsidal chapel farthest to the right of the chancel was dedicated by the Bernardo family in 1492, with a funerary monument on its right wall made for Girolamo Bernardo in 1500, probably by the Dalle Masegne family. The altarpiece is a polyptych signed by Bartolomeo Vivarini in 1482; in the centre are the enthroned Madonna and Child; on the left are St Andrew and St Nicholas and on the right St Paul and St Peter, with the Dead Christ above. The second chapel to the right of the chancel is dedicated to the Holy Sacrament. The tomb on the right-hand wall of the chapel is that of Duccio Alberti (d. 1336), Florentine ambassador to Venice; the one on the left wall is that of Arnoldo d'Este (d. 1337). The first chapel to the right of the chancel is dedicated to St John the Baptist, originally built in 1436 as the Altar of the Florentines. In the central niche of the chapel there is a statue in painted wood of St John the Baptist, carved by Donatello in 1443–53.

The altarpiece in the Great Chapel is *The Assumption*, a masterpiece begun by Titian in 1516 and placed in its present position on 19 May 1518, his first religious painting on a large scale. On the side walls of the chancel there are grandiose monuments to two Doges. High on the right wall is the monument of Doge Francesco Foscari (1423–57) attributed to Nicolò Giovanni Fiorentino. On the wall to the left is the

colossal monument of Doge Nicolò Tron (1471–3), completed
in 1476 by Antonio Rizzo, who created here what is generally
considered to be the major work of Renaissance sculpture in
Venice.

The first chapel to the left of the chancel is that of the
Franciscan Fathers. The altarpiece is a painting of the *Virgin
and Child Enthroned, with St Francis and Other Saints*, signed by
Bernardino Licinio and dated 1524. On the right-hand wall
of the chapel is the sarcophagus of Senator Nicolò Leoni (d.
1356). The second chapel to the left of the chancel was
dedicated to the Archangel Michael in 1384 by Michiel Marco.
On the altar there is a 15C tabernacle in painted wood with
three statues in niches with conch shells; in the centre is the
Archangel Michael trampling on Satan, flanked by the figures
of St Francis and St Sebastian. On the right-hand wall is the
monumental Lombardesque tomb of General Melchiore Trevisan (d. 1500); the statue of the deceased is attributed to
Lorenzo Bregno. The fresco in the ceiling is *The Resurrection*
by Giandomenico Tiepolo. The third chapel to the left of the
chancel is that of the Milanese, who dedicated the altar in
1421. The brethren of the Milanese Scuola commissioned
Alvise Vivarini to paint the grandiose altarpiece, which was
interrupted by his death in 1503 and finished by Marco
Basaiti. The painting depicts the enthroned *St Ambrose, Bishop
of Milan*, who is shown with saints and angel-musicians,
while in the vault above Christ crowns the Virgin. Among
the brethren of the Milanese Scuola buried here is the composer Claudio Monteverdi (d. 1543), whose tombstone is at
the front of the chapel.

At the end of the left transept a door leads into the Chapel
of St Mark; this was added to the church in 1417–20 through
a bequest of Federico Corner (d. 1376), whose funerary
monument is attributed to the Donatello school. The altarpiece is a triptych signed by Bartolomeo Vivarini and dated
1474; in the central panel is the enthroned St Mark with
angel-musicians; on the left are St John the Baptist and St

Jerome; and on the right are St Nicholas and St Peter. On the inner wall of the facade, above, is *Christ's Descent into Hell* by Palma il Giovane. Below there is a baptismal font with a beautiful marble statue of St John the Baptist by Sansovino.

Along the left wall of the transept there is a superb example of wainscot panelling in the Gothic style of the 15C, attributed to Lorenzo and Cristofolo Canozzi. Above this is the Lombard-esque monument of the Zen family, dated 1480. On the wall of the left aisle beside the choir there is an enormous canvas entitled *The Franciscan Tree*, painted in 1670 by Pietro Negri, depicting all the saints of the Franciscan order. In the first bay beyond the choir is the Chapel of St Peter, commissioned in 1432 by Pietro Emiliani, Bishop of Vicenza, who is buried there in a monumental tomb by the Dalle Masegne family, who also did the marble altarpiece with statues of the Madonna and Child, and saints.

Just to the left of the archway leading to the Chapel of St Peter is the funerary monument of Jacopo Pesaro (d. 1547), Bishop of Paphos in Cyprus, who in 1503 commanded a papal fleet that captured the Ionian island of Santa Maura from the Turks; the tomb was completed by Tullio and Antonio Lombardo in 1524, while the Bishop was still alive. Next to this is the Pesaro Altar, commissioned by Bishop Jacopo Pesaro and created by Tullio and Antonio Lombardo in 1519–26. The altarpiece is a masterpiece known as the *Ca' Pesaro Madonna*, done by Titian in 1519–26.

In the next bay, framing the middle door, is the colossal tomb of Doge Giovanni Pesaro (1658–9); this was erected in 1669 to a design attributed to Baldassare Longhena, with sculptural decoration by Melchiore Barthel and Bernardo Falcone. The next bay contains the funerary monument of the sculptor Antonio Canova (d. 1822), whose heart is contained therein. The monument, in the form of one side of a pyramid, was erected by Canova's followers to a design he had prepared for Titian's tomb in 1794, but which had not materialized. The last bay contains the Altar of the

Crucifixion, commissioned by Fra Maffei of Verona in 1672 and built by Giusto Le Court to a design by Baldassare Longhena. High on the wall of the chapel is the funerary urn of Senator Simeone Dandolo (d. 1360).

The building perpendicular to the main facade of the church is part of the State Archives. This is part of the former monastery of the Frari, known as Ca' Grandi, the principal cloisters being those of St Anthony and the Holy Trinity, two huge enclosures to the right of the church.

In the centre of Campo dei Frari there is a cylindrical *vera da pozzo* dated 1558.

We now pass along the side of the Frari and turn right on Salizzada San Rocco, which brings us behind the church into Campo San Rocco. This takes its name from the church and Scuola of San Rocco, the first of which is at the far end of the *campo* and the second at right angles to it on the corner to the left.

The church and Scuola were dedicated to St Roch of Montpellier, known in Italian as San Rocco, who died in Piacenza in 1327 after having devoted his life to caring for the sick. The cult of St Roch as a healer spread rapidly in Italy, and in 1475 his remains were brought to Venice. Three years later the Confraternity of San Rocco was founded, its mission being to relieve the suffering of the sick, particularly those stricken by the frequent plagues that Venice endured. Then in 1485 the Confraternity succeeded in obtaining the body of the saint, which greatly enhanced its prestige and enabled it to raise funds for the erection of a church and guildhall. During the years 1489–1508 the church of San Rocco was built under the supervision of Bartolomeo Bon, who also erected a small guildhall known today as the Scuoletta, the building opposite the present Scuola at No. 3032. Work on the present Scuola began in 1516 under the direction of Bartolomeo Bon, but in 1524 a dispute with the Confraternity led to him being replaced as chief architect by Sante Lombardo. Lombardo supervised the project until 1526, but then he too fell into

disagreement with the brethren and was replaced by Scarpagnino. Scarpagnino directed work on the Scuola until his
death in 1549, to be replaced by Gian Giacomo de' Grigi,
who finally completed the building in 1560. On 26 May 1564
the Confraternity initiated a competition, in which the leading
artists in Venice were invited to submit designs for paintings
to adorn the Sala dell'Albergo. Jacopo Tintoretto stole the
show by submitting within one month a completed painting,
which he donated to the Confraternity on 22 June 1564.
Then, without payment, Tintoretto decorated the rest of the
ceiling during the summer and autumn of that year. This led
the Confraternity to give him a commission to decorate the
entire hall, which he did within the space of three years. In
1575 Tintoretto donated another painting to be placed in the
centre of the ceiling of the Upper Hall, and two years later he
offered to donate two more canvases, subsequently suggesting
that the Confraternity commission him to decorate the entire
room and to grant him an annual income of one hundred
ducats a year for life. The Confraternity accepted, and on 2
November 1577 Tintoretto was commissioned to start work,
and despite other commissions he completed decorating the
Upper Hall by 1581, and then in the years 1582–7 he did
all of the paintings in the Lower Hall as well. Altogether
he did sixty-one paintings that still adorn the Scuola, finishing
the last one in 1588. Other painters and sculptors subsequently adorned the Scuola with their works, so that it
became the most splendidly decorated of all the Scuole Grande
in Venice.

After passing through a waiting-room we enter the Sala
Terrena. This great timber-roofed room is separated into a
nave and side aisles by twelve fluted columns in two rows of
six each, with an altar at the far end. Eight paintings by
Tintoretto are arrayed around the hall, all of them done in
the years 1582–7, depicting events from the New Testament.
The altar was built in 1587 by Girolamo Campagna, who also
did the statue of St Roch in the central arch.

The stairway to the upper floor was designed by Scarpagnino and built in 1544–60. The fresco in the cupola of the first landing was done *c.* 1700 by Giovanni Antonio Pellegrini, an allegory in which St Roch presents poor invalids to Charity. The walls on either side of the upper flight of the stairway are entirely filled with two large paintings that depict the terrible plague of 1630; the one on the left is by Pietro Negri and that on the right by Antonio Zanchi.

This brings us to Sala Grande Superiore, a magnificent room measuring 44 × 17 m, with a large chancel and altar at one end. The thirty-four large paintings on the walls and ceiling of the hall were done by Tintoretto in 1575–88, his scheme being to illustrate the relationship between episodes in the Old and New Testament and at the same time to glorify the Scuola through its efforts to alleviate the three great scourges of humanity: sickness, famine and thirst. The central arch of the altar frames *The Vision of St Roch*, completed by Tintoretto in 1588. The statues of St John the Baptist and St Sebastian on either side of the arch were done *c.* 1588 by Girolamo Campagna, who also did the figures of the prophets on pedestals at the sides, left unfinished at the time of his death in 1626. Within the chancel on either side of the altar there are four paintings on easels. One of the paintings on the left is the *Annunciation*, painted by Titian *c.* 1540 and bought by the Scuola in 1555; the other is *The Visitation*, done by Tintoretto in 1588. The two paintings on the right were done *c.* 1733 by Giambattista Tiepolo: *Hagar and Ishmael Succoured by the Angel* and *Abraham Visited by the Angels*.

There are two other paintings in the hall, both of them small. One of these is a picture of St Roch, done *c.* 1640 by Bernardo Strozzi. The other is a *Portrait of a Man*, painted by Tintoretto in 1573.

Along the sides of the hall there are a series of curious carvings, most of them allegorical figures, done in the second half of the 17C by Francesco Pianta il Giovane. Those along the wall facing the great stairway include amusing caricatures of Cicero, Tintoretto and Pianta himself, along with a make-believe bookcase showing sixty-four volumes. Twenty-three lanterns of the 18C are arrayed along the walls; these were carried together with the canopy and insignia of the Confraternity of San Rocco during religious and state ceremonies.

At the far end of the room on the same side as the stairway a door leads into Sala dell'Albergo, completed by Scarpagnino in 1536. The decoration of the hall began in 1564, when Tintoretto presented to the Confraternity the completed painting for the central panel in the ceiling, *The Glorification of St Roch*. This and the other twenty-two paintings on the ceiling and walls of the hall were done by Tintoretto in the period 1564–7; the most notable being *The Crucifixion*, one of the crowning masterpieces of his career.

In the hall there are also two paintings on easels, both of them of uncertain attribution. The first of these is *Christ Carrying the Cross*, which was the object of popular veneration in the church of San Rocco from the time that the building was first opened in 1508. The painting was attributed to Giorgione as early as the 16C, but general opinion now seems to be that it is an early work by Titian under the influence of Giorgione. The second painting is *Christ in Devotion*, dated c. 1510; this has also been attributed to both Giorgione and Titian, with current opinion being that it is a work of the school of Giorgione.

The classical facade of the church of San Rocco was erected in 1765–71 by Bernardino Maccaruzzi. The statues flanking the doorway are of St Pietro Orseolo and St Gherardo Sagredo, by Giovanni Marchiori. The sculptures in the upper order are by Gian Maria Morleiter.

Within the church a pair of statues flank the doorway, one of St Cecilia and the other of David holding the head of Goliath, both done in 1743 by Marchiori. The organ is suspended over the entrance on the *controfacciata* wall. On either side of it there are two small doors of the original organ painted by Jacopo Tintoretto, the one on the left depicting *The Annunciation* and the one on the right showing

St Roch being Presented to the Pope. The painting in the centre of the ceiling represents *The Charity of St Roch* by Giovanni Antonio Fumiani.

The first altar from the rear on the right has a painting of *St Francesco di Paola Reviving a Dead Child* by Sebastiano Ricci. Between the first and second altars there are two large canvases by Tintoretto; the upper one is *St Roch Captured after the Battle of Montpellier*; beneath it is *The Pool of Bethesda*. The altarpiece on the second altar, *St Anthony Healing a Youth*, is by Francesco Trevisani.

The high altar in the chancel was done in 1517–24 by Venturino Fantoni and his three sons; the statue of St Roch is attributed to Bartolomeo Bergamasco. The sarcophagus containing the body of St Roch has small panels by Andrea Schiavone, depicting *The Seizure, Captivity and Death of the Saint*. On the side walls of the chancel there are four paintings by Tintoretto, depicting scenes from the life of St Roch.

The painting on the first altar from the front on the left is *The Annunciation and Angels* by Francesco Solimena. The altarpiece on the second altar is *St Helena Discovering the True Cross* by Sebastiano Ricci.

Leaving by the side door of the church, we see the ancient portal and rose window erected by Bartolomeo Bon in 1489–1508.

We now retrace our way back across the *campo* to the street on the east side of the Scuola, Calle a Fianco de la Scuola, where we turn right. This takes us to Rio de la Frescada, where we turn right through Sottoportego de la Scuola, an arcaded portico that passes behind the Scuola di San Rocco, emerging in Campo Castelforte. This takes its name from the huge apartment house at the far end of the *campo* on the right. This is known as Castelforte, and was built by Scarpagnino in 1527–49 for the Scuola de San Rocco, as evidenced by the emblem SR on its facade.

At the far end of the *campo* we turn right on Calle de Castelforte, and at the first intersection we turn left into

Calle Larga de le Chiovere, where there is a *vera da pozzo* of the 14–15C. At the end of the *calle* we turn right on Calle drio l'Archivio, passing on the first corner to the right Ramo San Nicoleto. This is named for San Nicolò dei Frari, an ancient church suppressed in 1807 and demolished later in the 19C.

We continue along the *calle* as it bends to the left, and at its end we turn right on Calle del Campazzo. At the next corner we turn right on Calle de la Laca, which, after passing through a *sottoportego*, brings us into Corte Vitalba, and then after passing through another *sottoportego* we come to Corte de la Scuola. This is named for the Scuola Grande di San Giovanni Evangelista, which is on the left side of the *corte*, extending across the side that encloses the *sottoportego* to join the church of the same name. At the other end of the *corte* we pass through the portal of an ornate marble screen into Campiello San Giovanni Evangelista, where we turn to look back upon the complex.

According to tradition, the church, dedicated to St John the Evangelist, was founded in 970 by the Badoer family. The church in its present form dates from reconstructions in 1443–75 and 1758–9, the latter by Bernardino Maccaruzzi, who also rebuilt the campanile.

The Scuola di San Giovanni Evangelista was founded in 1261 and moved to its present location in 1301. The side facade of the present building dates from 1454; the marble screen with its archway and two windows was erected *c.* 1481 by Pietro Lombardo; the main entrance to the Scuola and its Lower Salon and stairway were built in the years 1498–1512 to a design by Mauro Coducci; while the Upper Salon in its present form was created *c.* 1727 by Giorgio Massari. On the outside wall of the Scuola there is an inscription dated 1349 and two reliefs, one representing the Virgin with Child and the other St John the Evangelist venerated by the brethren of the Confraternity.

The Scuola was suppressed at the beginning of the 19C by

the French, but the building was reopened in 1857 and the brotherhood was re-established as a Scuola Grande and Arch-Confraternity. It now houses the Society of Building Arts, and is open for lectures and exhibitions. The various rooms of the Scuola are still decorated with their original frescoes, along with paintings by a number of prominent artists of the 17–18C.

The entrance to the church is on the other side of the *corte*. Above the doorway in the interior is the sarcophagus and bust of Gian Andrea Badoer (d. 1566) by Danese Cattaneo; above the opposite door is the sarcophagus of Angelo Badoer (d. 1571). On the altar to the right of the chancel is a painting of *The Virgin and Angels* by Andrea Vicentino. The altarpiece on the high altar is *St John the Evangelist* by Pietro Liberi, who also did the paintings of *St James* and *St Matthias* between the ribs of the apse; the others are *Daniel*, *St John the Baptist*, and *The Virgin and Angel of the Annunciation* by Pietro Vecchia. On the wall to the right is *The Crucifixion*, signed by Domenico Tintoretto (1626); on the left is *The Last Supper* by Jacopo Marieschi, who also did the painting on the central panel of the ceiling, *The Exaltation of the Cross*.

From Campiello San Giovanni we turn right on Calle del Magazen. At the first corner we turn left on Calle del Tabacco, so called from a tobacconist's shop that was located here in the days of the Republic. Then at the end of the *calle* we enter Campo San Stin.

The *campo* is named for the ancient church of San Stin (Venetian dialect for St Stephen the Priest), suppressed by the French and demolished early in the 19C. In the centre of the *campo* there is a cylindrical *vera da pozzo* dated by an inscription to 1508. It is decorated with two reliefs, one showing St James and St Barbara standing on either side of the Cross, and a second with the figure of St Stephen the Priest, patron saint of the vanished church of San Stin.

We leave the *campo* at its north-eastern corner via Calle de la Vida, the Street of the Vine. This takes us into Campiello

17. The Grand Canal, with the church of San Simeon Piccolo in the foreground to the right

18. The Grand Canal, with the church of Santa Maria della Salute

19. The Palazzo Contarini del Bovolo and its extraordinary spiral staircase, unique in Venice

20. The Bacino Orseolo, a mooring place for gondolas close to the Piazza San Marco

21. The Gateway to the Arsenal, the great shipyard of the Venetian Arsenal, with ancient statues of lions brought back from Greece by the Venetians

22. A beautifully carved *vera da pozzo*, or well-head, in the Campo Santi Giovanni e Paolo

23. A gondola crossing the Grand Canal

24. The interior of the church of Madonna dell'Orto

25. (*below left*) The interior of the church of the Frari, with Titian's great painting of the Assumption framed in the arch of the choir

26. (*below right*) The interior of the church at Torcello, with the Byzantine mosaic of the Virgin and Child in the conch of the apse

27. An old wine merchant's on the Rio de San Trovaso, a canal in Dorsoduro

28. The church of the Zitelle in Giudecca, designed in 1570 by Andrea Palladio, the greatest of the Renaissance architects in Venice

29. (*facing*) Rio de la Fornace, a picturesque canal in Dorsoduro

30. The church of Santi Maria e Donato in Murano, founded in the seventh century and completed in its present form in 1140

31. The church of Santa Fosca in Torcello, built in the eleventh century

del Pozzo Longo, which leads to a *calle* and *sottoportego* of the same name. As we pass through the *calle* and *sottoportego* we have on our left Palazzo Molin and on our right Palazzo Giustinian, both of which have their main facades on Rio de Sant'Agostin. Palazzo Molin was rebuilt at the beginning of the 19C from a Veneto-Byzantine palace of the 13C. Palazzo Giustinian dates from the 17C.

We now cross the canal on Ponte Sant'Agostin, which takes us to the *campiello* of the same name. As we do so we see to our right Ponte de Ca' Donà, which also crosses to the *campiello*. This bridge takes its name from the palace just beyond it on the near side of the canal, the 16C Palazzo Donà delle Rose, restored at the beginning of the 19C.

The canal and bridge and *campiello* take their name from the former church of Sant'Agostino, which stood at the rear of the *campo* on the site now occupied by the house at No. 2306. This huge 19C apartment-house extends all the way back to Campo Sant'Agostin, which we approach from the *campiello* via Calle de la Chiesa.

According to tradition, the church of Sant'Agostin was founded by Pietro Marturio II, Bishop of Olivolo in the years 953–64. The church was suppressed by the French and demolished in the early 19C. In the centre of the *campo* there is a 16C *vera da pozzo*, which has on two of its panels reliefs of a bishop's mitre and pastoral staff, symbols of St Augustine, patron saint of the church of Sant'Agostino.

Some of the houses that now form the periphery of the *campo* stand on the site of Ca' Tiepolo. This was a large palace belonging to Bajamonte Tiepolo, destroyed by the Signoria after the failure of his plot to overthrow Doge Pietro Gradenigo in 1310. The Signoria then ordered the erection in the *campo* of a Column of Infamy; this monument is now in the Correr Museum, its site marked by a plaque in the pavement where Calle de la Chiesa enters the *campo*.

We leave the *campo* via Rio Terà Secondo, passing on our left Rio Terà Primo. The palatial building at the corner of these two streets, at No. 2279, is the 15C Palazzo Soranzo-Pisani. On the facade of the palace there is a 15C relief representing Faith and Justice Enthroned.

The *calle* on the right opposite Rio Terà Primo is Ramo dei Astori. At the end of the *calle* the house at No. 2313, has an inscription recording that Daniele Manin was born there in 1804.

Directly across the street from Palazzo Soranzo-Pisani, at No. 2311, is the house where in 1490 Aldus Manutius the Elder set up the first of his two printing shops in Venice. This was the famous Aldine Press, its symbol a dolphin and anchor, which published some of the finest editions of the classics during the Renaissance. Erasmus lived here in 1508 while one of his books was being printed by Manutius.

At the next corner we turn left on Calle del Calice, the Street of the Chalice. The *calle*, which passes alongside Palazzo Soranzo-Pisani, took its name from a wine shop that was doing business here as early as 1687, at 'the sign of the chalice'. At the back corner of the palace the *calle* bends to the right and comes to Calle San Boldo. Here we turn left and after a few steps come to Campo San Boldo, a picturesque square at the junction of two canals, Rio de San Giacomo and Rio de San Boldo.

The latter canal and the *campo* take their name from the ancient church of San Boldo (dedicated to St Ubaldo and St Agatha), suppressed in 1805 and demolished in 1826. The 14C campanile of the church has survived, adjoining the 17C Palazzo Grimani. In the centre of the *campo* there is a *vera da pozzo* dated 1712.

We leave the *campo* on Ponte San Boldo, which takes us to Fondamenta del Parucheta. This takes its name from the *parruccheta*, or periwig, worn by a local corn seller in the days of the Republic. At the end of the *fondamenta* we recross the canal on Ponte del Parucheta, continuing straight ahead on Rio Terà Primo. This takes us along the other side of Palazzo Soranzo-Pisani to Rio Terà Secondo, where we turn left;

then at the next corner we turn right on Calle del Scaleter. At the end of the *calle* we cross Rio de San Polo on Ponte Ca' Bernardo, named for the handsome palace to the right of the bridge on the other side of the canal. This is Palazzo Bernardo, a 15C Gothic edifice whose ground floor remains from a Veneto-Byzantine palace of the 13C. The palace to the right of that, separated from it by Rio de San Antonio, is the 16C Palazzo Turloni. The palace to the right of that, separated from it by Calle Pezzana, is Ca' Sanudo, which for a time may have been the residence of the diarist Marino Sanudo (1466–1536).

We continue straight ahead on Calle de Ca' Bernardo, which after a bend to the right brings us into Rio Terà San Antonio. There we turn left and enter Campo San Polo, where this first itinerary through the Sestiere di San Polo comes to an end.

SESTIERE DI SAN POLO II (*Map Route 14*)

Our next itinerary will begin where the last one ended, in Campo San Polo. San Polo, the largest *campo* in Venice, takes its name from the church at the south-western corner of the square.

The church, which is dedicated to St Paul the Apostle, was founded early in the reign of Doge Pietro Tradonico (836–64) and rebuilt in the 12C and again in the 15C. The entrance to the church is on its south side, on Salizzada San Polo. The Gothic entrance is adorned with the figures of two angels and a floral finial, surmounted by a half figure of St Paul, done by the workshop of the Bon family in the mid 15C.

The interior is divided into a central nave and two side aisles by two rows of six columns each. Recent restorations have uncovered the original sprung-beam wooden ceiling and opened up the rose window in the west wall, both of them part of the 15C Gothic church. At the rear of the nave is the organ, made in 1763 by Gaetano Callido. Beneath the organ there are paintings on either side of the door: to the left is *The Last Supper* by Jacopo Tintoretto; to the right is *St Silvester Baptizing the Emperor Constantine* by Paolo Piazza.

The door leads into a room that served as the narthex of the 12C church. This is now the Oratory of the Crucifix, decorated with paintings of the *Stations of the Cross*, done in 1749 by Giandomenico Tiepolo, who also did the two frescoes on the ceiling, a *Glory of Angels* and *The Resurrection of Christ*.

The first altar from the rear on the right side of the church has a painting of *The Assumption and Saints* by the workshop of Jacopo Tintoretto. The chapel to the right of the chancel, dedicated to the Holy Sacrament, is a Lombardesque work of the 16C; on its rear wall there are four paintings by Giuseppe Salviati: *The Washing of the Feet, Christ in the Garden, The Ascent to Calvary*, and *The Deposition*. The altarpiece on the high altar is a large *Crucifixion*, by an anonymous Venetian artist of the 14C; at the sides there are gilded bronze statues of St Paul and St Anthony Abbot by Alessandro Vittoria. At the end of the apse there is a painting of *The Conversion of St Paul*, by Palma il Giovane, who also did the four paintings on the side walls: on the right *The Temptation of St Anthony* and *The Liberation of the Saint*; on the left *The Giving of the Keys to St Peter* and *The Saint Invites St Mark to Preach in Aquileia*. The chapel to the left of the chancel has on its altar a panel depicting *The Marriage of the Virgin*, by Veronese. The painting on the second altar from the front on the left is *The Virgin Appearing to St John Nepomucene*, done in 1754 by Giambattista Tiepolo. On the third altar is a depiction of *The Sacred Heart and Saints*, done in 1802 by Jacopo Guarana.

The campanile dates from 1362. Set into its base there are figures of two crouching marble lions in the Romanesque style, one with a human head between its paws and the other with a snake. Venetian legend associates the first of these two statues with the famous *condottiere* Count Carmagnola, beheaded by the Republic in 1402, the story being that it is his head that the lion is holding.

The short stretch of street between the campanile and the south door of the church is where Lorenzino de' Medici and his friend Alessandro Soderini were assassinated on 28 February 1546. The assassin, a mercenary named Bibbioni, had been hired by Lorenzo's cousin, Cosimo de' Medici, Duke of Florence.

We now make our way back to the *campo*. As we do so we see on the building to our right at No. 2021–2 a statuette of a bishop set into the facade. A plaque on the facade records that this was the home of the sculptor Alessandro Vittoria (1525–1608).

As we pass around the apse of the church we see set into the facade a number of sculptures; the oldest, dating from the 13C, are on the right near the *canonica*: reliefs of the Baptism of Christ and the Madonna flanked by saints and angels. Beneath the latter relief there is an inscription, dated 10 August 1611:

All games whatsoever are prohibited: as also the sale of goods, or the erection of shops, round this church, by order of the most excellent *esecutori contra la biastema*: with the penalty of prison, the galleys, exile and also 300 lire de' picoli, to be divided between the accuser and captors.

The large size and central location of the *campo* made it a popular place for meetings and festivals of all sorts, including bullfights. One of the earliest public gatherings recorded here was on 26 July 1450, when a vast crowd came to hear a Franciscan friar who was a follower of St Bernardino of Siena inciting them to make a large fire in which they burned all of their fine clothes and wigs and false coils of hair and other such fripperies, a veritable bonfire of the vanities.

In the centre of the *campo* there is a hexagonal *vera da pozzo* on a three-stepped platform of the same shape. This is the largest well-head in Venice, 3.2 m in diameter, dated by an inscription to 1838. Its only decoration is a small shield with the relief of a 'prostrate' Lion of St Mark, which, together with the imperial eagle, was the emblem of Venice during the Austrian occupation.

There are several impressive palaces around the periphery of the *campo*. In the north-west corner is Palazzo Corner-Mocenigo (No. 2128). This was built for the Corner family in 1509 by Michele Sanmicheli, who erected it on the site of a 14C Gothic palace that had belonged to Francesco Sforza, Duke of Milan. The building at the north-east corner of the *campo* is Palazzo Donà (Nos. 2177). This Renaissance palace was erected at the beginning of the 16C on the site of a 14C Gothic *palazzo*, of which the fine pointed-arch doorway remains, decorated with reliefs of animals and floral designs. The middle of the west side of the *campo* is taken up with the huge Palazzo Soranzo (Nos. 2169–71). This splendid Gothic edifice is actually a double palace, one of the finest examples of this type in Venice. The palace on the left is the older of the two, built in the mid 14C, the lintels of its twin entrances carved with designs in the Byzantine style, as are the *paterae* on the floor above. The right-hand palace dates from the mid 15C, its design an imitation of that of the earlier building, with the Gothic string course extending along the full length of both facades. Both palaces were acquired in the mid 15C by the Soranzo, probably soon after the second *palazzo* was completed. The palace is still inhabited by descendants of the Soranzo, who number among their ancestors Doge Giovanni Soranzo (1312–28).

To the right of Palazzo Soranzo, separated from it by Sottoportego and Calle Cavalli, is Palazzo Tiepolo-Malfetti. This was built in the 18C by Giorgio Massari, who erected it on the site of an ancient Gothic palace of the Bernardo family. At the south-east corner of the *campo*, the building at No. 1992 is a graceful Lombardesque *palazzo* dating from the end of the 15C.

We leave the *campo* via Calle de la Madoneta, which is paralleled by an arcaded *sottoportego* under the building on the left. We cross Rio de la Madoneta on the bridge of the same name, passing through another *sottoportego* and continuing in the same direction on an extension of Calle de la Madoneta. The name comes from an ancient icon of the Virgin once enshrined in a tabernacle on the bridge, which as early as 1393 was known as Ponte Virginis Mariae; the image was stolen in the 19C and has since been replaced by a relief.

We continue straight ahead through Campiello dei Meloni, so called because sellers of melons once had their shops here. We then cross Rio dei Meloni on the broad bridge of the same name, continuing in the same direction on Calle de Mezo into Campo Sant'Aponal. The *campo* is named for the church of Sant'Aponal, whose Gothic facade we see straight ahead on the far side of the square.

The church was founded in the first half of the 11C by refugees from Ravenna, who dedicated it to their patron saint, Sant'Apollinare, who in Venetian dialect became Sant' Aponal. The church in its present form dates from a rebuilding in the mid 15C. It was suppressed in 1810 by the French and stripped of all of its works of art. The church was reconsecrated in 1851 and restored in 1929, but in 1984 it was closed, and now serves as an archive of the Venetian Commune.

The church retains its 15C Gothic facade. Above the rose window in the centre of the main facade there is a large marble relief of the Crucifixion, dating from the late 14C. Below the window there is a large and elaborate relief framed in a Gothic arch flanked by the figures of saints in spired niches; in the lunette is the figure of Christ on the Cross with the Virgin on one side and St John the Baptist on the other, with two reliefs below showing scenes from the life of Christ dated 1294.

The house to the left of the church, at No. 1252, is the former Scuola dell'Arte dei Tagliapietra, the Guild of Stone-cutters. High on the facade of the building there is a relief of four crowned figures.

The narrow street to the left of the house is Calle dei

Campaniel; this is named for the campanile of the church, which dates from the 12–13C, its upper part rebuilt in 1467. At the north-west corner of the *campo* a *sottoportego* leads into Calle de la Madona. A plaque over the entrance to the *sottoportego* records that Pope Alexander III stayed in a house in the *calle* when he visited Venice in 1177. In the centre of the *campo* there is a cylindrical *vera da pozzo*, dating from the 16–17C.

We leave the *campo* at its south-east corner via Calle del Luganegher, which takes us into Campo San Silvestro. This is named for the church of San Silvestro, which forms the western side of the square, its main facade on the street to its north, Rio Terà San Silvestro. The former Scuola dei Mercanti di Vino, the Guild of Wine-merchants, extends along the entire length of the church on that side of the *campo*, a 16C building attributed to Giannantonio Chiona. The eastern side of the square, where Sottoportego Pasina leads to Pontile San Silvestro, was the site of the palace of the Bishop of Grado, exiled from his own seat because of pirate raids. Sottoportego Pasina is one of the oldest byways in Venice, first referred to in 1182. In the centre of the *campo* there is a *vera da pozzo* dating from the first half of the 14C.

The church of San Silvestro was founded in the 9C and rebuilt in the first half of the 15C. It was reconstructed in the first half of the 17C and again in 1837–43 by Lorenzo Santi. The present facade was erected in 1909, with a large statue of St Silvester in a niche over the doorway.

The first altar from the rear on the right has a painting of *The Baptism of Christ* by Jacopo Tintoretto. The altarpiece on the second altar is a painting of *The Virgin and St Joseph Showing the Child Jesus to the Holy Father* by Carl Loth. Between the two altars an iron grille closes the entrance to the former Scuola dei Mercanti di Vino. On the second altar from the front on the left is a painting of *St Thomas à Becket Enthroned with Angel-musicians*, done in 1520 by Girolamo da Santacroce, with the figures of St John the Baptist and St Francis added by Leonardo Gavagnin.

The house opposite the church at No. 1022 on Rio Terà San Silvestro is the 17C Palazzo Valier. The painter Giorgione (*c.* 1478–*c.* 1510) is believed to have resided in the house to the left at No. 1091.

We now turn right on Rio Terà San Silvestro and then right again at the first corner on to Rio Terà San Silvestro o del Fontego. At the end of the street we come to the Grand Canal, where we turn left on Riva del Vin, named for the wine that was unloaded there in times past. As we walk along the *fondamenta* we pass a number of *sottoporteghi* leading into the narrow *calli* behind. The first of these is Sottoportego del Paradiso, named for a pharmacy located here in the 18C. The second is Sottoportego del Sturion, named for the Albergo Sturion (sturgeon), an inn mentioned in Venetian records of 1398 as having been fined for watering its wine. The sign of the inn can be seen in Carpaccio's painting of 1494, *The Healing of a Man Possessed of the Devil*. The name of the inn is perpetuated in that of a hotel on the site.

The last building on Riva del Vin before the Rialto Bridge is Palazzo Dieci Savi, named for the ten magistrates in charge of the public tithes who had their headquarters here. This edifice, which is now the headquarters of the Water Board and the City Council Works, was built by Scarpagnino in 1520–22. The foundation date is recorded in an inscription on the facade under a modern Lion of St Mark; on the corner of the building near the bridge there is a small statue of Justice, dating from the end of the 16C.

We now come to Ruga dei Oresi, the street that begins at the foot of the Rialto Bridge and leads through the heart of the Rialto market quarter. Its original name was Ruga Orefici, the Street of the Goldsmiths, who were allowed to set up their shops here by a decree of the Senate on 23 March 1331.

Across the street from Palazzo Dieci Savi, is Palazzo dei Camerlenghi, built by Guglielmo Bergamasco in 1525–8. The palace took its name from the Camerlenghi del Comun, three magistrates in charge of the State Treasury, though it also housed the more important magistrates *dei Governatori all'En-trade*, who were responsible for the financial administration of the Republic. The rooms on the ground floor also served as the state prison. The palace now houses the Department of Public Revenues for the Veneto region.

The arcaded building that extends along the entire left side of Ruga dei Oresi as one walks in from the Rialto Bridge is the Fabbriche Vecchie di Rialto, which under the Republic was the headquarters of the magistrates in charge of trade, navigation and supplies, as well as of the Tribunal of Justice and other offices. It was erected by the Signoria in 1520–22, to a design by Scarpagnino, replacing earlier buildings that had been destroyed by a fire in 1514.

The first street that leads off to the right from Ruga dei Oresi is Naranzaria, named for the shops selling oranges (*naranze* in Venetian dialect) that were once located there. Naranzaria leads to the Erbaria, or wholesale vegetable market. The long market building that bounds the Erbaria on the landward side is a wing of the Fabbriche Vecchie, also erected in 1520–22 by Scarpagnino. An inscription on a pillar, dated 1726, records a list of prices to be observed by the public weigher.

Continuing along Ruga dei Oresi, some 20 m beyond Naranzaria on our right we come to Campiello San Giacomo de Rialto, a colourful little market square with a marble fountain in its centre. The *campiello* is bounded on two sides by arcades of the Fabbriche Vecchie, and on a third, to the south-east, by the main facade of the church of San Giacomo di Rialto, also known as San Giacometto.

According to tradition, San Giacomo (St James) is the oldest church in Venice, founded in 421, as recorded in an inscription on the left-hand pillar in the chancel. This is part of the foundation legend of Venice, which has it that three consuls from Padua established a trading post on one of the Rialtine islands at that time. The legend goes on to say that the consuls built a church on the island dedicated to St James, consecrating it at the stroke of noon on 21 March 421, which during the Republic was celebrated as Venice's *dies natalis*, or birthday. No archaeological evidence has been found to support this legend, which still has its believers. The present church was erected during the reign of Doge Domenico Selvo (1071–84), its main purpose being to serve the merchants in the Rialto market. An inscription of the 12C on the outside of the apse bids the merchants to be honest in their dealings, to use true weights and to honour their bargains. The church survived the fire of 1514, but it seems to have suffered some damage because it was restored in 1531. It was rebuilt again in 1599–1601, but without altering its original plan.

The small Roman-style campanile, erected in the 17C, rises from the centre of the main facade. Under the bells there is a Gothic relief of the Virgin and Child, dating from the early 16C. The huge clock beneath this was put in place in 1410 and restored in the 17C. The church is preceded by a penthouse porch, with its wooden architrave carried on five columns of Greek marble surmounted by magnificent Gothic capitals. This dates from the 14C, and is the only Gothic church porch in Venice that has survived intact.

The interior plan is a Greek cross in a square, the central nave separated from the side aisles by two rows each of three columns in Greek marble surmounted by 11C Veneto-Byzantine capitals. The four columns to the east support a hemispherical dome on pendentives. The altar on the right side of the nave was originally dedicated by the Guild of the Grain Winnowers and Porters, as recorded in an inscription on the parapet. The altarpiece is *The Annunciation*, signed by Marco Vecellio, who also did one of the two paintings on the side walls, *The Marriage of the Virgin*, while the one on the other side, *The Nativity of the Virgin*, was done by Leandro Bassano. The chapel to the right of the chancel was commissioned by the Guild of the Oil Decanters, who dedicated it to their patron saint, St Anthony of Padua. The high altar in the chancel was commissioned by the Guild of Cheese Merchants, who dedicated it to their patron saint, St James the Elder, and the Senate commissioned the 18C tabernacle; the marble tracery and the statue of St James were carved by Alessandro Vittorio. The altar on the left side of the nave was commissioned by the Guild of Goldsmiths in 1601 and built by Vincenzo Scamozzi; the statue of St Anthony Abbot, patron saint of goldsmiths, is by Girolamo Campagna.

At the rear of the *campo* is the Colonna del Bando, the Proclamation Stone, from which in the days of the Republic a herald read official proclamations to those assembled in the market-place. The stone is known popularly as 'Gobbo di Rialto', or 'the Dwarf of the Rialto', from the bent figure that supports it, done in the 16C by Pietro da Salò.

The arcade that extends along the two wings of the Fabbriche Vecchie is called the Sottoportego Banco Giro. The portico takes its name from the Banco Giro, or circulating bank, which was established here in the 12C by the Republic, the first state bank in history. Here we are reminded of the lines from Shakespeare's *The Merchant of Venice*, where Shylock remarks:

> Signor Antonio, many a time and oft
> In the Rialto you have rated me
> About my monies . . .

At the corner of the arcade we pass through a *sottoportego* to emerge in Campo de la Cordaria. This was named for the shops that sold ropes, cables and rigging for the ships of the Venetian Merchant fleet; with the passing of sail it became an appendage to the Erbaria. Beyond the far right-hand corner of the *campo* is the Casaria, or cheese market, where the Guild of the Cheese Merchants was first permitted to do business by a decree of the Senate on 18 October 1436, and where many of them continue to operate today, along with numerous other merchants, principally of food.

Campo de la Cordaria and the Casaria are bounded to the

right by the Fabbriche Nuove di Rialto. This is a long and monotonous building that stretches for 65 m along the Grand Canal, fronted by an arcade of twenty-five round arches in rusticated stone; it was built in 1552–5 to a design attributed to Jacopo Sansovino, and was erected as an addition to the Fabbriche Vecchie. Today the Fabbriche Nuove houses the law courts, police court and the court of assizes.

Beyond the Casaria and the Fabbriche Nuove is Campo de la Pescaria, and at the far end of that is the arcaded building of the Pescaria, or fish market. The Pescaria was established on this site in a wooden structure in 1332, rebuilt in stone in 1398, appearing in Barbari's view of 1500. The building that now houses the Pescaria is a neo-Gothic arcade erected in 1907 by Domenico Rupolo and Cesari Laurenti, who also did the bronze statue of St Peter on the facade.

The streets leading into the Casaria and Campo de la Pescaria are named after famous inns and taverns that were located there in the days of the Republic. The first two that we pass as we walk through the Casaria are Calle de la Simia, the Street of the Monkey, and Calle drio la Simia. These are named for an inn 'at the sign of the monkey', established here as early as the 14C. The next two are both called Calle de la Donzella, named for the Osteria de Donzella, one of two 18C inns of that name in the area, both kept by Piero de Pieri. The next one is Calle de l'Osteria de la Campana, named for a famous inn 'at the sign of the bell' (campana), functioning here as early as 1341.

At the far end of Campo de la Pescaria we turn left into Calle de le Becarie, which leads to the *campo* of the same name, taking us along the side of the Pescaria to its inner end. The *calle* and *campo* are named for the Becarie, or public slaughterhouse, which was established here in 1339. The side of the *campo* by the Pescaria was originally the site of Casa dei Querini. At the beginning of the 13C this was divided between three brothers of the Querini family: Marco, Piero and Giovanni. Marco and Piero were implicated in the abortive plot of Bajamonte Tiepolo in 1310, as a result of which they were exiled and their portions of the palace were confiscated by the government. The state purchased the remaining third of the building in 1339 and turned the entire palace into a public slaughterhouse; later it was used as a city market hall and eventually it became part of the fish market, to be demolished when the present Pescaria was erected. At the centre of Campo Becarie there is an octagonal *vera da pozzo* dating from the first half of the 16C.

We leave the *campo* at its south-east corner via Calle dell'Anzelo, the Street of the Angel. The *calle* takes its name from an inn at 'the sign of the angel', an inn used by Turkish merchants before they acquired the Fontego dei Turchi in 1621.

After a few steps we turn left into Calle de Do Spade, the Street of the Two Swords. This is named after another ancient inn, which was opened here by Carlo de Zuane in 1488 at 'the sign of the two swords', mentioned by Giacomo Casanova in his *Memoirs* in connection with an amorous adventure of his during Carnival in 1745. At the end of the *calle* we turn right into Calle San Matio. This takes its name from the church of San Mattio, founded in 1156 and demolished in the 19C.

At the end of Calle San Matio we turn left on Calle del Volto and then right on Ramo de la Donzela, named after the second of the two inns kept by Piero de Pieri in this neighbourhood in the 18C.

At the end of the *calle* we turn right on Calle del Sansoni, which brings us into the long *campiello* of the same name. At the end of the *campiello* we come to Rio de le Becarie, which we cross on Pontecello Raspi. Pausing on the bridge, we see to our left on the near side of the canal Palazzetto Sansoni, a little 14C Gothic palace with trilobate windows, a Gothic shield with the family crest, and a Byzantine cornice of the 9C. Opposite this, on the far side of the canal to the left of the bridge, is Palazzo Raspi, built at the end of the 16C on the site of an earlier palace, of which only the 15C Gothic doorway remains.

After crossing the bridge we continue straight ahead on Calle de Ca' Raspi, passing on our left the side of Palazzo Raspi. At the end the *calle* we turn right on the wide Calle dei Botteri, the Street of the Cask-makers, named for the artisans who made casks here in the 13–14C. The first building that we pass on our right is the 17C Palazzo Priuli-Pesaro (No. 1560). Farther along on the right we pass a 15C Gothic *palazzetto* (No. 1565), its doorway surmounted by a terracotta archway.

We continue along Calle dei Botteri to the Grand Canal, where we turn left on Riva de l'Ogio. This *fondamenta* takes its name (in Venetian *ogio* is 'oil') from the fact that the principal stores of olive oil were on this quay. At the end of the *fondamenta*, where we turn left on to Calle del Campaniel, we see the Palazzo Morosini-Brandolin. This Gothic palace was built in the early 15C by the Morosini family of San Cassiano on the site of an earlier Veneto-Byzantine *palazzo* of the 13C; later it passed to the Brandolin. The upper floor was demolished in the 19C.

Some 40 m along Calle del Campaniel we take a detour by turning right into Calle de Ca' Michiel; then at the first corner we make a right into Calle del Teatro Vechio, followed by a left into the *corte* of the same name. The name comes from the ancient Teatro Michiel of San Cassiano; this was also known as the Teatro Vecchio, the first opera house in Venice, founded here in 1580. The first musical drama in Venice was produced here in 1637; this was Ferrari's *Andromeda*, with music by Francesco Manelli. In the centre of the *corte* there is a *vera da pozzo* in pink Verona marble dating from the latter half of the 13C. Along the left side of the *corte* there is a walled-in colonnade in the Byzantine style of the 13C, once part of a portico on the ground floor of the Veneto-Byzantine palace that originally stood on this site.

We now return to Calle del Campaniel and continue

walking in the same direction. The *calle* is named for the 13C campanile of the church of San Cassiano, which we pass on our right at the far end of the street, just before turning right into Campo San Cassan. The main facade of the church is around the corner to the right, facing Rio de San Cassan and Ponte de la Chiesa, with its side entrance on the *campo*.

The church was founded in the 9C and reconstructed in the 13–14C. It was restored and redecorated at the beginning of the 17C, when it took on its present appearance, except for the demolition of its portico in the 19C. The doorposts of the main entrance are in the Veneto-Byzantine style, perhaps preserved from the original church.

The ceiling is decorated with numerous frescoed panels by Costantino Cedini, the main scene depicting *San Cassiano in Glory*; above the two side chapels in the chancel there are large monochrome lunettes, possibly by Giandomenico Tiepolo, depicting *Incidents in the Life of Abraham*. The altarpiece in the chapel to the right of the chancel is *The Visitation* by Leandro Bassano, who also did the two paintings on the walls: *The Annunciation to St Zacharias* and the *Birth of the Virgin*, along with twelve portraits of brethren of the Scuola della Visitazione. The high altar is a baroque work richly decorated with fine marbles and sculptures, done in 1684–9 by Bartolomeo Nardi and Heinrich Meyring. The altarpiece is *The Resurrection, with St Cassiano and St Cecilia*, attributed to Jacopo Tintoretto and dated 1575. On the side walls of the chancel there are two paintings done in 1568 by Tintoretto: *The Descent into Limbo* and *The Crucifixion*.

The altarpiece on the first altar from the front on the right is *Christ on the Cross and Four Saints* by Matteo Ponzone. Beyond this we pass through the sacristy to reach a chapel commissioned in 1746 by the Abbot Carlo del Medico. The altarpiece is *The Virgin and Child with St Charles Borromeo and St Philip Neri*, signed and dated 1763 by Giambattista Pittoni, who also did the fresco on the ceiling, depicting *St Cassiano and St Cecilia*. The paintings on the walls of the chapel are

SESTIERE DI SAN POLO

The Martyrdom of St Cassiano by Antonio Balestra and *Christ in the Garden* by Leandro Bassano.

Returning to the nave, we see on the second altar a painting of *St Anthony and the Child Jesus* by Lattanzio Querena. We leave Campo San Cassan at its south-east corner via Calle de Ca' Muti. After the first corner on the left we see on our right Palazzo Muti-Baglioni, a large palace dating from the end of the 16C. Halfway along the side of the palace we turn left on Calle del Bota, at the end of which we turn right on Calle dei Boteri. At the end of the *calle* we turn right and then after a few steps left into Corte Carampane. At the end of the *corte* we pass through a *sottoportego* and then turn right on Rio Terà Carampane, following it to its end at Rio de San Cassan, where we turn right on Fondamenta de le Tette. Then after a few steps we come on our left to Ponte de le Tette, the Bridge of Breasts, the name referring to an edict passed by the Council of Ten in 1482. At that time the Council decreed that the city's prostitutes, when displaying themselves from the windows of their bordellos, must leave their breasts uncovered. The parish of San Cassiano was notorious for the number of its bordellos, and there were apparently several along the *fondamenta* by the bridge.

Crossing the bridge and turning left on Fondamenta de la Stua, we see across the canal and to the right the main facade of Palazzo Albrizzi. The palace was built in the 16C by the Bonomo, a wealthy *cittadini* family who sold it to the Albrizzi in the second half of the 17C. The Albrizzi were extremely wealthy merchants from Crete who bought their way into the Venetian nobility in 1692, their descendants continuing to reside in the palace to the present day. The most distinguished of the family was the Countess Isabella Teotochi Albrizzi, who established a celebrated literary salon that at one time or another included Ippolito Pindemonte, Ugo Foscolo, Madame de Staël, Sir Walter Scott, Lord Byron and Antonio Canova. She was also a literary figure in her own right, her best-

known work being her *Ritratti* ('Portraits'), published in
several editions between 1807 and 1826. Across the canal is
the walled garden of the palace, once connected to it by a
private bridge. This was the site of the Teatro Nuovo di San
Cassiano, founded in 1636, whose early productions included
works by Claudio Monteverdi, Francesco Manelli and
Francesco Cavalli.

We now go back across Ponte de le Tette and retrace our
steps along Rio Terà de le Carampane as far as Calle Albrizzi,
where we turn right and enter the *campiello* of the same name.
The right side of the *campiello* is taken up with the landward
facade of Palazzo Albrizzi. At the far end of the *campiello* we
turn left into Calle Stretta, which brings us to Rio de
Sant'Aponal. There we turn left into Sottoportego de la
Furatola, an arcaded walkway that extends for some 50 m
along the canal, ending at Fondamenta Banco Salviati. The
fondamenta is named for the Florentine bankers Salviati, who
in the 16C did business here in Palazzo Camin (No. 1500).
This Gothic palace was built in the 14C by the Camin family,
which became extinct in 1420; their coat of arms in marble
was discovered in restorations in the late 19C and put back on
the facade of the building. The last house on the *fondamenta*,
at No. 1510, is an older building completely restored in the
19C; its facade is decorated with the busts of two Roman
emperors, four Byzantine *paterae*, and two reliefs with the
heads of lions. Directly across the canal from the *fondamenta*
are two 17C *palazzi*; the first is Palazzo Piatti and the second
Palazzo Bernardi.

At the end of the *fondamenta* we cross the canal on Ponte
Storto. Directly on the left of the bridge, at an angle of the
canal, is Palazzo Molin-Cappello. The palace was built towards
the end of the 15C by the Molin family and later it passed to
a branch of the Cappello. The famous Bianca Cappello was
born here in 1548, and it was from one of the canal-side
windows of the palace that she first saw Pietro Bonaventuri, a
young clerk who was then working at the Salviati bank

across the way. Bianca was only fifteen at the time, but on 29 November 1563 she eloped with Pietro and married him in Florence, causing her family to disown her and the Republic to forbid her ever to return to Venice. Some years later, after Pietro was killed in a duel, Bianca became the wife of Francesco I de' Medici, Grand Duke of Tuscany, having been his mistress since the beginning of her stay in Florence. As soon as she was married to the Duke the Cappello family welcomed Bianca back into the fold and the Venetian government cancelled her exile, declaring her a 'true and noble daughter of the Republic'. Bianca died in Florence on 20 October 1587, the day after her husband, the general suspicion being that they had both been poisoned by Francesco's brother, Cardinal Ferdinando de' Medici, who thereupon succeeded to the dukedom.

After crossing the bridge we turn left into Rio Terà Sant'Aponal, following it as it bends to the right at each intersection, at its end passing behind the church of Sant' Aponal. We then turn left on Rughetta del Ravano. After about 90 m the street widens and changes its name to Ruga Vecchia San Giovanni. This name comes from the church of San Giovanni Elemosinario, St John the Almoner, whose barrel-vaulted doorway we see on the right near the end of the street.

According to tradition, the church was founded in the 9–10C, and though the earliest record of it is dated 1050, it is already referred to as an ancient church. The church was destroyed in the great fire that ravaged the Rialto market quarter in 1514, after which it was rebuilt by Scarpagnino in the years 1514–28. The church is at present closed for restoration. The altarpiece on the high altar in the chancel is a painting of *St John the Almoner* giving alms to a beggar, done by Titian *c.* 1545.

The alley across the street from the church is Calle dei Do Mori, the Street of the Two Moors. This took its name from a café under 'the sign of the Two Moors', which operated here in the latter half of the 18C. The Osteria Do Mori now occupies the same site.

Continuing to the end of Ruga Vechia San Giovanni, we turn right on Ruga dei Oresi. Thirty metres along the street we turn right into a *sottoportego* that that takes us into Campo Rialto Nova, where we turn left. In the centre of the *campo* there is a *vera da pozzo* dated *c.* 1520–30.

We leave the *campo* at its far end via Calle del Gambaro, which takes us once again out on to Riva del Vin. There we turn left and walk to the Rialto Bridge, where we end the second and last of our strolls through the Sestiere di San Polo.

[11] Sestiere di Santa Croce

SESTIERE DI SANTA CROCE I (*Map Route 15*)

We now set out on the first of two strolls through the Sestiere di Santa Croce. We begin at Campo San Cassan, approaching it from the Rialto Bridge by walking along the bank of the Grand Canal to the end of Rio de l'Ogio and then turning left on Calle del Campaniel.

We leave the *campo* by the bridge to the right, Ponte de la Chiesa, which crosses Rio de San Cassan to Calle dei Morti. At the end of the *calle* we turn right on Calle de la Regina, continuing straight ahead on Calle de Ca' Corner. This brings us to the land entrance of Palazzo Corner della Regina (No. 2214), now the Archive of Contemporary Art.

Queen Caterina Cornaro was born here in 1454 on the site of an earlier Palazzo Corner. Caterina married King James II de Lusignan of Cyprus in 1468, but the marriage was performed by proxy in the Palazzo Ducale and she did not actually join her husband until 1472. The following year the king died suddenly, leaving his wife with child. The Venetians sent Pietro Mocenigo, the future Doge, to look after Caterina on Cyprus, and he acted as regent for her and her infant son, King James III, who died just a year after his birth. Then in October 1488 Caterina abdicated and returned to Venice, whereupon Cyprus became part of the Venetian Empire. Caterina was given possession of Asolo in the Veneto, where she lived until 1509. She then returned to Venice to spend her last year in Palazzo Corner, where she died on 10 July 1510. The present *palazzo* was built for the Corner family by Domenico Rossi beginning in 1724; then in the last quarter of the 18C it was decorated with frescoes by Costantino Cedini, Domenico Fossati and Giuseppe Montanari, with stucco work by Vincenzo Colomba. The frescoes in the main reading room can be seen by applying at the entrance.

We now retrace our steps along Calle de Ca' Corner and Calle de la Regina, along which we pass on our right Palazzo Moro (No. 2265), a 15C palace in the Lombardesque style. At the next corner we turn right on Ramo de la Regina, passing on our left Palazzo Gozzi (No. 2268). The palace was built in 1550 by the Gozzi, originally silk-merchants from a noble family in Bergamo who remained in the *cittadini* class after they moved to Venice. The brothers Gasparo (1713–86) and Carlo Gozzi (1720–1806) were born here.

We cross Rio de le Do Torre on Ponte Maria Mater Domini, which brings us to the *campo* of the same name. The name comes from the church of Santa Maria Mater Domini, whose main facade and entrance are on the narrow extension of the *campo* to the right at the far end.

Before walking around to visit the church, let us first look at the old houses around the periphery of the *campo*. The first building on the right is Casa Barbaro (No. 2177), a Gothic house of the 14C with pointed arches, the family arms set into the facade. The last building on the left is Casa Zane (No. 2172), a house in the Veneto-Byzantine style of the 13C, with a three-mullioned window decorated with *paterae* and crosses. At the far end of the *campo* is Palazzetto Viaro-Zane (No. 2123), dating from the beginning of the 14C; on the first floor there is a remarkable row of trilobate Gothic windows. In the centre of the *campo* there is a *vera da pozzo* dating from the first half of the 15C.

The church was founded *c.* 960 and dedicated to Santa Maria Mater Domini. It was rebuilt in a project whose first stage began at the end of the 15C and ended at the beginning of the 16C, perhaps to a design by Mauro Coducci. The project was completed in a second stage during the years 1512–24, perhaps by Jacopo Sansovino, and the new church was finally consecrated in 1640. Over the doorway of the church there is a half-length figure of the Virgin, a 14C carving in the Byzantine style.

The first altar from the rear on the right was begun by Lorenzo Bregno, who carved the statues of St Peter and St Paul; after his death in 1524 it was completed by Antonio Minello de' Bardi, who did the statue of St Andrew. On the second altar there is a painting of the *Martyrdom of St Christina*, done in 1520 by Vincenzo Catena. Over the side door is a painting of *The Last Supper* by Bonifacio de' Pitati. On the high altar there is a coloured stucco in the Donatello style, a 15C work of the Tuscan school. On the altar to the left of the chancel are statues of St Mark and St John by Lorenzo Bregno. In the transept is a gilded marble relief of the Virgin Praying, a Veneto-Byzantine work of the 13C. Above is a painting of *The Invention of the Cross*, a youthful work of Jacopo Tintoretto. The first altar from the front on the left side was done in 1536 from a model by Sansovino. The altarpiece on the second altar is *The Transfiguration*, done in 1512 by Francesco Bissolo.

The building directly opposite the church is Casa Leoni (No. 2180); this dates from the end of the 15C or the beginning of the 16C and is partly in the Gothic style and partly in that of the Renaissance.

We now turn left into Calle de la Chiesa, which takes us past the side of the church to Ponte del Cristo. This brings us to Campiello de lo Spezier, which extends across to Rio de San Stae. There we turn right on Fondamenta Rimpetto, passing on our left on the other side of the canal the colossal Palazzo Mocenigo, dating from the 17C. The Mocenigo inhabited the palace from the time it was built until the family became extinct in 1954 with the death of Count Alvise Nicolò Mocenigo, who bequeathed it to the Commune of Venice. The San Stae branch of the family who lived in this palace were descended from the third of the seven Mocenigo Doges, Giovanni Mocenigo (1478–85); the last of his descendants to rule was Alvise Mocenigo IV (1763–78). The palace preserves its sumptuous decoration throughout, including ceiling frescoes by Jacopo Guarana, Giambattista Canal and G. A. Zanetti, along with portrait busts and paintings of the many distinguished members of the family, most notably Doge Alvise Mocenigo IV. The palace now houses the Centre for the History of Fabric and Costume Studies; the main entrance is on Salizzada San Stae, which we will pass presently.

At the next corner we turn right into Calle va al Forno, which takes us back to Ponte del Forner. Towards the end of the *calle* on the left we pass the 14C Palazzo Agnusdio (No. 2060). The palace takes its name from the tondo over the ogive-arched door on the canal, where there is a relief of the Agnus Dei, the mystic Lamb of God. Over the land-door, framed in a lunette bordered with a carved floral design, there is a beautiful Romanesque relief of the 13C, showing an angel in majesty over a Gothic shield supported by two kneeling angels. On the facade overlooking the canal there is a superb pentaforium, or five-light balcony window, with reliefs of the Virgin and Angel of the Annunciation over the end pilasters and the symbols of the four Evangelists in the spandrels of the arches, dating from the mid 14C.

After crossing the bridge we turn left on Fondamenta de Ca' Pesaro, from which we can see the canal-side facade of Palazzo Agnusdio. At the end of the *fondamenta* we come on our right to Ca' Pesaro, which now houses the Museums of Modern and Oriental Art.

In the courtyard of the palace there is a monumental *vera da pozzo* surmounted by a triumphal arch and a statue of Apollo. This once stood in the courtyard of the Zecca and was moved here in 1905. The well-head and its arch were made by Jacopo Sansovino in 1537–45, along with the triumphal arch, while the statue was added by Danese Cattaneo. The great stairway leading to the piano nobile is by Antonio Gaspari, while the richly carved wooden ceilings are by

Baldassare Longhena. Some of the original 18C art works of the palace are preserved in the various rooms of the piano nobile, including frescoes by Nicolò Bambini and Girolamo Brusaferro.

After leaving the palace we cross Rio de la Pergola on Ponte Ca' Pesaro, continuing straight ahead on the *calle* of the same name, which brings us to Rio San Stae. There we turn right into Sottoportego de Ca' Giovanelli, at the end of which we turn left on the bridge of the same name, bringing us to Campo San Stae. Here we come to the church of San Stae, whose neoclassical facade faces across the *campo* to the Grand Canal.

A medieval source, the Savinin Chronicle, says that the church was founded in 966; it was dedicated to San Eustachio (St Eustace), who in Venetian dialect became San Stae. The original church was demolished in 1678 and a new one erected by Giovanni Grassi, with the facade completed in 1710 by Domenico Rossi, aided by seven sculptors.

A large tombstone in the centre of the nave covers the tomb of Doge Alvise Mocenigo II (d. 1709). The altarpiece in the first chapel from the rear on the right shows *The Madonna with Sts Lorenzo Giustinian, Anthony of Padua and Francis of Assisi* by Nicolò Bambini. The altar in the second chapel has a painting of *St Eustace Adoring the Crucifix* by Giuseppe Camerata. On the altar in the third chapel is *St Eustace in Glory* by Antonio Balestra; on the ceiling is *The Triumph of Faith* by Bartolomeo Letterini.

The paintings on the ceiling of the chancel were done in 1708 by Sebastiano Ricci. On the right wall of the chancel, below, there is a painting by Giambattista Tiepolo, depicting *The Martyrdom of St Bartholomew*. The other paintings on the walls of the chancel include two by Giuseppe Angeli and individual works by Gregorio Lazzarini, Giovanni Antonio Pellegrini, Pietro Uberti, Nicolò Bambini, Angelo Trevisani, Giambattista Piazzetta, Sebastiano Ricci, Antonio Balestra, Silvestro Manaigo, Giambattista Pittoni and Giambattista Mariotti.

The first chapel from the front on the left was dedicated by the Foscarini, who are commemorated by four funerary monuments with portrait busts. One of these marks the tomb of Antonio Foscarini, who was reinterred here with great honours after he was exonerated of the charge of treason for which he was executed in 1622; his portrait bust is by Giuseppe Torretti, who also did the altarpiece, a carving of Christ on the Cross. The altarpiece in the second chapel is *The Assumption of the Virgin* by Francesco Migliori. The painting on the altar of the third chapel is *St Catherine and St Andrew* by Jacopo Amigoni.

In the centre of the *campo* in front of the church there is a handsome *vera da pozzo* dating from the mid 18C. The quaint building just to the left of the church is the former Scuola dei Tiraoro e Battiloro, founded in 1711 by the guild of the drawers and beaters of gold.

We leave the *campo* via Salizzada San Stae, passing the 18C campanile of the church. On the base of the campanile there is the figure of an angel carved at the end of the 13C. On the second block beyond the church we once again pass Palazzo Mocenigo, whose entrance is at No. 1992. Opposite the palace, at No. 1920, there are the remains of a 13C house, with a handsome row of Gothic windows with pointed arches and a door surmounted by a 15C brick arch.

We now turn right on Calle del Tentor, which takes us to Ponte del Tentor, continuing straight ahead on the *ramo* of the same name. At the end of the block we turn left and then right to come to Ponte Megio, where we turn right on the *fondamenta* of the same name. The first building on the left is Casa Sanudo (No. 1757), the house in which Marino Sanudo (1466–1536) died. Sanudo left to posterity a diary in which he recorded each day all that happened in Venice during the years 1482–1533, an incomparable record of Venetian life at the beginning of the Renaissance.

Continuing along the *fondamenta*, we see to our right across the canal Palazzo Stazio-Priuli, built in the 16C to a design by

Sansovino. Opposite the *palazzo* we turn left into Ramo del Megio, at the end of which we turn right on Salizzada del Fontego dei Turchi. The street takes its name from the enormous old building that forms its right side for the last 50 m down to the Grand Canal. This is the Fontego dei Turchi, now the Museum of Natural History.

The original building was erected early in the 13C for Giuseppe Palmieri of Pesaro, who used it as a *fontego*, a combination of palace, warehouse and place of business, where ships could load and unload at the quay on the Grand Canal and their cargos could be bought and sold in the great hall on the ground floor. The Republic acquired the building in 1381 for the use of Nicolò V, the Marquis of Ferrara, and after his departure it was used to house other notables and heads of state visiting Venice. The Byzantine Emperor John VIII Palaeologus stayed here when on his way to and from the Council of Ferrara (and later Florence) in 1438. Then in 1621 it was rented by the state to the community of Turkish merchants in Venice, who used it as their residence and place of business up until 1838. The building was then abandoned and during the next two decades it fell into decay. It was purchased by the Venetian Commune in 1858, after which it was restored so badly as to lose virtually all of its original architectural distinction and interest.

We now retrace our steps along Salizzada del Fontego dei Turchi, pausing at the entrance to the alleyway on the right leading to the house at No. 1721, Casa Correr. This was the home of Teodoro Correr (1750–1830), who spent most of his life in collecting works of art, documents, memorabilia and other objects associated with Venetian history. He bequeathed his collections to the city of Venice, and from 1836 they were exhibited here at Casa Correr. The collections were subsequently moved to the Fontego dei Turchi, and then in 1922 to the Procuratie Nuove in the Piazza San Marco, where today they constitute the core of the Correr Civic Museum.

At the next corner we turn right into Calle dei Preti,

which leads to Campo San Zan Degolà. This is named for the church of San Zan Degolà, whose main facade we see to our left on entering the *campo*.

The church is dedicated to San Giovanni Decollato (St John Beheaded), who in Venetian dialect became San Zan Degolà. The church was founded in the 8C and rebuilt in the 14C.

The church is divided into a central nave and side aisles by two colonnades each of four columns of Greek marble with Byzantine capitals of the 11C. The nave is covered by a wooden 'ship's keel' ceiling. In the chapel to the right of the chancel the altarpiece is a marble statue of the Saviour dating from the second half of the 16C, possibly by Giulio del Moro. On the walls of the chancel there are two paintings by the school of Veronese: *The Annunciation* and *The Meeting of the Virgin with St Elizabeth*. In the chapel to the left of the chancel restorations have uncovered some important frescoes, the oldest dating to the 11C. On the outside of the arch that frames the chapel there is a fragmentary fresco of *The Annunciation* dating from the 13C.

In the centre of the *campo* there is a Gothic *vera da pozzo* of the 14C, with an inscription recording that it was restored in 1727.

We leave the *campo* at its south-west corner via Ponte Bembo. On the far side of the bridge to the right we see the 17C Palazzo Gidoni-Bembo. We continue straight ahead on Calle de Ca' Bembo, at the end of which we turn left on Rio Terà. At the first corner we turn right into Campiello Rielo, which after the first corner on the left becomes Lista Vechia dei Bari. Near the end of the street we pass on our right the entrance to Corte Pisani, a 13C archway with finials and capitals and reliefs of animals.

At the end of Lista Vechia dei Bari we turn right into Salizzada de la Chiesa, which takes us behind the church of San Simeon Grande. We then turn left into Sottoportego de la Chiesa, where on the wall to the right we see a 13C relief with the figure of a bishop, originally a tombstone. Beyond this the *sottoportego* becomes an arcaded portico that on its right side opens into Campo San Simeon Grande. At the inner end of the *campo*, which extends out to the Grand Canal, there is an 18C *vera da pozzo*. We continue on into Campo Santo, where immediately to our left we see the main facade of the church of San Simeon Grande.

The church is dedicated to San Simeon Profeta (St Simon the Apostle), but it is called San Simeon Grande to distinguish it from the nearby church of San Simeon Piccolo. The church was founded in 967 and reconstructed in the 12–13C. It was rebuilt again at the beginning of the 18C by Domenico Margutti, and its interior was renovated in 1750–55. The facade is in the form of a Greek temple front.

The interior retains its original basilica plan, with the central nave separated from the side aisles by antique columns with Byzantine capitals surmounted by 19C statues of the Apostles. On the wall to the right of the entrance there is a painting of *The Presentation in the Temple, with Donors*, by Palma il Giovane. In the right aisle, beyond the first altar from the rear, is the modern baptistery, with two reliefs in roundels showing the *Virgin and Angel of the Annunciation*, dating from the beginning of the 15C. Beside the baptistery to the left there is a 15C Lombardesque statuette of St Valentine. In the chapel to the left of the chancel there is a recumbent statue of St Simon on top of a sarcophagus, with a long inscription dating the monument to 1317. The altarpiece in the sacristy is a painting of *The Holy Trinity*, attributed to Giovanni Mansueti. The first altar from the front on the left side was dedicated by the Guild of Wool-carders; the altarpiece is *The Annunciation* by a follower of Palma il Giovane. On the second altar is *The Visitation* by Leonardo Corona, and on the wall beyond that *The Last Supper*, done by Jacopo Tintoretto *c.* 1560.

We leave the *campo* via Ponte de la Bergama, looking to the left on the other side of the canal to see Palazzo Gradenigo, built in the 18C by Domenico Margutti. After crossing the bridge we continue in the same direction on Calle Longa Bergama, which at the end of the first block bends to the right to bring us out to the Grand Canal at Ponte dei Scalzi. There we come to the end of the first of our two strolls through the Sestiere di Santa Croce.

SESTIERE DI SANTA CROCE II (*Map Route 16*)

Our second and final stroll through the Sestiere di Santa Croce starts where the last one ended, at Ponte dei Scalzi, and from there we will begin walking westwards along Fondamenta San Simeon Picolo.

Ponte dei Scalzi was first constructed in iron by the Austrians in 1855; the present stone bridge was completed in 1958.

At the beginning of the *fondamenta*, just past the foot of Ponte dei Scalzi, we pass in succession three 17C *palazzi*: Palazzo Foscari (No. 715), Palazzo Foscari-Contarini (No. 714), and Casa Adoldo (No. 712). Palazzo Foscari-Contarini was erected on the site of an earlier palace dating back to the 12C; tradition has it that Doge Francesco Foscari was born here in 1375.

We then come to the church of San Simeon Piccolo, whose large green dome is the most prominent landmark at the upper end of the Grand Canal.

The church is dedicated to St Simon and St Jude, the Apostles, but in Venetian dialect it came to be known as San Simeon Piccolo, the 'Little', to distinguish it from the nearby San Simeon Grande. According to tradition, the church was founded in the 10C, though the first documented reference to it dates from the second half of the 11C. The church was rebuilt in 1718–38 by Giovanni Scalfarotto, who erected it on a high platform facing the Grand Canal. Scalfarotto was inspired by the Pantheon in Rome, copying its dome on a miniature scale in the church. The porch is in the form of the *pronaos* of a classical Greek temple, with pillars at the corners and four columns between them in front and two on the sides. Within the triangular pediment there is a relief showing *The Martyrdom of St Simon and St Jude* by Francesco Penso, called Cabianca.

The circular nave is completely covered by the dome. At the ends of the diagonals there are four side altars framed in *aediculae*. The first altar on the right has a painting of *St Francesco di Paola and St Gaetano of Thiene* by Antonio Marinetti. On the second altar there is a painting of *Sts Simon, Jude and John the Baptist* by Francesco Polazzo. The high altar in the chancel is adorned with rich marbles; on either side there are statues of St Simon and St Jude, flanking an elegant tabernacle decorated with putti and two paintings on gold backgrounds, *The Three Maries at the Tomb* and *Mary Magdalene*, possibly by Domenico Maggiotto. A door in the exedra to the right leads to the sacristy, where the altarpiece is a marble Crucifix attributed to Giovanni Marchiori.

The building just to the right of the church, at No. 697, is the former Scuola dei Panni di Lana, the Guild of Woollen Cloth Makers, dating from the second half of the 16C. On either side of the facade on the third floor there are small *paterae* with reliefs of St Simon and St Thaddeus, the patron saints of the guild, which was suppressed in 1787.

On the right side of the guildhall Calle a Fianco de la Chiesa leads to a tiny *campiello* behind the church, where we find a graceful *vera da pozzo* dating from the second half of the 14C. Continuing along the *fondamenta*, after the second *calle* we pass Palazzo Emo-Diedo (No. 561). The palace, which has a central loggia surmounted by a triangular pediment, dates from the end of the 17C and is attributed to Andrea Tirali. Angelo Emo, the last admiral of the Venetian Navy, was born here in 1731. He died here in 1792, the last of his line, after which the palace passed to the Diedo family.

We walk over Ponte de la Croce, and continue in the same direction on Fondamenta de la Croce. This takes us past the Papadopoli Public Gardens, once part of the grounds of

Palazzo Foresti-Papadopoli, whose main facade is on Rio de la Croce. The park was first laid out in 1834 to a plan by Francesco Bagnara, and in 1863 it was redone by Marc Guignon. It was once rich in exotic plants and flowers, and in times past it was the scene of nocturnal festivals, but now it is neglected and forlorn.

We now cross Rio Novo on Ponte del Monastero. The bridge is named for the monastery of the church of Santa Croce, the Holy Cross, for which the Sestiere di Santa Croce was named. According to tradition, the church was founded in the 8–9C by refugees from the mainland. At the beginning of the 12C the Badoer family donated land for the foundation of a monastery, erected along with a new and larger church of Santa Croce. It was then that the church gave its name to the whole of the surrounding *sestiere*, which up until 1271 also included the island of Murano. The complex was suppressed in 1808 and subsequently both the church and the monastery were destroyed, with the monastic gardens being included with those of Palazzo Foresti-Papadopoli in what are now the Papadopoli Public Gardens. All that remains of the complex is a crenellated wall abutting the hotel on the far side of Ponte del Monastero, along with a granite column and Byzantine capital built into the corner of the structure at the angle of the Papadopoli Gardens by Ponte de la Croce.

After crossing the bridge we continue along Fondamenta Santa Chiara, which takes us past the northern end of Piazzale Roma, the vast traffic circle occupied by the bus terminal, with a huge car park at its western end. The bus terminal and car park, along with the enormous complex of the former tobacco company to their west and the other commercial enterprises around the Piazzale Roma, take up virtually all of what was once known as the Isola di Santa Croce, which in old prints appears as picturesque as any other quarter in Venice, though today it is a wasteland, an eyesore at the western end of the Grand Canal. But there are still a few remnants of its more felicitous past to be seen here and there, and we will come upon these as we walk around the periphery of the island.

We find one of these monuments between the two flights of steps that lead down from the traffic circle to the first of the *vaporetto* landings at Piazzale Roma. This is a superb *vera da pozzo* dated *c.* 1470. It appears in Barbari's view of 1500, where it is shown in the middle of a small *campo* behind the church and convent of Santa Croce. The *campo* disappeared when Piazzale Roma was developed in the years 1930–33, after the completion of the highway bridge connecting Venice with the mainland. The little square was known as Campo Morto, indicating that it was on the site of an old cemetery.

Continuing along Fondamanta Santa Chiara, we pass the several *vaporetto* stations of Piazzale Roma, and just beyond the last of them we come to the confluence of the Canale Santa Chiara and the Grand Canal. Across the side canal we see the former convent of Santa Chiara, now a military hospital, approached by a private bridge. The convent and church of Santa Chiara were founded in 1236. The complex was suppressed by the French in 1808 and the church was subsequently demolished, with the convent surviving first as a barracks and then as the present military hospital.

The *fondamenta* continues along the east bank of the Canale Santa Chiara, taking us under the easternmost span of Ponte della Libertà, the highway bridge built in 1930–33 by Eugenio Miozzi. A few steps beyond the bridge we come to the church of the Santissimo Nome di Gesù, the Most Sacred Name of Jesus, its gateway surmounted by the statues of two angels. The church was begun in 1815 by Giannantonio Selva, and after his death in 1819 work was continued by Antonio Diedo, who completed the building in 1834, adhering strictly to Selva's original neoclassical design.

At the end of the *fondamenta* we come to Campo San Andrea, named for the church of Sant'Andrea della Zirada, whose Gothic facade looks out across the little square towards the canal.

The church is dedicated to St Andrew the Apostle, the added name *zirada*, or 'bend', coming from the fact that the shoreline here made a sharp bend at what was originally one of the westernmost points of Venice. Sant'Andrea was founded in 1329 as an oratory associated with a hospice for impoverished women. The present church was begun in 1475. In the lunette over the door there is a 14C relief showing the calling of the Apostles Peter and Andrew, with the figure of the Dead Christ above, and on the crown of the arch the head of God the Father. Unfortunately the church is now closed.

We now make our way by the most direct route to Campo Santa Maria Maggiore, which is located at the intersection of three canals. Here we come to the church of Santa Maria Maggiore, which is at the south-west corner of the penitentiary to which it has given its name.

The church was built in 1498, probably by Tullio Lombardo, and the monastery was added in 1500–1505. At the beginning of the 19C the complex was suppressed by the French and its works of art removed, after which the church was used for a time as a warehouse for the tobacco factory, while the monastery served as a military barracks. The monastery was badly damaged by a fire in 1817 and then demolished in 1900; the penitentiary was built on its site in 1920–30.

On the south side of the church we cross Ponte Santa Maria Maggiore, after which we turn left on Fondamenta de Procuratie. This and the *fondamenta* on the other side are lined with rows of houses dating back to the 16–17C. On the north bank of Rio de Santa Maria Maggiore, just beyond the side canal, we see Palazzo Rizzi (No. 316). This was built in the late 17C by the Rizzi, a wealthy family of Rialto goldsmiths who bought their way into the nobility in 1687. The Rizzi continued to inhabit their palace until 1790; it was subsequently divided up into a congeries of flats. The long row of contiguous four-storey houses beyond Palazzo Rizzi also dates from the 17C, designed and still operating as multiple dwellings for people of the *cittadini* class.

Directly across the canal from Palazzo Rizzi we pass a huge four-storey apartment building that straddles Calle Larga dei Volti, which passes through the middle of the structure under an arch at the roof-line. This enormous structure, built in 1553 as an apartment house, stretches across the width of the island to the *fondamenta* on Rio del Tentor, the next canal to the south.

We turn right into Calle Cappello, which takes us through to Rio del Tentor at its intersection with Rio Briati. There we turn left on Fondamenta dei Cereri, named for the *cereri*, or wax-makers, who had their workshops here in times past. The first house that we pass on the Fondamenta dei Cereri is Case Cappello (No. 2508), built in 1547–53 as an apartment house. The entrance to Case Cappello faces Ponte Rossa, which crosses Rio del Tentor to Fondamenta Rossa on the east bank of Rio Briati. The large building to the left of the bridge at the junction of the two canals is Casa Bonazza, erected in 1563 as an apartment house.

Continuing along Fondamenta dei Cereri, on the next block we turn left through a *sottoportego* which takes us into Corte San Marco. In the centre of the *corte*, which is surrounded by contiguous houses of the 16C, there is a *vera da pozzo* dated 1599. The well-head and all the houses around the *corte* belonged to the Scuola di San Marco, built from an endowment by one of the brethren, Pietro Oliveri, who died in 1515.

Returning to the *fondamenta*, we continue in the same direction as far as the next corner, where we turn right to cross Ponte dei Ragusei. This takes us across the intersection of three canals to a little *campiello*, where we turn left into Calle Larga dei Ragusei. The *calle* and the bridge take their name from the Ragusei, a family who are recorded as living here in 1319.

At the end of the *calle* we cross Rio Nova on Ponte de la Sbiaca, after which we turn right on Fondamenta del Passamonte. We then bear left into Campiello del Basego, at the inner end of which we turn right into the *calle* of the same name. At the end of the *calle* we enter Corte del Basego, in the centre of which there is *vera da pozzo* in pink Verona marble, dated by an inscription to 1436.

At the outer end of the *corte* we come to Rio del Malcanton, where we turn left on the *fondamenta* and then left again into Calesela ai Malcanton, which bends to the right midway along its course. The ancient house at No. 3604 in the *calle* has an inscription recording that it was rebuilt in 1475. The *calle* brings us out to Rio del Malcanton, which here makes two perpendicular bends before it joins Rio del Gaffaro. Malcanton in Venetian dialect means 'the bad corner', referring to the corner of the canal bank at the southernmost of the two bends. The generally accepted theory as to the origin of this name traces it back to an incident in the 14C when the Bishop of Castello, trying to collect the death tithes from the parish priest of the church of San Pantalon, Bartolomeo Dandolo, was set upon and murdered by a group of angry locals, thus giving rise to the long-lived conflict between the Castellani and the Nicoletti.

Looking across Rio del Malcanton and to the right, we see at the angle of the canal the 17C Palazzo Arnaldi. We then turn left on the *fondamenta*, where after a few steps we pass Palazzo Surian (No. 3552), which also dates from the 17C. Just beyond Palazzo Surian we go through a little *ramo* and court to enter Corte de Ca' Surian, in the middle of which there is an elegant *vera da pozzo* dating from the second half of the 14C.

We leave the *corte* at its north-east corner via a *sottoportego*, after which we turn left on the *fondamenta*. We then continue straight ahead and cross the canal on Ponte de Ca' Marcello. The bridge is named for the handsome Gothic palace directly opposite its far end, the 14C Palazzo Marcello (No. 134A). The building to the left of this is Palazzo Minotto (No. 143), dating from the 17C. And to the left of that is Palazzo Oddoni (No. 151), a Gothic edifice dating from the 15C.

Looking to the right from the bridge, at the angle of Rio del Malcanton we see a picturesque Gothic house of the 14C, the balustrade of its canal-side garden surmounted by the statue of a saint. The land entrance to the house is at No. 49 on Salizzada San Pantalon. Directly across the street from the house, at No. 131, we see the former Scuola dei Lanieri, a handsome neoclassical edifice built for the Guild of Wool-makers in 1631–3 by Baldassare Longhena.

We now turn left from the bridge on to Fondamenta Minotto, which takes us along the north bank of Rio del Gaffaro. As we pass the Palazzo Minotto we see directly opposite it on the other side of the canal an unusual house known as Casa Torres, built in the neo-Byzantine style in 1907–8 by Giuseppe Torres.

At the end of Fondamenta Minotto we come to the intersection of Rio del Gaffaro with Rio del Magazen (to the left) and Rio dei Tolentini (to the right). Here the first of these canals is spanned by Ponte del Gaffaro and the second by Ponte dei Squartai, the Bridge of the Cutthroats, so called because of the murderous gangs who used to waylay people here in the old days.

At Ponte del Gaffaro we turn right on to Fondamenta dei Tolentini. This brings us to Campo dei Tolentini, which is dominated by the imposing classical porch of the church of San Nicolò da Tolentino.

After the sack of Rome by Charles V in 1527, St Gaetano of Thiene took refuge in Venice with some of his monks, one of whom was Giovanni Pietro Carafa, the future Pope Paul IV, and the year after their arrival they built a small oratory here dedicated to St Nicholas of Tolentino. In 1591 Vincenzo Scamozzi was commissioned to build the present church, which was consecrated in 1602, though the interior construction and decoration were not completed until 1671, with the great classical porch being added in 1706–14 by Andrea Tirali. The porch, which is raised on a flight of six steps, is in the form of a Greek hexastyle *pronaos*, with six Corinthianesque columns in front and two on the sides, counting corner columns twice, supporting an entablature and a triangular pediment with an oval window in the tympanum.

The high altar in the chancel was built by Baldassare Longhena in 1661, with the statues of the two angels on the sides and the six angel-caryatids done by Giusto Le Court. On the right wall of the chancel there is a painting of *The Annunciation*, a masterpiece by Luca Giordano. On the left wall is the elaborately decorated baroque funerary monument of Patriarch Francesco Morosini (d. 1678) by Filippo Parodi. The vault is decorated with a fresco of *San Gaetano in Glory* attributed to Mattia Bortolini. On the external wall of the chancel to the right is a painting of *St Gregory the Great and Angels* by Girolamo Forabosco and *The Blessed Giovanni Marinoni* by Palma il Giovane. On the external wall to the left is *St Gaetano* by Palma il Giovane and *St Jerome Visited by an Angel* by Johann Liss.

Looking out from the church porch over the *campo*, on the other side of the canal we see two *palazzi* side by side just to the left of Ponte dei Tolentini. The one immediately to the left of the bridge is Palazzo Foresti-Papadopoli, dating from the mid 16C. Next to it is the 18C Palazzo Condulmer; the most notable member of this family was Gabriele Condulmer, who became Pope Eugenio IV (1431–47).

Leaving by the north side of the porch, we step down into Campazzo dei Tolentini. On our right is the entrance to the School of Architecture of the University of Venice, housed in the former monastery of San Nicolò da Tolentino.

We walk diagonally across the *campazzo* to the northern stretch of Fondamenta dei Tolentini, which takes us along the east bank of Rio de la Croce. We then turn right into the second *sottoportego*, which takes us into Corte del Tagiapiera. In the centre of the *corte* there is a *vera da pozzo* in pink Verona marble dating from the beginning of the 15C.

At the far end of the *corte* we continue into Campo de la Lana, turning left at the first corner into the *ramo* of the same name. The name (*lana* is 'wool') comes from the Arte dei Tessitori di Panni di Lana Tedeschi, the Guild of German Wool-workers, who founded a hospice here in 1566.

At the end of the *ramo* we take a right turn into Calle de le Case Nove, then a right again into Calle dei Bergamaschi. We then turn left into Ramo de le Muneghe, where we see a *vera da pozzo* of the 15C. The well-head appears in an engraving done in the early 19C by Giovanni Pividor, who shows it against the background of a church that once stood on the north side of Ramo de le Muneghe. This was the church of Gesù e Maria, which, with its convent, was founded early in the 17C. The complex was suppressed by the French in 1805 and then demolished later in the 19C. The name of the church is commemorated in that of Calle de Gesù e Maria, which leads off from the middle of the north side of Ramo de le Muneghe.

We now turn right into Calle Sechere, after which we make a left into Corte Canal. Along the middle of this long *corte* there are two identical bowl-shaped *vere da pozzo*, both dated 1730.

At the far end of the *corte* we pass through a *sottoportego* into Campiello dei Nerini, at the end of which we come to Rio Marin and Ponte Cappello. As we do so we pass on our left Palazzo Cappello, pausing to look back upon it from the bridge. The palace was built in the 17C by the Bragadin family, and then passed in turn to the Soranzo and the Cappello, by whose name it is now known. It was once famous for its magnificently decorated rooms, its rich marbles, elegant furniture and beautiful paintings, and above all for its garden, described by Henry James in *The Aspern Papers* and by Gabriele d'Annunzio in *Il Fuoco*. D'Annunzio, describing its bewitching atmosphere in spring, writes that the garden 'enclosed like an exiled thing by its girdle of water, becomes all the more intense from its banishment, like the soul of an exile'.

After crossing the bridge we turn right on Fondamenta dei

Garzoti, named for the *garzotti*, wool-carders, who founded a *scuola* here in 1611. Looking across the canal, on the second block beyond Ponte Cappello on Fondamenta Rio Marin, we see the 17C Palazzo Contarini (No. 803), where a Freemasons' Lodge was established secretly in 1785. Beyond that we see a five-storey apartment block whose side facade extends the full length of Calle Larga Contarina, erected as apartments in 1559–66 and still serving the same purpose today. On the second block beyond this is the 18C Palazzo Malipiero (Nos. 836–8).

At the end of Fondamenta Garzoti we come to Campiello del Cristo, named for an icon depicting Christ that was venerated here in a wayside shrine.

Looking eastwards along the canal on its opposite side, where it is joined by Rio de San Zuan Evangelista, we see Ponte de le Late. This bridge and the *fondamenta* to its east are named for the Dalle Late family, who lived here as early as 1379. Marino Sanudo writes of a bizarre incident that took place on this bridge, which he notes in his diary for 31 August 1505:

Today the execution took place of the Albanian who treacherously murdered Zuan Marco. First his hand was cut off at Ponte de le Late. And mark that this gave rise to a curious incident; to wit, while his wife was taking leave of him, he made as if he wanted to kiss her and bit off her nose. It is said that she was responsible for bringing his crime to light.

At the inner corner of the *campiello* we enter Calle del Cristo, at the end of which we turn right into Campiello de le Strope. This was named for Antonio di Stropi, a draper who opened a shop here in 1456. In the centre of the *campiello* there is a pretty *vera da pozzo* dating from *c.* 1500, one of its reliefs representing the bearded head of a Silenus, one of the followers of Dionysus.

Continuing for a few steps through the *campiello*, we turn left through a *sottoportego* that takes us into the Corte de l'Anatomia o Fiorenzuola. The *corte* takes the first part of its name from the nearby Theatre of Anatomy of the School of Medicine, while the second part comes from Cristofolo Fiorenzuola, an official of the Scuola Grande di San Giovanni Evangelista who is recorded as residing here in 1473.

At the far right-hand corner of the *corte* we pass through a *sottoportego* which brings us to Rio Sant'Agostin and Ponte de l'Anatomia. On the other side of the bridge to the left we see the Teatro Anatomico, built in 1671 as an anatomical theatre for the Collegio dei Medici, endowed by a bequest of Lorenzo Loredan.

On the other side of the bridge we come to Campo San Giacomo de l'Orio, one of the most picturesque *campi* in Venice, a large area of highly irregular shape surrounding the church for which it is named. The church turns its back to the *campo*, with its main facade facing Rio Sant'Agostin on Campiello del Piovan, which extends around the north side of the church. The church also has entrances on both sides, but we will bypass these to enter the building by the front door, exploring the *campo en route* from Ponte de l'Anatomia.

There are three *vere da pozzo* in the *campo*, all of them dating from the 14–15C. There are two *palazzi* on the east side of the *campo*. One of these, the 17C Palazzo Mariani, is behind the apse of the church at Nos. 1584–6. The second, Palazzo Pemma, is near the north-east corner of the *campo*, at No. 1624. This dates from the early 18C, and now serves as the University Institute of Architecture; in its interior courtyard there is a beautiful Gothic *vera da pozzo* of the 14C.

We now continue around the church, passing the campanile and turning left into the canal-side part of Campiello del Piovan to come to the main entrance of the church.

According to tradition, the church was founded in the 9–10C, although the first documented reference to it is dated 1089. It was dedicated to San Giacomo (St James, in this case the Greater), the 'dell'Orio' apparently being a corruption of *del lauro*, 'of the bay tree', which tradition says was growing on the site of the church when it was founded. The church was rebuilt in 1225 through funds provided by the Badoer and Da Mula families. It was rebuilt again at the turn of the 14–15C, and once more at the beginning of the 16C, each time adding to the Gothic structure of the 13C. The campanile dates from the rebuilding of 1225. Over the main entrance in Campiello del Piovan there is a statuette of St James, dating from the 17C.

The interior plan of the church is a Latin cross, separated into a central nave and side aisles by two rows of granite columns surmounted by Veneto-Byzantine capitals of the 13C. Two columns of the colonnade extend into the south transept, with the one on the right made of verd-antique and topped by a classical Ionic capital, probably taken from an ancient temple. Near the front of the nave on the left the last column has a Ravenna-style capital dating from the 6C. Next to it there is an octagonal chalice-shaped pulpit of rich marbles in the Lombardesque style. Both the nave and the transept are covered by a beautiful ship's-keel roof dating from the 14C.

The organ is suspended above the main entrance on the *controfacciata* wall. On its front there are three paintings: *Jesus Disputing in the Temple, The Calling of the Apostles* and *The Martyrdom of St James*, all attributed to Andrea Schiavone, who also did the portraits of the two prophets flanking the door. On the baroque altar on the right side of the nave there is a polychrome wooden statue of the Virgin, an anonymous work of the 15C. On the right wall of the south transept there is a huge painting of *The Multiplication of Loaves and Fishes* by Palma il Giovane. The painting on the altar is *The Madonna and Child in Glory with Saints* by Giambattista Pittoni; on the wall to the left is *Christ Sustained by an Angel* by Palma il Giovane.

The apsidal area to the right of the chancel is the Cappella Santissimo, where frescoes by Jacopo Guarana are being restored. The two lunettes in the upper zone of the side walls are, to the right, *The Flagellation* by Tizianello and, on the left,

Ecce Homo by Giulio del Moro. The two paintings below are by Palma il Giovane: on the left, *Christ and St Veronica*; on the right, *The Deposition in the Sepulchre*.

The side walls of the chancel are decorated by two huge crosses in polychrome marble, Lombardesque works from the beginning of the 16C. At the centre of the apse is a painting of the *Madonna and Child* with *Sts Andrew, James the Greater, Cosmas and Damian*, signed by Lorenzo Lotto and dated 1546. On the wall just to the left of the chancel there is a beautiful statuette of the Madonna Annunciata, dating from the beginning of the 14C.

The altarpiece in the chapel at the end of the north transept is a painting of *Sts Lawrence, Jerome and Prospero* by Veronese. On the side walls of the chapel are two paintings by Palma il Giovane: on the right, *St Lawrence Presents the Poor of Rome to the Emperor Valerian*; on the left, *The Martyrdom of St Lawrence*. On the altar on the left side of the nave there is a large marble Crucifixion of the 17C.

The Old Sacristy was decorated in the years 1575–81 by Palma il Giovane; on the ceiling is *The Eucharist Adored by the Four Evangelists*; on the walls, *The Deposition, The Passage of the Red Sea, The Madonna and Saints, The Plague of Serpents, The Fall of Manna, Elijah and the Angel* and *The Passover*.

Permission can be obtained from the custodian to visit the New Sacristy. At the centre of the panelled ceiling is an *Allegory of Faith* and at the sides are *Doctors of the Church*, all by Veronese. On the walls there are paintings by Giovanni Buonconsiglio, Francesco Bassano, Palma il Giovane, Bonifacio de' Pitati and the school of Veronese.

We leave the church and cross Campiello del Piovan to Ponte Ruga Vechia, which takes us across the canal to the street of the same name. Halfway along Ruga Vechia we come to a *vera da pozzo* of the late 15C or the early 16C. The only unusual feature of the well-head is that one side of its base is rounded and the other squared, the latter having two circular troughs to provide water for cats, dogs and birds. An ordinance of 1795 specifies that these drinking-bowls for animals and birds should be kept clean by the porters who looked after the *vere da pozzo* in each parish.

At the end of the street we turn right on Ramo Orsetti, continuing straight ahead in the *campiello* of the same name, noticing the unusual coat of arms on the left at No. 1135 at the junction of the two streets. At the far left-hand corner of the *campiello* we pass through an extremely narrow gap to emerge on Lista Vechia dei Bari, where we turn right and continue to the first corner on the left. There we turn left into a narrow *ramo* that takes us into Campiello Zen. In the centre of the little *campiello* there is a *vera da pozzo* of the 18C.

We continue to the end of the *calle*, which brings us out to the Grand Canal on Riva di Biasio and the *pontile* of the same name. Here we come to the end of our second and last stroll through the Sestiere di Santa Croce, completing our final walk through the Venetian labyrinth.

As we emerge here on the Grand Canal after our last stroll, we sense that perhaps it will be the enduring vision of the Venetian labyrinth that we will carry away with us in our exile from this bewitching city born of the lagoon, as Proust wrote in *Albertine disparue*:

After dinner I went out by myself into the heart of the enchanted city where I found myself wandering in strange regions like a character in the Arabian Nights . . . I had plunged into a network of little alleys, *calli* dissecting in all directions by their ramifications the quarter of Venice isolated between a canal and the lagoon, as if it had crystallized along these innumerable slender capillary lines. All of a sudden, at the end of one of these little streets, it seemed as though a bubble had occurred in the crystallized matter. A vast and splendid *campo*, of which I would never, in this network of little streets, have guessed the importance, or even found room for, spread out before me flanked with charming palaces silvery in the moonlight. It was one of those architectural wholes towards which, in any other town, the streets converge, lead you and point the way.

Here it seemed to be deliberately concealed in a labyrinth of alleys, like those palaces in oriental tales to which mysterious agents convey by night a person who, taken home again before daybreak, can never find his way back to the magic dwelling, which he ends by supposing that he visited only in a dream.

On the following day I set out in search of my beautiful nocturnal *piazza*. I followed *calli* which were exactly like one another and refused to give me any information, except such as would lead me farther astray. Sometimes a vague landmark which I seemed to recognize led me to suppose that I was about to see appear, in its seclusion, solititude and silence, the beautiful exiled *piazza*. At that moment some evil genie which had assumed the form of a fresh *calle* made me turn unconsciously from my course, and I found myself suddenly brought back to the Grand Canal. And as there is no great difference between the memory of a dream and the memory of a reality, I ended by asking myself whether it was not during my sleep that there had occurred in a dark patch of Venetian crystallization that strange interruption which offered a vast *piazza* flanked by romantic palaces, to the mediative eye of the moon.

[12] The Islands of the Lagoon

Venice begins and ends in its all-embracing lagoon. And so in this last chapter we will explore the lagoon and its islands, some of which preserve monuments that go back to the earliest days of Venice.

THE LIDO

Many tourists who come to Venice in the summer head directly out to the Lido, on the boats that leave from the Riva degli Schiavone. The boats stop at Pontile Santa Maria Elisabetta, and from there the No. 11 bus goes south along the whole length of the island to Alberoni; from Alberoni, the bus is transported on a shuttle ferry to Santa Maria del Mare on Pellestrina, and from there it continues on to the south end of that island, from where there is a connecting ferry to Chioggia on the mainland.

The Lido is some 12 km long and only 300–1,000 m wide, fringed on its sea side by a sand beach. Until the second half of the 19C the Lido was inhabited almost exclusively by fishermen and farmers. The first bathing establishment on the Lido opened in 1857 and then, with the beginning of the *vaporetto* service in 1881, the island became extremely popular as a summer resort, leading to the building of grand hotels, restaurants, cafés, and summer villas.

As the *vaporetto* approaches the Lido at Pontile Santa Maria Elisabetta the principal landmark is the huge green dome of the votive temple of Santa Maria della Vittoria, Our Lady of

Victory. This was begun in 1925 by the architect Giuseppe Torres as a memorial to those who died in the service of Italy during the First World War.

Pontile Santa Maria Elisabetta is named for the little church directly across from the landing stage. The church was founded in the mid 16C and rebuilt in its present form in 1620. A short distance to the right of the church is the beginning of the Gran Viale Santa Maria Elisabetta, which extends across the waist of the island from the lagoon to the sea coast. At the end of the Gran Viale we come to the coastal road, which leads on the right to two famous hotels of the Lido, the Grand Hôtel des Bains and the Excelsior. Both are mentioned by Thomas Mann in *Death in Venice*, published in 1912. Mann himself stayed at the Hôtel des Bains in 1911, and it is there that he houses his protagonist, the doomed Aschenbach.

One can walk out towards the northern end of the Lido along the lagoon road to the church of San Nicolò di Lido, a distance of 1.5 km. The original church here, dedicated to St Nicholas of Myra, was founded in 1044 by Doge Domenico Contarini, whose monument is over the main doorway; the Benedictine monastery was established nine years later. The present church dates from a complete rebuilding in 1626. The only painting of note that now remains is on the first altar from the front on the left, *The Ascension of Christ* by Pietro Vecchia. In the chancel there is a large wooden Crucifix dating from the early 14C.

In the *campo* in front of the church there is a bowl-shaped *vera da pozzo* dating from the 16–17C. The large building beyond the church is the 16C Casa Rossa, identified by an inscription on the architrave of its doorway as the Palazzo del Consiglio dei Dieci.

Returning along the lagoon road, some 400 m from the church we pass the wall of the ancient Jewish cemetery. This is closed to the public except by special appointment, but one can see a number of old and interesting tombstones through the

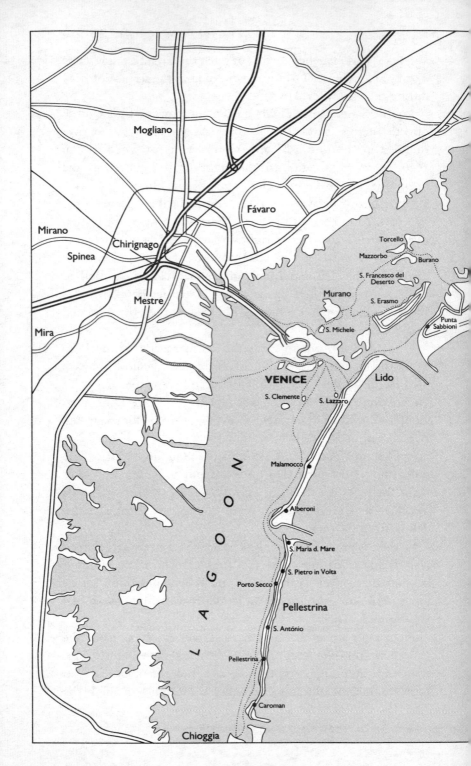

The Lagoon

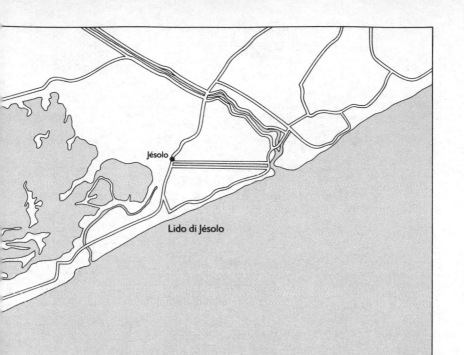

Jésolo

Lido di Jésolo

A D R I A T I C

S E A

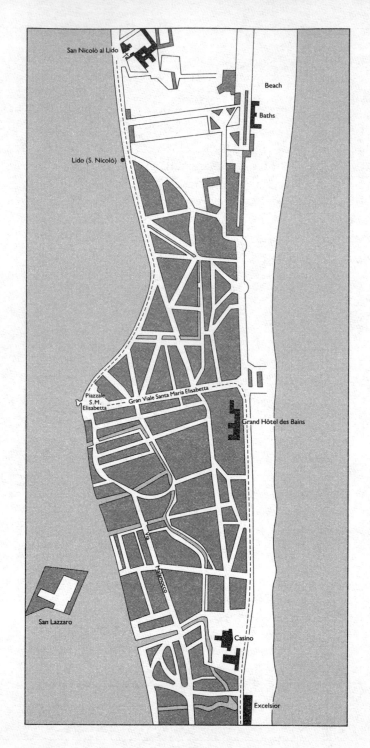

The Lido

gateway. The cemetery was founded in 1386, when the Venetian government gave the Jews permission to open a graveyard here.

From Pontile Santa Maria Elisabetta it is 5.5 km south to Malamocco. The present village of Malamocco originated as the Roman town of Metamaucus, which during the years 742–811 was the capital of the Venetian Republic. Metamaucus was utterly destroyed by a great tidal wave in 1106, and not a trace of it remains. The present village was built closer to the lagoon, protected on its outer side by the Murazzi, the great sea wall constructed by the Republic in the late 18C. As early as 1159 this was known as 'the new Malamocco', a semi-autonomous town with its own Podestà, or Mayor. Malamocco still retains its individuality; as Horatio Brown wrote nearly a century ago, it is 'quiet and sleepy and clean; the people with a type distinctly their own; very gentle and friendly to strangers, but at heart seeming to say, "we are not Venetians, but Malamocchini"'.

The principal monuments in the picturesque village are grouped around the contiguous Campo della Chiesa and Piazza Maggiore; these are the Palazzo del Podestà and the church of Santa Maria Assunta, both of them Gothic edifices dating from the 15C. There are two *vere da pozzo* in the Campo della Chiesa and one in the Piazza Maggiore, all dating from the 15–16C. All three have reliefs of the Lion of St Mark, which also appears in ten other places around the two squares. These lions escaped destruction by the French in 1797 because of the remoteness of Malamocco at that time.

From Malamocco it is another 3 km to Alberoni, from where a shuttle ferry crosses the narrow channel of Porto di Malamocco to the northern tip of Pellestrina.

PELLESTRINA

The island is 11.3 km long and varies in width from 320 m at its northern end to only 50 m along its tenuous southern strip.

The road runs along the eastern side of the island beside the Murazzi. On the western side half a dozen fishing villages are strung out along the lagoon, the last of them being Pellestrina. The village of Pellestrina is the largest community on the island, and has three churches, the oldest of which is Ognissanti, founded in the 10C and rebuilt in 1535.

Pellestrina is inhabited almost entirely by the families of fishermen, whose boats line the quay as far as the eye can see. Like the Mallamocchini, the people of Pellestrina are a race apart, with their own distinctive dialect and customs. In times past they were renowned singers, particularly the women. Goethe was informed of this by his gondolier one evening when he heard two boatmen singing verses by Tasso, as he writes in his *Italian Journey*:

He wanted me to hear the women on the Lido, especially those from Malamocco and Pellestrina. They too, he told me, sing verses by Tasso to the same or a similar melody, and added: 'It is their custom to sit on the seashore while their husbands are out sea-fishing, and sing these songs in penetrating tones until from far out over the sea, their men reply, and in this way they converse with one another.' Is this not a beautiful custom?

The last bus stop on Pellestrina island is Caroman, which takes its name from Ca' Roman, an ancient fortress that guarded the strait of Porto di Chioggia. There a ferry meets the No. 11 bus to take passengers across the strait to Chioggia, a beautiful and historic city, but beyond the bounds of the present book.

SAN LAZZARO AND OTHER SOUTHERN ISLETS

Vaporetti also leave Riva degli Schiavone for a quartet of islets in the lagoon between Venice and the Lido, stopping in succession at La Grazia, San Servolo, San Lazzaro and San Clemente, and then returning in the reverse order. Most tourists who travel this route are headed for the Armenian monastery on San Lazzaro, while the other islands are visited by those who have business there. La Grazia, San Servolo and San Clemente all were the site of monasteries in the early days of the Republic. Later La Grazia became the site of a hospital for highly infectious diseases, which still functions today; San Servolo's monastery became an asylum for the insane, now converted into a school for architectural restorers; while San Clemente is abandoned.

The island of San Lazzaro degli Armeni is the headquarters of the Mechitarist Order. The island was first used in the 12C as a hospital for pilgrims; then later, under the supervision of the abbot of the Sant'Ilario monastery, it became a hospital for poor lepers, dedicated to St Lazarus. The lepers were eventually moved to the new Ospedale di San Lazzaro dei Mendicanti at Santi Giovanni e Paolo, after which the island was deserted for several centuries. Then in 1717 the island was given to an Armenian monk named Manouk Bedrosian (1675–1749), better known as Mechitar, or the Consoler, who was born in the Turkish Anatolian city of Sivas and educated in Istanbul, where in 1700 he founded his own religious order, the Mechitarist Fathers, which was approved by Pope Clement XI as an Armenian congregation in union with Rome. Mechitar and his monks restored the existing church and built the monastic complex that we see today, which includes a library with 150,000 books and 5,000 Armenian manuscripts, a printing-press that has been publishing works of Armenian culture since 1789, many of them by renowned scholars of the Mechitarist Order, an archaeological museum, a gallery of Armenian art, and numerous other works of art that adorn the various buildings of the complex, which is surrounded by a beautiful garden.

A small room off the modern library contains memorabilia of Lord Byron, who often visited the monastery during his stay in Venice in 1816–17. While here he studied Armenian under the tutelage of Father Pascal Aucher ('a learned and pious soul'), with whom he worked on the publication of an

Armenian grammar. Byron writes of the Mechitarist Fathers in a fragmentary document found among his papers:

The society of the Convent of St Lazarus appears to unite all the advantages of the monastic institution without any of its vices. The neatness, the comfort, the gentleness, the unaffected devotion, the accomplishments, and the virtues of the brethren of the order, are well fitted to strike the man of the world with the conviction that there are other and better things even in this life . . .

SAN MICHELE

The islands in the northern part of the lagoon are approached from Pontile Fondamente Nove. *Vaporetti* go out to San Michele (Cimitero) and Murano; to Murano, Mazzorbo, Burano, Torcello and Treporti (on the Cavallino peninsula); and to Murano, Le Vignole and Sant'Erasmo, the latter two islands being almost entirely given over to vineyards and farms.

The cemetery isle of San Michele is just 420 m off the Fondamente Nove, and the *vaporetto* passes along its western side on the way to the landing by the church of San Michele in Isola.

The present church of San Michele in Isola was erected in 1469–78 by Mauro Coducci, his first building in Venice. It was also the first church in Venice to be built in the classical style of the Renaissance. The doorway is surmounted by a 15C statue of the Madonna and Child. Just to the left of the facade, projecting from the corner of the island, there is a domed hexagonal structure that houses the Cappella Emiliani, added in 1530 by Guglielmo Bergamasco; on two sides of the building there are statues of St Margaret and St John the Baptist attributed to Bartolomeo Bergamasco. The chapel was repaired by Jacopo Sansovino in 1560–62. To the right of the church facade there is an ornate Gothic doorway, with a high triangular arch framing a 15C sculptural group of St

Michael Killing the Dragon. The doorway leads to the cloister of the 15C monastery.

There are numerous tombstones and funerary monuments within the church, with the chapel in the apse containing the tomb of Andrea Loredan (d. 1513). In the vestibule we see the tombstone of Paolo Sarpi (d. 1623), whose remains were reinterred here in 1828 after the church of the Servites was demolished.

The cemetery of San Michele contains the remains of a number of famous foreign visitors who died in Venice, including Serge Diaghilev, Igor Stravinsky, Ezra Pound and Frederick Rolfe, alias Baron Corvo, as well as the painter Leopold Robert, who committed suicide in 1835, apparently because of his unrequited love for Napoleon's niece.

MURANO

We continue on to Murano, disembarking at Piazzale alla Colonna. This is named for the granite column on the *fondamenta*, once surmounted by a statue of Doge Domenico Contarini (1659–75).

Murano is the ancient Amuranium, which up until 1271 was a semi-autonomous state. Then from 1272 onwards, under the aegis of the Venetian Doge, it had its own Podestà, assisted by a major and minor *arengo*, or council. In 1291 all glass-blowing establishments were moved to Murano from Venice because of the danger of fire in the densely settled city. Thenceforth the prosperity of Murano was based on its craft of glass-making, its products being famous throughout the world for more than seven centuries.

We now walk eastwards along Fondamenta dei Vetrai, which follows the north bank of the canal of the same name. *Vetrai* means 'glass-maker', and indeed both sides of the canal are lined with glass-works and shops selling Murano glass. A short way along we pass on our left the 16C Palazzo dei Contarini (No. 27). We then pass on our right Ponte Santa

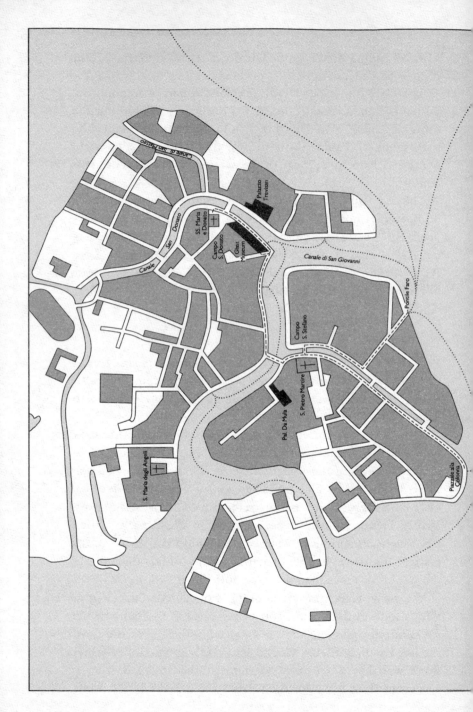

Burano and Torcello

Chiara, which leads to Fondamenta Daniele Manin. The name of the bridge comes from that of the ancient conventual church of Santa Chiara that once stood on the *fondamenta*. The church was founded in the 15C and renovated in 1519; it was suppressed in 1826 and then subsequently converted into a glass factory and warehouse. This now houses the Consorzio Museo Vetraio, an adjunct to the Murano Glass Museum that displays the contemporary products of the island's glassworks. At No. 4 on Fondamenta Daniele Manin we see Casino Mocenigo, built in 1591–1617 by a follower of Palladio, probably Vincenzo Scamozzi, and most recently restored in 1984. At No. 6 on the same *fondamenta* there is a 14C Gothic house, with its upper floors suspended over an arcaded portico, its facade decorated with crests of the Obizzi and Sodeci families.

Continuing along Fondamenta dei Vetrai, we pass a 15C Gothic house at No. 37 and a Renaissance dwelling at No. 41, after which we come to Ponte Ballarin. In the days of the Republic this was the focal point of Murano, and public proclamations were made here by a herald, with the spot still marked by a marble Lion of St Mark on a column.

Continuing along Fondamenta dei Vetrai, at the first corner we pass Campiello de la Pescaria, the ancient site of the Murano fish market. Then after walking for 150 m we come to San Pietro Martire, the parish church of Murano.

The original church on this site, dedicated to St John the Baptist, was founded in 1348 by the nobleman Marco Michiel, along with a Dominican monastery. The church was destroyed by a fire in 1474 and then completely rebuilt, after which it was reopened in 1511 and dedicated to St Peter Martyr. The complex was suppressed in 1808 and stripped of all of its works of art, only to be reopened five years later. The church was redecorated with works of art from other suppressed churches on Murano, and then in 1922–8 its fabric was restored.

On the first altar from the rear on the right there is a

painting of *Sts Nicholas, Charles Borromeo and Lucy* signed by Palma il Giovane. Beyond this in the right aisle there are two notable paintings by Giovanni Bellini, *The Assumption of the Virgin with Eight Saints*, done in the years 1505–13, and *The Madonna with Doge Agostino Barbarigo*, signed and dated 1488. A little farther on is *The Baptism of Jesus*, a late work by Jacopo Tintoretto. On the wall in front of the left aisle there are two paintings done *c.* 1565–6 by Paolo Veronese, *St Agatha in Prison Visited by St Peter and an Angel*, and *St Jerome in the Desert*.

Beside the church, in Corte de la Chiesa, there is a splendid *vera da pozzo* dated 1348.

We now return to Fondamenta dei Vetrai and continue past the side of the church, passing Ponte San Pietro Martire. Fifty metres beyond the bridge we come to the junction of Rio dei Vetrai and the Canale Grande di Murano, which we cross on Ponte Vivarini.

Looking back and to our left we see the impressive Palazzo Da Mula, a 15C Gothic palace altered in the 16C, with *paterae*, panels, sculptural fragments and the remains of a portico and archway from an earlier Veneto-Byzantine palace of the 12–13C.

After crossing the bridge we turn right on the opposite *fondamenta*, which eventually takes us to Palazzo Giustinian (No. 8). This was built in 1680 for Marco Giustinian, Bishop of Torcello, who had received permission to move the bishop's residence to Murano. After Giustinian's death in 1735 his successors as bishop lived here until 1805, when the bishoprics of Torcello and Venice were combined under the aegis of the Venetian Patriarch. The palace was acquired by the Commune of Murano, and then in 1861 it was converted to its present function, housing the Murano Glass Museum.

In the entrance hall and arcade there are architectural and sculptural fragments dating back to the 7C, including coats of arms of prominent Murano families. The exhibits in the ten rooms of the palace are principally examples of Murano glass ranging from 15C to 18C, the jewel of the collection being the 15C marriage cup traditionally attributed to the Barovier family. Other exhibits include objects from archaeological excavations, including examples of ancient Egyptian, Phoenician and Roman glass; foreign glass, principally Spanish and Bohemian; and memorabilia associated with the history and life of Murano. There are also a number of paintings; the most notable are *The Madonna of the Roses* by Veronese and *The Virgin Praying* by Bartolomeo Vivarini.

After leaving the museum we continue along the *fondamenta* for another 50 m or so to Campo San Donato, where we see the ancient church of Santi Maria e Donato, with its graceful arcaded apse facing Canale San Donato at its junction with Canale di San Matteo.

The church seems to have been founded in the 7C by refugees from the mainland, who dedicated it to the Virgin, as recorded in a document dated 999. Then in 1125 the body of St Donatus was brought from the Ionian island of Cephalonia to Venice and enshrined here, whereupon the church was re-dedicated to St Mary and St Donatus. The church seems to have been rebuilt in its present form at that time, to be completed in 1140, a date recorded in its mosaic floor. The interior was redecorated in the baroque style in the first half of the 18C by Bishop Marco Giustinian, who was buried in the nave. The building was restored in the years 1858–73, recreating the original form of the 12C church. The original baptistery, which stood outside the church, was demolished in 1719. The isolated campanile, which stands at the rear of Campo San Donato beside the church, dates from the 12–13C. Beside the tower is a war memorial created by the Murano sculptor Napoleone Martinuzzi. In the middle of the *campo* there is a remarkable *vera da pozzo* dating from the second half of the 13C.

The most remarkable aspect of the church exterior is its apse, encircled by two tiers of blind arcades, their double marble columns flanking brick niches below and enclosing a gallery above, the two orders separated by decorative zigzag terracotta patterns and dog-tooth mouldings. The main facade is that of a basilica of the Ravenna type; over the doorway there is a relief depicting St Donatus and a devotee, dating from the beginning of the 14C.

The interior is basilical with a Latin-cross plan, the central nave separated from the side aisles by two rows of columns of Greek marble with Veneto-Byzantine capitals. The magnificent polychrome mosaic pavement in the nave bears an inscription recording that it was laid down in 1140, which is also presumed to be the date when the present church was completed. The wooden ship's-keel ceiling dates from the beginning of the 16C. The high altar in the elevated chancel enshrines the remains of St Donatus. (The bones of the dragon he is supposed to have killed are behind the altar.) The only remaining work of the original 12C decoration that has survived in the chancel is the beautiful Byzantine mosaic in the conch of the apse, depicting the Virgin Praying. Around the peripheral walls of the apse there are four panels with frescoes of the Evangelists, done by Nicolò di Pietro at the beginning of the 15C. Over the door of the 19C baptistery, in a lunette, there is a painting of *The Madonna and Child Enthroned, with Saints and the Donor* signed by Lazzaro Bastiani and dated 1484. Near the rear of the left aisle of the nave there is a painted and gilded wooden altarpiece depicting St Donatus flanked by two donors, with an inscription giving the date 1310. Beside the main doorway there is a marble holy-water stoup supported on the stump of a column dating from the 7–8C

After leaving the church we retrace our steps to Ponte San Pietro Martire, where we now turn left and cross the canal to Campo San Stefano. The *campo* is named for the ancient church of San Stefano, suppressed by the French at the beginning of the 19C and subsequently demolished. In the *campo* there is a *vera da pozzo* dated 1428.

We leave the *campo* at its south-western corner via Fondamenta Daniele Manin, which we follow along Rio dei Vetrai as far as Viale Giuseppe Garibaldi, where we turn left. Halfway along this wide street, just after passing on our right Calle Miotti, we see on our left Ospizio Briati. This was erected in 1754 through the generosity of the glass-maker G. Briati to house the indigent widows of glass-blowers.

At the end of the street we come to Pontile Faro, named for the lighthouse (in Italian, *faro*), the principal landmark of Murano. Here we come to the end of our tour of Murano, after which we can take the *vaporetto* to go on to Mazzorbo, Burano and Torcello.

MAZZORBO

After a voyage of some four nautical miles we enter Canale di Mazzorbo, the right side of which is formed by the island of Mazzorbo. Mazzorbo is the ancient Roman Maiurbum, long known for its orchards and vineyards. In times past Mazzorbo was a favourite retreat for wealthy Venetians who had summer villas here, but now there is only a scattering of fishermen's houses along the surrounding canals.

We disembark at Pontile Mazzorbo, after which we turn right on Fondamenta di Santa Caterina. This takes us back along the Canale di Mazzorbo to its junction with a side canal, where we turn left and follow the *fondamenta* to its end at the south-western tip of the island.

At the end of the *fondamenta* we come to the church of Santa Caterina, a Romanesque-Gothic structure of the early 15C, restored in the 16C. Over the doorway to the church there is a Gothic marble relief of 1368 showing *The Marriage of St Catherine*. On the high altar there is a painting of *The Baptism of Christ, with St Catherine and St Mary Magdalene* by Giuseppe Salviati.

We now make our way to the eastern side of the island, to the wooden bridge that links Mazzorbo and Burano. Before crossing the bridge we look left to see a campanile standing by itself in a field on the northern end of Mazzorbo. This is all that is left of the ancient church and convent of Santa Maria Valverde, demolished in the 19C.

BURANO AND SAN FRANCESCO DEL DESERTO

Burano is the most populous of all the lagoon islands after Murano, contrasting dramatically with neighbouring Mazzorbo. The ancient lace industry of Burano has been revived, and its fine products are displayed in numerous shops as well as in the local houses, which are the most colourful in the lagoon, a palette of pastels that make this the most picturesque community in the environs of Venice. The men of Burano make their living from the sea, and as you walk around the town you see moored before their blue and yellow and green and pink canal-side houses the fishing-boats and barges in which they spend their working lives, as have their ancestors since time immemorial. The town is particularly lively and colourful at the time of the annual regatta on the third Sunday in July, when people come from all over the lagoon to watch the races in the Canale di Burano, with the town band playing and the choir singing old boating songs.

The path from the bridge leads along the shore to the Burano *vaporetto* station, where we turn right on Via Adriano Marcello to head into the centre of the town. As we do so we pass on our right a *vera da pozzo*, dated 1588.

At the end of Via Marcello we continue in the same direction along Calle San Mauro, which brings us to the *fondamenta* of the same name, where we turn left. A short way along we pass on our right Ponte dei Assassini, whose baleful name probably perpetuates the villainy of some Buranei of times past, for, as Horatio Brown noted, their 'evil repute is hereditary'.

After crossing Ponte San Marco we come to Via Baldassare Galuppi, the broad main avenue of Burano, which leads to the vast piazza of the same name. Across the piazza we see

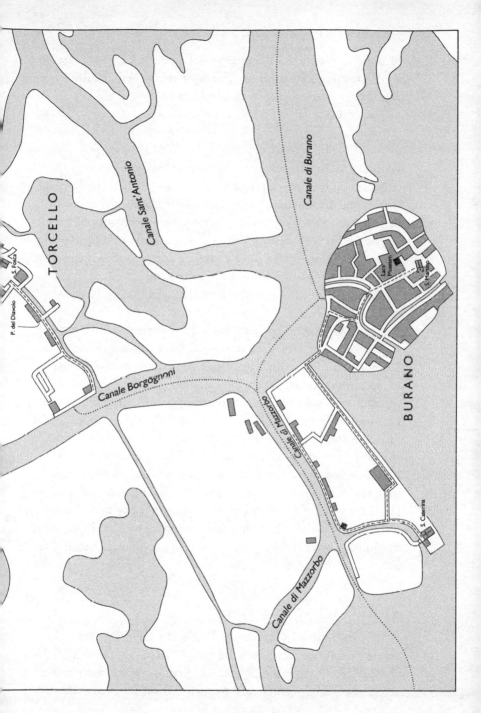

Murano

Murano's principal monument, the church of San Martino, whose leaning campanile is the most prominent landmark in the northern part of the Venetian lagoon.

The church was founded in the 16C, and was enlarged and restored in later times. The most notable painting is hung on the wall of the second bay from the front on the right side, a *Crucifixion*, done *c.* 1725, by Giambattista Tiepolo.

Next to the church is the 17C oratory of St Barbara. Across the piazza from the church is Palazzo del Podestà, a 14C Gothic palace that was the government centre of Burano in the days of the Republic. The palace now houses the School and Museum of Lace-making, with exhibits displaying the island's ancient tradition of lace-making.

In the centre of the piazza there is a *vera da pozzo* in white marble dated 1568.

We now make our way back to the ferry landing-stage, where one can hire a boat to go out to San Francesco del Deserto, an islet about half a mile south of Burano. Contrary to its name, the island is a little Eden, shaded by groves of spectral cypresses, inhabited by Franciscan monks who live harmoniously in what must be one of the oldest monasteries of their order. Tradition holds that their founder himself stopped here on a voyage in 1220, and that the monastery was founded two years after his death in 1226, with the island donated to them by the nobleman Jacopo Michiel. The church and monastery were dedicated in 1233 and continue to function to the present day, though the buildings have obviously been rebuilt and restored several times in the interim.

TORCELLO

After returning to Burano we board the ferry for Torcello, a voyage of about half a mile, taking us to the isolated dock on the Canale Borgognoni. After landing we turn right and go along the shore a short way to turn left on a path by the side canal, from where it is a 500 m walk to the site of the town. Some 300 m along we pass the old stone span known as Ponte del Diavolo, the Devil's Bridge. Then finally we cross another bridge to come to what was once the Piazzetta di Torcello, a grass-grown *campo* dominated on its far side by the cathedral of Santa Maria Assunta and the church of Santa Fosca; together with the Palazzo del Consiglio and the Palazzo dell'Archivio on the left of the square, this is all that remains of the ancient island township of Torcello, now a virtually uninhabited ghost town surrounded by the desolate wastes of the lagoon.

The founding legend of Torcello, the ancient Turricellum, has it that it was settled by refugees from Altino, driven from their homes by the last wave of Lombard invasions in 568. The Bishop of Altino transferred his seat here in 638, and Torcello became one of the most important communities in the lagoon, one of the twelve townships that together created the Venetian Republic. Torcello prospered, particularly because of its thriving wool industry, and it became an important ecclesiastical centre with many churches and monasteries, governed by its own Podestà and Council under the aegis of the Venetian Doge. At its peak the population of Torcello reached 20,000, but then eventually the dwindling of its trade, the silting up of its navigational channels and the spread of malaria by the miasmal swamps around it led to an inexorable dwindling of its population as its people moved to Venice. In 1689 Bishop Marco Giustinian moved his seat from Torcello to Murano, leaving the ancient bishopric vacant, to be abolished in 1805 when it was combined with that of Venice under the Venetian Patriarch. Then in 1810 the surviving churches and monasteries on Torcello were suppressed, for by that time the island had been almost completely abandoned by its populace.

An inscription preserved in the cathedral records that the first church on this site was erected in 639 on orders from Isaac, Exarch of Ravenna in the reign of the Byzantine

Emperor Heraclius, and that it was dedicated to the Blessed Virgin Theotokos, the Mother of God. The chronicler John the Deacon records that the church was completed at the beginning of the 8C by Bishop Adeodato I, who adorned it with marble decorations. Other sources record that the church was enlarged by Bishop Adeodato II (864–7), who extended the central apse and enlarged the two side apses, created the crypt beneath the chancel, and added the front porch. The church was given its present form *c.* 1008 by Bishop (later Doge) Otto Orseolo who also erected the splendid campanile. Subsequent adornments included the mosaic pavement and mosaics on the walls, the paintings on the iconostasis and the altars, and the sculptural decoration, all of which were completed by the early 15C. The church was restored in 1423 by Bishop Pietro Nani, and again in 1646, when the basilica and campanile were damaged by lightning. The Emperor Francis I of Austria left a bequest that allowed repairs to be done to the basilica in 1821 and again in 1827, and then in 1929–39 the cathedral and the church of St Fosca were restored to their original condition, ridding them of the baroque superstructures that had been added to them.

The ruined circular structure in front of the cathedral is the baptistery, which dates back to the 7C, part of the original church.

The present entrance to the cathedral is approached from the right side of the porch. Before entering there through the side door, look out through the window at the end of the corridor to see the stone shutters on the windows of the south side of the church, massive slabs rotating on iron hinges in stone sockets on their left side.

The interior of the basilica is vast and empty, the central nave covered by a pitched roof of uncovered sprung beams. The floor is paved with beautiful multicoloured marble mosaics in geometrical patterns, dating from the 11C. The church is basilical in plan, with the central nave divided from the side aisles by two rows of nine columns each, made of Proconnesian marble and capped with Byzantine capitals. The iconostasis forms a screen between the seventh column on either side to enclose the chancel, which is raised on a two-stepped platform, its central portal flanked by three columns on either side, also of Proconnesian marble and surmounted by Byzantine capitals that support the actual icon screen. The pulpit is between the sixth and seventh columns on the left side of the central aisle by the iconostasis. It is supported on four marble columns and approached by a stairway with a balustrade adorned with elaborately carved panels. The lower part of the iconostasis on either side of the entrance has a parapet consisting of four marble panels, intricately carved with the figures of lions, peacocks and other birds amidst the dense foliage of grape vines, all dating from the 11C. The icon screen above the columns of the iconostasis is decorated with thirteen portraits, and the *Madonna and Child Flanked by the Twelve Apostles*, done in the early 15C by Zannino di Pietro. Above the centre of the iconostasis rises a huge Crucifixion in polychrome wood, dating from the 11C. Set into the pavement in front of the entrance of the iconostasis is the 15C tombstone of Bishop Paolo d'Altino.

The 1929–39 restoration of the church demolished the baroque altar and replaced it with an altar table made mostly from the fragments of the original one of the 7C. Under the altar table is a Roman sarcophagus of the 2–3C; this contains the body of St Heliodorus, first Bishop of Altino and friend of St Jerome, brought to Torcello in 635. Beneath the altar a metal grille covers the crypt, which can be approached from the side apses. On the wall to the left of the altar is a plaque with an inscription recording the foundation of the church in 639, the oldest written record in Venetian history.

Behind the altar is the *synthronon*, a feature of early Byzantine churches, consisting of six tiers of seats for the clergy around the apse, with a flight of steps leading up to the bishop's throne.

The upper zone of the apse is decorated with mosaics in the

Byzantine style. The conch of the apse is adorned with the huge figure of the Virgin Theotokos, the Mother of God, who is holding in her arms the Christ Child. Above in the spandrels of the arch are the Angel and Virgin of the Annunciation. On the upper wall of the apse are the standing figures of the twelve Apostles, six on either side of the east window, below which is a half-figure of St Heliodorus, a modern replacement of the original. The Apostles are dated to the 12C; the Virgin and Child to *c.* 1230; the Annunciation is probably of the 12–13C.

The apsidal chapel to the right of the chancel is also decorated with mosaics. In the conch of the apse is the enthroned Christ Pantocrator, the All-Powerful, flanked by the Archangels Michael and Gabriel. Below on either side of the east window are figures of four Doctors of the Latin Church; from right to left: Sts Augustine, Ambrose, Martin and Gregory the Great. The groined vault of the chapel has at its focal point a circle representing a copper shield, with the figure of the Mystic Lamb, supported in the four segments by figures of angels, separated by floral bands representing the four rivers of Paradise. These mosaics have been dated to the 12C, but are based on much earlier works of the Byzantine era in Ravenna.

The rear wall of the nave is entirely covered by a vast mosaic composition depicting the Apotheosis of Christ and the Last Judgement, a magnificent work of the Veneto-Byzantine school dating from the 12–13C. The composition, known as the Doomsday Mosaic, is divided into six bands, beginning at the top under the peak of the roof with a depiction of Christ on the Cross between the Virgin and St John the Evangelist. The two lower zones flank the main doorway, in the lunette of which there is a mosaic of the Virgin at Prayer.

We now walk over to the church of Santa Fosca. The church was built as a martyrium dedicated to St Fosca, the virgin martyr of Ravenna, whose remains were brought here some time before 1011, along with those of St Maura, her nurse and companion in martyrdom. The nucleus of the church dates from the early 11C, with the porch around its front and sides added in the 12C.

The interior plan of the church is a Greek cross, with pendentives making the transition to the circular drum of the wooden conical dome, which is tiled on the exterior. The dome is supported by four piers at the corners of a square and by a circlet of eight columns of Greek marble with Byzantine capitals, freestanding in pairs athwart the diagonals of the square. Two additional columns combine with the two on the front side of the square to form colonnades in the deep chancel, dividing it into a wide central apsidal chapel flanked by narrow side aisles. The only altar is a marble table at the front of the chancel.

The little palace on the north side of the *piazzetta* near the baptistery is the Palazzo dell'Archivio, a 14C structure with a double portico and an elegant triforium. The one on the west side of the square is Palazzo del Consiglio, also dating from the 14C, with a trilobate window and a little campanile. The two palaces now comprise the Torcello Museum, with the Palazzo dell'Archivio housing the archaeological collection, which includes Greek, Roman and Etruscan works; and the Palazzo del Consiglio devoted to medieval and modern works of art associated with the Venetian lagoon. A number of the sculptural and architectural fragments in the collections are arrayed in the lower portico of the Palazzo dell'Archivio, while others are scattered around the lawn in the *piazzetta*. These include five *vere da pozzo*, all but one of them dating from the 14–15C. The exception is a cubical *vera da pozzo* with crosses inscribed on its sides; this is dated to the 8–9C, and is probably the oldest well-head in the Venetian lagoon.

In the centre of the lawn there is a rough-hewn marble seat known traditionally as the 'Throne of Attila'. The throne is believed to have been used in the early days of Torcello as the seat of the island tribune administering justice in the name of the Byzantine emperor, when the horrible memories of the raids of Attila and other barbarian warlords were still fresh in the minds of those who had taken refuge here and on the other islands of the lagoon. As Ruskin wrote in *The Stones of Venice*, in an elegaic passage at the end of his description of the view from the campanile, gazing over the deserted site of Torcello:

Thirteen hundred years ago, the grey moorland looked as it does this day, and the purple mountains stood in the deep distance of evening; but on the line of the horizon there were strange fires mixed with the light of sunset, and the lament of many human voices mixed with the fretting of the waves on their ridges of sand. The flames rose from the ruins of Altinum; the lament from the multitudes of its people seeking, like Israel of old, a refuge from the sword in the paths of the sea.

The cattle are feeding and resting upon the site of the city that they left; the mower's scythe swept this day at dawn over the chief street of the city that they built, and the swathes of soft grass are now sending up their scent into the night air, the only incense that fills the temple of their ancient worship . . .

And thus Venice ends as it begins, in the whispering marshes of its all-embracing lagoon, where the jade-green waters stir as the salt wind breathes in from the east. '*Il mare la chiama.*' The sea is calling, eternally calling for his lost bride.

Glossary

acqua alta: exceptionally high tide that floods Venice

aedicula (pl. *aediculae*): kiosk with a neoclassical frame

atlantes (also *telamones*): male figures used as supporting members

baldachino: canopy supported by columns, usually over an altar

barbacani: extended wooden supports of the upper floor of a building

barco: suspended choir in church, used by nuns or monks

calesela: narrow *calle*

calle: rather long, narrow street

campanile: bell-tower

campazzo: abandoned place, though some are now once again in use

campiello: small *campo*

campo: square, generally next to a church

canale: name used only for the larger canals, most notably the Canale Grande

canonica: house of the clergy next to a church

casa (*ca'*): palace, or large house

casino: place used for assignations, gambling or social gatherings

chiovere: dyer's drying-ground

cittadini: family of the citizen class

Consiglio dei Dieci: Council of Ten

controfacciato: interior of facade wall of church

corte: courtyard

cortile: large court

exedra (pl. *exedrae*): rectangular or semicircular recess

felze: wooden cabin once used on a gondola

fontego (or *fondaco*): large warehouse with offices and living quarters used by foreign merchants

fondamenta: sidewalk along the bank of a canal

intrado: interior curve of an arch

lidi: the islands that separate the Venetian lagoon from the sea

lunette: space within arch

Maggior Consiglio: Great Council of the Venetian Republic

merceria (or *marzaria*): busy street flanked by shops

Molo: the quay by the Piazzetta and Ducal Palace

motonave: the largest ferry-boats

naiskos: tabernacle in the form of a classical temple front

palazzetto: small palace

palazzo: palace

pali: wooden piles used to moor boats and mark channels

parrocchia: parish

patera (pl. *paterae*): circular stone plaque or ornament on facade of building

pendentive: spherical segment between arches and circular drum of dome

piano nobile: main floor of a palace, usually the first floor

piazza: large square, the Piazza San Marco being the only one in the historic centre of Venice

piazzetta: small piazza, there being only two in Venice, one beside the Ducal Palace and the other, the Piazzetta Leoni, beside the Basilica of San Marco

piscina: street formed by filling in a pond

pluteus (pl. *plutei*): marble panel, usually decorated, on parapet

polyptych: painting or panel in more than three sections

ponte: bridge

pontile: landing-stage on a *vaporetto* line

pozzo (pl. *pozzi*): a well or cistern

portego: central hall of a palace

porti: channels between the *lidi* leading out from the lagoon to the sea

predella: small painting attached below a larger one

Procuratie: offices and apartments of the Procurators of San Marco

Provveditori: the officials in charge of the civic administration of the city

punta: promontory or point

ramo: short extension of a street

reredos: ornamental screen behind an altar

ridotto: gambling saloon

rio: canal

rio terà: street formed by filling in a canal

riello: small rio

riva: quayside street

ruga: some of the older *calli* have this name, said to be derived from the French *rue* or the Portugese *rua*

rughetta: diminutive of *ruga*

salizzada: the principal street in a parish, first paved (in Venetian, *salizai*) with brick *c.* 1260

scoazzera: enclosed place for rubbish, generally near a canal

scuola: guild or confraternity; also the hall that housed these

sestiere (pl. *sestieri*): one of the six districts of Venice

soffit: the underside of an arch

sottoportego: a street that passes under a building, also a portico

spandrel: space between arches in an arcade

squero: boatyard where gondolas are made and repaired

telamones: see *atlantes*

terraferma: the mainland of the Venetian lagoon

tondo: circular panel

traghetto: gondola ferrying passengers across the Grand Canal

triptych: painting or tablet in three sections

vaporetto: ferry-boat

vera da pozzo: well-head

Opening Hours of Monuments and Museums

Most churches are open 9–12 and 16–19, though less frequented ones may be open only for services on Sunday and evening rosary; all opening times are liable to change (D. = daily; Sun. = Sunday and holidays; cl. = Closed; sum. = summer)

Accademia Galleries: D. 9–14 (sum. 9–19.15); Sun. 9–13

Archaelogical Museum: D. 9–14; Sun. 9–13

Burano Lace Museum: D. 9–18; Sun. 10–16; cl. Mon.

Byzantine Sacred Painting Museum: D. 9–13 and 14–17; cl. Sun.

Ca' d'Oro (Franchetti Gallery): D. 9–13.30; Sun. 9–12.30

Ca' Pesaro (Gallery of Modern Art): D. and Sun. 9–16; cl. Mon.

Ca' Pesaro (Oriental Museum): D. 9–14; Sun. 9–13; cl. Mon.

Ca' Rezzonico (Museum of Eighteenth-century Venice): D. and Sun. 10–16; cl. Fri.

Carmini, Scuola dei: D. 9–12 and 15–18; cl. Sun.

Casa Goldoni: D. 8.30–13.30; cl. Sun.

Cini Palazzo Gallery: sum. only

Correr Museum: D. and Sun. 10–17; cl. Tue.

Diocesan Museum of Sacred Art: D. and Sun. 10.30–12.30

Doge's Palace: D. and Sun. 9–19 (ticket booth closes 18)

Fortuny Museum: D. and Sun. 9–19; cl. Mon.

Frari, Church of the: D. 9–12 and 14.30–18; Sun. 15–17.30

Guggenheim Museum: D. and Sun. 9–14; Sat. 9–13; cl. Mon.

Jewish Museum: D. and Sun. 10–16.30; cl. Sat.; guided tours of synagogues 10.30, 11.30, 12.30, 13.30, 14.30, 15.30 (except Fri.)

Murano Glass Museum: D. and Sun. 10–17; cl. Wed.

Natural History Museum: D. and Sun. 9–13; cl. Mon.

Naval Historical Museum: D. 9–13; cl. Sun.

Palazzo Mocenigo a San Stae: Tue., Wed. and Sat. 8.30–13.30

Querini-Stampalia Gallery: D. and Sun. 10–12.30; cl. Mon.

Oratorio dei Crociferi: Apr.–June, Oct.: Fri., Sat. and Sun. 10–12; July–Sept.: Fri., Sat. and Sun. 16.30–18.30

San Francesco del Deserto, Monastery of: D. and Sun. 9–11 and 15–17

San Giorgio Maggiore, Campanile of: D. and Sun. 9–13 and 14–18

San Giorgio degli Schiavone, Scuola di: D. 10–12.30 and 15.30–18; Sun. 10–12.30

San Lazzaro degli Armeni Monastery: D. and Sun. 15–17

San Marco Basilica; Gallery: D. and Sun. 9.45–18.30; Pala d'Oro and Treasury: D. 9.45–18.30; Sun. 14–17.30

San Marco, Campanile of: D. and Sun. 9–13 and 14–18

San Rocco, Scuola di: D. and Sun. 9–17

Torcello Cathedral: D. and Sun. 10–12.30 and 14–18.30

Index

A = architect; C = ceramicist; D = decorator; E = engraver; Med. = medallist; Mos. = mosaicist; P = painter; S = sculptor; Stuc. = stucco worker; aft. = after; b. = born; bef. = before; beg. = beginning; d. = died; n. = noted, or only record of

LAGUNA

S. M. dei
Penitenti

Canal de Cannaregio

2)

S.
Giobbe

Rio de S. Giobbe

9

9

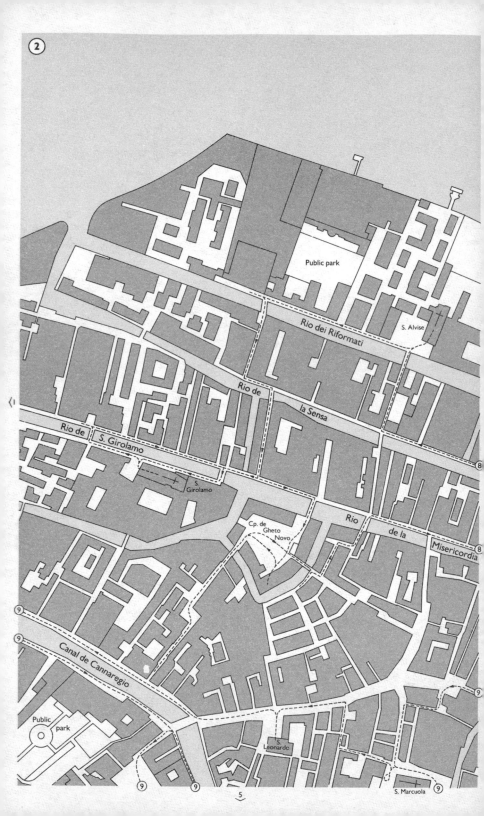

Public park

Rio dei Riformati

S. Alvise

Rio de

la Sensa

Rio de S. Girolamo

S. Girolamo

Cp. de Gheto Novo

Rio

de la

Misericordia

8

8

9

9

Canal de Cannaregio

Public park

9

S. Leonardo

S. Marcuola

9

9

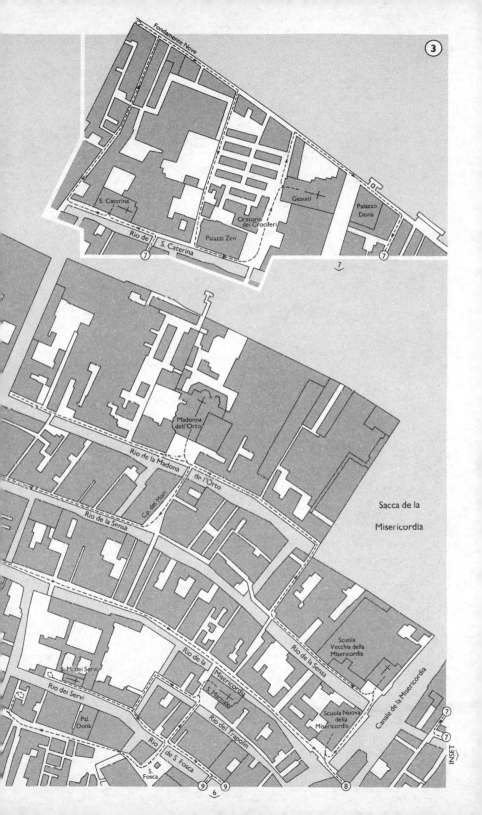

Fondamente Nove

③

S. Caterina

Gesuiti

Oratorio
dei Crociferi

Palazzo Zen

Palazzo
Donà

Rio de

S. Caterina

⑦

⑦

⑦

Madonna
dell'Orto

Rio de la Madona

de l'Orto

Ca' dei Mori

Rio de la Sensa

Sacca de la

Misericordia

S. M. dei Servi

Rio de la

Rio de la Sensa

Scuola
Vecchia della
Misericordia

Rio dei Servi

Misericordia

S. Marzial

Pal.
Donà

Rio del Trapolin

Scuola Nuova
della
Misericordia

Canale de la Misericordia

⑦

⑦

Rio

de S. Fosca

S.
Fosca

⑨

⑥

⑨

⑧

INSET

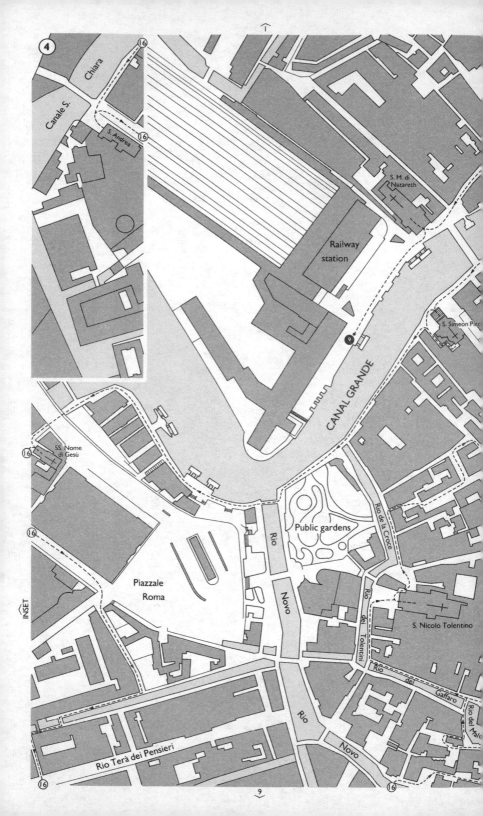

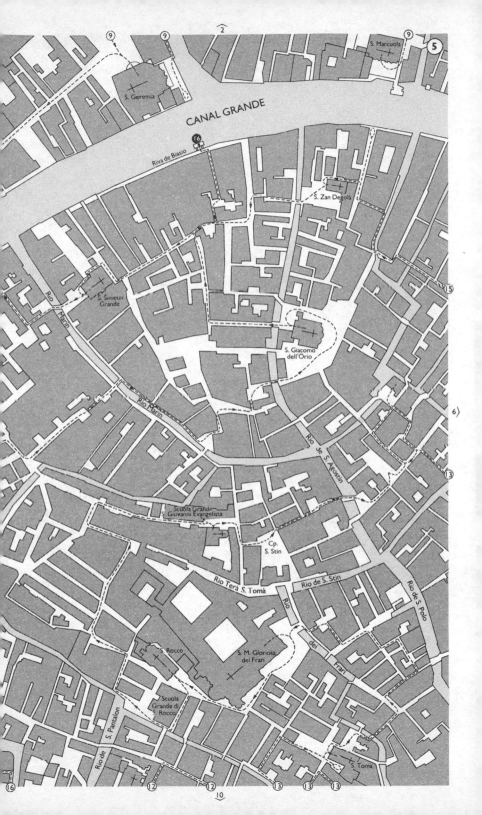

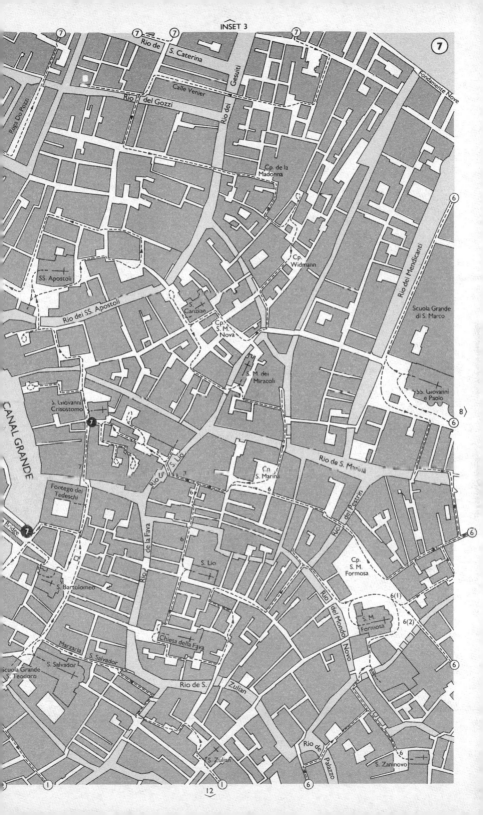

⑦ ⑦ ⑦ Rio de S. Caterina ⑦

Calle Venier

Rio del Gozzi

Rio dei Gesuiti

Fondamente Nove

Rega Do Pozzi

Cp. de la Madonna

⑥

Cp. Widmann

Rio dei Mendicanti

SS. Apostoli

S. Canzian

Scuola Grande di S. Marco

Rio dei SS. Apostoli

Cp. S. M. Nova

S. M. dei Miracoli

SS. Giovanni e Paolo

S. Giovanni Crisostomo

⑦

8)

⑥

CANAL GRANDE

⑦

Rio de S. Marina

Rio Co

S. Lio

Cn. S. Marina

Ric dei Pestrin

Fontego dei Tedeschi

⑥

⑥

7

S. Bartolomeo

Rio de la Fava

Cp. S. M. Formosa

Endre

⑦

S. Lio

6(1)

S. M. Formosa

6(2)

Rio del Mondo Novo

⑥

Marzaria

S. Salvador

S. Salvador

Chiesa della Fava

Scuola Grande S. Teodoro

Rio de S. Zulian

Rio de Palazzo

S. Zaninovo

⑥

S. Zulian

① ① ⑥

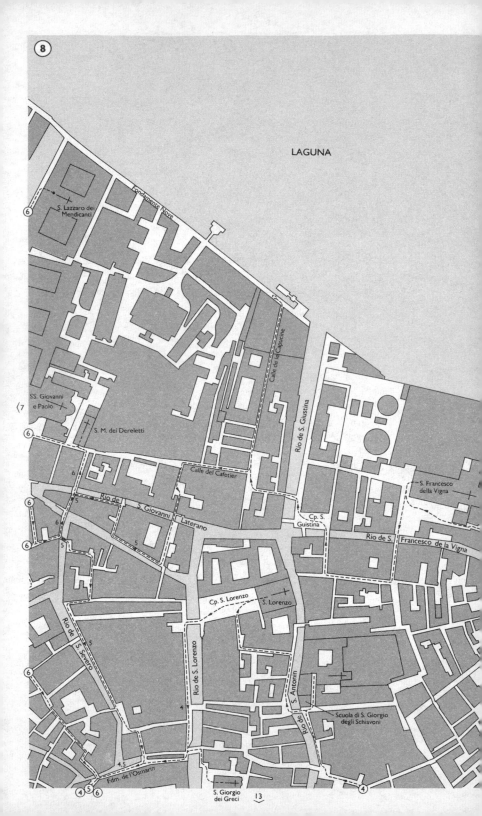

LAGUNA

Fondamenta Nove

S. Lazzaro dei
Mendicanti

SS. Giovanni
e Paolo

S. M. dei Dereletti

Calle del Cafetier

Calle de le Capucine

Rio de S. Giustina

S. Francesco
della Vigna

Rio de' S. Giovanni

Laterano

Cp. S.
Guistina

Rio de S. Francesco de la Vigna

Cp. S. Lorenzo

S. Lorenzo

Rio de S. Severo

Rio de S. Lorenzo

Rio de S. Antonin

Scuola di S. Giorgio
degli Schiavoni

Fdm. de l'Osmarin

S. Giorgio
dei Greci

13

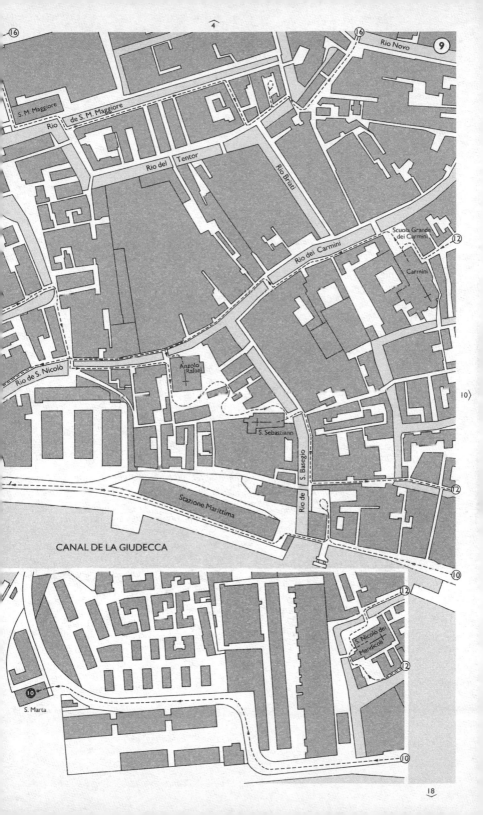

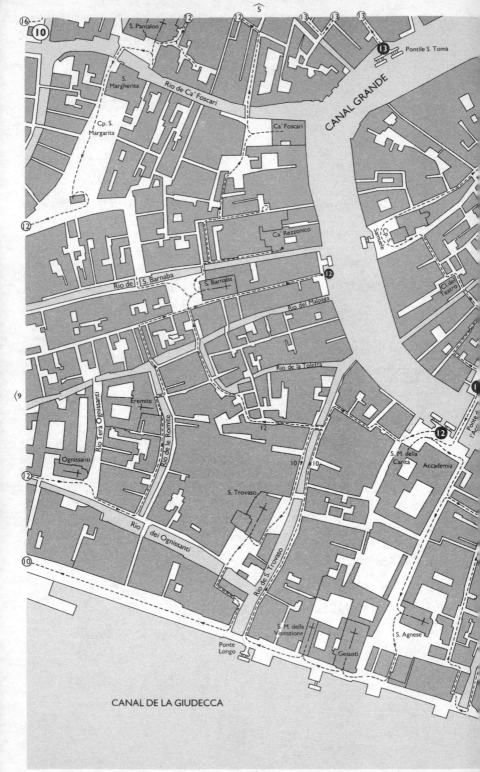

16
10

S. Pantalon

12   12   13   13   13

13   Pontile S. Tomà

S. Margherita

Rio de Ca' Foscari

CANAL GRANDE

Cp. S. Margarita

Ca' Foscari

12

Ca' Rezzonico

Cp. S. Samuele

Rio de S. Barnaba   S. Barnaba

12

Ct. del Teatro

Rio del Malpaga

Rio de la Toletta

9

Rio Terà Ognissanti

Rio de le Romite

Eremite

1

12

Ognissanti

S. M. della Carità

12

Accademia

Ponte d. l'Acc

10   10

12

S. Trovaso

Rio dei Ognissanti

10

Rio de S. Trovaso

S. M. della Visitazione

S. Agnese

Ponte Longo

Gesuati

CANAL DE LA GIUDECCA

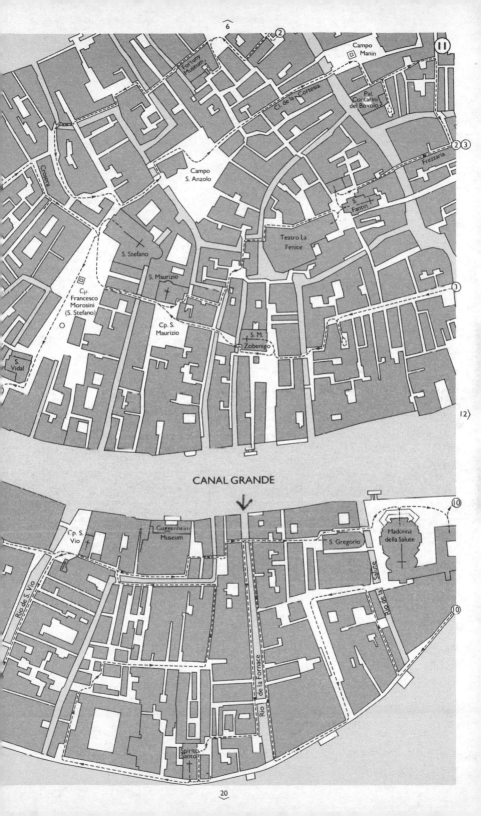

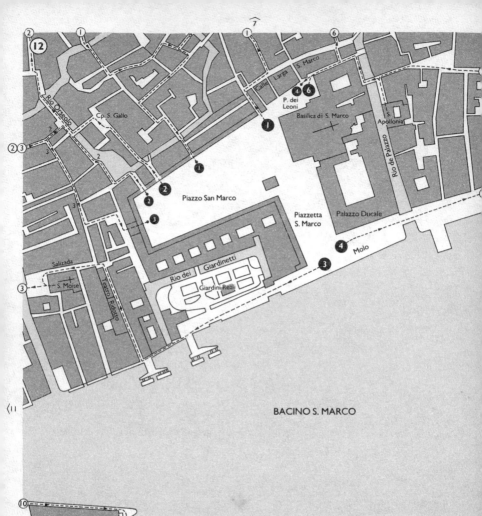
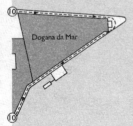

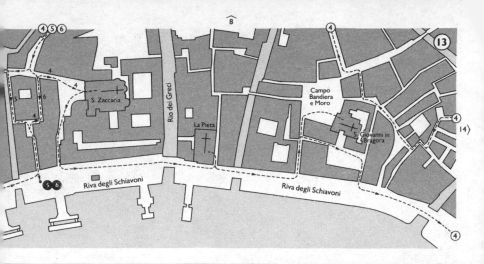

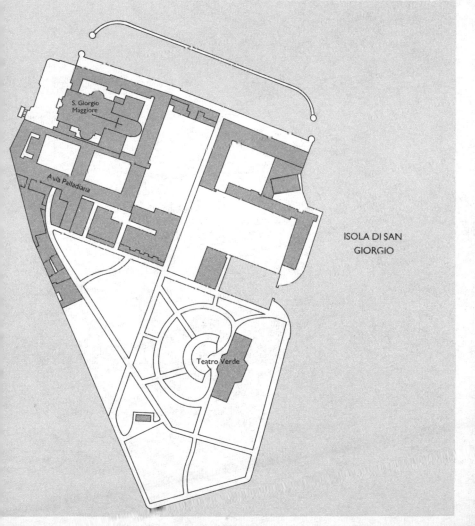

ISOLA DI SAN
GIORGIO

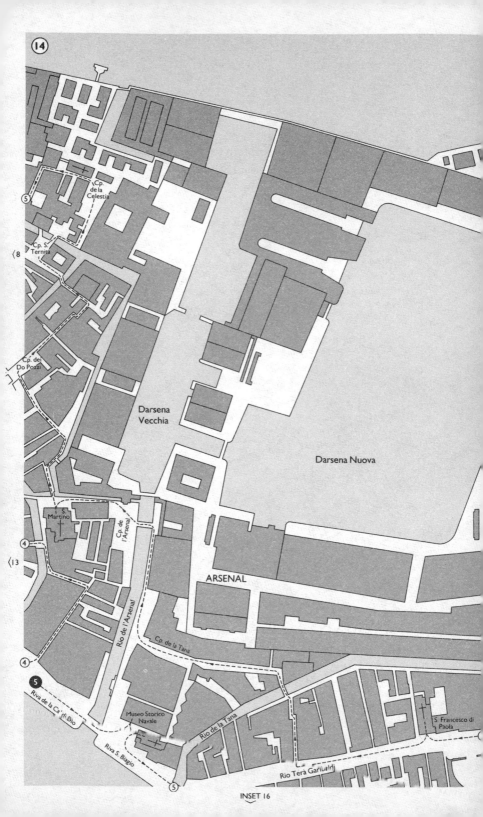

(14)

(5)

Cp.
de la
Celestia

Cp. S.
Ternità

(8)

Cp. dei
Do Pozzi

Darsena
Vecchia

Darsena Nuova

S.
Martino

Cp. de
l'Arsenal

(4)

(13)

ARSENAL

Rio de l'Arsenal

Cp. de la Tana

Rio de la Tana

(4)

(5)

Riva de la Ca' di Dio

Museo Storico
Navale

Riva S. Biagio

Rio Terà Gari(aldi)

S. Francesco di
Paola

(5)

INSET 16

S. Francesco di
Paola

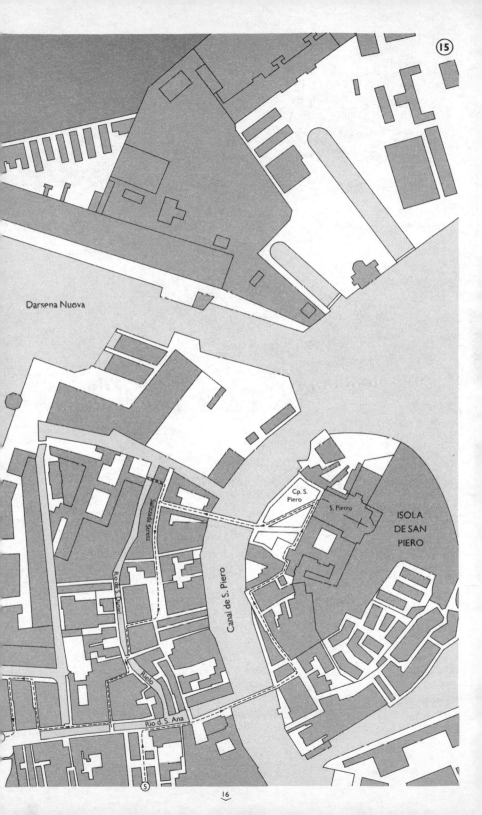

Darsena Nuova

Salizzada Streta

R.o de S. Danl

Rielo

Rio d. S. Ana

Canal de S. Piero

Cp. S. Piero

S. Pietro

ISOLA DE SAN PIERO

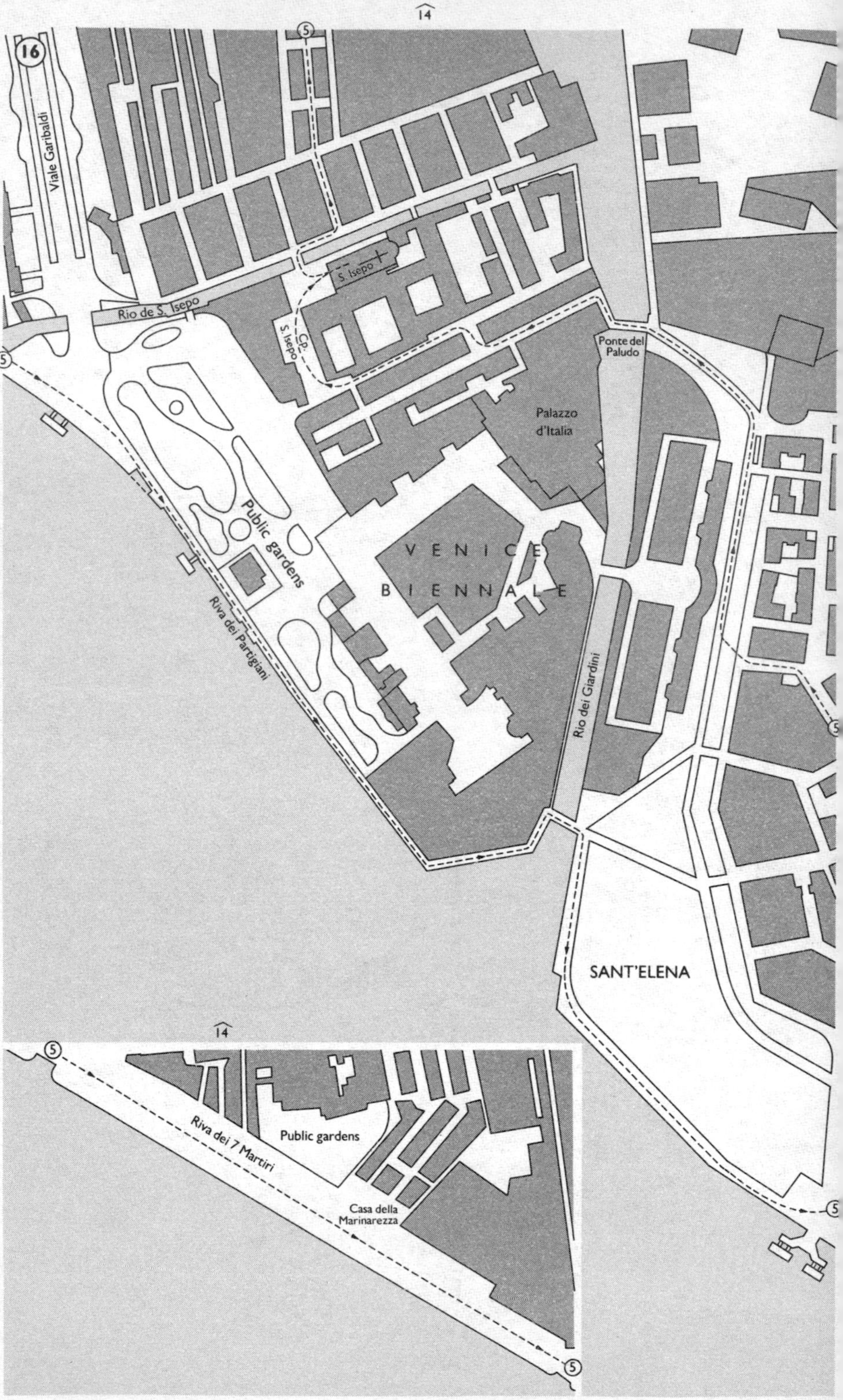

16

INSET

Viale Garibaldi

5

S. Isepo

Rio de S. Isepo

S. Isepo

Cp.

Ponte del
Paludo

Palazzo
d'Italia

Public gardens

V E N I C E

B I E N N A L E

Riva dei Partigiani

Rio dei Giardini

5

SANT'ELENA

5

Riva dei 7 Martiri

Public gardens

Casa della
Marinarezza

5

5

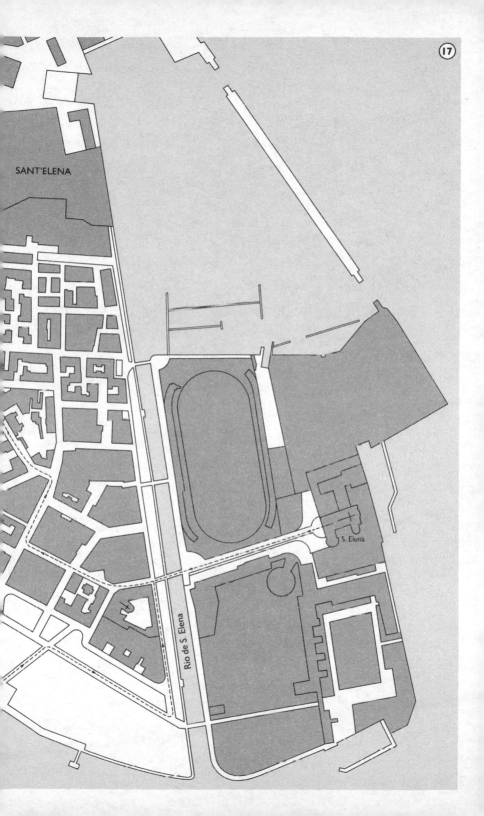

SANT'ELENA

S. Elena

Rio de S. Elena

⑰

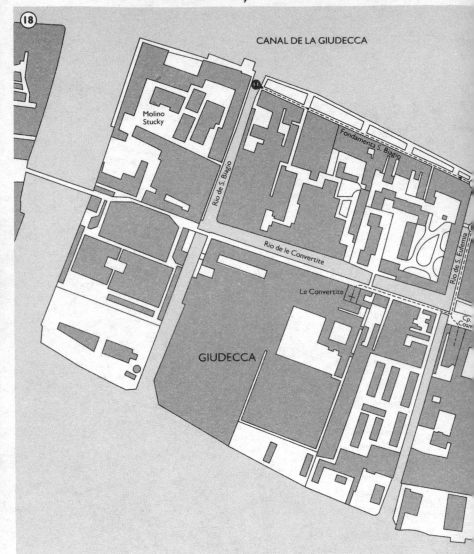

CANAL DE LA GIUDECCA

Molino
Stucky

Rio de S. Biagio

Fondamenta S. Biagio

Rio de le Convertite

Le Convertite

Rio de S. Eufemia

Cp.
Cosn

GIUDECCA

LAGOON

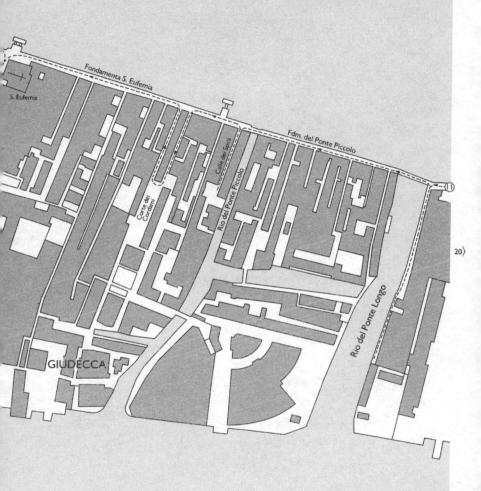

CANAL DE LA GIUDECCA

Fondamenta S. Eufemia

S. Eufemia

Fdm. del Ponte Piccolo

Corte dei Cordami

Calle dei Spiri

Rio del Ponte Piccolo

Rio del Ponte Longo

GIUDECCA

LAGOON

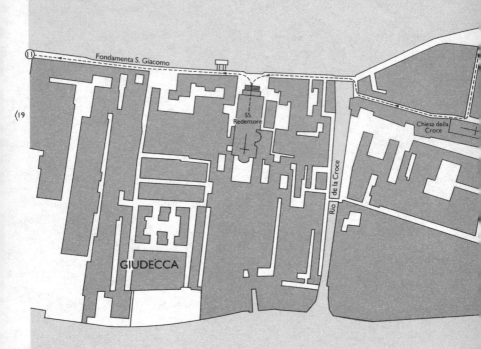

CANAL DE LA GIUDECCA

11
Fondamenta S. Giacomo

19

SS.
Redentore

Chiesa della
Croce

Rio de la Croce

GIUDECCA

LAGUNA

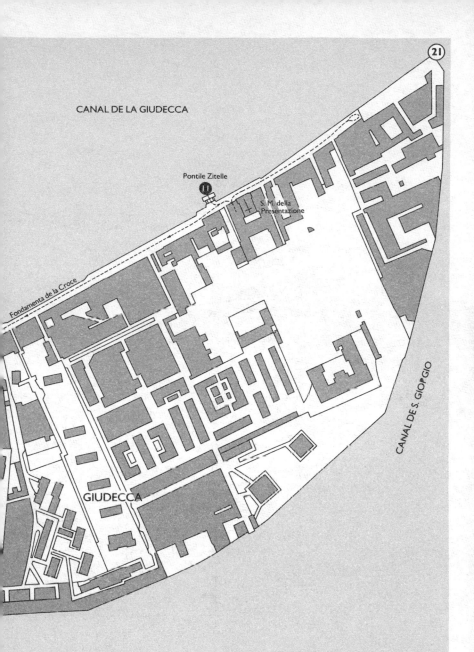

21

CANAL DE LA GIUDECCA

Pontile Zitelle

S. M. della
Presentazione

Fondamenta de la Croce

CANAL DE S. GIORGIO

GIUDECCA

LAGUNA

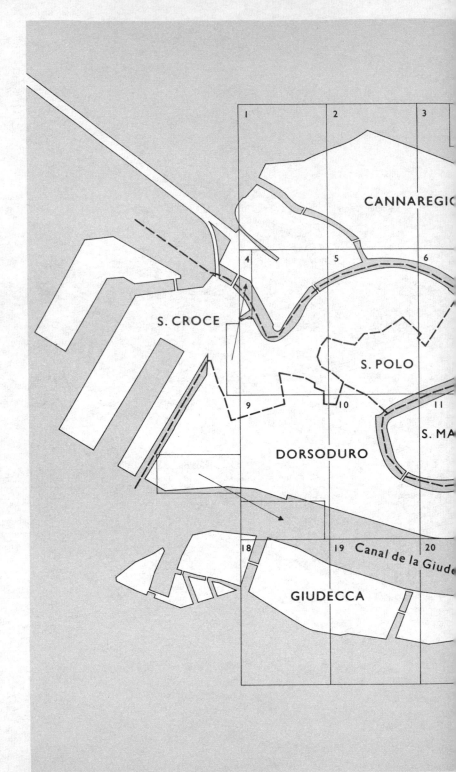

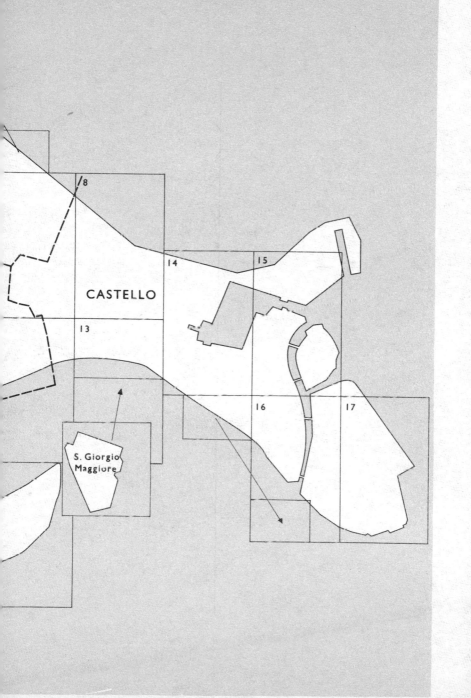

/8

14   15

CASTELLO

13

S. Giorgio
Maggiore

16   17